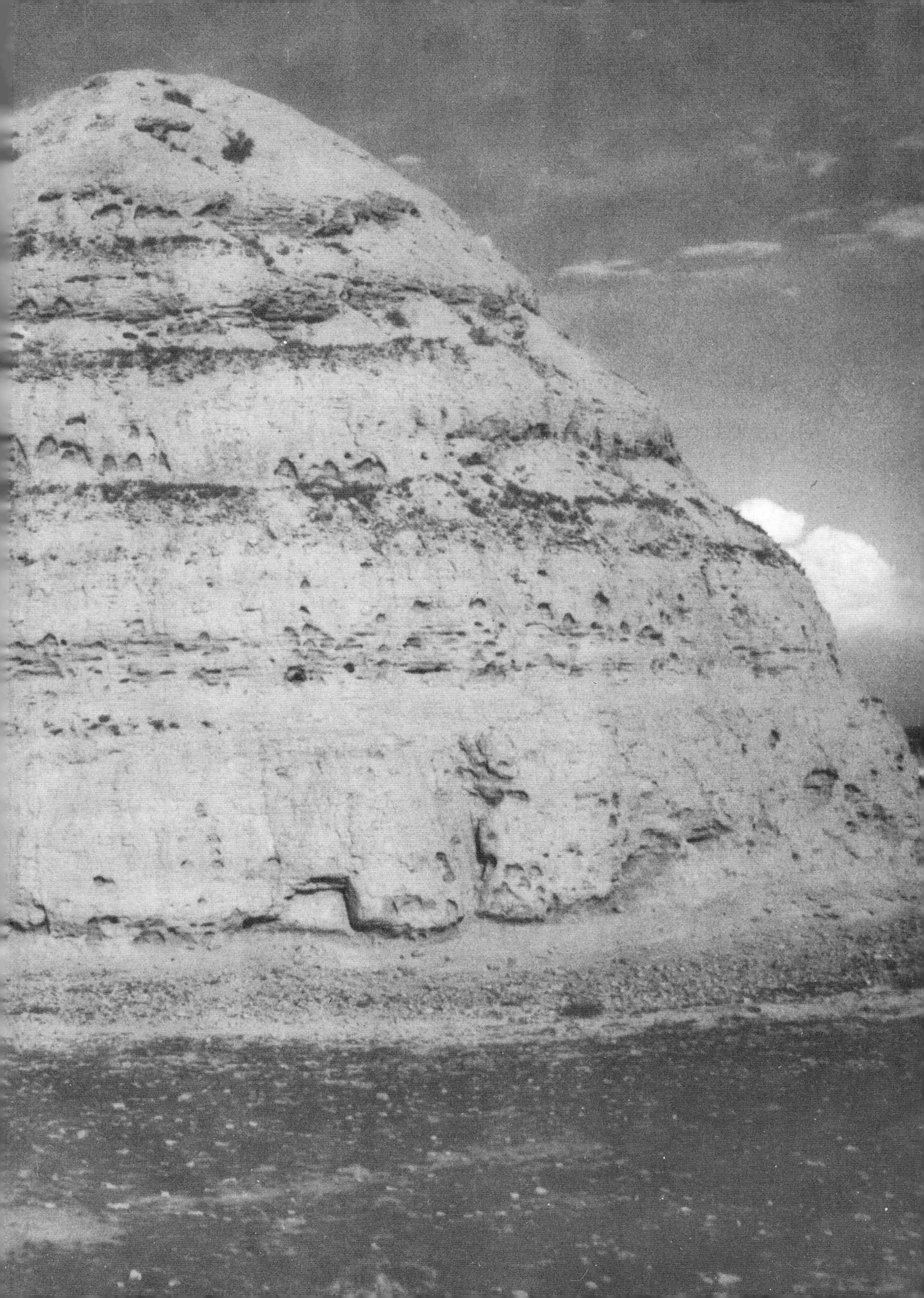

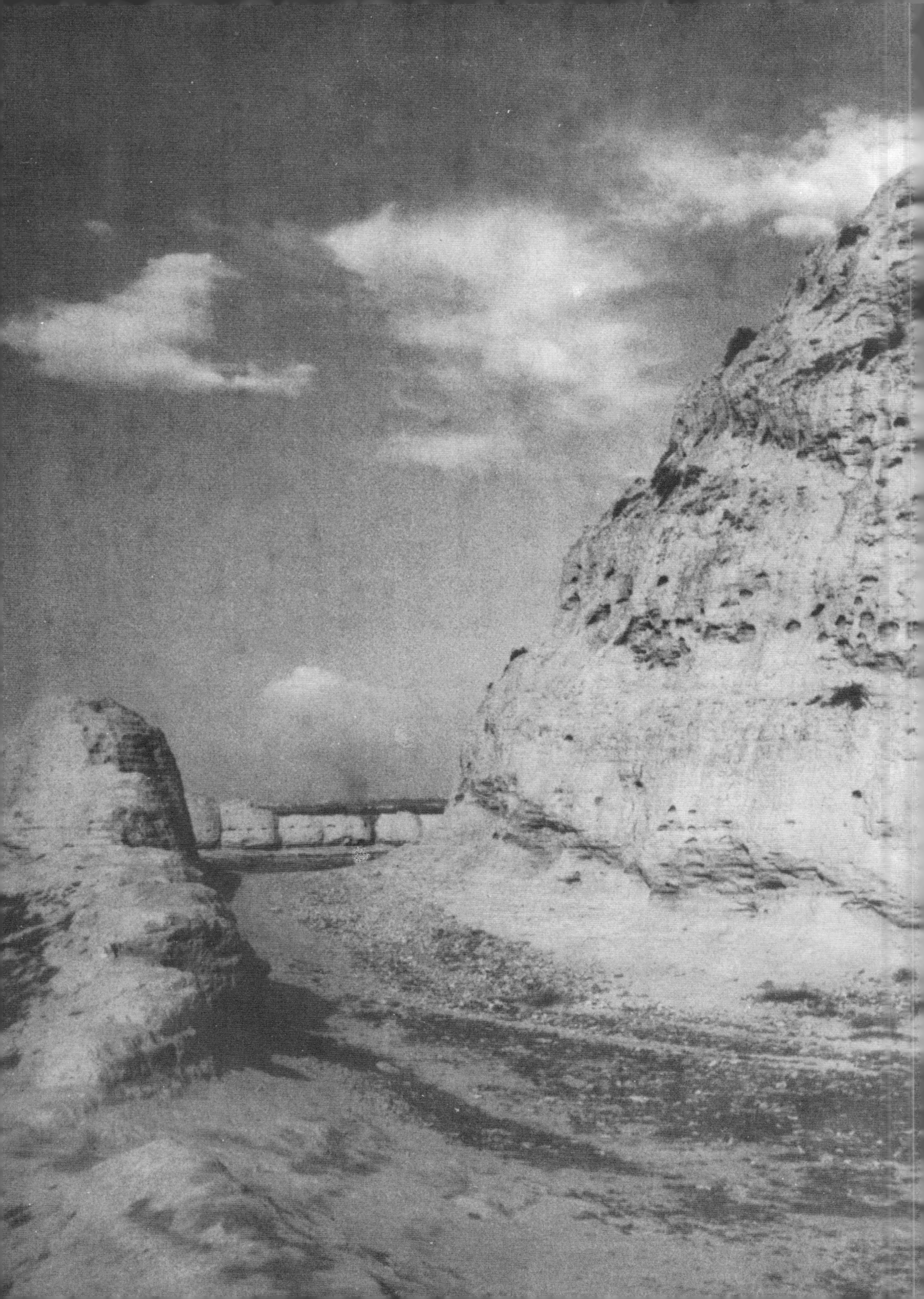

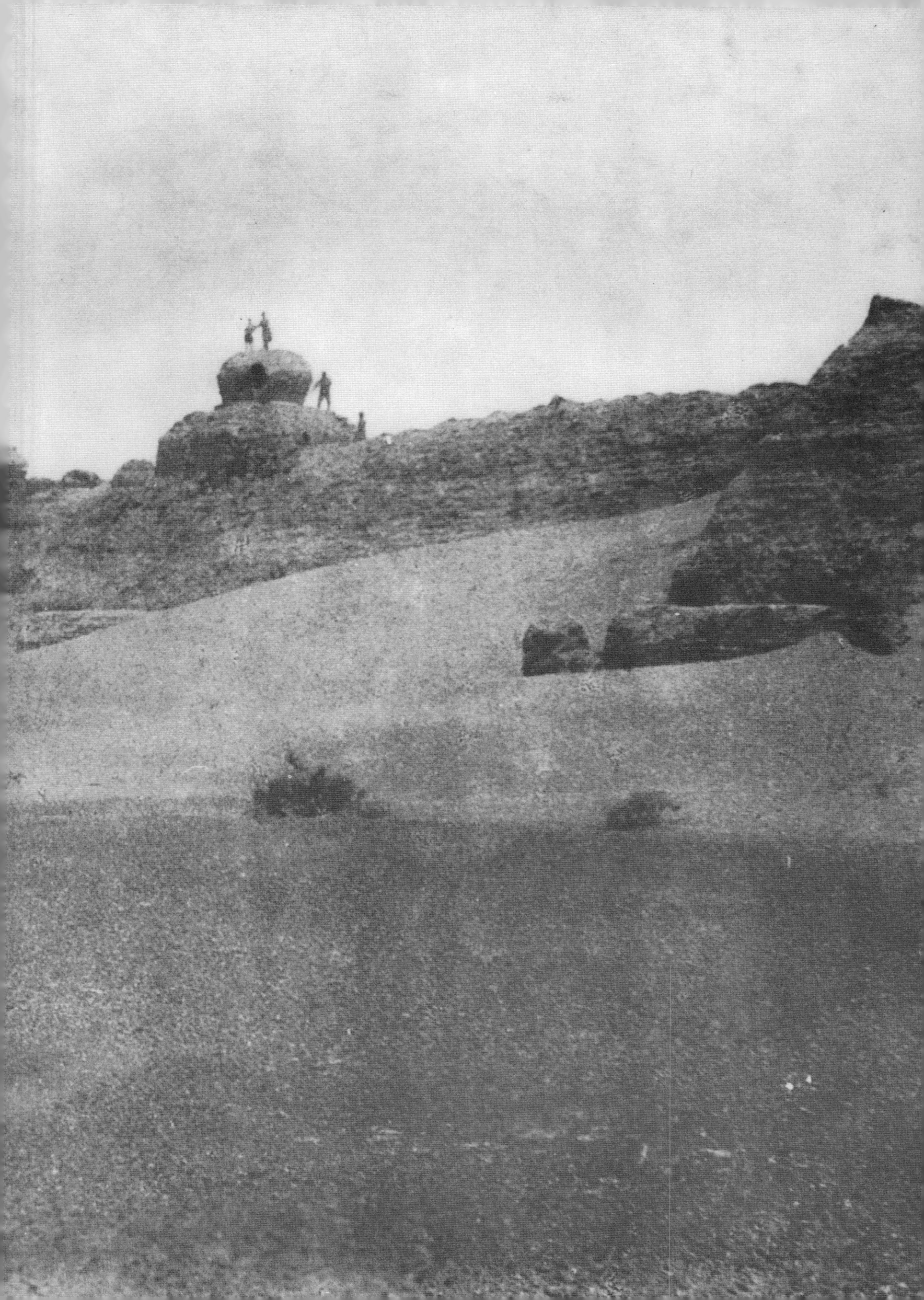

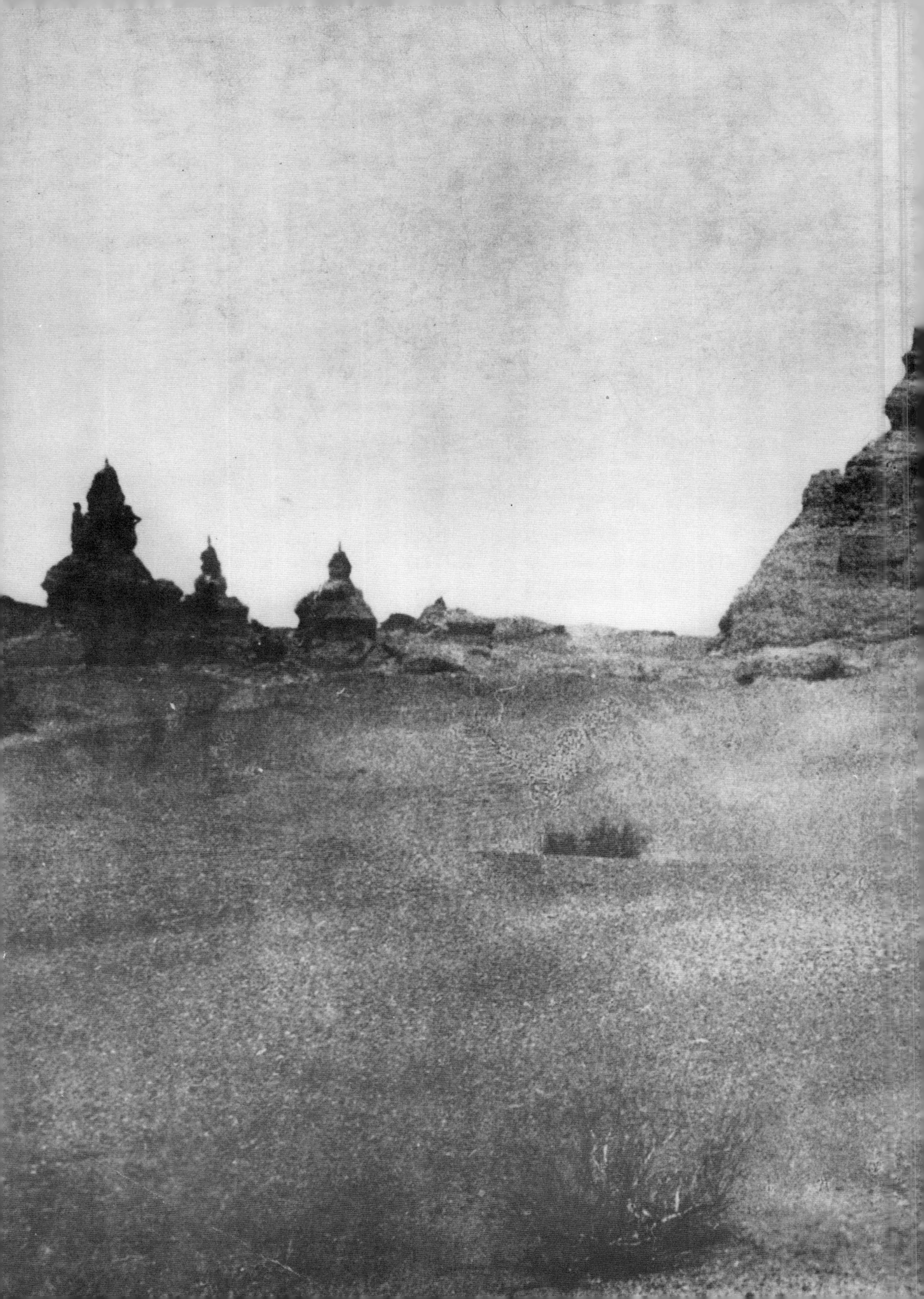

俄羅斯科學院東方文獻研究所
中國社會科學院民族學與人類學研究所
上 海 古 籍 出 版 社 編

俄羅斯科學院東方文獻
研究所藏黑水城文獻

㉓

西夏文
佛教部分

上 海 古 籍 出 版 社
二〇一四年·上海

圖書在版編目(CIP)數據

俄藏黑水城文獻.23,西夏文佛教部分/俄羅斯科學院
東方文獻研究所,中國社科院民族學與人類學研究所,
上海古籍出版社編.—上海：上海古籍出版社,2014.8
ISBN 978 - 7 - 5325 - 7391 - 2

Ⅰ.①俄… Ⅱ.①俄… ②中… ③上… Ⅲ.①出土文
物-文獻-額濟納旗-西夏-圖錄②佛教-文獻-額濟納旗-
西夏-圖錄 Ⅳ.①K877.92

中國版本圖書館 CIP 數據核字(2014)第 200035 號

國家古籍整理出版專項經費資助項目
俄藏黑水城文獻自第十五册起受中國社會科學院出版基金資助

俄藏黑水城文獻 ㉓

編者　俄羅斯科學院東方文獻研究所
　　　中國社會科學院民族學與人類學研究所
　　　上海古籍出版社

主編　史金波(中)
　　　魏同賢(中)
　　　E.И.克恰諾夫(俄)

出版　上海古籍出版社
　　　中國上海瑞金二路 272 號郵政編碼 200020

印製　上海麗佳製版印刷有限公司

©　俄羅斯科學院東方文獻研究所
　　中國社會科學院民族學與人類學研究所
　　上海古籍出版社

開本 787 × 1092 mm　1/8　印張 39.5　插頁 28
二○一四年八月第一版　二○一四年八月第一次印刷
ISBN 978 - 7 - 5325 - 7391 - 2/K · 1930
定價：二二○○圓

Памятники письменности
из Хара-Хото хранящиеся
в Институте восточных рукописей РАН

㉓

Коллекции буддийской части тангутского языка

Институт восточных рукописей
Российской академии наук
Институт национальностей и антропологии
Академии общественных наук Китая
Шанхайское издательство "Древняя книга"

Шанхайское издательство
"Древняя книга"
Шанхай 2014

Памятники письменности
нз Хара-Хото хранящиеся в России ㉓

Составнтели
Институт восточных рукописей РАН
Институт национальности и антропологии
АОН Китая
Шанхайское издательство
"Древняя книга"

Главные редакторы
Е. И. Кычанов (Россия)
Ши Цзинь-бо (Китай)
Вэй Тун-сянь (Китай)

Издатель
Шанхайское нздательство
"Древняя книга"
Китай Шанхай ул. Жуйцзиньэр 272
Почтовый индекс 200020

Печать
Шанхайская гравировальная и полиграфическая компания
"Ли Цзя" с ограниченной ответственностью

© Институт восточных рукописей РАН
Институт национальности и антропологии
Академии общественных наук Китая
Шанхайское нздательство "Древняя книга"

Формат 787×1092 mm 1/8
Печатный лист 39.5
Вкладка 28
Первое издание Ⅷ.2014г.
Первая печать Ⅷ.2014г.

Heishuicheng Manuscripts
Collected in
the Institute of Oriental Manuscripts of
the Russian Academy of Sciences

㉓

Tangut Buddhist Manuscripts

The Institute of Oriental Manuscripts of
the Russian Academy of Sciences
Institute of Ethnology and Anthropology of
the Chinese Academy of Social Sciences
Shanghai Chinese Classics Publishing House

Shanghai Chinese Classics Publishing House
Shanghai, 2014

Heishuicheng Manuscripts
Collected in Russia
Volume ㉓

Participating Institutions
The Institute of Oriental Manuscripts of
the Russian Academy of Sciences
Institute of Ethnology and Anthropology of
the Chinese Academy of Social Sciences
Shanghai Chinese Classics Publishing House

Editors-in-Chief
Shi Jinbo (on Chinese part)
Wei Tongxian (on Chinese part)
E. I. Kychanov (on Russian part)

Publisher
Shanghai Chinese Classics Publishing House
(272 Ruijin Second Road, Shanghai 200020, China)

Printer
Shanghai Pica Plate Making & Printing Co., Ltd

© The Institute of Oriental Manuscripts of
the Russian Academy of Sciences
Institute of Ethnology and Anthropology of
the Chinese Academy of Social Sciences
Shanghai Chinese Classics Publishing House

8 mo 787×1092mm 39.5 printed sheets 28 insets
First Edition: August 2014   First Printing: August 2014
ISBN 978 - 7 - 5325 - 7391 - 2/K · 1930
Price: ￥2200.00

俄藏黑水城文獻

主　編　　史金波（中）

魏同賢（中）

E.И.克恰諾夫（俄）

編輯委員會（按姓氏筆畫爲序）

中方　　　魏同賢

聶鴻音

李偉國

李國章

白　濱

史金波

俄方　　　E.И.克恰諾夫

孟列夫

К.Б.克平

執行編輯　　蔣維崧

俄藏黑水城文獻 ㉓

本卷主編　史金波
　　　　　Е.И.克恰諾夫

本卷副主編　聶鴻音　蘇　航

責任編輯　蔣維崧

裝幀設計　嚴克勤

攝　　影　嚴克勤

技術編輯　耿瑩褘

Памятники письменности
из Хара-Хото хранящиеся в России ㉓

Главный редактор этого тома
Е. И. Кычанов
Ши Цзинь-бо
Заместитель главного редактора этого тома
Не Хун-инь
Су Хан

Ответственный редактор
Цзян Вэй-сун
Художественный и технический редактор
Янь Кэ-цинь
Фотограф
Янь Кэ-цинь
Технический редактор
Гэн Ин-и

Heishuicheng Manuscripts

Collected in Russia

Volume ㉓

Editor-in-Chief for this Volume
Shi Jinbo
E. L. Kychanov
Deputy Editor-in-Chief for this Volume
Nie Hongyin
Su Hang
Editor-in-Charge
Jiang Weisong
Cover Designer
Yan Keqin
Photographer
Yan Keqin
Technical Editor
Geng Yingyi

一 Инв.No.4271 大方廣佛華嚴經名略

二 Инв.No.5740 大方廣佛華嚴經卷第八十

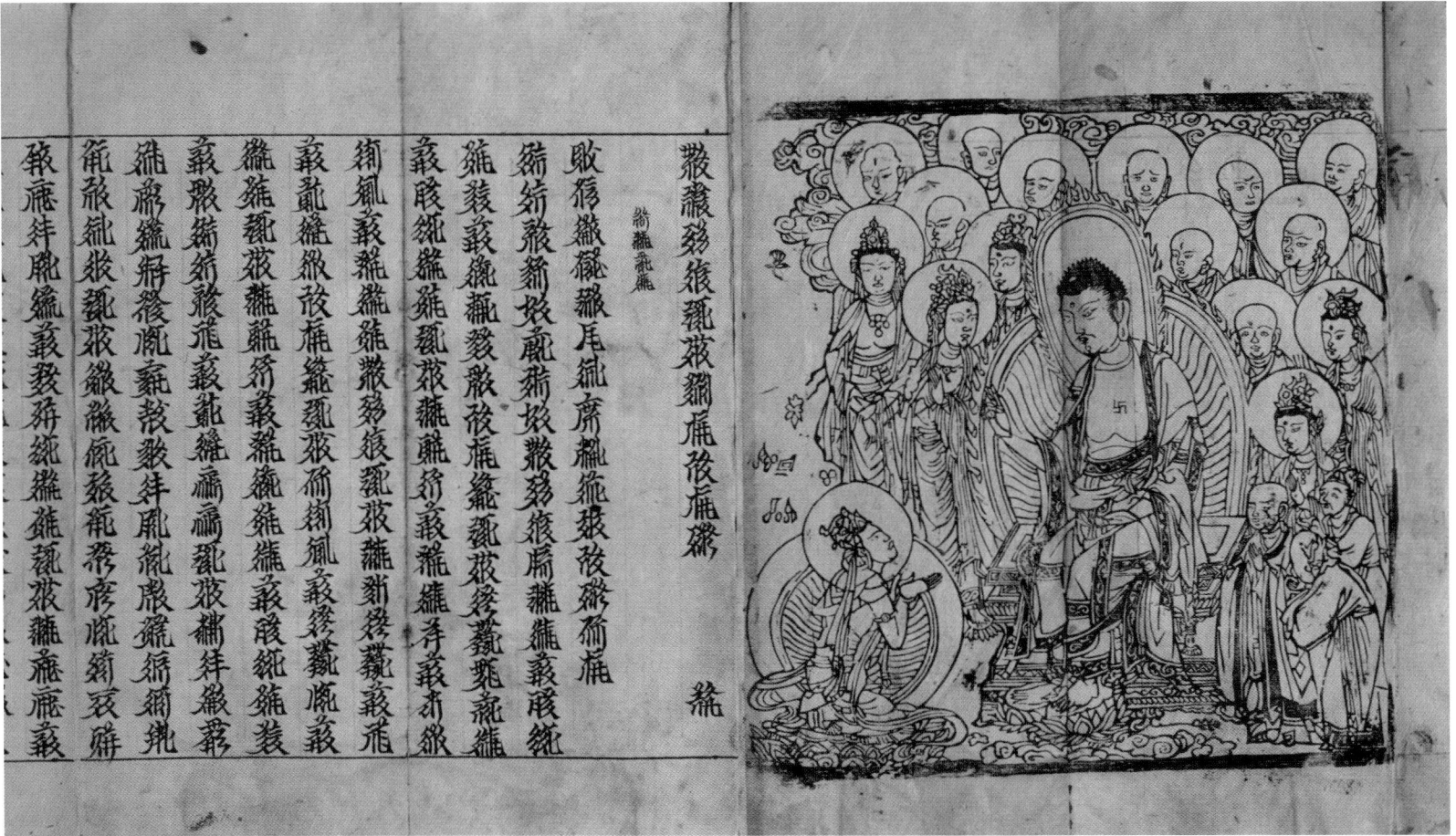

三　Инв.No.420　大般涅槃經卷第二十二經圖卷首

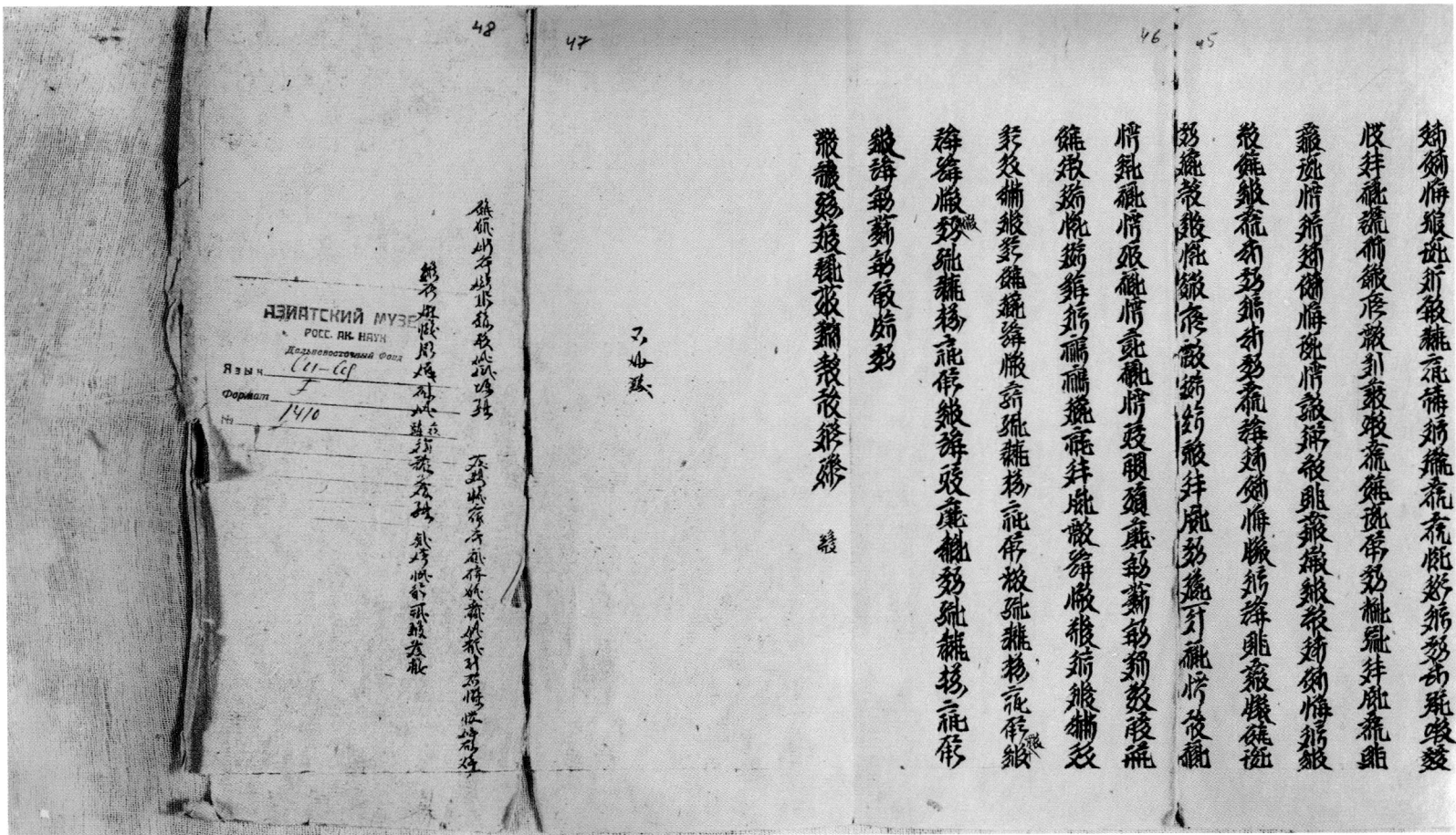

四　Инв.No.469　大般涅槃經卷第三十六題記

五　Инв.No.6331　大般涅槃經卷第十題記

六　Инв.No.4631　妙法蓮華經序卷第一

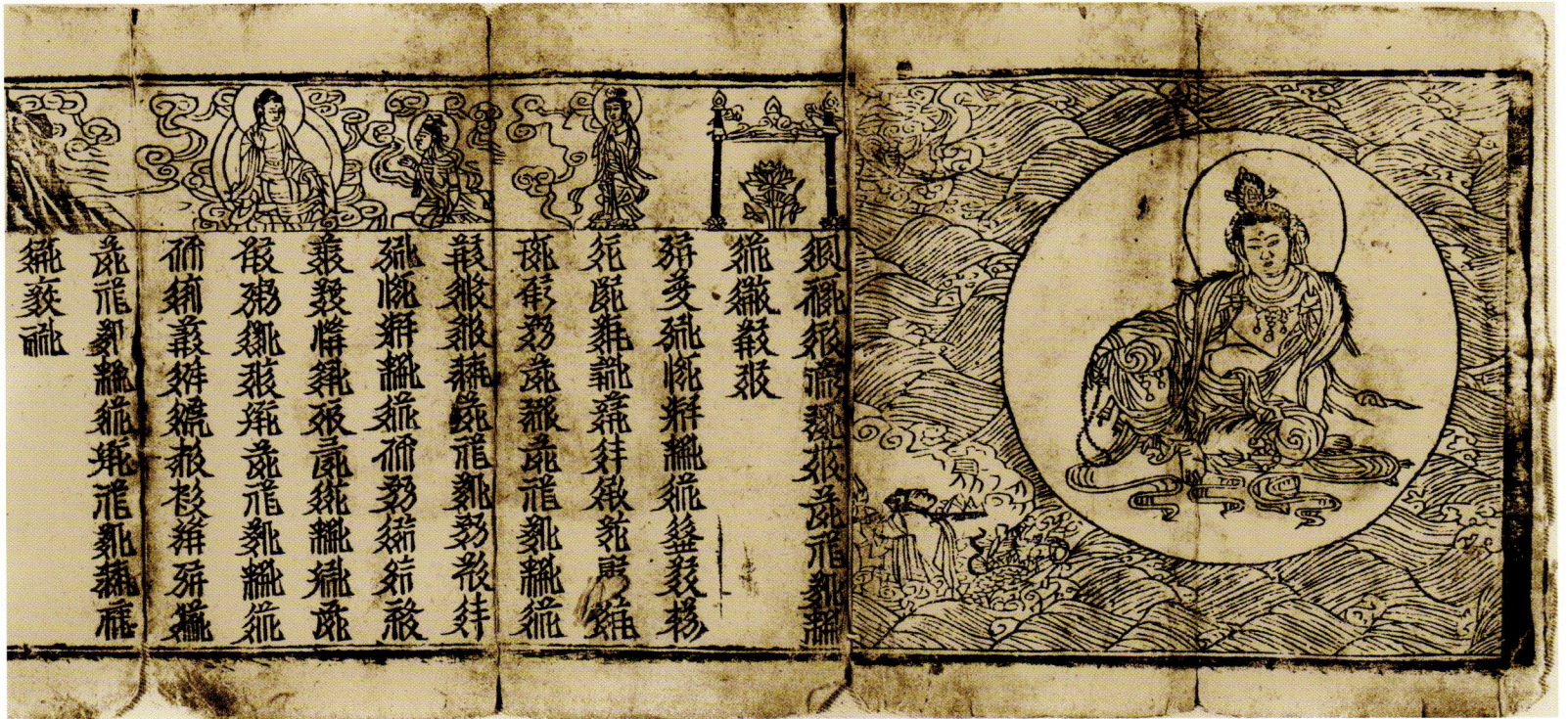

七　Инв.No.940　妙法蓮華經觀世音菩薩普門品卷首

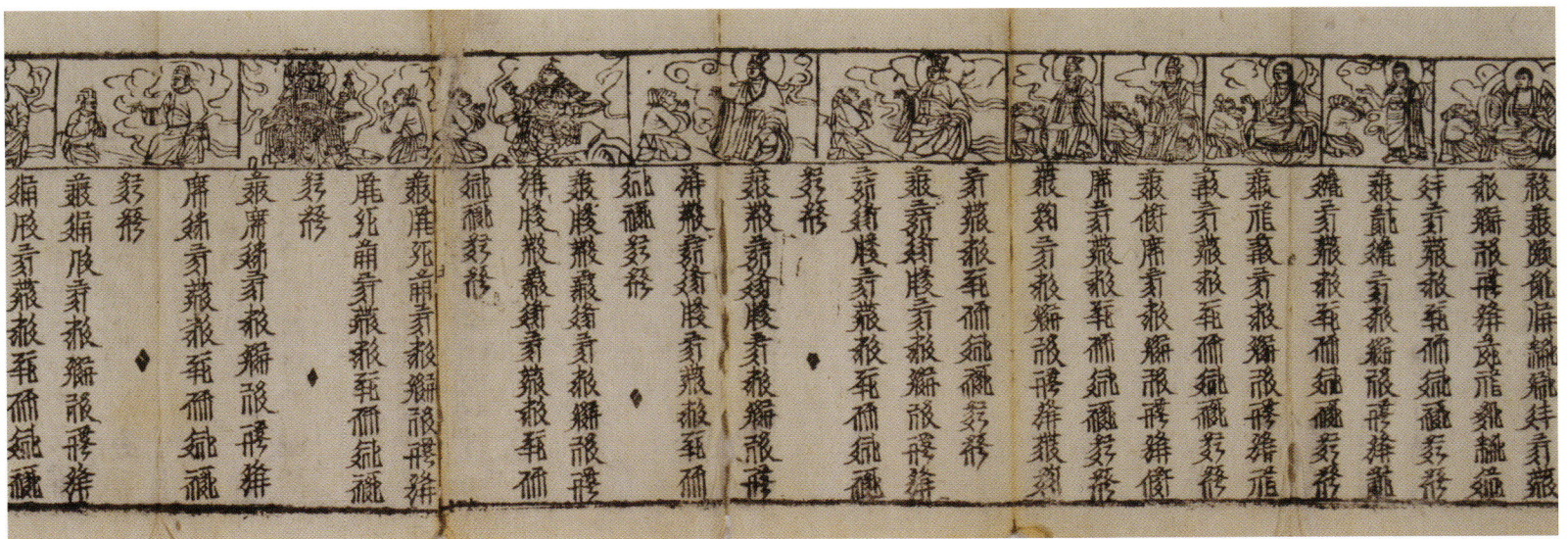

八　Инв.No221　妙法蓮華經觀世音菩薩普門品

彩色圖版目録

俄 Инв.No.4271 4272 4273 4274 4275 4276 4277 4278 4279 4280 4281 4282 4283 4284 4295 4297 5322 5326
5333 5758 6330 6337 6338 7357 7650 7651　1.大方廣佛華嚴經名略　　(82-1)

俄 Инв.No.4271 4272 4273 4274 4275 4276 4277 4278 4279 4280 4281 4282 4283 4284 4295 4297 5322 5326
5333 5758 6330 6337 6338 7357 7650 7651　1.大方廣佛華嚴經名略　　(82-2)

俄 Инв.No.4271 4272 4273 4274 4275 4276 4277 4278 4279 4280 4281 4282 4283 4284 4295 4297 5322 5326
5333 5758 6330 6337 6338 7357 7650 7651　1.大方廣佛華嚴經名略　　(82-3)

俄 Инв.No.4271 4272 4273 4274 4275 4276 4277 4278 4279 4280 4281 4282 4283 4284 4295 4297 5322 5326
5333 5758 6330 6337 6338 7357 7650 7651　2.大方廣佛華嚴經卷第一　　(82-4)

俄 Инв.No.4271 4272 4273 4274 4275 4276 4277 4278 4279 4280 4281 4282 4283 4284 4295 4297 5322 5326
5333 5758 6330 6337 6338 7357 7650 7651　3.大方廣佛華嚴經卷第二　　(82-5)

俄 Инв.No.4271 4272 4273 4274 4275 4276 4277 4278 4279 4280 4281 4282 4283 4284 4295 4297 5322 5326
5333 5758 6330 6337 6338 7357 7650 7651　4.大方廣佛華嚴經卷第四　　(82-6)

俄 Инв.No.4271 4272 4273 4274 4275 4276 4277 4278 4279 4280 4281 4282 4283 4284 4295 4297 5322 5326
5333 5758 6330 6337 6338 7357 7650 7651　5.大方廣佛華嚴經卷第五　　(82-7)

俄 Инв.No.4271 4272 4273 4274 4275 4276 4277 4278 4279 4280 4281 4282 4283 4284 4295 4297 5322 5326
5333 5758 6330 6337 6338 7357 7650 7651　6.大方廣佛華嚴經卷第六　　(82-8)

俄 **Инв**.No.4271 *4272 4273 4274 4275 4276 4277 4278 4279 4280 4281 4282 4283 4284 4295 4297 5322 5326*
5333 5758 6330 6337 6338 7357 7650 7651 7.大方廣佛華嚴經卷第九 (82-9)

俄 **Инв**.No.4271 *4272 4273 4274 4275 4276 4277 4278 4279 4280 4281 4282 4283 4284 4295 4297 5322 5326*
5333 5758 6330 6337 6338 7357 7650 7651 8.大方廣佛華嚴經卷第十 (82-10)

俄 **Инв**.No.4271 *4272 4273 4274 4275 4276 4277 4278 4279 4280 4281 4282 4283 4284 4295 4297 5322 5326*
5333 5758 6330 6337 6338 7357 7650 7651 8.大方廣佛華嚴經卷第十 (82-11)

俄 **Инв**.No.4271 *4272 4273 4274 4275 4276 4277 4278 4279 4280 4281 4282 4283 4284 4295 4297 5322 5326*
5333 5758 6330 6337 6338 7357 7650 7651 9.大方廣佛華嚴經卷第十一 (82-12)

俄ИнⅡв.No.4271 4272 4273 4274 4275 4276 4277 4278 4279 4280 4281 4282 4283 4284 4295 4297 5322 5326 5333 5758 6330 6337 6338 7357 7650 7651　17.大方廣佛華嚴經卷第二十　　　(82-21)

俄ИнⅡв.No.4271 4272 4273 4274 4275 4276 4277 4278 4279 4280 4281 4282 4283 4284 4295 4297 5322 5326 5333 5758 6330 6337 6338 7357 7650 7651　18.大方廣佛華嚴經卷第二十一　　(82-22)

俄ИнⅡв.No.4271 4272 4273 4274 4275 4276 4277 4278 4279 4280 4281 4282 4283 4284 4295 4297 5322 5326 5333 5758 6330 6337 6338 7357 7650 7651　19.大方廣佛華嚴經卷第二十二　　(82-23)

俄ИнⅡв.No.4271 4272 4273 4274 4275 4276 4277 4278 4279 4280 4281 4282 4283 4284 4295 4297 5322 5326 5333 5758 6330 6337 6338 7357 7650 7651　20.大方廣佛華嚴經卷第二十三　　(82-24)

俄 **Инв.**No.4271 *4272 4273 4274 4275 4276 4277 4278 4279 4280 4281 4282 4283 4284 4295 4297 5322 5326*
5333 5758 6330 6337 6338 7357 7650 7651 21.大方廣佛華嚴經卷第二十四 (82-25)

俄 **Инв.**No.4271 *4272 4273 4274 4275 4276 4277 4278 4279 4280 4281 4282 4283 4284 4295 4297 5322 5326*
5333 5758 6330 6337 6338 7357 7650 7651 22.大方廣佛華嚴經卷第二十六 (82-26)

俄 **Инв.**No.4271 *4272 4273 4274 4275 4276 4277 4278 4279 4280 4281 4282 4283 4284 4295 4297 5322 5326*
5333 5758 6330 6337 6338 7357 7650 7651 22.大方廣佛華嚴經卷第二十六 (82-27)

俄 **Инв.**No.4271 *4272 4273 4274 4275 4276 4277 4278 4279 4280 4281 4282 4283 4284 4295 4297 5322 5326*
5333 5758 6330 6337 6338 7357 7650 7651 23.大方廣佛華嚴經卷第二十七 (82-28)

俄ИНВ.No.4271 4272 4273 4274 4275 4276 4277 4278 4279 4280 4281 4282 4283 4284 4295 4297 5322 5326 5333 5758 6330 6337 6338 7357 7650 7651　24.大方廣佛華嚴經卷第二十八　　(82-29)

俄ИНВ.No.4271 4272 4273 4274 4275 4276 4277 4278 4279 4280 4281 4282 4283 4284 4295 4297 5322 5326 5333 5758 6330 6337 6338 7357 7650 7651　25.大方廣佛華嚴經卷第二十九　　(82-30)

俄ИНВ.No.4271 4272 4273 4274 4275 4276 4277 4278 4279 4280 4281 4282 4283 4284 4295 4297 5322 5326 5333 5758 6330 6337 6338 7357 7650 7651　26.大方廣佛華嚴經卷第三十一　　(82-31)

俄ИНВ.No.4271 4272 4273 4274 4275 4276 4277 4278 4279 4280 4281 4282 4283 4284 4295 4297 5322 5326 5333 5758 6330 6337 6338 7357 7650 7651　27.大方廣佛華嚴經卷第三十二　　(82-32)

俄 Инв.No.4271 *4272 4273 4274 4275 4276 4277 4278 4279 4280 4281 4282 4283 4284 4295 4297 5322 5326 5333 5758 6330 6337 6338 7357 7650 7651*　28.大方廣佛華嚴經卷第三十三　　(82-33)

俄 Инв.No.4271 *4272 4273 4274 4275 4276 4277 4278 4279 4280 4281 4282 4283 4284 4295 4297 5322 5326 5333 5758 6330 6337 6338 7357 7650 7651*　29.大方廣佛華嚴經卷第三十四　　(82-34)

俄 Инв.No.4271 *4272 4273 4274 4275 4276 4277 4278 4279 4280 4281 4282 4283 4284 4295 4297 5322 5326 5333 5758 6330 6337 6338 7357 7650 7651*　30.大方廣佛華嚴經卷第三十五　　(82-35)

俄 Инв.No.4271 *4272 4273 4274 4275 4276 4277 4278 4279 4280 4281 4282 4283 4284 4295 4297 5322 5326 5333 5758 6330 6337 6338 7357 7650 7651*　31.大方廣佛華嚴經卷第三十六　　(82-36)

俄 Инв.No.4271 4272 4273 4274 4275 4276 4277 4278 4279 4280 4281 4282 4283 4284 4295 4297 5322 5326
5333 5758 6330 6337 6338 7357 7650 7651　32.大方廣佛華嚴經卷第三十七　　　(82-37)

俄 Инв.No.4271 4272 4273 4274 4275 4276 4277 4278 4279 4280 4281 4282 4283 4284 4295 4297 5322 5326
5333 5758 6330 6337 6338 7357 7650 7651　33.大方廣佛華嚴經卷第三十八　　　(82-38)

俄 Инв.No.4271 4272 4273 4274 4275 4276 4277 4278 4279 4280 4281 4282 4283 4284 4295 4297 5322 5326
5333 5758 6330 6337 6338 7357 7650 7651　34.大方廣佛華嚴經卷第三十九　　　(82-39)

俄 Инв.No.4271 4272 4273 4274 4275 4276 4277 4278 4279 4280 4281 4282 4283 4284 4295 4297 5322 5326
5333 5758 6330 6337 6338 7357 7650 7651　35.大方廣佛華嚴經卷第四十　　　(82-40)

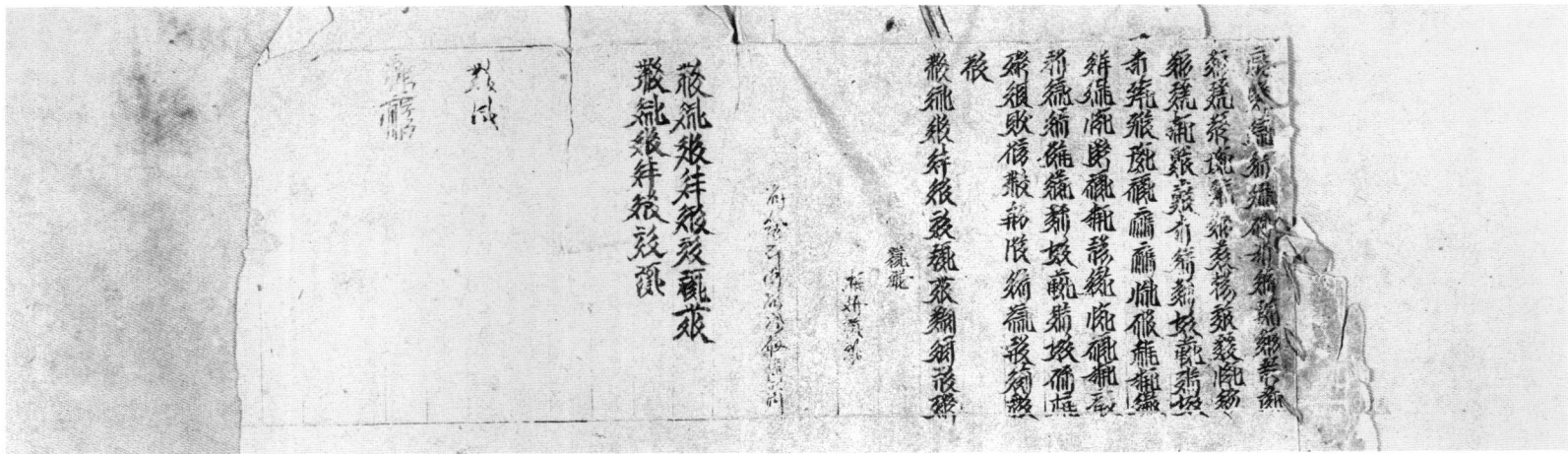

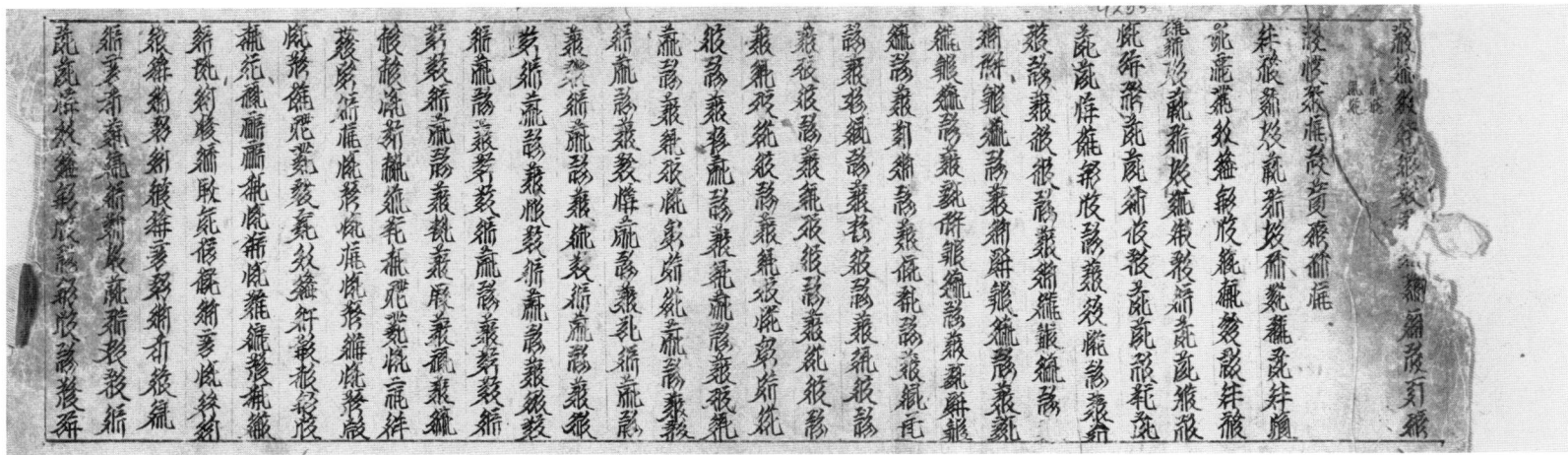

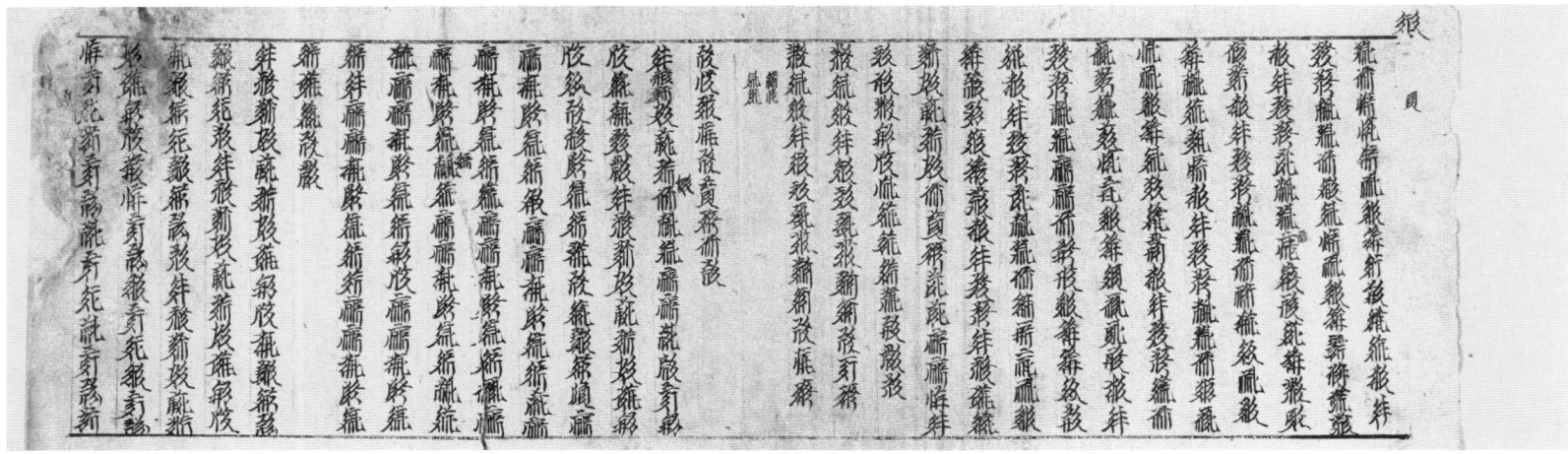

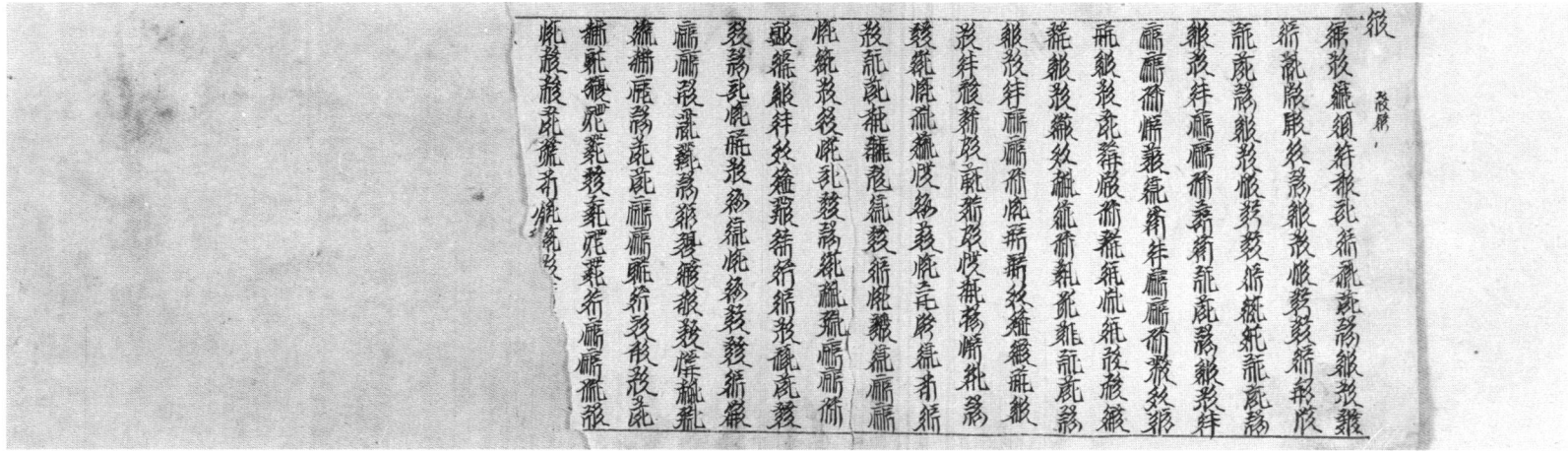

11

俄 Инв.No.4271 4272 4273 4274 4275 4276 4277 4278 4279 4280 4281 4282 4283 4284 4295 4297 5322 5326 5333 5758 6330 6337 6338 7357 7650 7651　42.大方廣佛華嚴經卷第四十九　　(82-49)

俄 Инв.No.4271 4272 4273 4274 4275 4276 4277 4278 4279 4280 4281 4282 4283 4284 4295 4297 5322 5326 5333 5758 6330 6337 6338 7357 7650 7651　43.大方廣佛華嚴經卷第五十　　(82-50)

俄 Инв.No.4271 4272 4273 4274 4275 4276 4277 4278 4279 4280 4281 4282 4283 4284 4295 4297 5322 5326 5333 5758 6330 6337 6338 7357 7650 7651　44.大方廣佛華嚴經卷第五十一　　(82-51)

俄 Инв.No.4271 4272 4273 4274 4275 4276 4277 4278 4279 4280 4281 4282 4283 4284 4295 4297 5322 5326 5333 5758 6330 6337 6338 7357 7650 7651　45.大方廣佛華嚴經卷第五十二　　(82-52)

俄 Инв.No.4271 4272 4273 4274 4275 4276 4277 4278 4279 4280 4281 4282 4283 4284 4295 4297 5322 5326
5333 5758 6330 6337 6338 7357 7650 7651　45.大方廣佛華嚴經卷第五十二　　　(82-53)

俄 Инв.No.4271 4272 4273 4274 4275 4276 4277 4278 4279 4280 4281 4282 4283 4284 4295 4297 5322 5326
5333 5758 6330 6337 6338 7357 7650 7651　46.大方廣佛華嚴經卷第五十三　　　(82-54)

俄 Инв.No.4271 4272 4273 4274 4275 4276 4277 4278 4279 4280 4281 4282 4283 4284 4295 4297 5322 5326
5333 5758 6330 6337 6338 7357 7650 7651　47.大方廣佛華嚴經卷第五十四　　　(82-55)

俄 Инв.No.4271 4272 4273 4274 4275 4276 4277 4278 4279 4280 4281 4282 4283 4284 4295 4297 5322 5326
5333 5758 6330 6337 6338 7357 7650 7651　48.大方廣佛華嚴經卷第五十六　　　(82-56)

俄Инв.No.4271 4272 4273 4274 4275 4276 4277 4278 4279 4280 4281 4282 4283 4284 4295 4297 5322 5326
5333 5758 6330 6337 6338 7357 7650 7651　52.大方廣佛華嚴經卷第六十　　(82-61)

俄Инв.No.4271 4272 4273 4274 4275 4276 4277 4278 4279 4280 4281 4282 4283 4284 4295 4297 5322 5326
5333 5758 6330 6337 6338 7357 7650 7651　53.大方廣佛華嚴經卷第六十二　　(82-62)

俄Инв.No.4271 4272 4273 4274 4275 4276 4277 4278 4279 4280 4281 4282 4283 4284 4295 4297 5322 5326
5333 5758 6330 6337 6338 7357 7650 7651　54.大方廣佛華嚴經卷第六十三　　(82-63)

俄Инв.No.4271 4272 4273 4274 4275 4276 4277 4278 4279 4280 4281 4282 4283 4284 4295 4297 5322 5326
5333 5758 6330 6337 6338 7357 7650 7651　55.大方廣佛華嚴經卷第六十四　　(82-64)

俄Инв.No.4271 4272 4273 4274 4275 4276 4277 4278 4279 4280 4281 4282 4283 4284 4295 4297 5322 5326 5333 5758 6330 6337 6338 7357 7650 7651　59.大方廣佛華嚴經卷第六十九　　　(82-69)

俄Инв.No.4271 4272 4273 4274 4275 4276 4277 4278 4279 4280 4281 4282 4283 4284 4295 4297 5322 5326 5333 5758 6330 6337 6338 7357 7650 7651　60.大方廣佛華嚴經卷第七十　　　(82-70)

俄Инв.No.4271 4272 4273 4274 4275 4276 4277 4278 4279 4280 4281 4282 4283 4284 4295 4297 5322 5326 5333 5758 6330 6337 6338 7357 7650 7651　60.大方廣佛華嚴經卷第七十　　　(82-71)

俄Инв.No.4271 4272 4273 4274 4275 4276 4277 4278 4279 4280 4281 4282 4283 4284 4295 4297 5322 5326 5333 5758 6330 6337 6338 7357 7650 7651　61.大方廣佛華嚴經卷第七十一　　　(82-72)

俄 Инв.No.4271 4272 4273 4274 4275 4276 4277 4278 4279 4280 4281 4282 4283 4284 4295 4297 5322 5326
5333 5758 6330 6337 6338 7357 7650 7651　66.大方廣佛華嚴經卷第七十七　　　(82-81)

俄 Инв.No.4271 4272 4273 4274 4275 4276 4277 4278 4279 4280 4281 4282 4283 4284 4295 4297 5322 5326
5333 5758 6330 6337 6338 7357 7650 7651　67.大方廣佛華嚴經卷第七十九　　　(82-82)

俄 Инв.No.5319 5733 5735 5736 5737 5738 5739 5740 5741 7335 7547 7652
1.大方廣佛華嚴經名略　　　(72-1)

俄 Инв.No.5319 5733 5735 5736 5737 5738 5739 5740 5741 7335 7547 7652
1.大方廣佛華嚴經名略　　　(72-2)

1.大方廣佛華嚴經名略　　（72-3）

2.大方廣佛華嚴經卷第一　　（72-4）

3.大方廣佛華嚴經卷第二　　（72-5）

4.大方廣佛華嚴經卷第三　　（72-6）

5.大方廣佛華嚴經卷第四　　　(72-7)

6.大方廣佛華嚴經卷第五　　　(72-8)

7.大方廣佛華嚴經卷第六　　　(72-9)

8.大方廣佛華嚴經卷第七　　　(72-10)

俄 Инв.No.5319 *5733 5735 5736 5737 5738 5739 5740 5741 7335 7547 7652*

9.大方廣佛華嚴經卷第八　　(72-11)

俄 Инв.No.5319 *5733 5735 5736 5737 5738 5739 5740 5741 7335 7547 7652*

10.大方廣佛華嚴經卷第九　　(72-12)

俄 Инв.No.5319 *5733 5735 5736 5737 5738 5739 5740 5741 7335 7547 7652*

11.大方廣佛華嚴經卷第十三　　(72-13)

俄 Инв.No.5319 *5733 5735 5736 5737 5738 5739 5740 5741 7335 7547 7652*

12.大方廣佛華嚴經卷第十四　　(72-14)

15.大方廣佛華嚴經卷第十七　　　(72-19)

16.大方廣佛華嚴經卷第十八　　　(72-20)

17.大方廣佛華嚴經卷第二十　　　(72-21)

18.大方廣佛華嚴經卷第二十二　　　(72-22)

19.大方廣佛華嚴經卷第二十三　　(72-23)

20.大方廣佛華嚴經卷第二十四　　(72-24)

21.大方廣佛華嚴經卷第二十五　　(72-25)

22.大方廣佛華嚴經卷第二十六　　(72-26)

俄 **Инв**.No.5319 *5733 5735 5736 5737 5738 5739 5740 5741 7335 7547 7652*

23.大方廣佛華嚴經卷第二十八　　　(72-27)

俄 **Инв**.No.5319 *5733 5735 5736 5737 5738 5739 5740 5741 7335 7547 7652*

24.大方廣佛華嚴經卷第二十九　　　(72-28)

俄 **Инв**.No.5319 *5733 5735 5736 5737 5738 5739 5740 5741 7335 7547 7652*

25.大方廣佛華嚴經卷第三十　　　(72-29)

俄 **Инв**.No.5319 *5733 5735 5736 5737 5738 5739 5740 5741 7335 7547 7652*

26.大方廣佛華嚴經卷第三十一　　　(72-30)

俄 Инв.No.5319 *5733 5735 5736 5737 5738 5739 5740 5741 7335 7547 7652*

27.大方廣佛華嚴經卷第三十二　　　(72-31)

俄 Инв.No.5319 *5733 5735 5736 5737 5738 5739 5740 5741 7335 7547 7652*

28.大方廣佛華嚴經卷第三十三　　　(72-32)

俄 Инв.No.5319 *5733 5735 5736 5737 5738 5739 5740 5741 7335 7547 7652*

29.大方廣佛華嚴經卷第三十四　　　(72-33)

俄 Инв.No.5319 *5733 5735 5736 5737 5738 5739 5740 5741 7335 7547 7652*

30.大方廣佛華嚴經卷第三十五　　　(72-34)

俄 Инв.No.5319 *5733 5735 5736 5737 5738 5739 5740 5741 7335 7547 7652*

31.大方廣佛華嚴經卷第三十六　　(72-35)

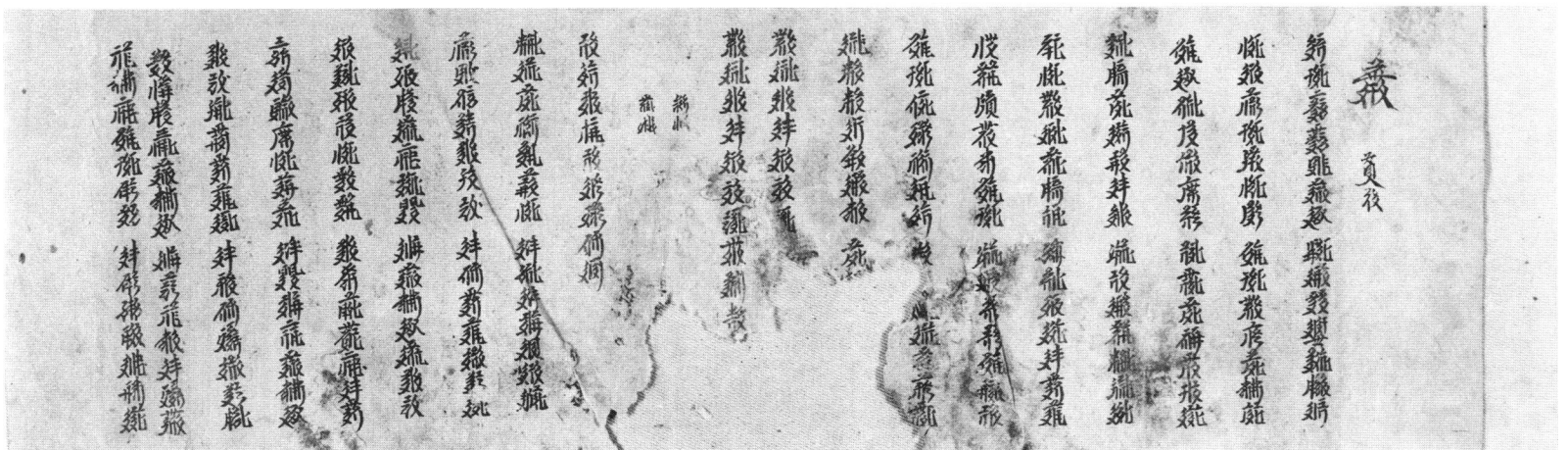

俄 Инв.No.5319 *5733 5735 5736 5737 5738 5739 5740 5741 7335 7547 7652*

32.大方廣佛華嚴經卷第三十七　　(72-36)

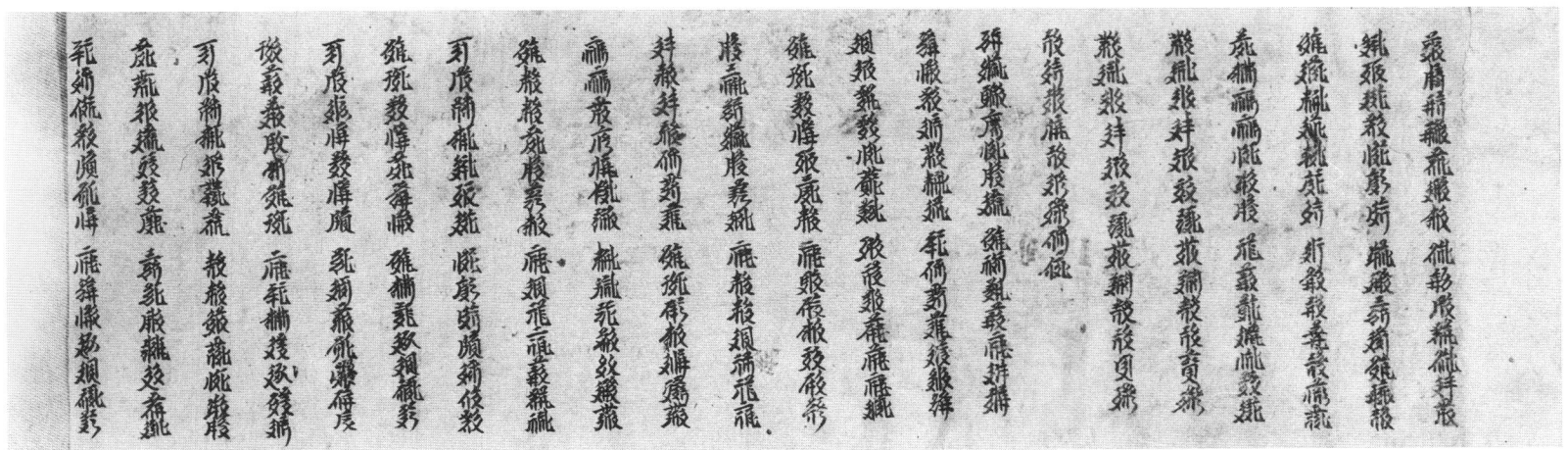

俄 Инв.No.5319 *5733 5735 5736 5737 5738 5739 5740 5741 7335 7547 7652*

33.大方廣佛華嚴經卷第三十八　　(72-37)

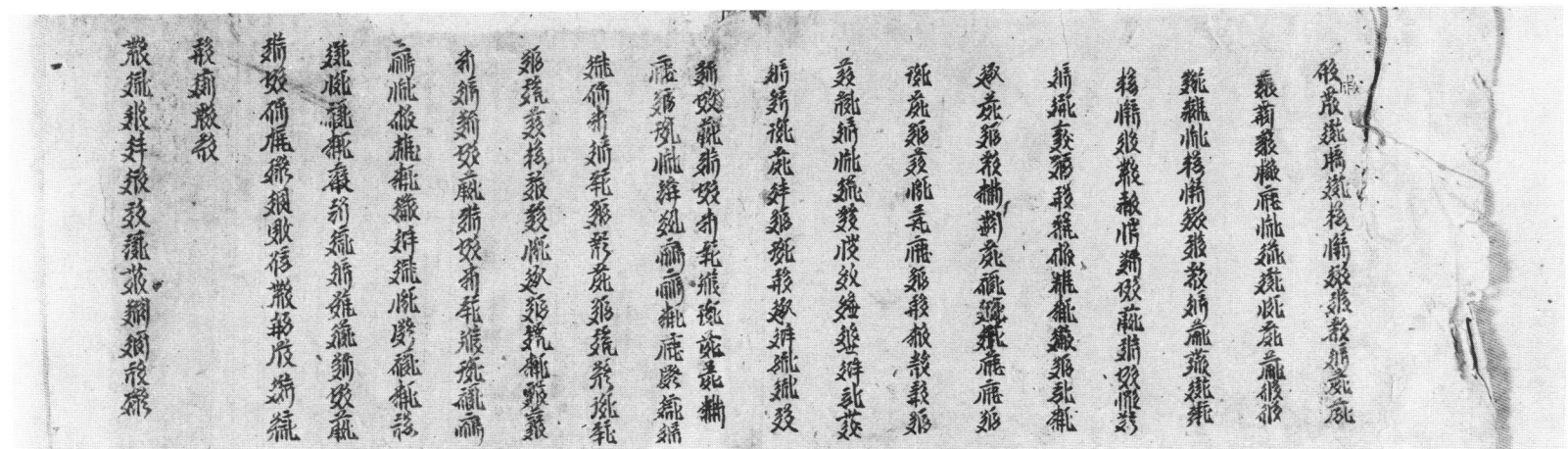

俄 Инв.No.5319 *5733 5735 5736 5737 5738 5739 5740 5741 7335 7547 7652*

34.大方廣佛華嚴經卷第四十　　(72-38)

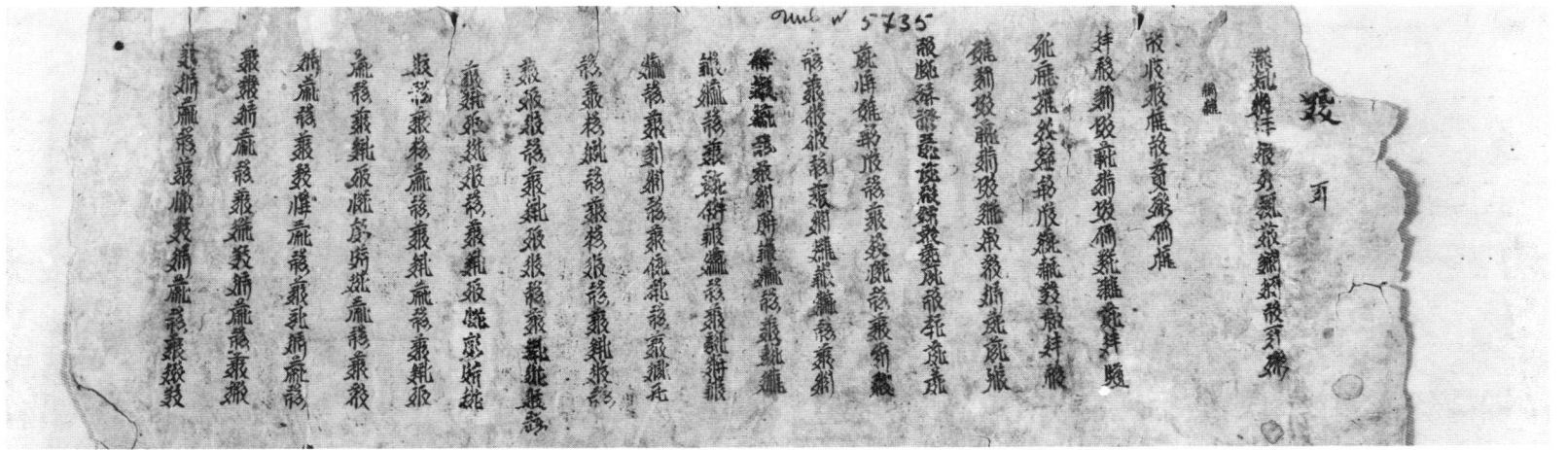

35.大方廣佛華嚴經卷第四十一　　　(72-39)

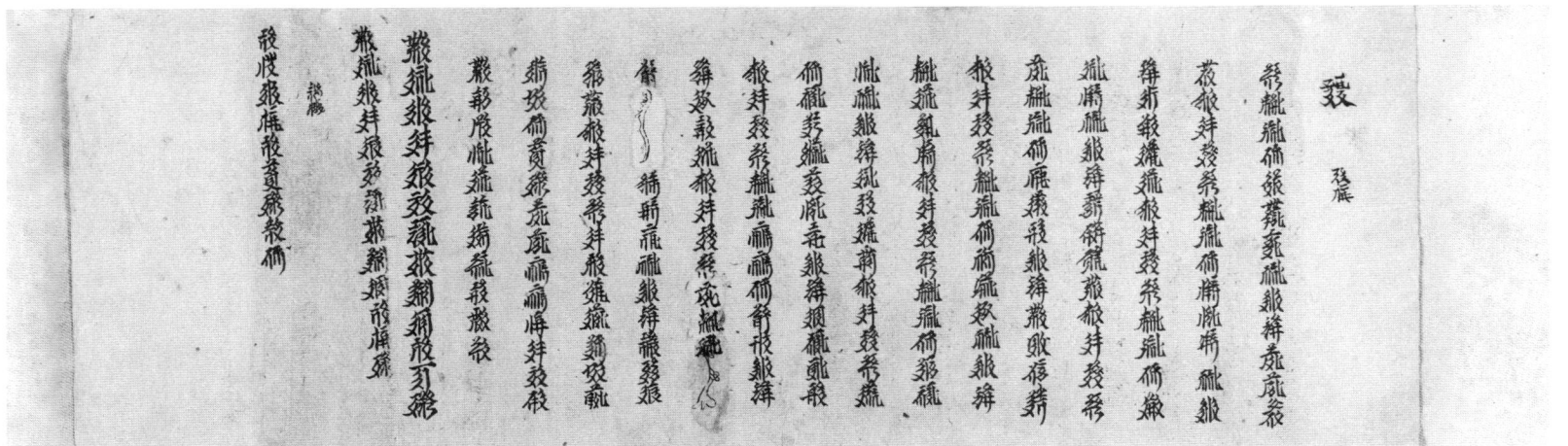

36.大方廣佛華嚴經卷第四十二　　　(72-40)

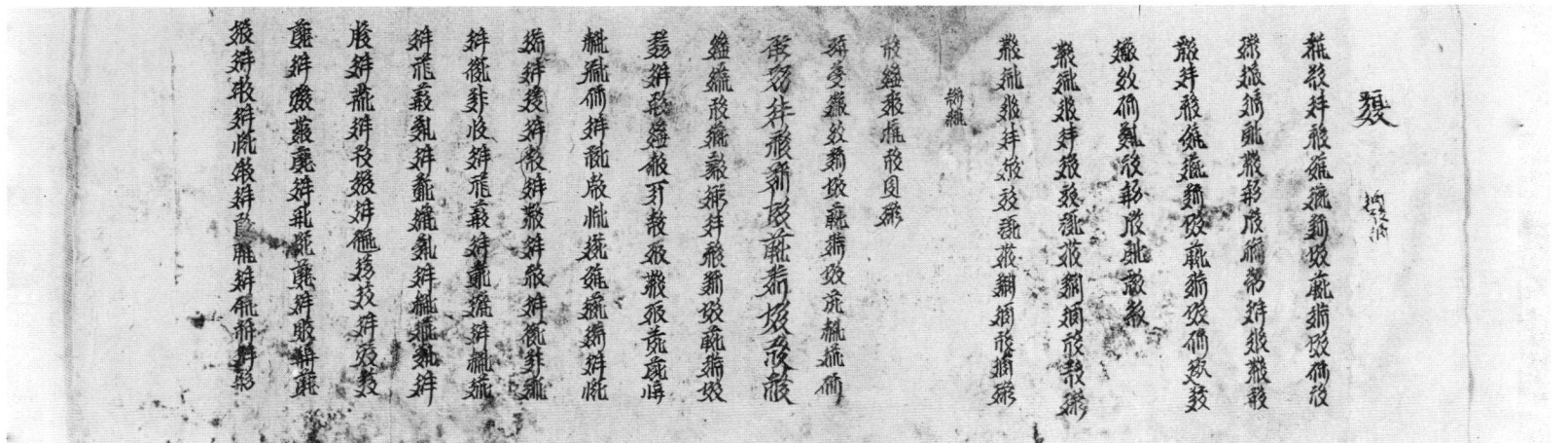

37.大方廣佛華嚴經卷第四十四　　　(72-41)

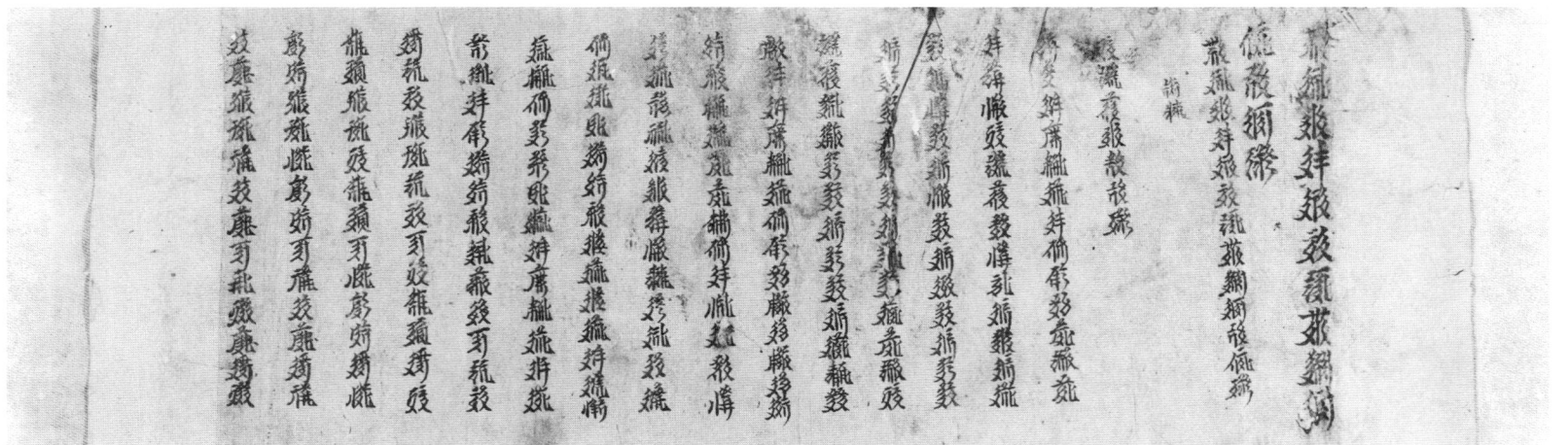

38.大方廣佛華嚴經卷第四十五　　　(72-42)

俄 Инв.No.5319 5733 5735 5736 5737 5738 5739 5740 5741 7335 7547 7652

39.大方廣佛華嚴經卷第四十六　　　(72-43)

俄 Инв.No.5319 5733 5735 5736 5737 5738 5739 5740 5741 7335 7547 7652

40.大方廣佛華嚴經卷第四十七　　　(72-44)

俄 Инв.No.5319 5733 5735 5736 5737 5738 5739 5740 5741 7335 7547 7652

41.大方廣佛華嚴經卷第四十八　　　(72-45)

俄 Инв.No.5319 5733 5735 5736 5737 5738 5739 5740 5741 7335 7547 7652

42.大方廣佛華嚴經卷第五十　　　(72-46)

47.大方廣佛華嚴經卷第五十五　　　(72-51)

48.大方廣佛華嚴經卷第五十六　　　(72-52)

49.大方廣佛華嚴經卷第五十八　　　(72-53)

50.大方廣佛華嚴經卷第五十九　　　(72-54)

Инв. No.5319 *5733 5735 5736 5737 5738 5739 5740 5741 7335 7547 7652*

51.大方廣佛華嚴經卷第六十 　　　(72-55)

俄**Инв.**No.5319 *5733 5735 5736 5737 5738 5739 5740 5741 7335 7547 7652*

52.大方廣佛華嚴經卷第六十二 　　(72-56)

俄**Инв.**No.5319 *5733 5735 5736 5737 5738 5739 5740 5741 7335 7547 7652*

53.大方廣佛華嚴經卷第六十三 　　(72-57)

俄**Инв.**No.5319 *5733 5735 5736 5737 5738 5739 5740 5741 7335 7547 7652*

54.大方廣佛華嚴經卷第六十四 　　(72-58)

55.大方廣佛華嚴經卷第六十五　　(72-59)

56.大方廣佛華嚴經卷第六十六　　(72-60)

57.大方廣佛華嚴經卷第六十八　　(72-61)

58.大方廣佛華嚴經卷第六十九　　(72-62)

俄 **Инв**.No.5319 *5733 5735 5736 5737 5738 5739 5740 5741 7335 7547 7652*

59.大方廣佛華嚴經卷第七十一　　　(72-63)

俄 **Инв**.No.5319 *5733 5735 5736 5737 5738 5739 5740 5741 7335 7547 7652*

60.大方廣佛華嚴經卷第七十二　　　(72-64)

俄 **Инв**.No.5319 *5733 5735 5736 5737 5738 5739 5740 5741 7335 7547 7652*

61.大方廣佛華嚴經卷第七十三　　　(72-65)

俄 **Инв**.No.5319 *5733 5735 5736 5737 5738 5739 5740 5741 7335 7547 7652*

62.大方廣佛華嚴經卷第七十四　　　(72-66)

俄 **И**нв.No.5319 *5733 5735 5736 5737 5738 5739 5740 5741 7335 7547 7652*

63.大方廣佛華嚴經卷第七十五　　　(72-67)

俄 **И**нв.No.5319 *5733 5735 5736 5737 5738 5739 5740 5741 7335 7547 7652*

64.大方廣佛華嚴經卷第七十六　　　(72-68)

俄 **И**нв.No.5319 *5733 5735 5736 5737 5738 5739 5740 5741 7335 7547 7652*

65.大方廣佛華嚴經卷第七十七　　　(72-69)

俄 **И**нв.No.5319 *5733 5735 5736 5737 5738 5739 5740 5741 7335 7547 7652*

66.大方廣佛華嚴經卷第七十九　　　(72-70)

俄 Инв.No.5319 5733 5735 5736 5737 5738 5739 5740 5741 7335 7547 7652

66.大方廣佛華嚴經卷第七十九　　　(72-71)

俄 Инв.No.5319 5733 5735 5736 5737 5738 5739 5740 5741 7335 7547 7652

67.大方廣佛華嚴經卷第八十　　　(72-72)

俄 **И**нв.No.972　　大般涅槃經卷第七

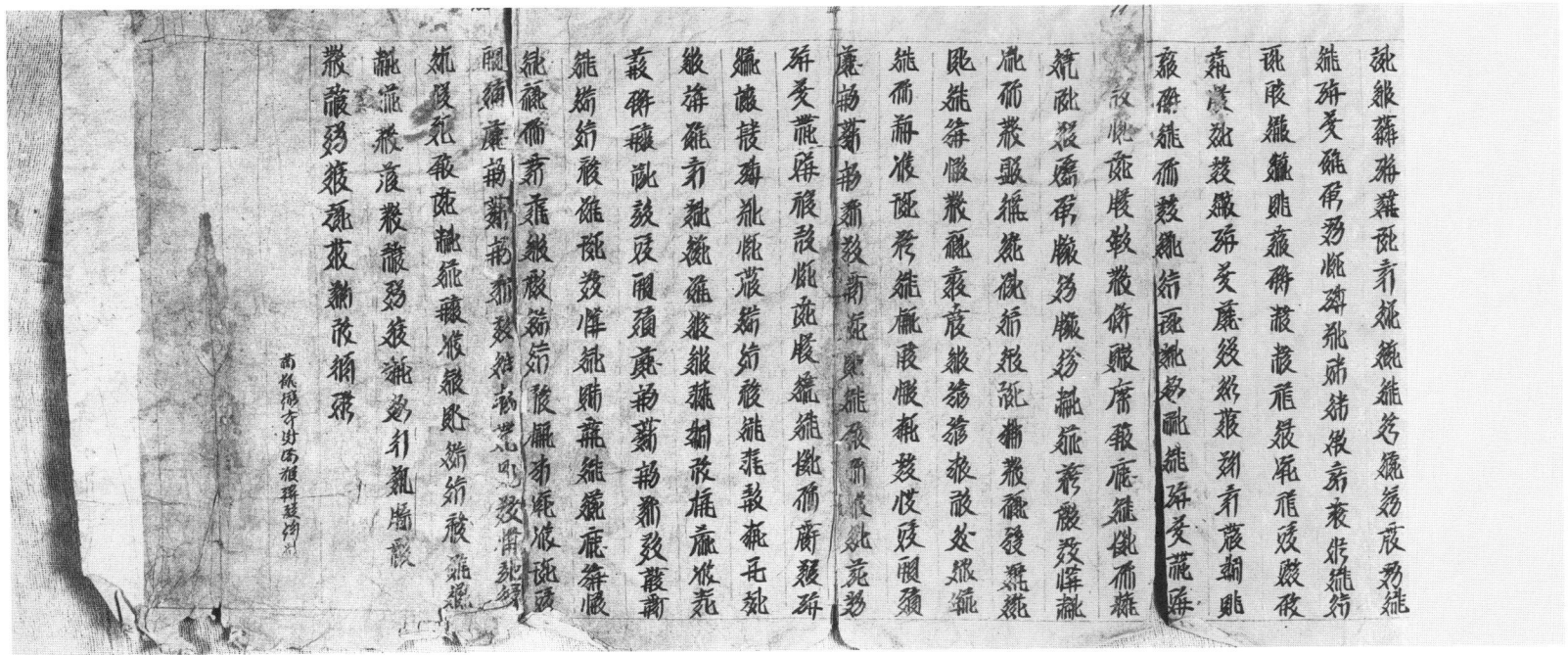

俄 **И**нв.No.2002　　大般涅槃經卷第十四

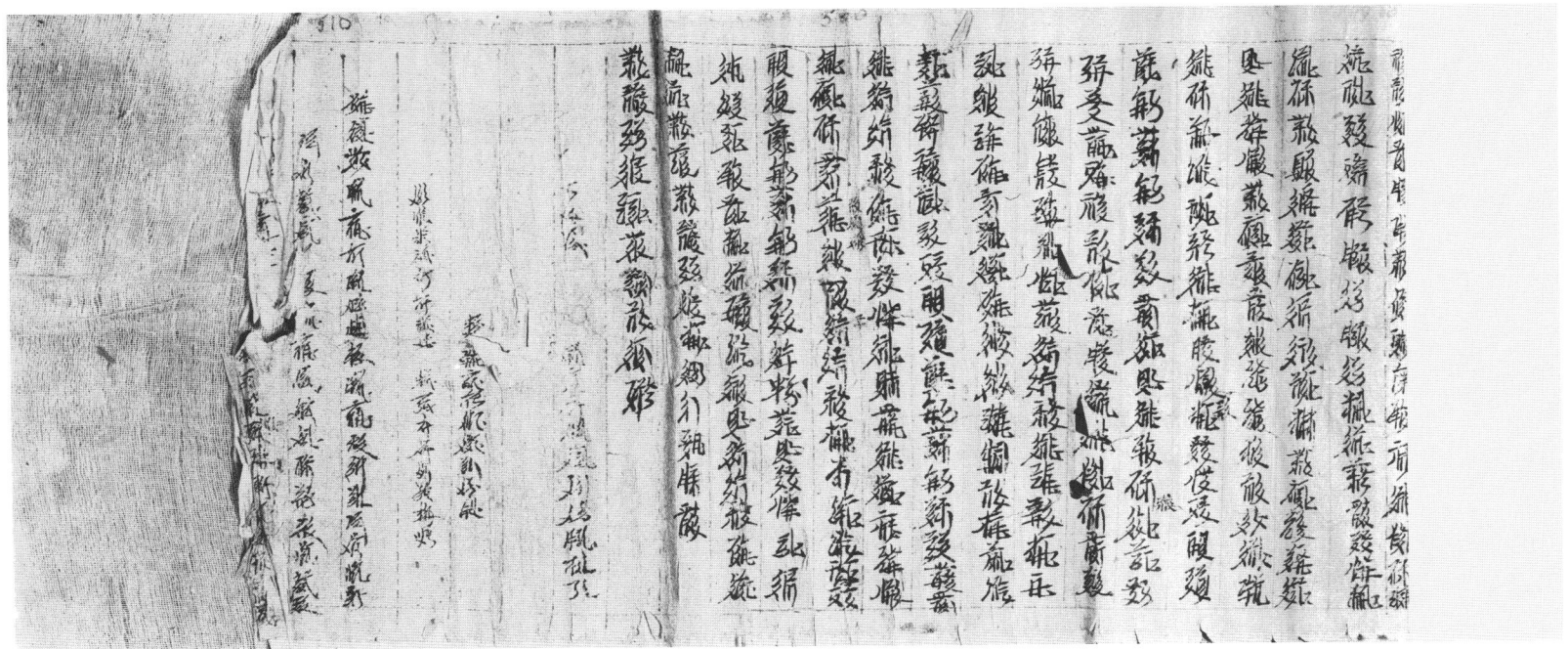

俄 **И**нв.No.4878　　大般涅槃經卷第十四

俄 Инв.No.4574　大般涅槃經卷第十六　　(17-1)

俄 Инв.No.4574　大般涅槃經卷第十六　　(17-2)

俄 Инв.No.4574　大般涅槃經卷第十六　　(17-3)

俄 **И**нв.No.4574　大般涅槃經卷第十六　　　　(17-4)

俄 **И**нв.No.4574　大般涅槃經卷第十六　　　　(17-5)

俄 **И**нв.No.4574　大般涅槃經卷第十六　　　　(17-6)

俄 Инв.No.4574　大般涅槃經卷第十六　　　　(17-7)

俄 Инв.No.4574　大般涅槃經卷第十六　　　　(17-8)

俄 Инв.No.4574　大般涅槃經卷第十六　　　　(17-9)

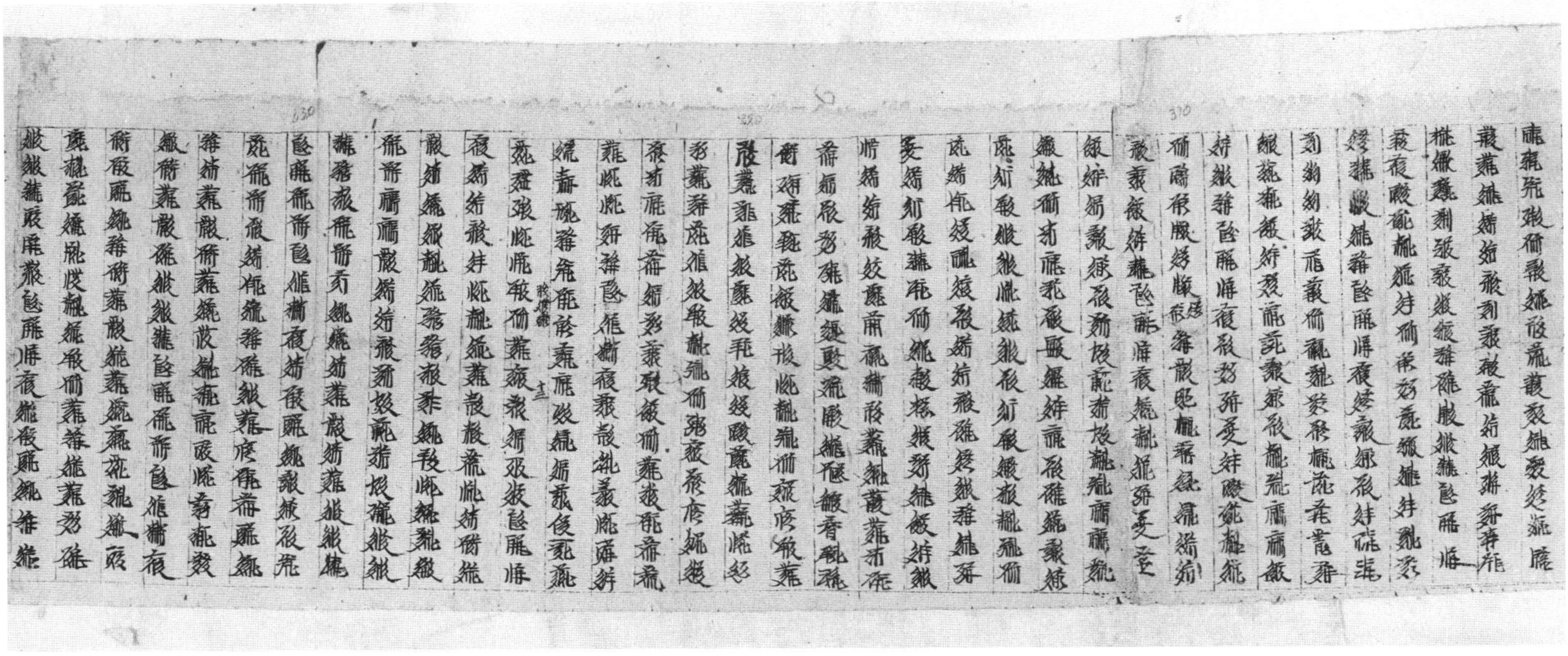

俄 Инв.No.4574　大般涅槃經卷第十六　(17–10)

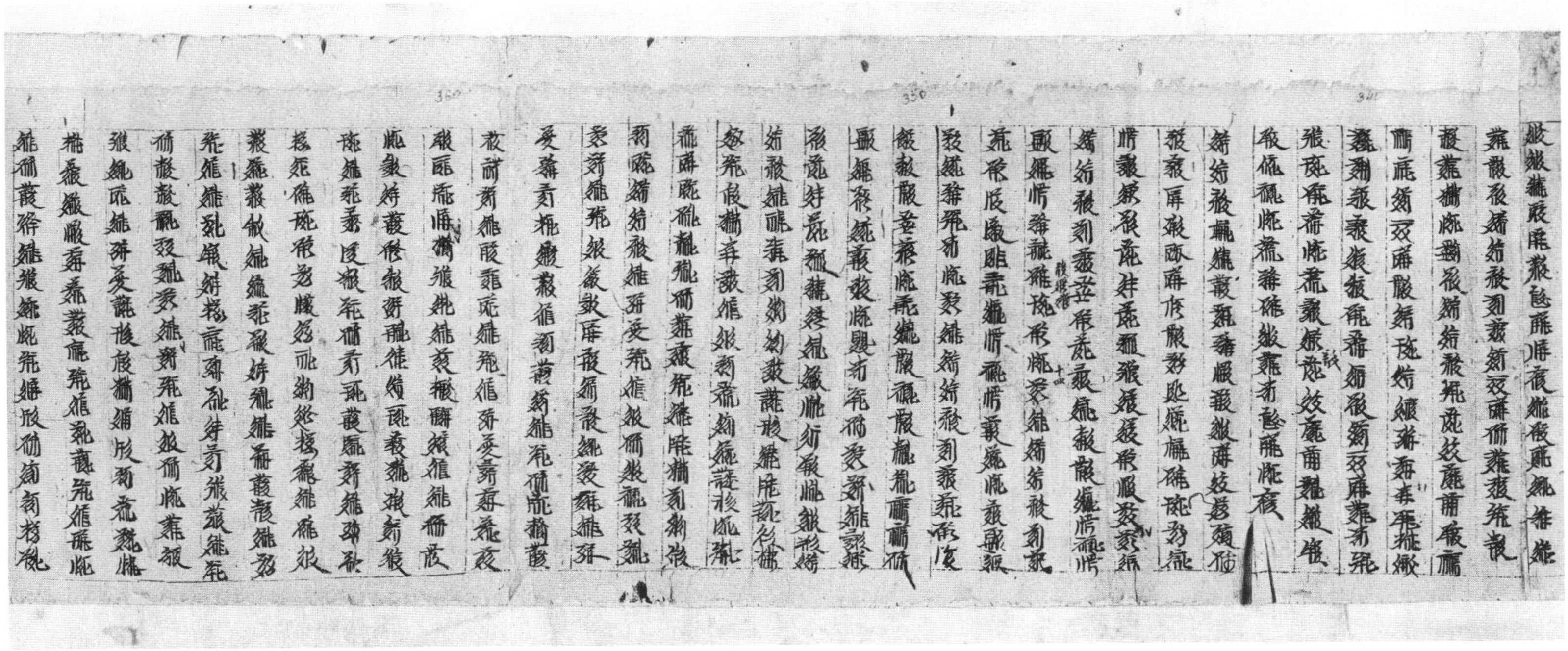

俄 Инв.No.4574　大般涅槃經卷第十六　(17–11)

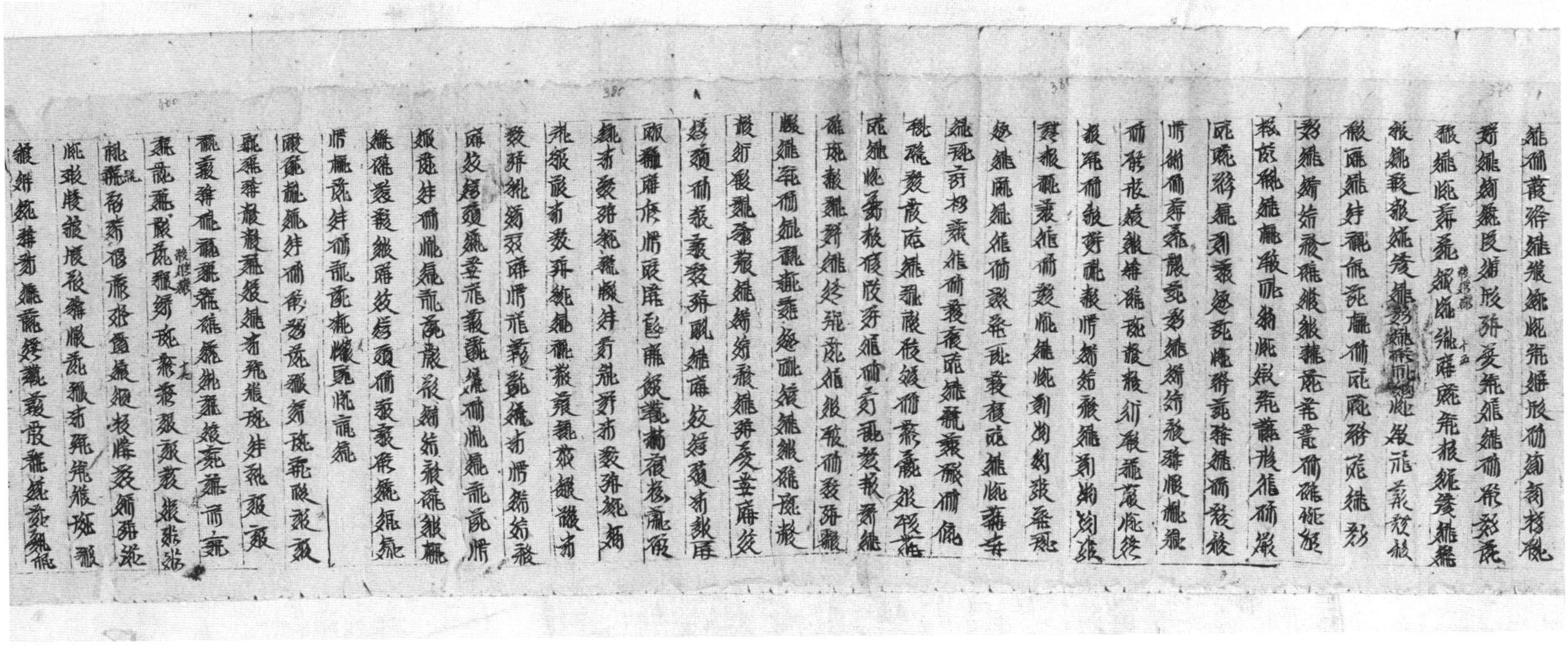

俄 Инв.No.4574　大般涅槃經卷第十六　(17–12)

俄 Инв.No.4574　大般涅槃經卷第十六　　　(17-16)

俄 Инв.No.4574　大般涅槃經卷第十六　　　(17-17)

俄 Инв.No.1191　大般涅槃經卷第十七　　　(13-1)

俄 Инв.No.1191　大般涅槃經卷第十七　　　(13-2)

俄 Инв.No.1191　大般涅槃經卷第十七　　　(13-3)

俄 Инв.No.1191　大般涅槃經卷第十七　　　(13-4)

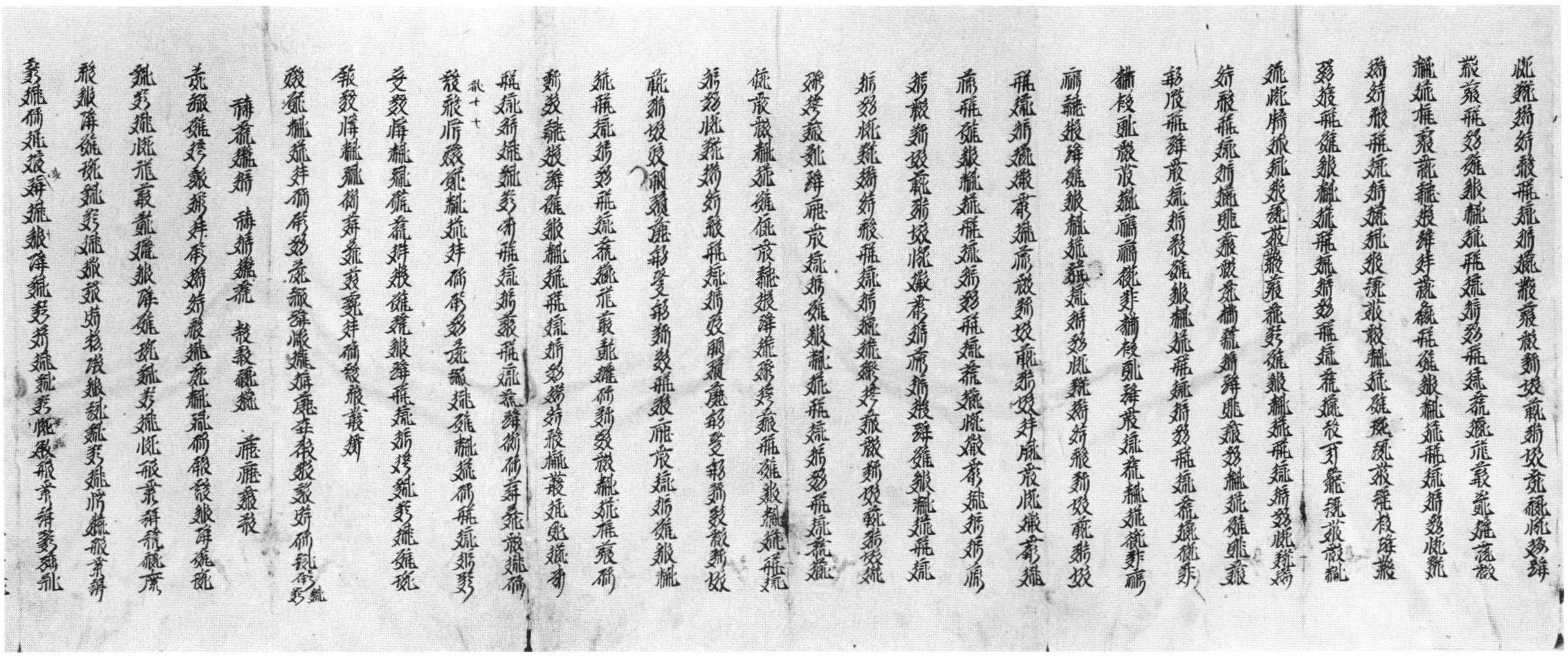

俄 Инв.No.1191　大般涅槃經卷第十七　(13–5)

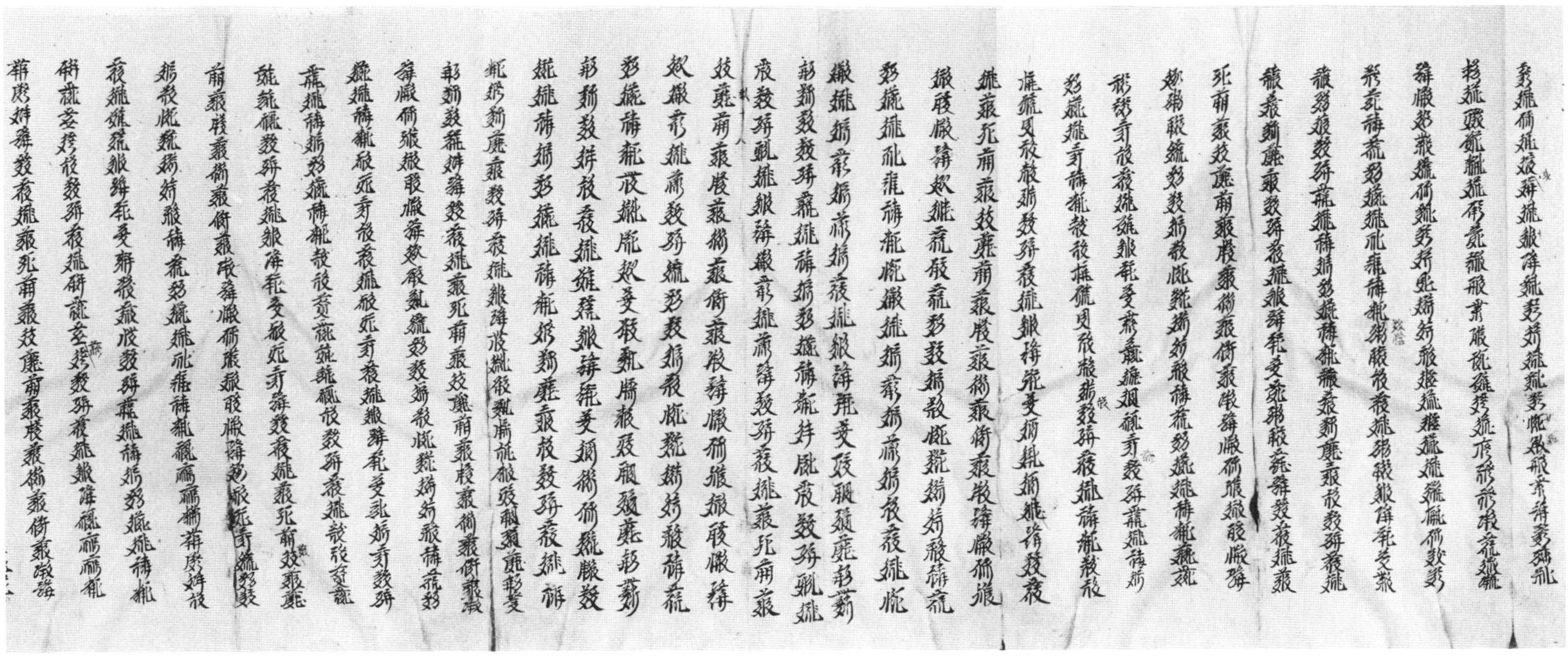

俄 Инв.No.1191　大般涅槃經卷第十七　(13–6)

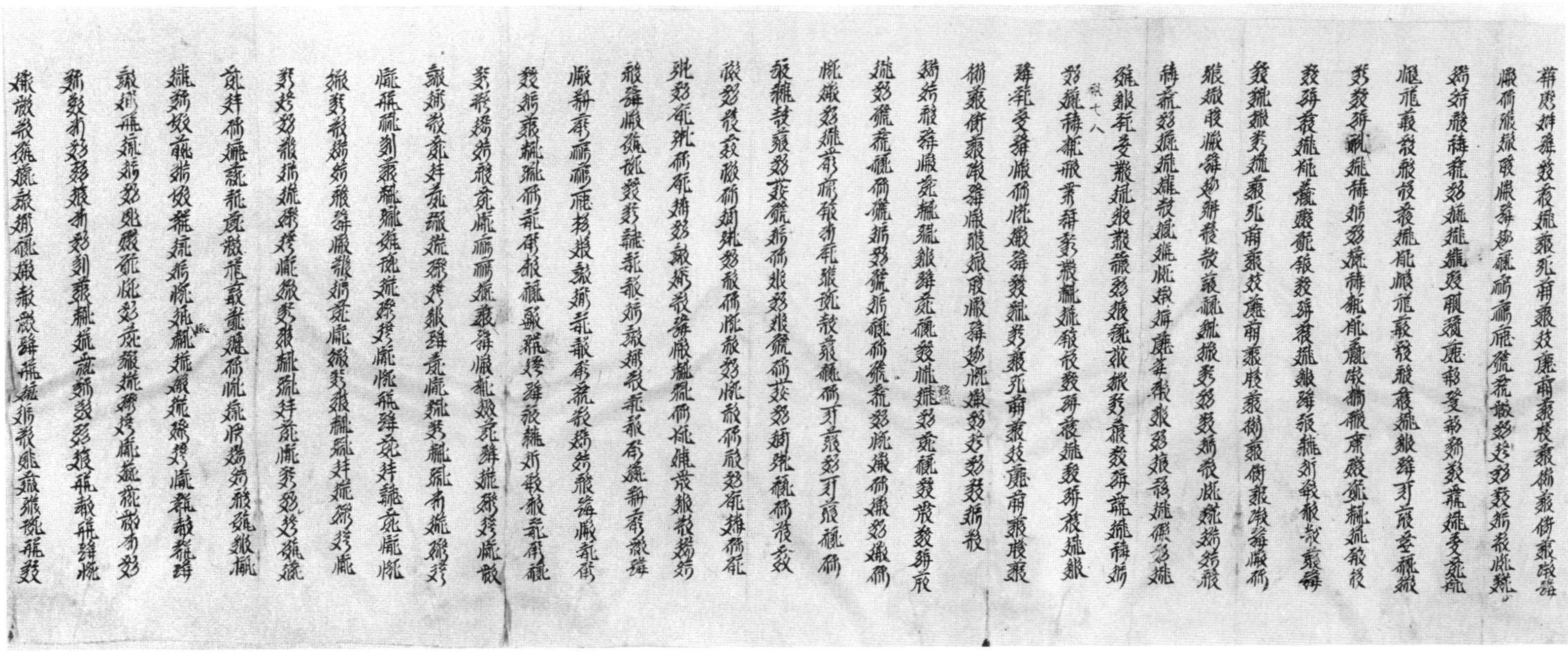

俄 Инв.No.1191　大般涅槃經卷第十七　(13–7)

俄 Инв.No.1191　大般涅槃經卷第十七　　(13-8)

俄 Инв.No.1191　大般涅槃經卷第十七　　(13-9)

俄 Инв.No.1191　大般涅槃經卷第十七　　(13-10)

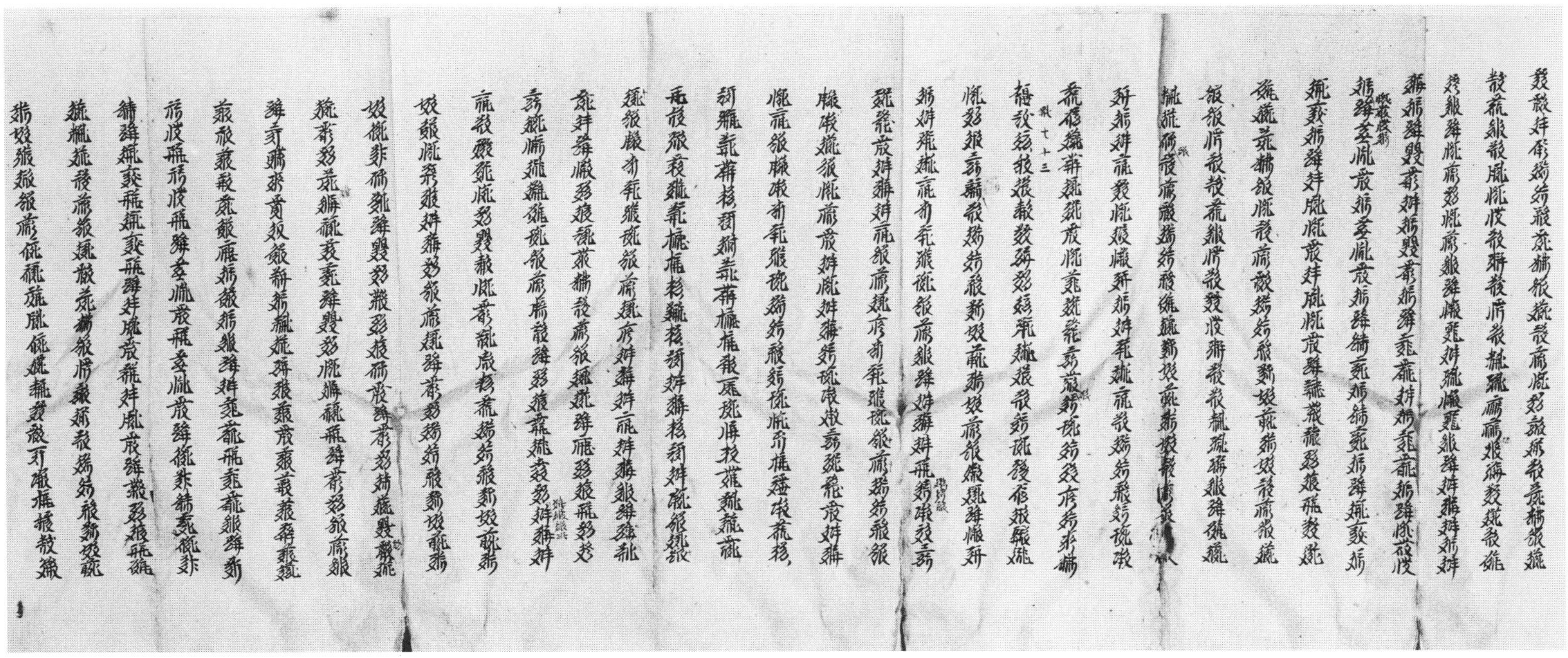

俄 Инв.No.1191　大般涅槃經卷第十七　(13–11)

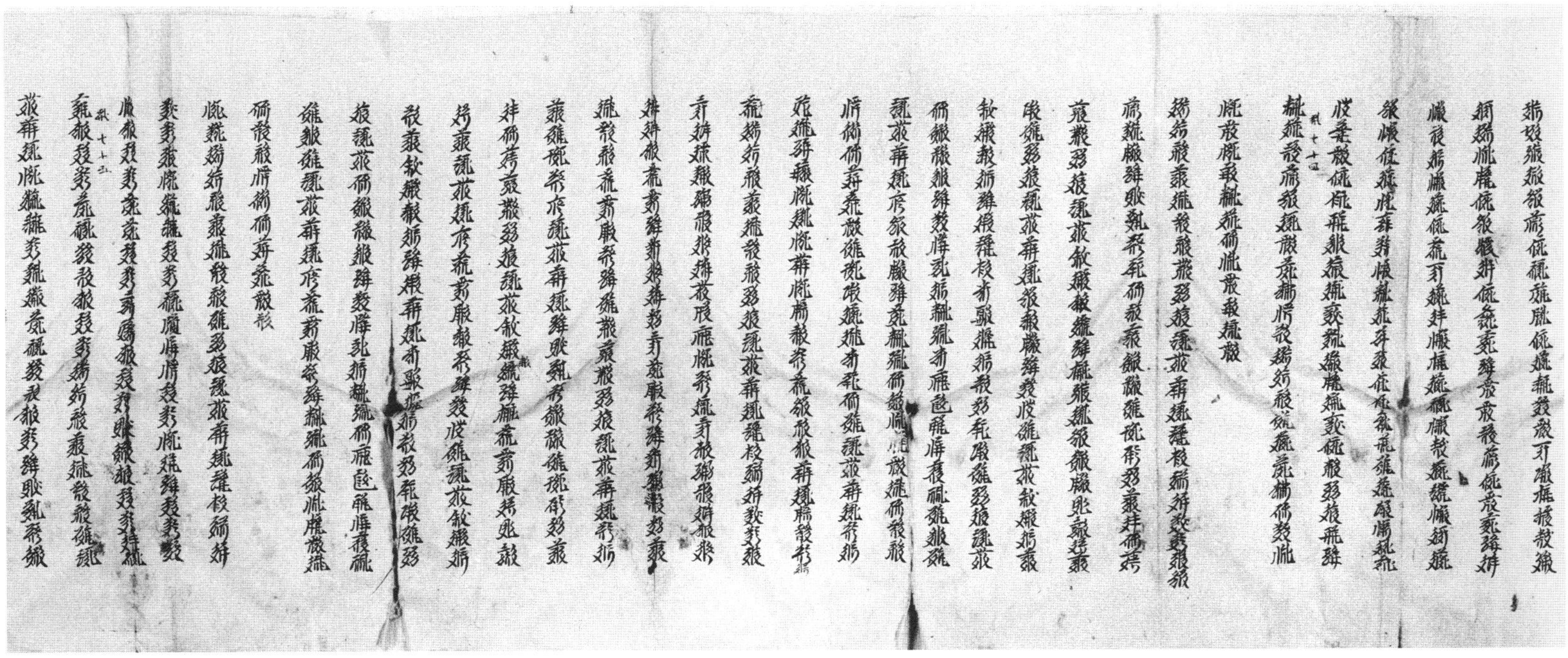

俄 Инв.No.1191　大般涅槃經卷第十七　(13–12)

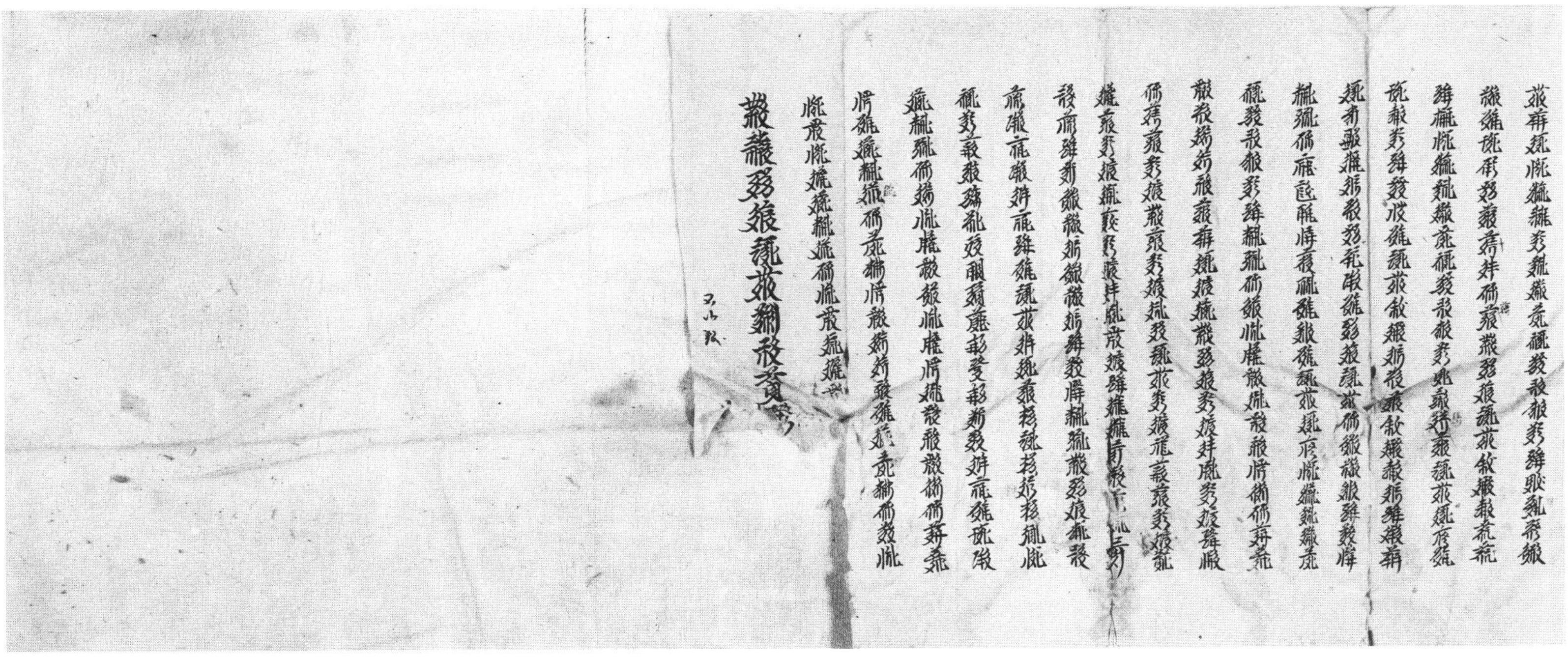

俄 Инв.No.1191　大般涅槃經卷第十七　(13–13)

俄 **И**нв.No.390　大般涅槃經卷第十八　　　　(16-1)

俄 **И**нв.No.390　大般涅槃經卷第十八　　　　(16-2)

俄 **И**нв.No.390　大般涅槃經卷第十八　　　　(16-3)

俄 Инв.No.390　大般涅槃經卷第十八　　　(16-4)

俄 Инв.No.390　大般涅槃經卷第十八　　　(16-5)

俄 Инв.No.390　大般涅槃經卷第十八　　　(16-6)

俄 **И**нв.No.390　大般涅槃經卷第十八　　　(16-7)

俄 **И**нв.No.390　大般涅槃經卷第十八　　　(16-8)

俄 **И**нв.No.390　大般涅槃經卷第十八　　　(16-9)

俄 Инв.No.390　大般涅槃經卷第十八　　　(16-10)

俄 Инв.No.390　大般涅槃經卷第十八　　　(16-11)

俄 Инв.No.390　大般涅槃經卷第十八　　　(16-12)

俄 **И**нв.No.390　大般涅槃經卷第十八　　　　(16-13)

俄 **И**нв.No.390　大般涅槃經卷第十八　　　　(16-14)

俄 **И**нв.No.390　大般涅槃經卷第十八　　　　(16-15)

俄 **И**нв.No.390　大般涅槃經卷第十八　　　（16-16）

俄 **И**нв.No.930　大般涅槃經卷第十九　　　（5-1）

俄 **И**нв.No.930　大般涅槃經卷第十九　　　（5-2）

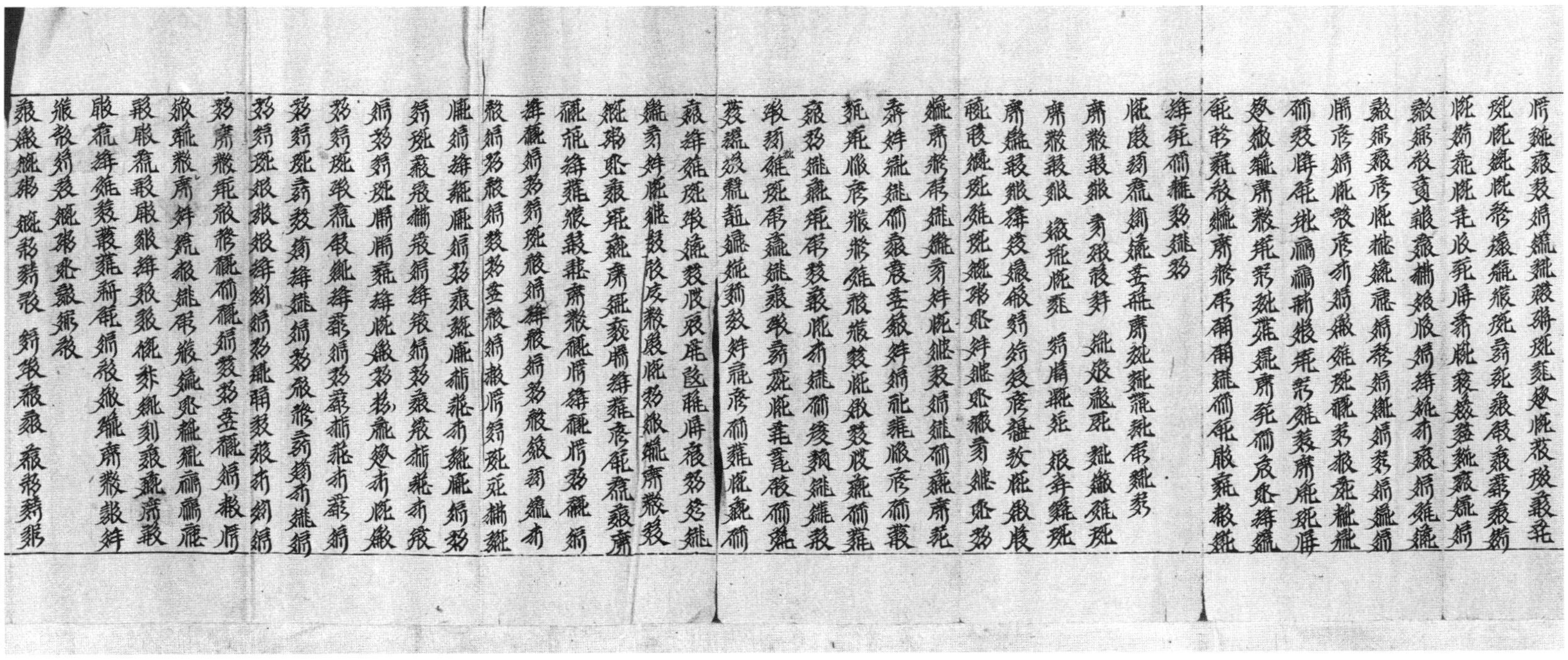

俄 Инв.No.930　大般涅槃經卷第十九　(5-3)

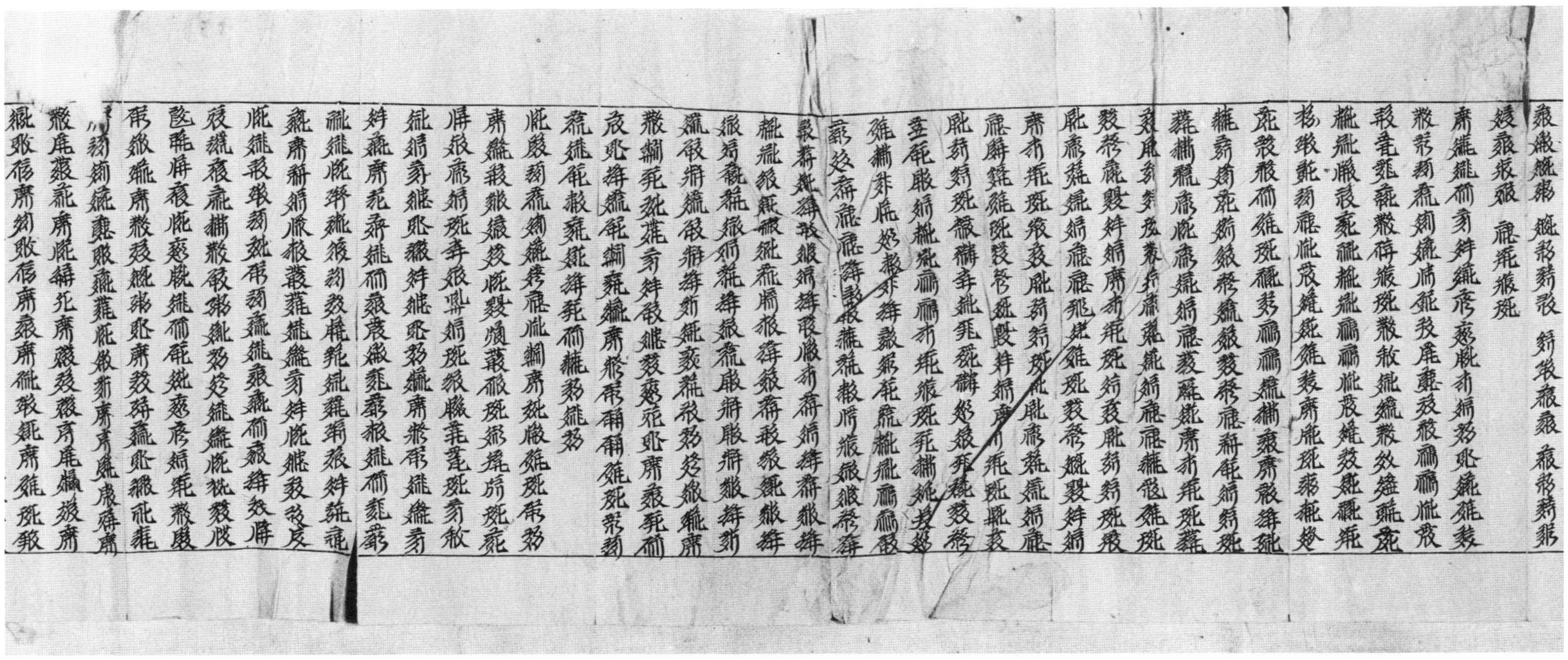

俄 Инв.No.930　大般涅槃經卷第十九　(5-4)

俄 Инв.No.930　大般涅槃經卷第十九　(5-5)

俄 Инв.No.1985　大般涅槃經卷第十九　　　(12-1)

俄 Инв.No.1985　大般涅槃經卷第十九　　　(12-2)

俄 Инв.No.1985　大般涅槃經卷第十九　　　(12-3)

俄 Инв.No.1985　大般涅槃經卷第十九　　　(12-4)

俄 Инв.No.1985　大般涅槃經卷第十九　　　(12-5)

俄 Инв.No.1985　大般涅槃經卷第十九　　　(12-6)

俄 Инв.No.1985　　大般涅槃經卷第十九　　(12-7)

俄 Инв.No.1985　　大般涅槃經卷第十九　　(12-8)

俄 Инв.No.1985　　大般涅槃經卷第十九　　(12-9)

俄 Инв.No.1985　大般涅槃經卷第十九　　　　(12-10)

俄 Инв.No.1985　大般涅槃經卷第十九　　　　(12-11)

俄 Инв.No.1985　大般涅槃經卷第十九　　　　(12-12)

俄 **И**нв.No.6650a+1991　大般涅槃經卷第二十　(3-1)

俄 **И**нв.No.6650a+1991　大般涅槃經卷第二十　(3-2)

俄 **И**нв.No.6650a+1991　大般涅槃經卷第二十　(3-3)

俄 **И**нв.No.422　大般涅槃經卷第二十一　　　(16-1)

俄 **И**нв.No.422　大般涅槃經卷第二十一　　　(16-2)

俄 **И**нв.No.422　大般涅槃經卷第二十一　　　(16-3)

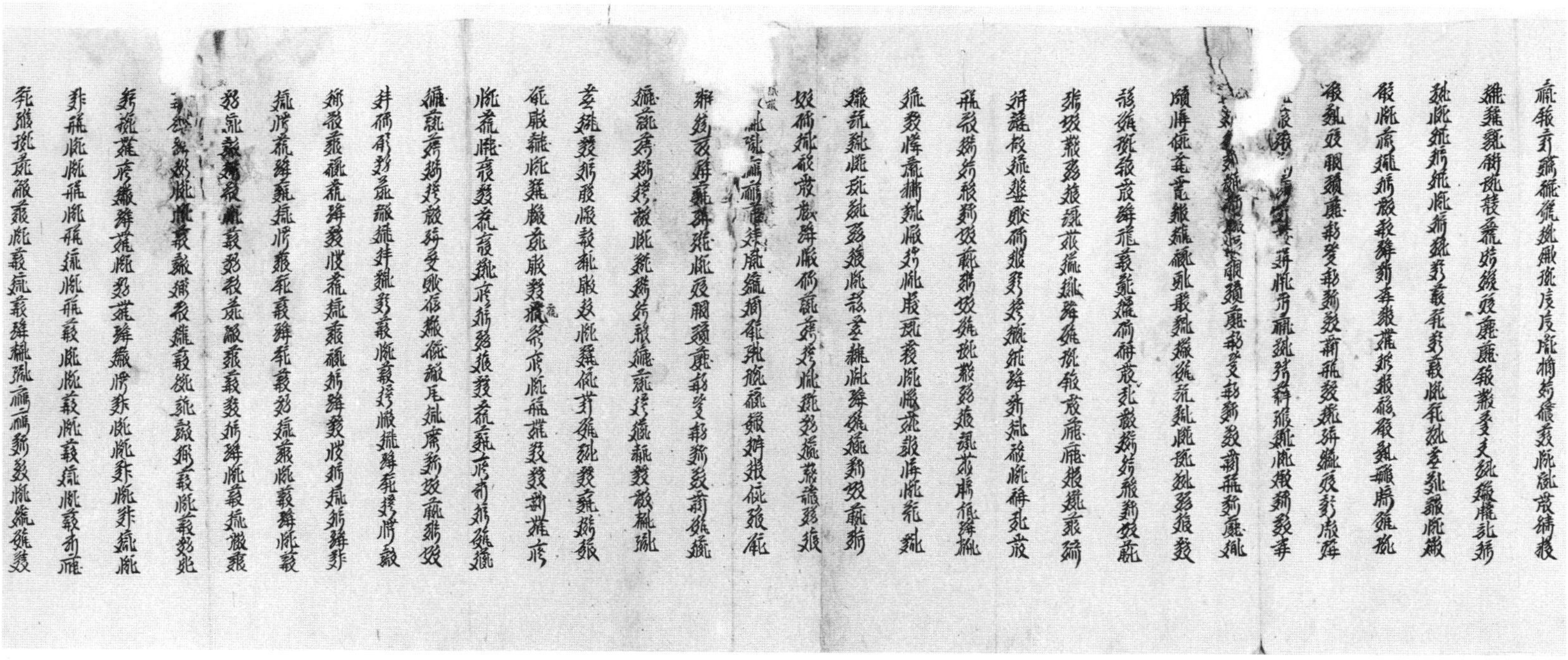

俄 Инв.No.422　大般涅槃經卷第二十一　(16-4)

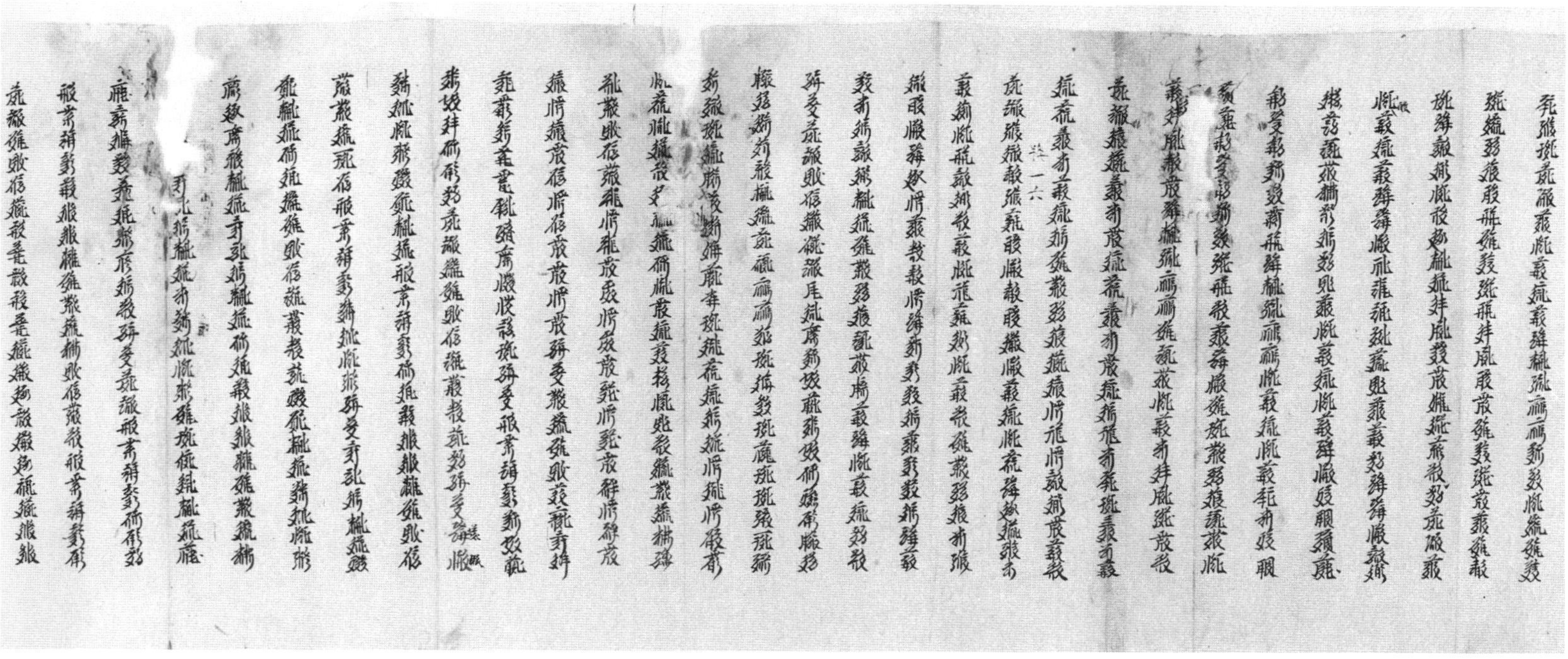

俄 Инв.No.422　大般涅槃經卷第二十一　(16-5)

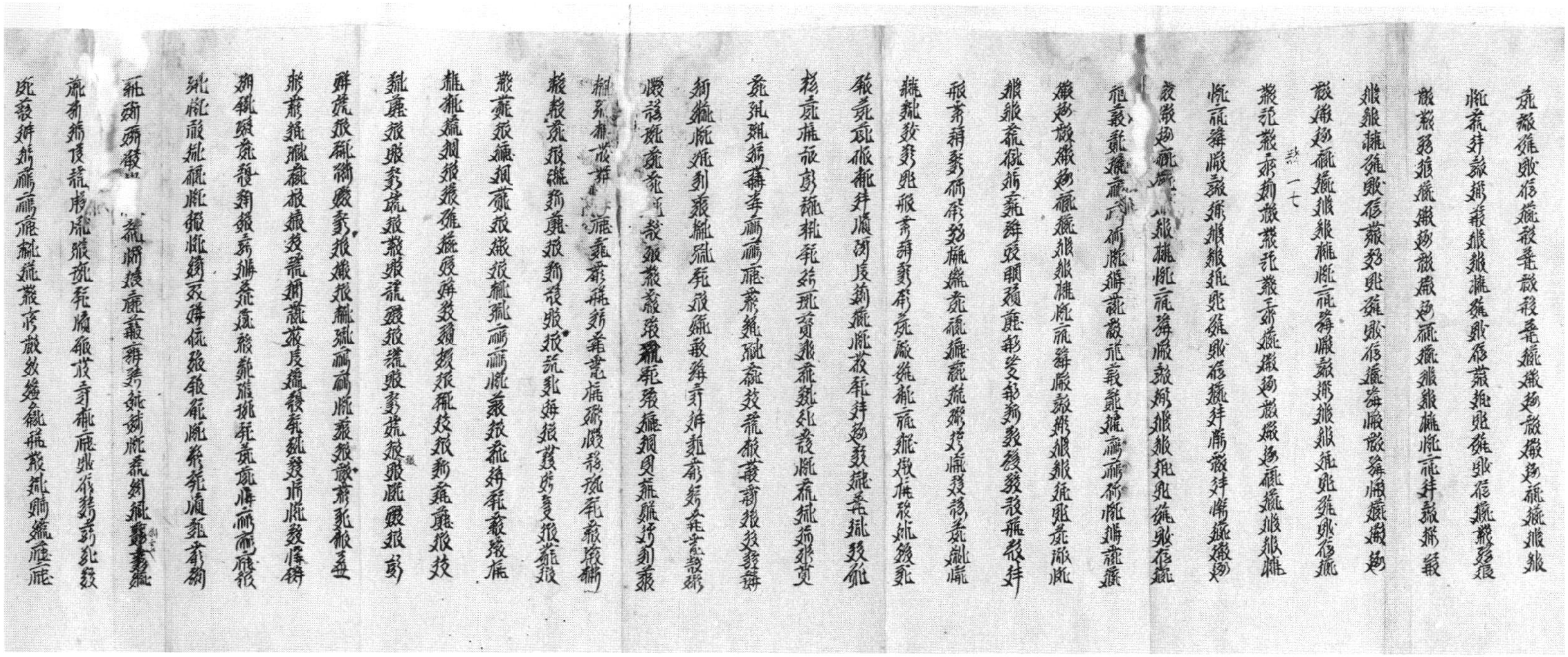

俄 Инв.No.422　大般涅槃經卷第二十一　(16-6)

俄 Инв.No.422　大般涅槃經卷第二十一　　　(16-7)

俄 Инв.No.422　大般涅槃經卷第二十一　　　(16-8)

俄 Инв.No.422　大般涅槃經卷第二十一　　　(16-9)

俄 Инв.No.422　大般涅槃經卷第二十一　　(16-10)

俄 Инв.No.422　大般涅槃經卷第二十一　　(16-11)

俄 Инв.No.422　大般涅槃經卷第二十一　　(16-12)

俄Инв.No.422　大般涅槃經卷第二十一　　　(16-13)

俄Инв.No.422　大般涅槃經卷第二十一　　　(16-14)

俄Инв.No.422　大般涅槃經卷第二十一　　　(16-15)

俄 Инв.No.422　大般涅槃經卷第二十一　　　(16-16)

俄 Инв.No.420+6650　大般涅槃經卷第二十二　　(12-1)

俄 Инв.No.420+6650　大般涅槃經卷第二十二　　(12-2)

俄 **Инв**.No.420+6650　大般涅槃經卷第二十二　　　(12-3)

俄 **Инв**.No.420+6650　大般涅槃經卷第二十二　　　(12-4)

俄 **Инв**.No.420+6650　大般涅槃經卷第二十二　　　(12-5)

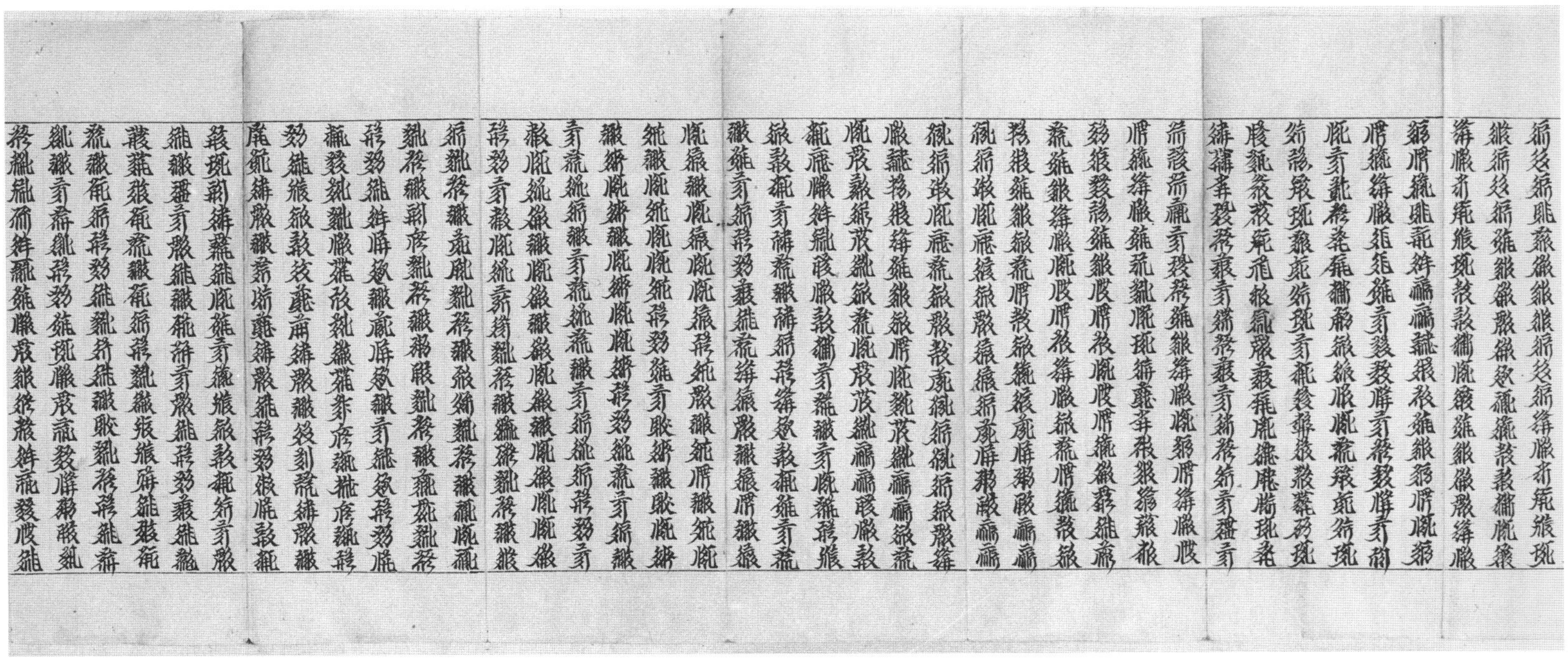

俄 Инв.No.420+6650 大般涅槃經卷第二十二 (12–6)

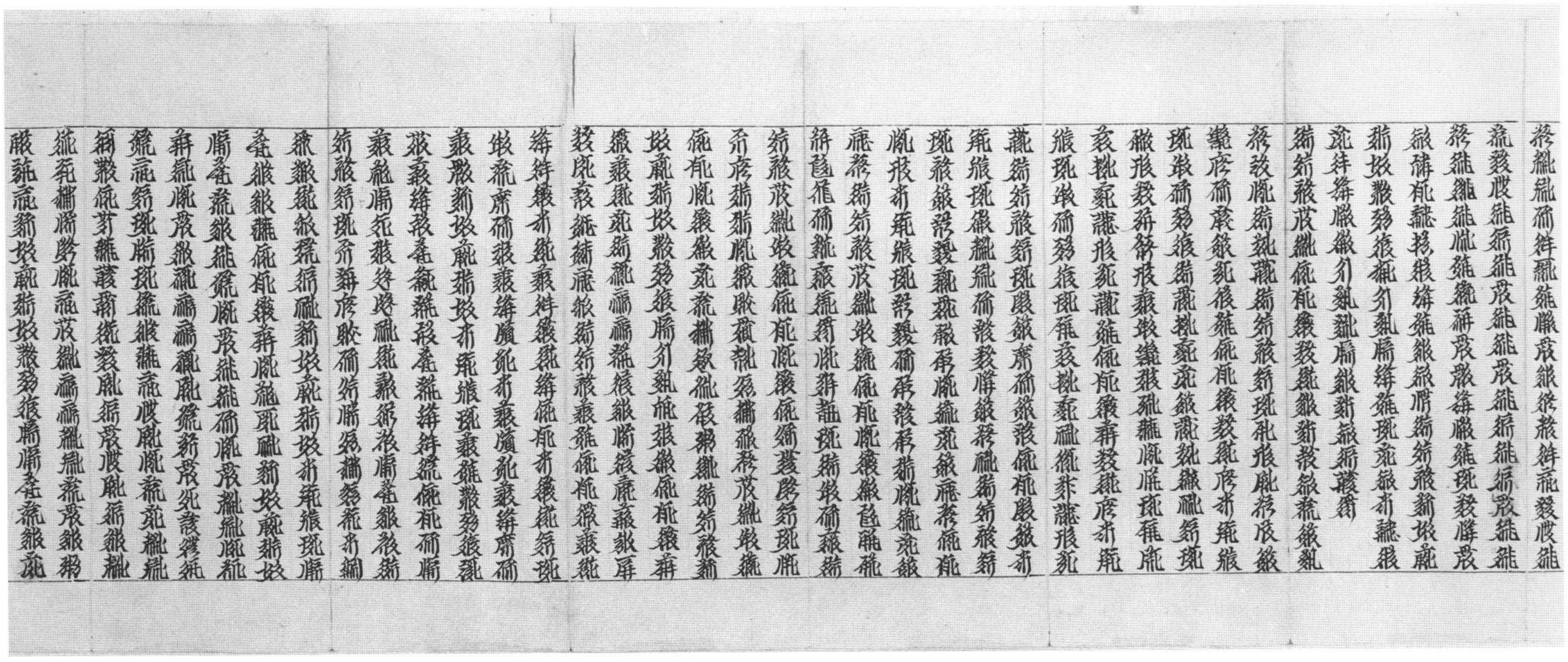

俄 Инв.No.420+6650 大般涅槃經卷第二十二 (12–7)

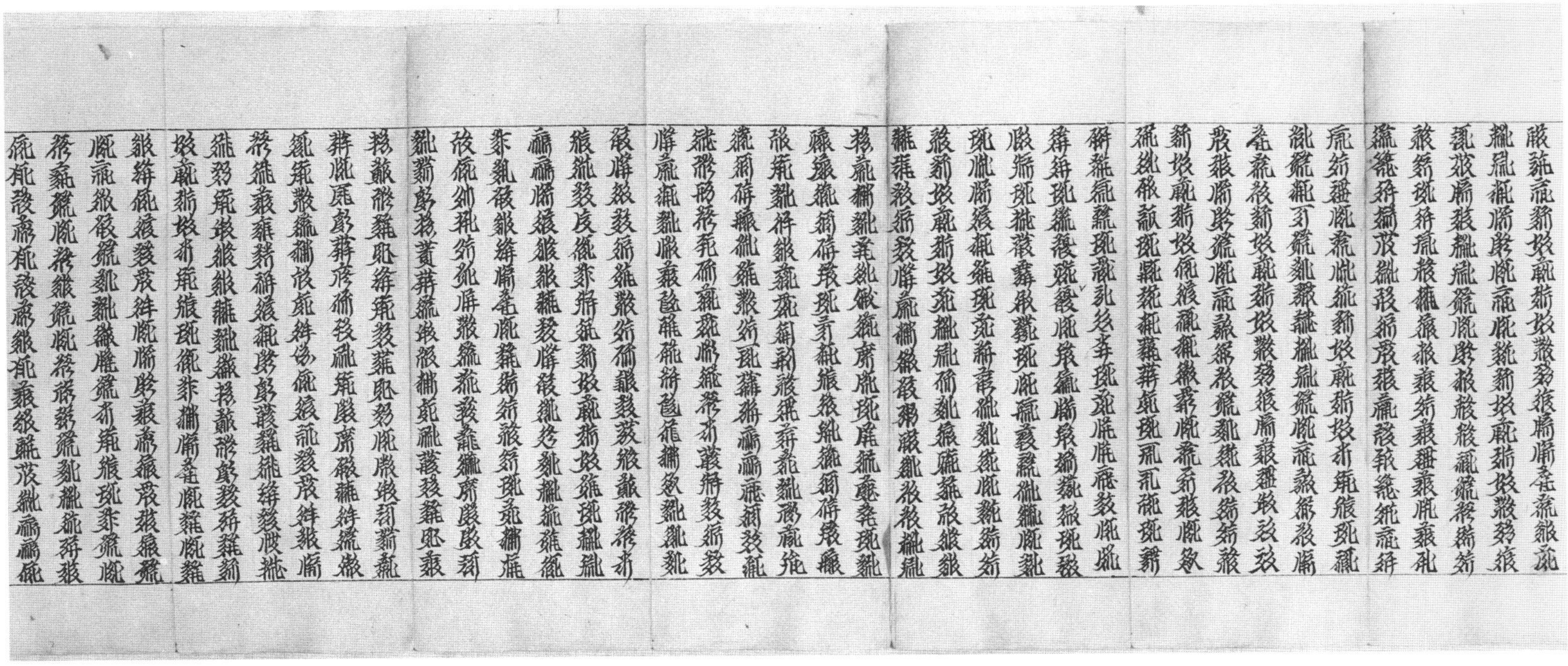

俄 Инв.No.420+6650 大般涅槃經卷第二十二 (12–8)

俄 **Инв**.No.420+6650　大般涅槃經卷第二十二　　　(12-9)

俄 **Инв**.No.420+6650　大般涅槃經卷第二十二　　　(12-10)

俄 **Инв**.No.420+6650　大般涅槃經卷第二十二　　　(12-11)

俄 Инв.No.420+6650　大般涅槃經卷第二十二　　　(12-12)

俄 Инв.No.5068　大般涅槃經卷第二十三　　　(16-1)

俄 Инв.No.5068　大般涅槃經卷第二十三　　　(16-2)

俄 Инв.No.5068　大般涅槃經卷第二十三　　　(16-3)

俄 Инв.No.5068　大般涅槃經卷第二十三　　　(16-4)

俄 Инв.No.5068　大般涅槃經卷第二十三　　　(16-5)

俄 Инв.No.5068 　大般涅槃經卷第二十三 　　　　(16-6)

俄 Инв.No.5068 　大般涅槃經卷第二十三 　　　　(16-7)

俄 Инв.No.5068 　大般涅槃經卷第二十三 　　　　(16-8)

俄 **И**нв.No.5068　大般涅槃經卷第二十三　　　　(16−9)

俄 **И**нв.No.5068　大般涅槃經卷第二十三　　　　(16−10)

俄 **И**нв.No.5068　大般涅槃經卷第二十三　　　　(16−11)

俄 **И**нв.No.5068　大般涅槃經卷第二十三　　　(16-12)

俄 **И**нв.No.5068　大般涅槃經卷第二十三　　　(16-13)

俄 **И**нв.No.5068　大般涅槃經卷第二十三　　　(16-14)

俄 Инв.No.5068　大般涅槃經卷第二十三　　(16-15)

俄 Инв.No.5068　大般涅槃經卷第二十三　　(16-16)

俄 Инв.No.959　大般涅槃經卷第二十四　　(16-1)

俄Инв.No.959　大般涅槃經卷第二十四　　(16-2)

俄Инв.No.959　大般涅槃經卷第二十四　　(16-3)

俄Инв.No.959　大般涅槃經卷第二十四　　(16-4)

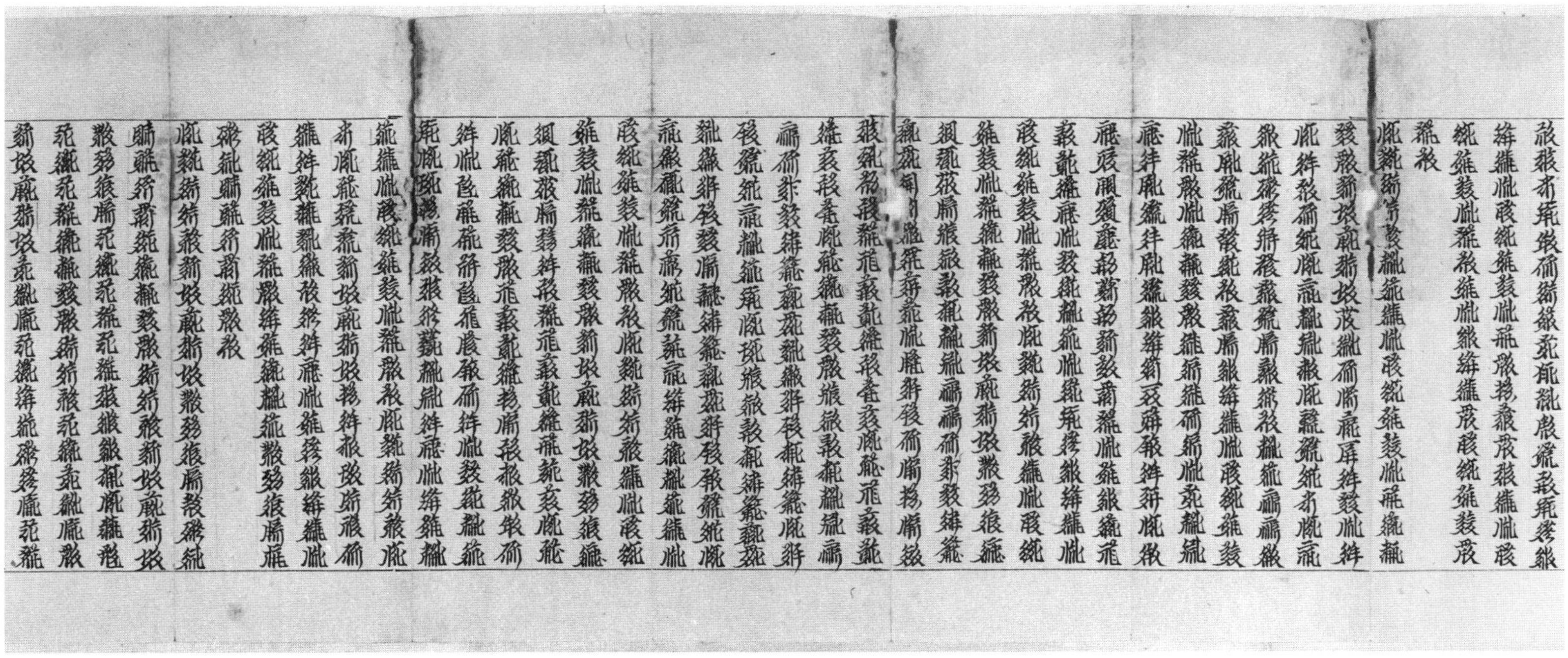

俄 Инв.No.959　大般涅槃經卷第二十四　(16–5)

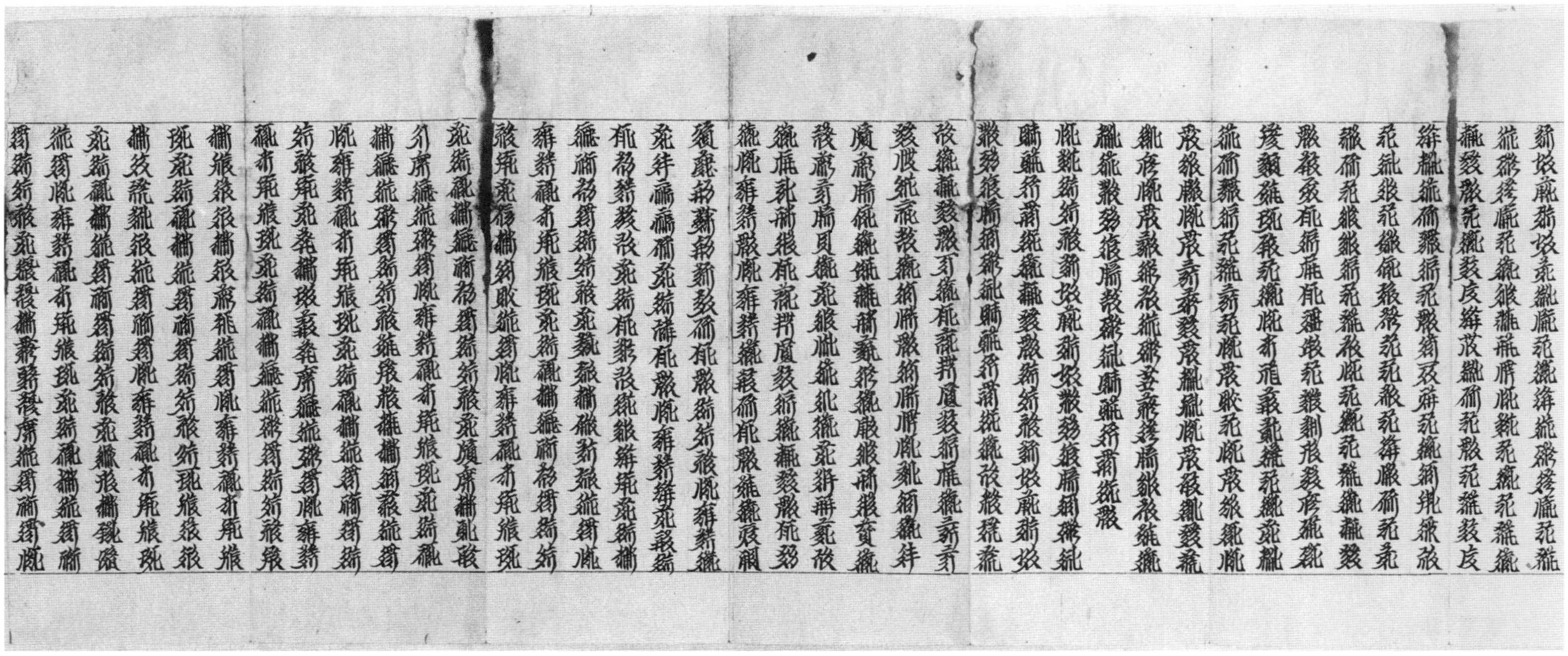

俄 Инв.No.959　大般涅槃經卷第二十四　(16–6)

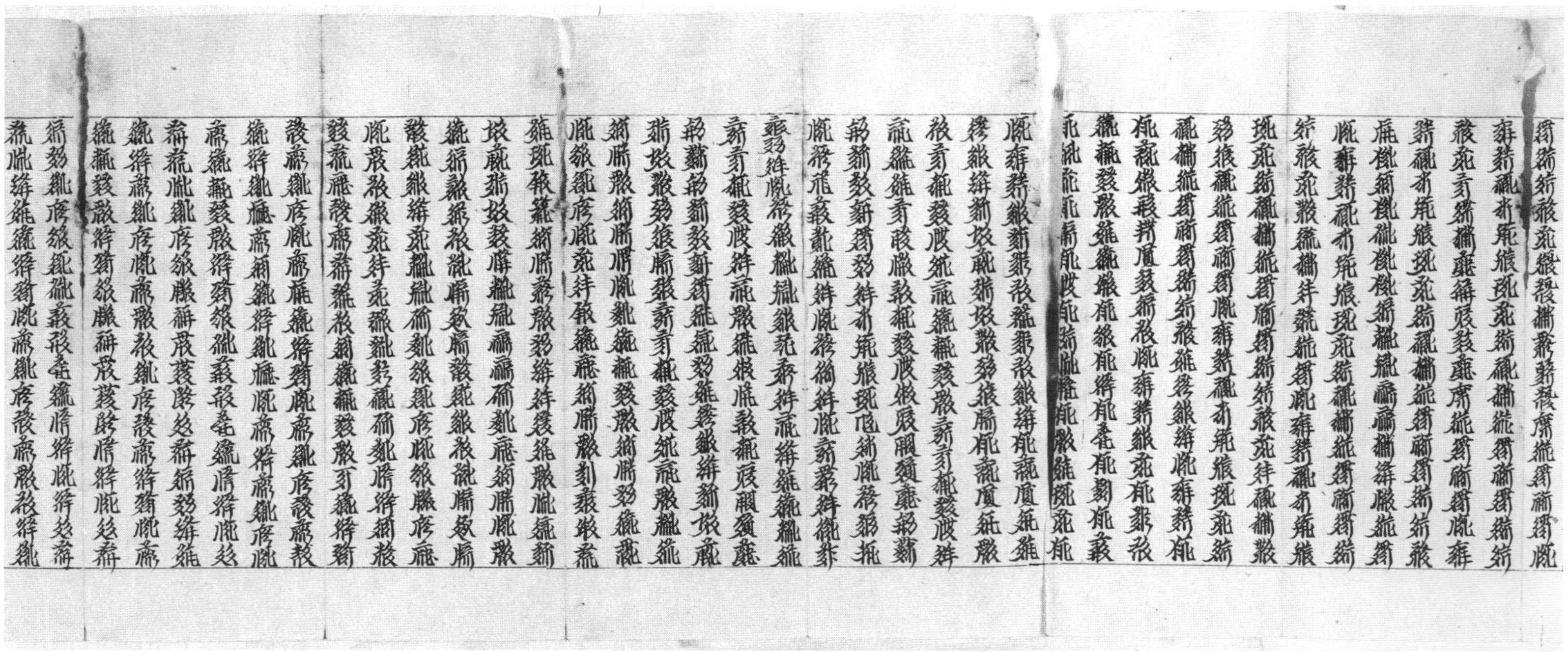

俄 Инв.No.959　大般涅槃經卷第二十四　(16–7)

俄 Инв.No.959　大般涅槃經卷第二十四　(16-8)

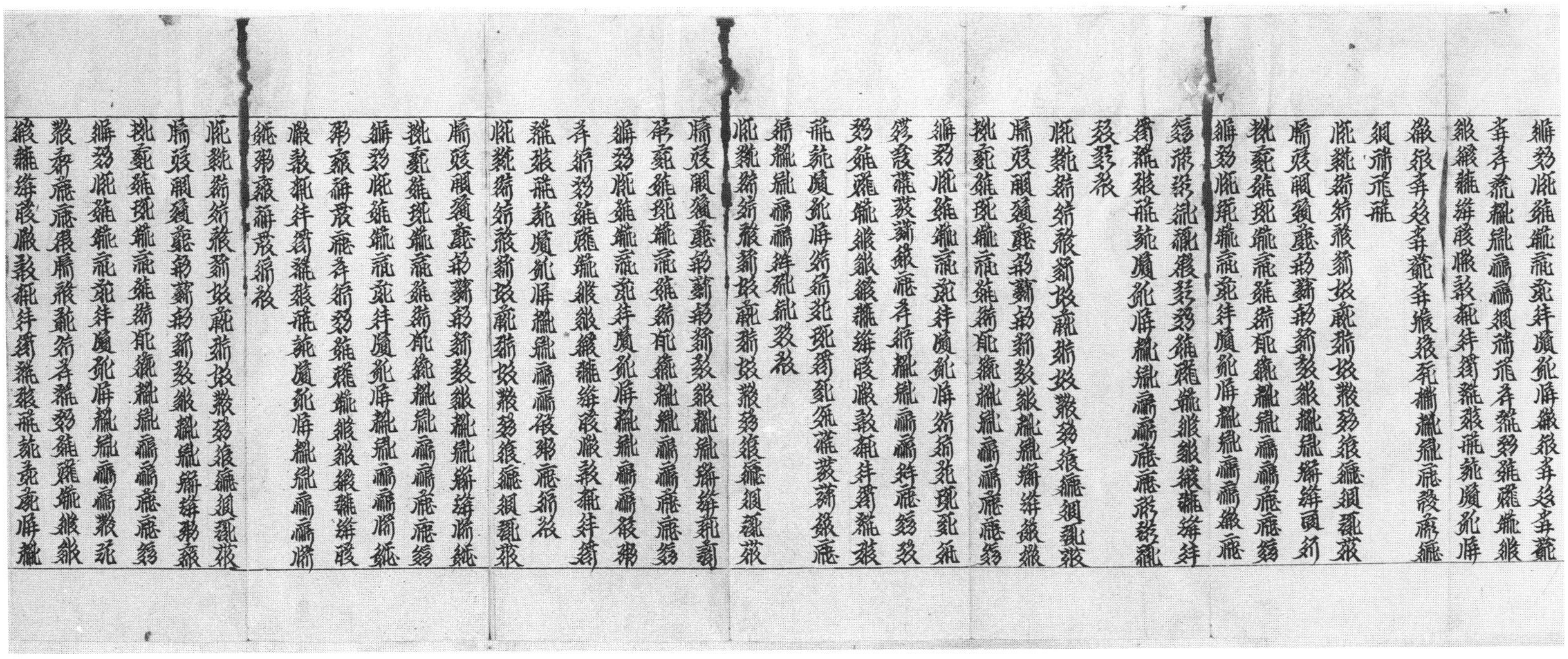

俄 Инв.No.959　大般涅槃經卷第二十四　(16-9)

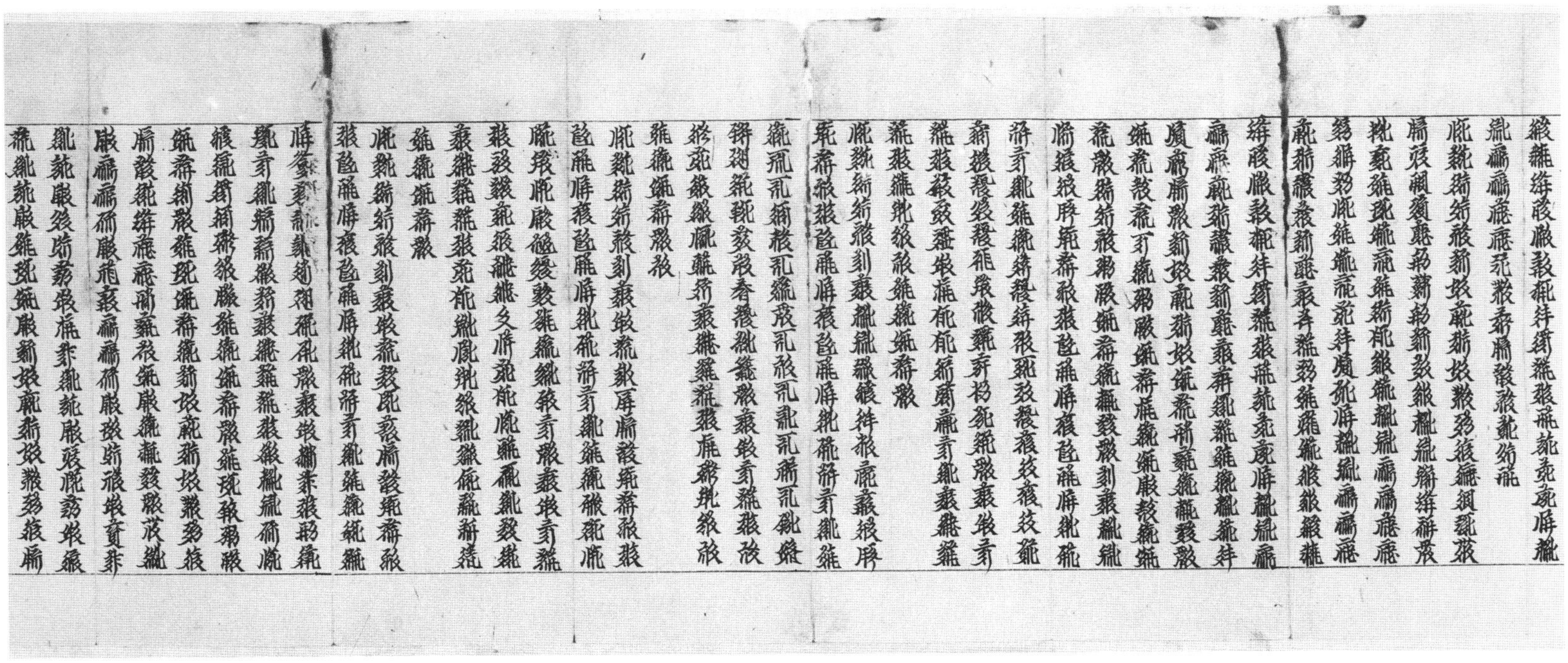

俄 Инв.No.959　大般涅槃經卷第二十四　(16-10)

俄 Инв.No.959　大般涅槃經卷第二十四　　(16-11)

俄 Инв.No.959　大般涅槃經卷第二十四　　(16-12)

俄 Инв.No.959　大般涅槃經卷第二十四　　(16-13)

俄 ИнB.No.959　大般涅槃經卷第二十四　　　（16-14）

俄 ИнB.No.959　大般涅槃經卷第二十四　　　（16-15）

俄 ИнB.No.959　大般涅槃經卷第二十四　　　（16-16）

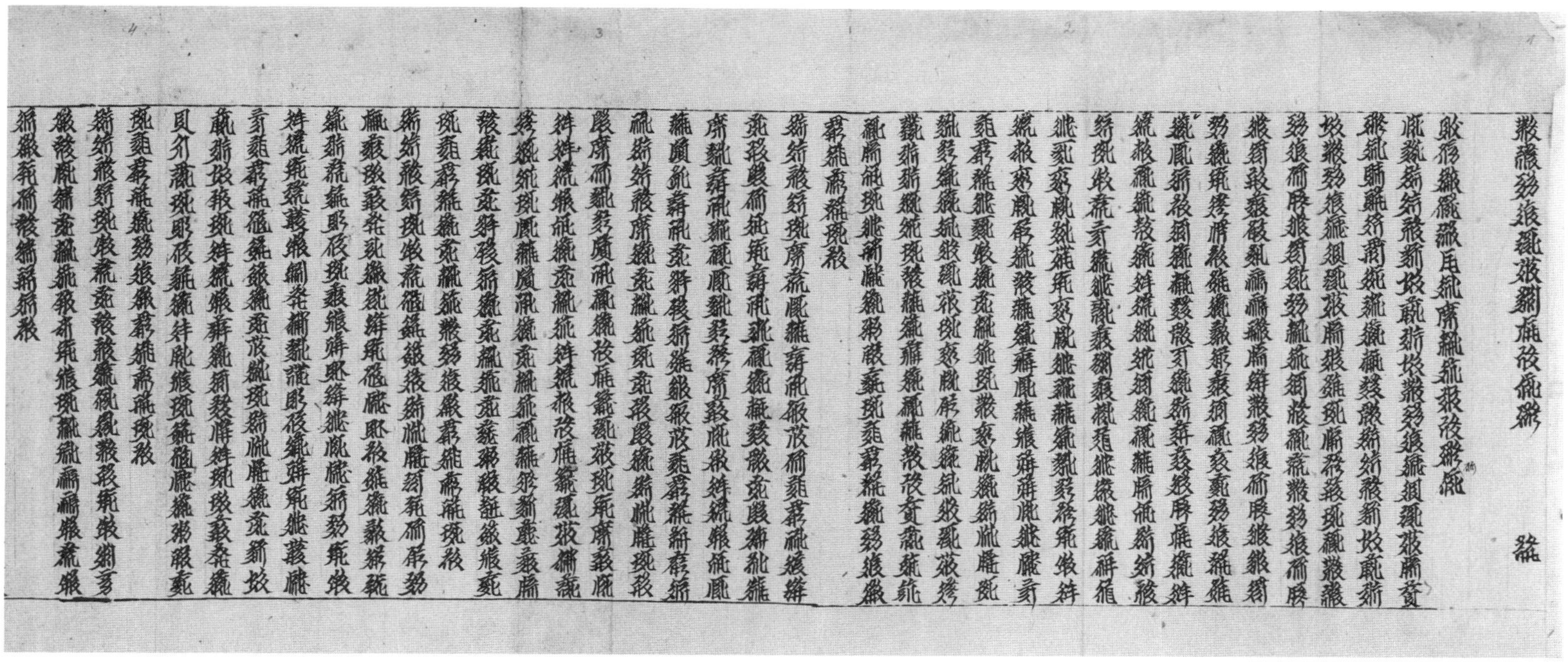

俄 Инв.No.1994　大般涅槃經卷第二十五　(15–1)

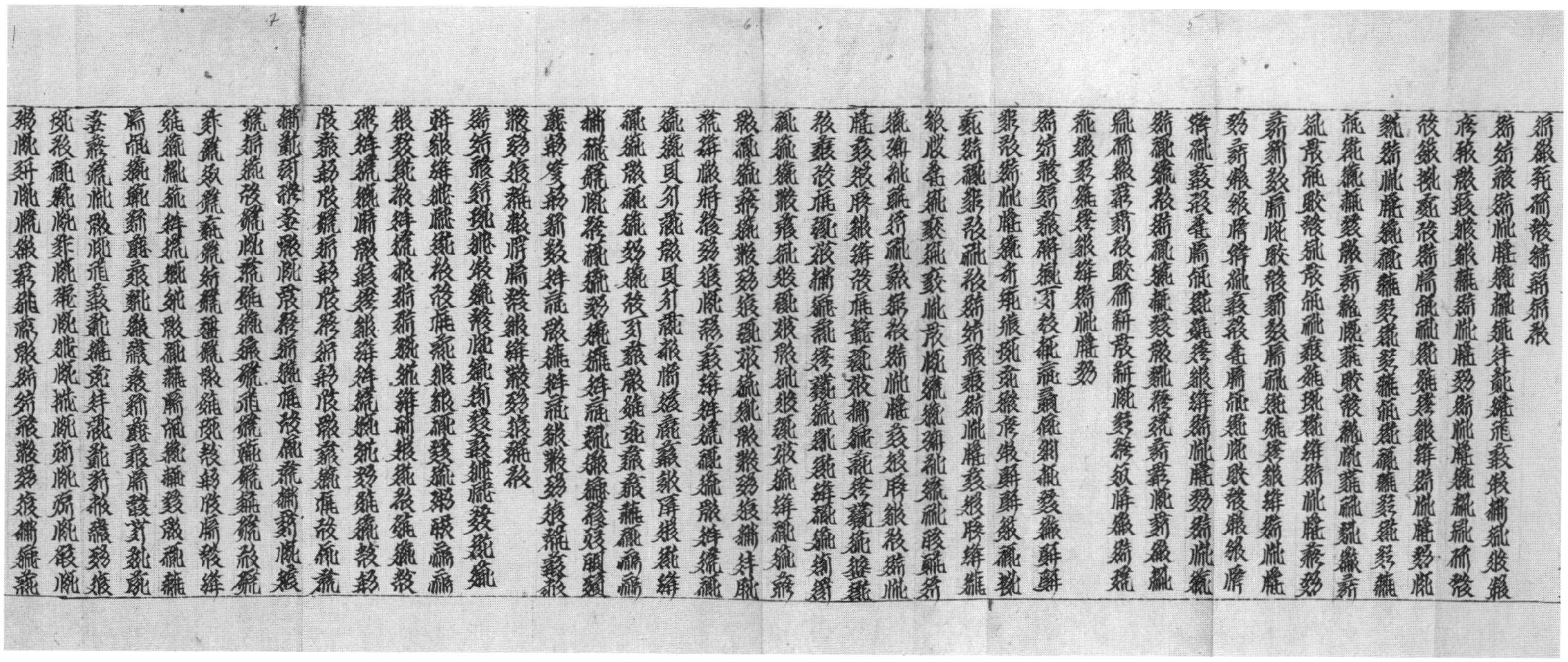

俄 Инв.No.1994　大般涅槃經卷第二十五　(15–2)

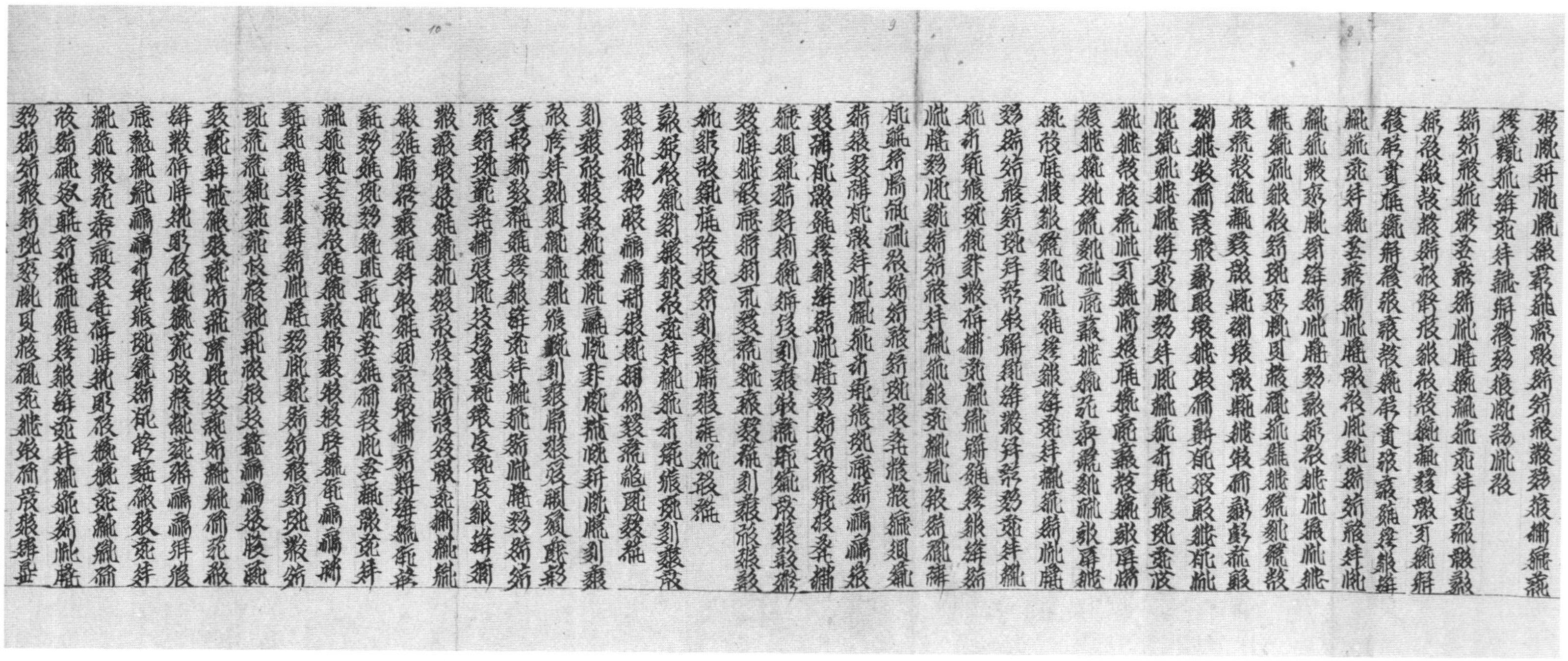

俄 Инв.No.1994　大般涅槃經卷第二十五　(15–3)

俄 **И**нв.No.1994　大般涅槃經卷第二十五　　　(15-4)

俄 **И**нв.No.1994　大般涅槃經卷第二十五　　　(15-5)

俄 **И**нв.No.1994　大般涅槃經卷第二十五　　　(15-6)

俄 Инв.No.1994　大般涅槃經卷第二十五　　　(15-7)

俄 Инв.No.1994　大般涅槃經卷第二十五　　　(15-8)

俄 Инв.No.1994　大般涅槃經卷第二十五　　　(15-9)

俄 **И**нв.No.1994　大般涅槃經卷第二十五　　　(15-10)

俄 **И**нв.No.1994　大般涅槃經卷第二十五　　　(15-11)

俄 **И**нв.No.1994　大般涅槃經卷第二十五　　　(15-12)

俄 Инв.No.1994　大般涅槃經卷第二十五　　　(15-13)

俄 Инв.No.1994　大般涅槃經卷第二十五　　　(15-14)

俄 Инв.No.1994　大般涅槃經卷第二十五　　　(15-15)

俄 **И**нв.No.5131　大般涅槃經卷第二十五

俄 **И**нв.No.418　大般涅槃經卷第二十六　　(10-1)

俄 **И**нв.No.418　大般涅槃經卷第二十六　　(10-2)

俄Инв.No.418　大般涅槃經卷第二十六　　　(10-3)

俄Инв.No.418　大般涅槃經卷第二十六　　　(10-4)

俄Инв.No.418　大般涅槃經卷第二十六　　　(10-5)

俄**И**нв.No.418　大般涅槃經卷第二十六　　　(10-6)

俄**И**нв.No.418　大般涅槃經卷第二十六　　　(10-7)

俄**И**нв.No.418　大般涅槃經卷第二十六　　　(10-8)

俄 **Инв**.No.418　大般涅槃經卷第二十六　　　(10-9)

俄 **Инв**.No.418　大般涅槃經卷第二十六　　　(10-10)

俄 **Инв**.No.423　大般涅槃經卷第二十七　　　(14-1)

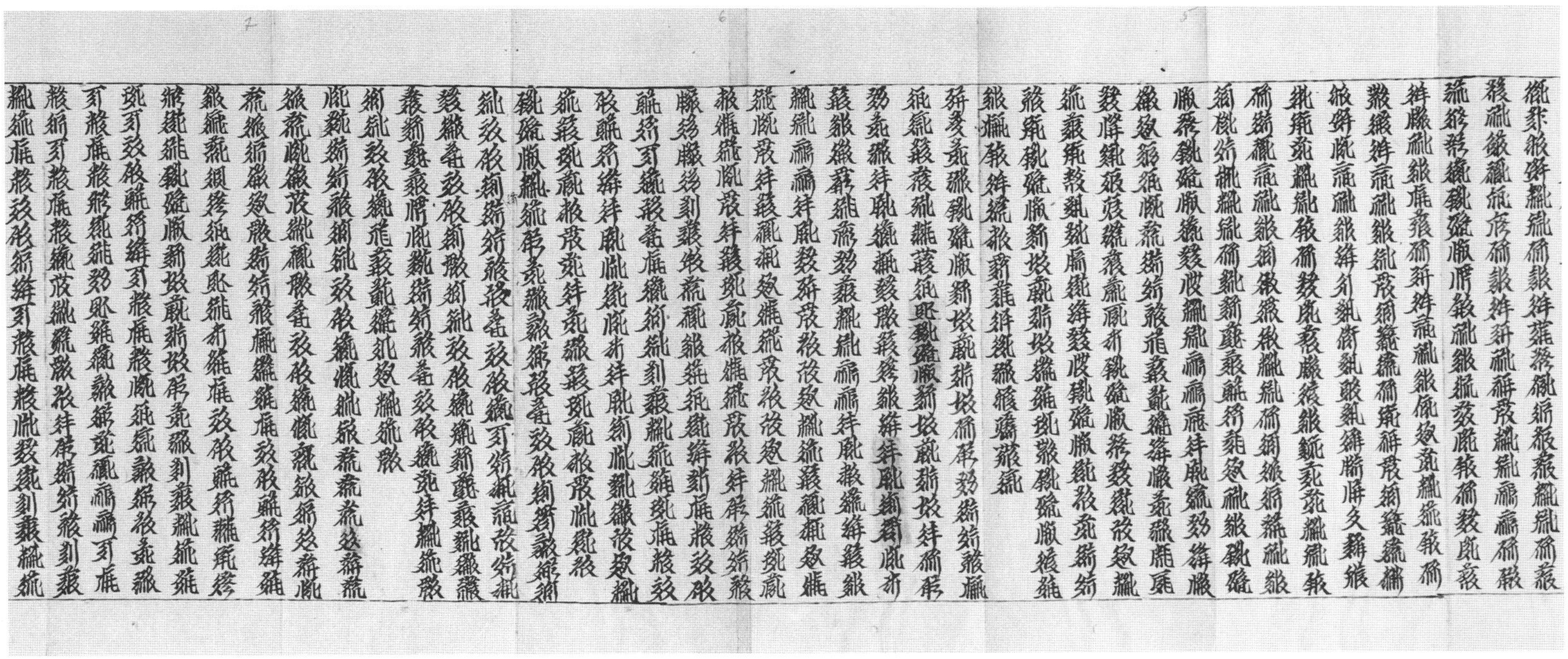

俄Инв.No.423　大般涅槃經卷第二十七　　(14-2)

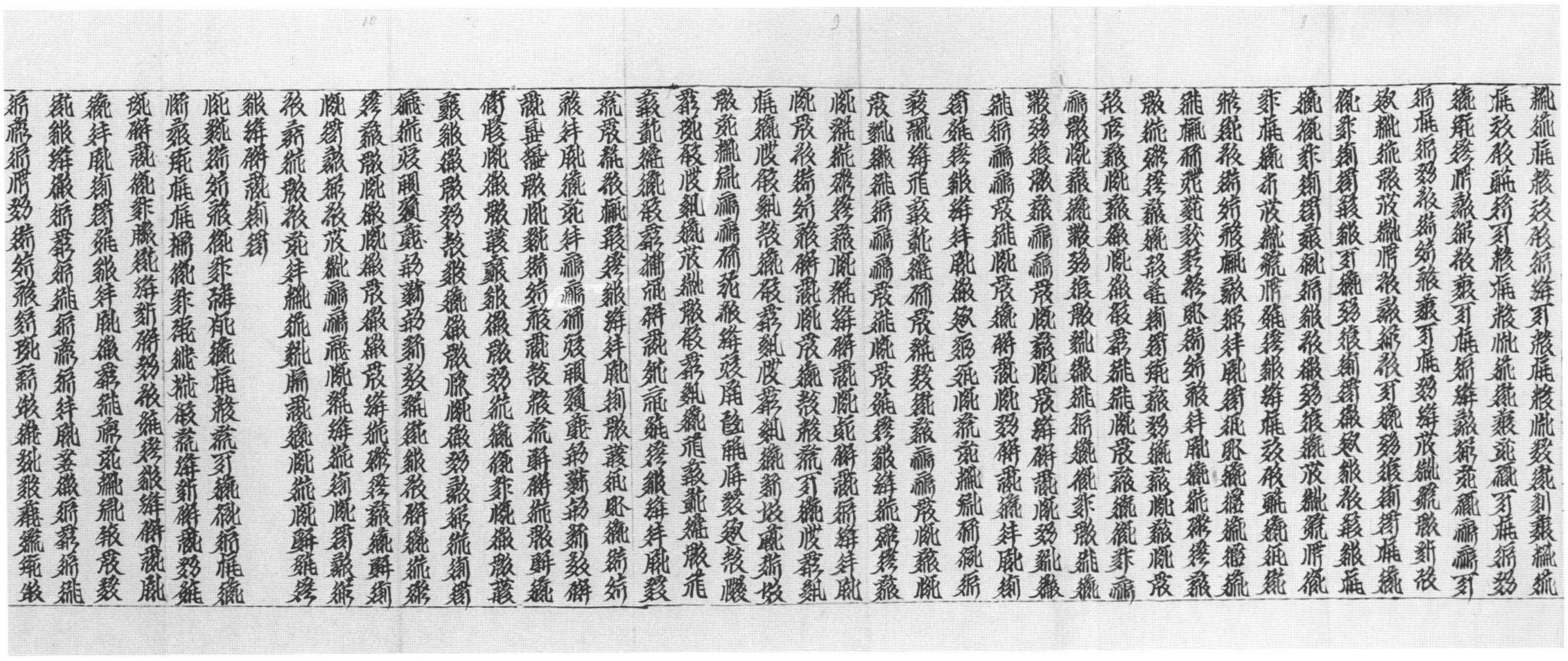

俄Инв.No.423　大般涅槃經卷第二十七　　(14-3)

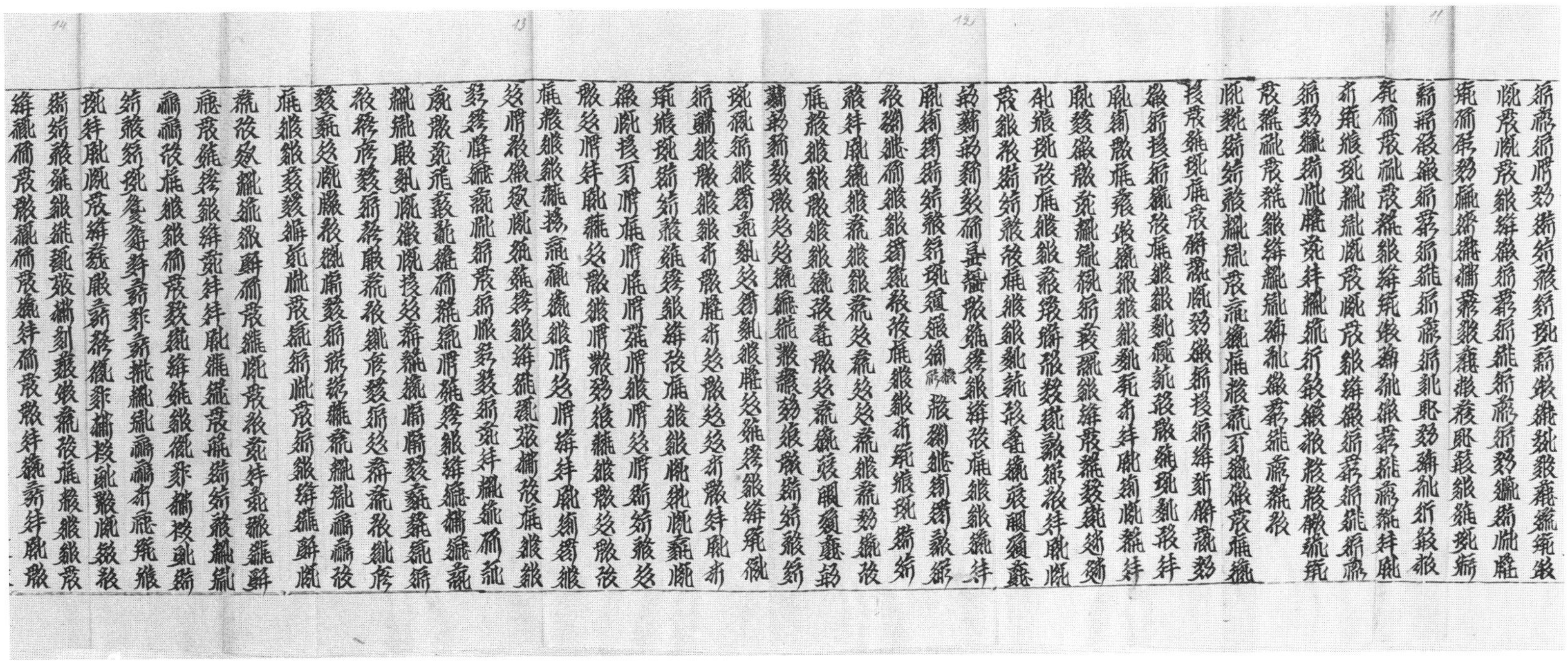

俄Инв.No.423　大般涅槃經卷第二十七　　(14-4)

俄 Инв.No.423　大般涅槃經卷第二十七　　　(14-5)

俄 Инв.No.423　大般涅槃經卷第二十七　　　(14-6)

俄 Инв.No.423　大般涅槃經卷第二十七　　　(14-7)

俄 **И**нв.No.423　大般涅槃經卷第二十七　　　(14-8)

俄 **И**нв.No.423　大般涅槃經卷第二十七　　　(14-9)

俄 **И**нв.No.423　大般涅槃經卷第二十七　　　(14-10)

俄 **И**нв.No.423　大般涅槃經卷第二十七　　　(14-11)

俄 **И**нв.No.423　大般涅槃經卷第二十七　　　(14-12)

俄 **И**нв.No.423　大般涅槃經卷第二十七　　　(14-13)

俄 **И**нв.No.423　大般涅槃經卷第二十七　　(14-14)

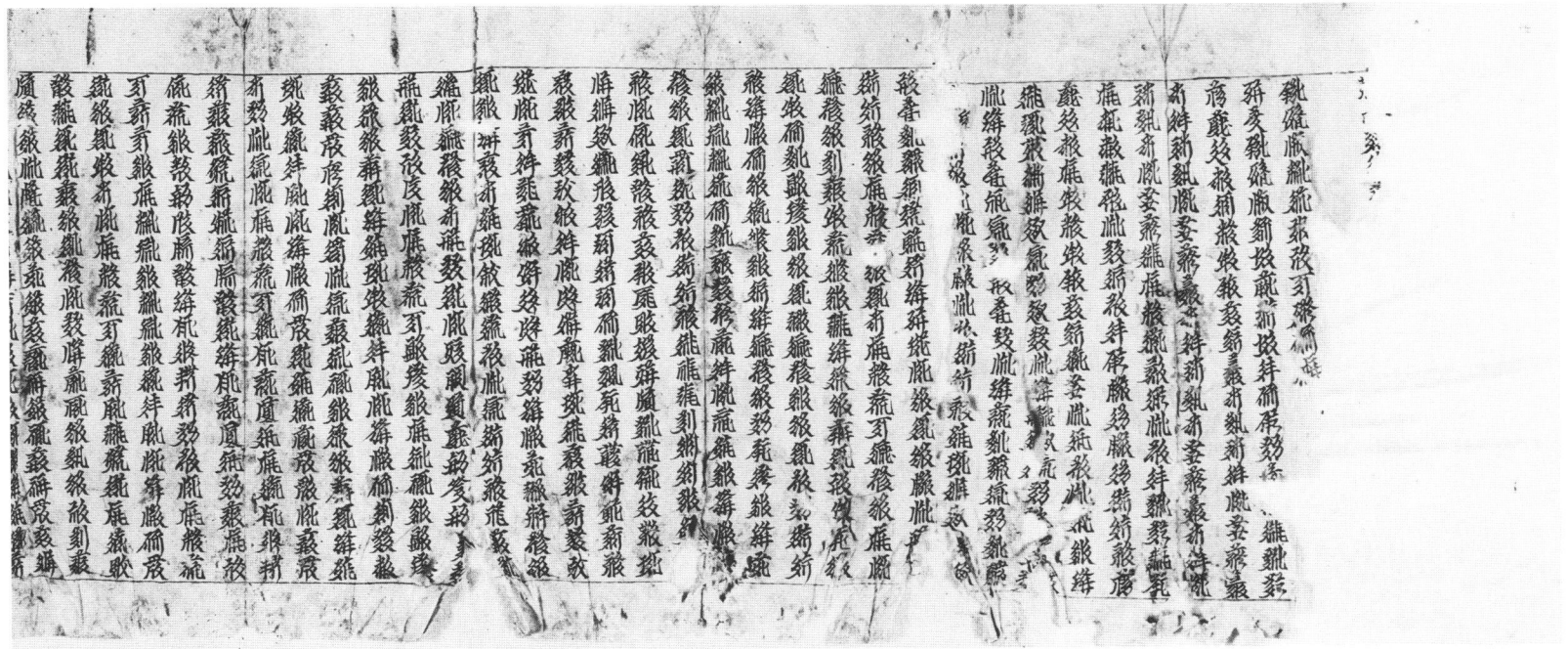

俄 **И**нв.No.961　大般涅槃經卷第二十八　　(14-1)

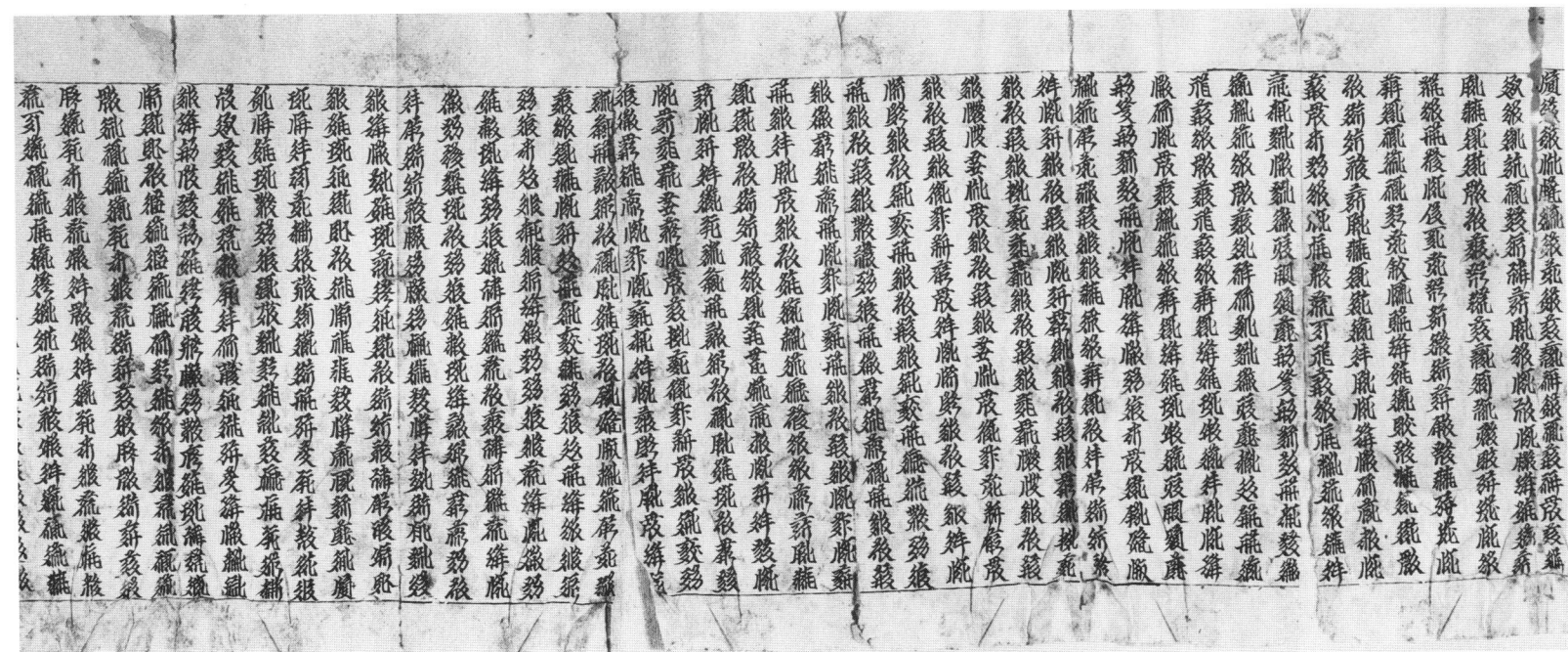

俄 **И**нв.No.961　大般涅槃經卷第二十八　　(14-2)

俄 Инв.No.961　大般涅槃經卷第二十八　　(14-3)

俄 Инв.No.961　大般涅槃經卷第二十八　　(14-4)

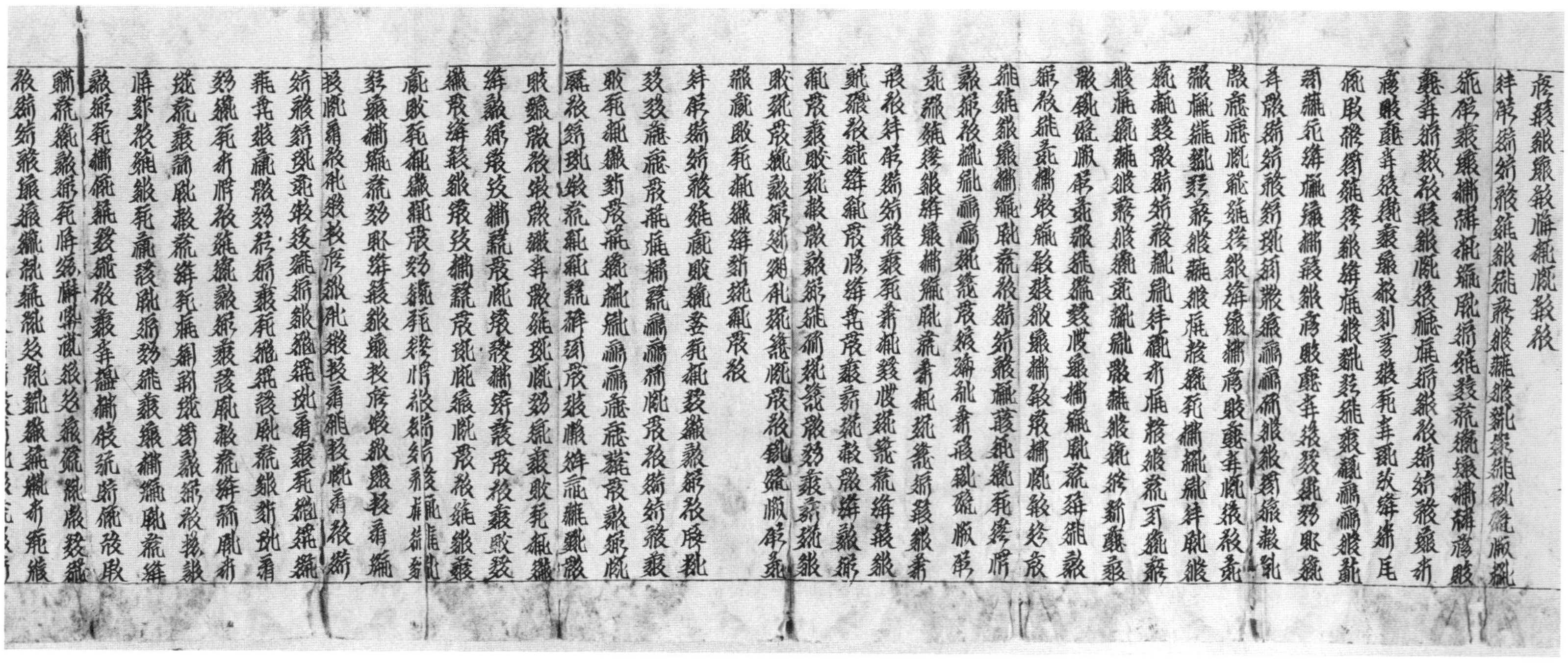

俄 Инв.No.961　大般涅槃經卷第二十八　　(14-5)

俄 ИнВ.No.961　大般涅槃經卷第二十八　　(14-6)

俄 ИнВ.No.961　大般涅槃經卷第二十八　　(14-7)

俄 ИнВ.No.961　大般涅槃經卷第二十八　　(14-8)

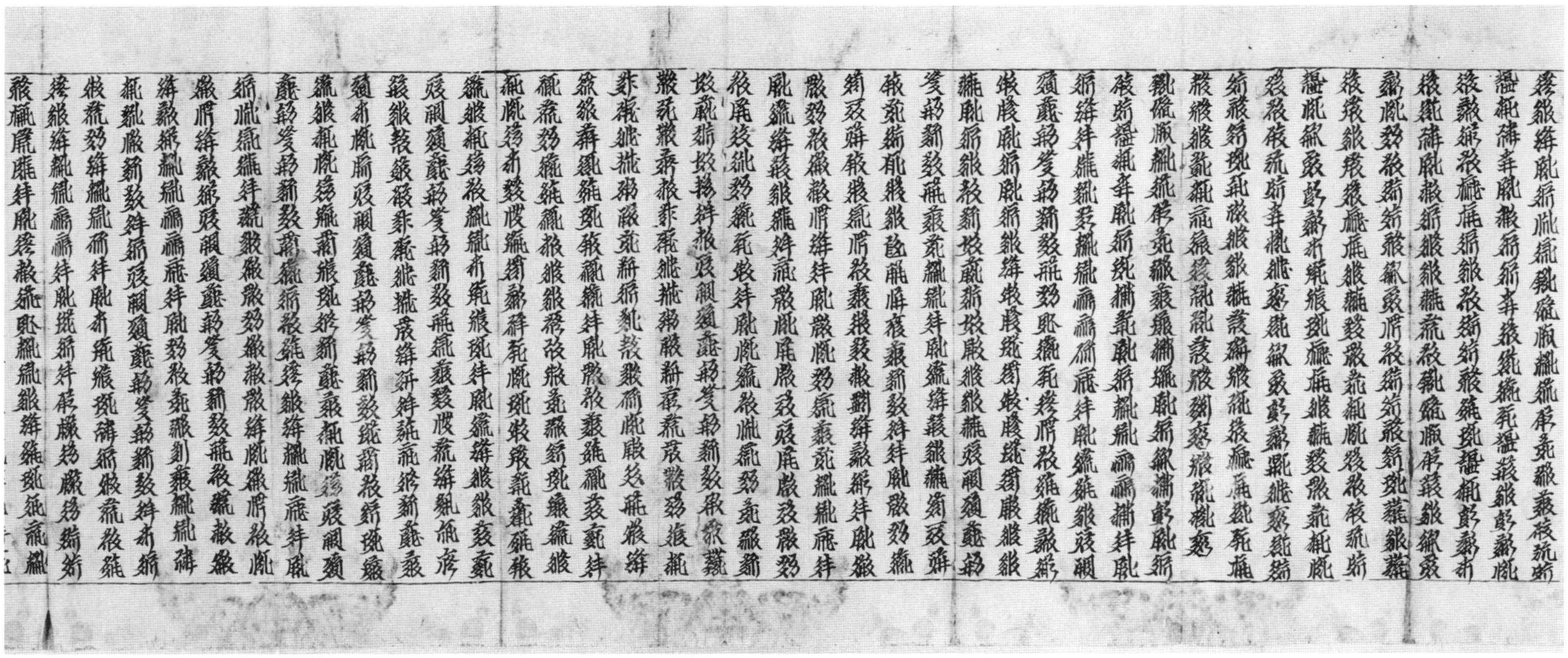

俄 Инв.No.961　大般涅槃經卷第二十八　(14-9)

俄 Инв.No.961　大般涅槃經卷第二十八　(14-10)

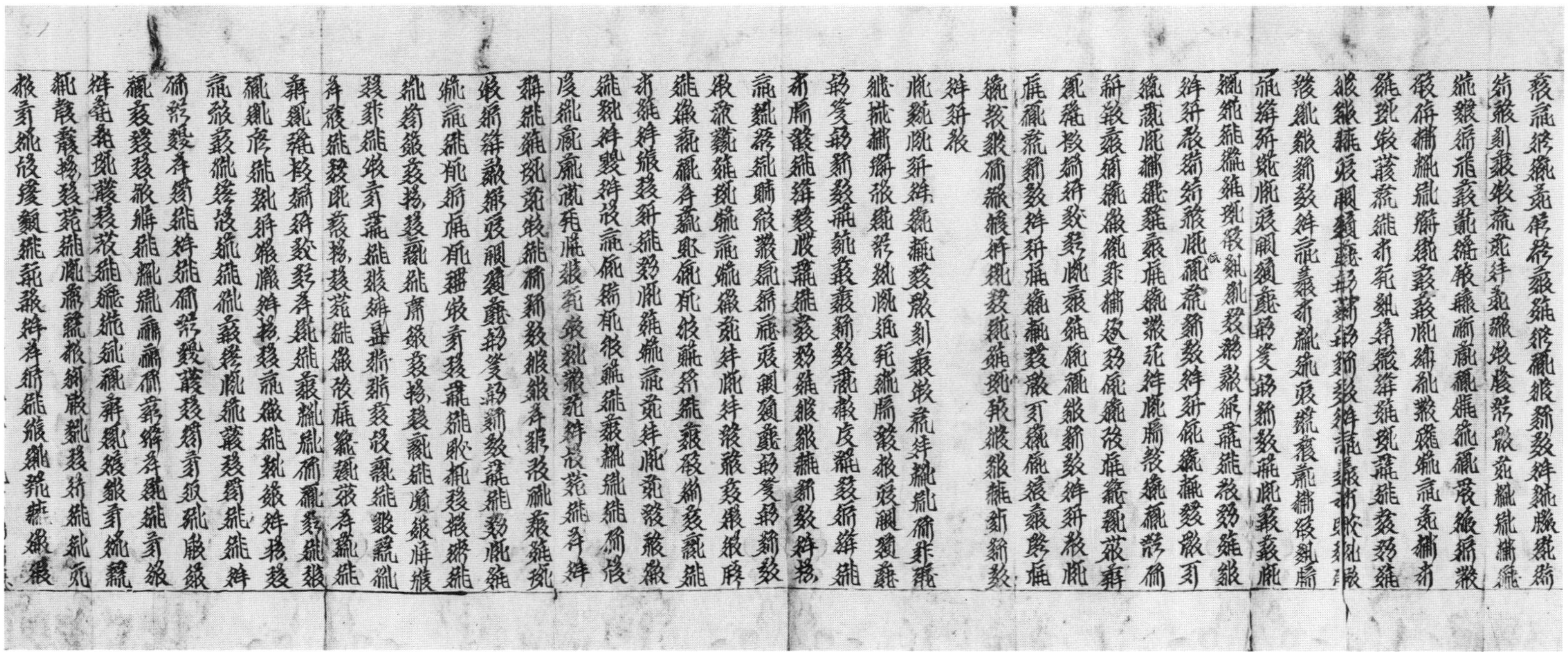

俄 Инв.No.961　大般涅槃經卷第二十八　(14-11)

俄 Инв.No.961　大般涅槃經卷第二十八　　　(14-12)

俄 Инв.No.961　大般涅槃經卷第二十八　　　(14-13)

俄 Инв.No.961　大般涅槃經卷第二十八　　　(14-14)

俄 **И**нв.No.920　大般涅槃經卷第二十九　　　(16-1)

俄 **И**нв.No.920　大般涅槃經卷第二十九　　　(16-2)

俄 **И**нв.No.920　大般涅槃經卷第二十九　　　(16-3)

俄 Инв.No.920 大般涅槃經卷第二十九 (16-4)

俄 Инв.No.920 大般涅槃經卷第二十九 (16-5)

俄 Инв.No.920 大般涅槃經卷第二十九 (16-6)

俄 Инв.No.920　大般涅槃經卷第二十九　　(16-7)

俄 Инв.No.920　大般涅槃經卷第二十九　　(16-8)

俄 Инв.No.920　大般涅槃經卷第二十九　　(16-9)

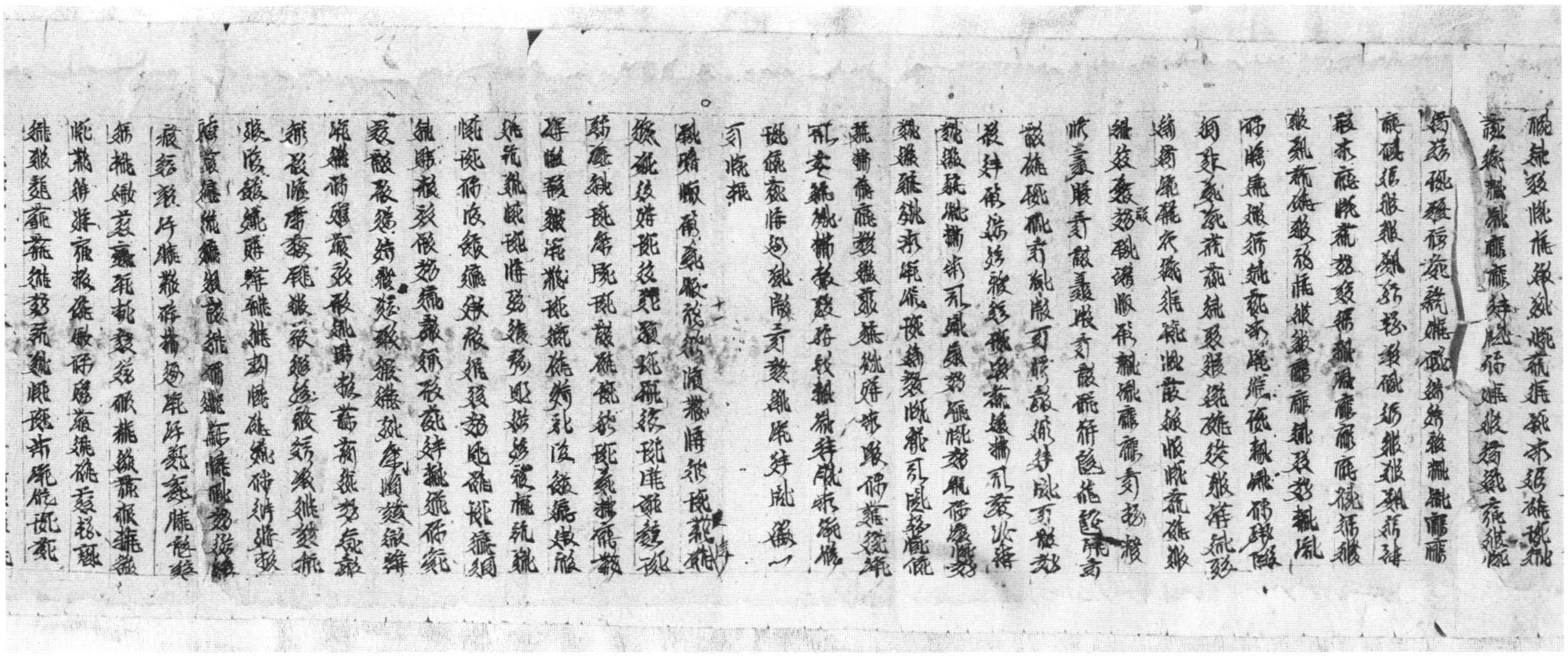

俄 Инв.No.920　大般涅槃經卷第二十九　(16–10)

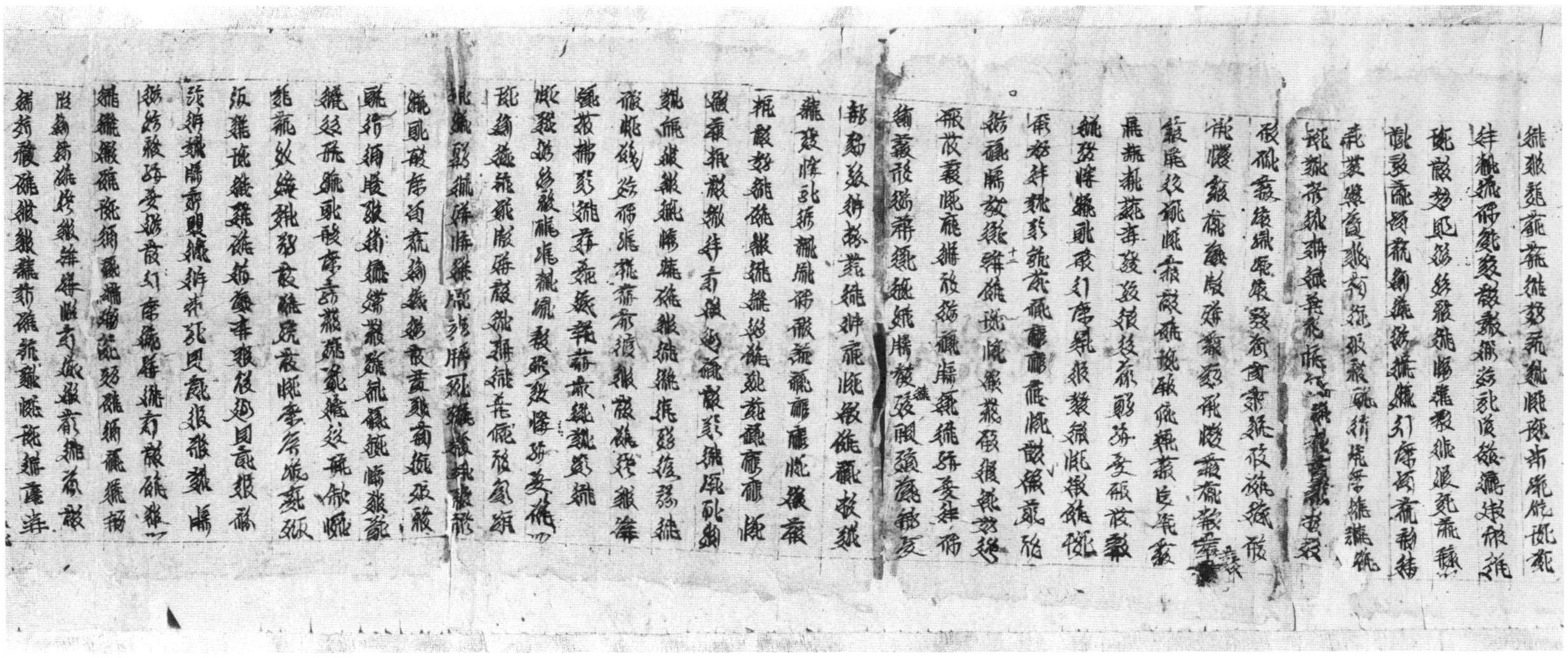

俄 Инв.No.920　大般涅槃經卷第二十九　(16–11)

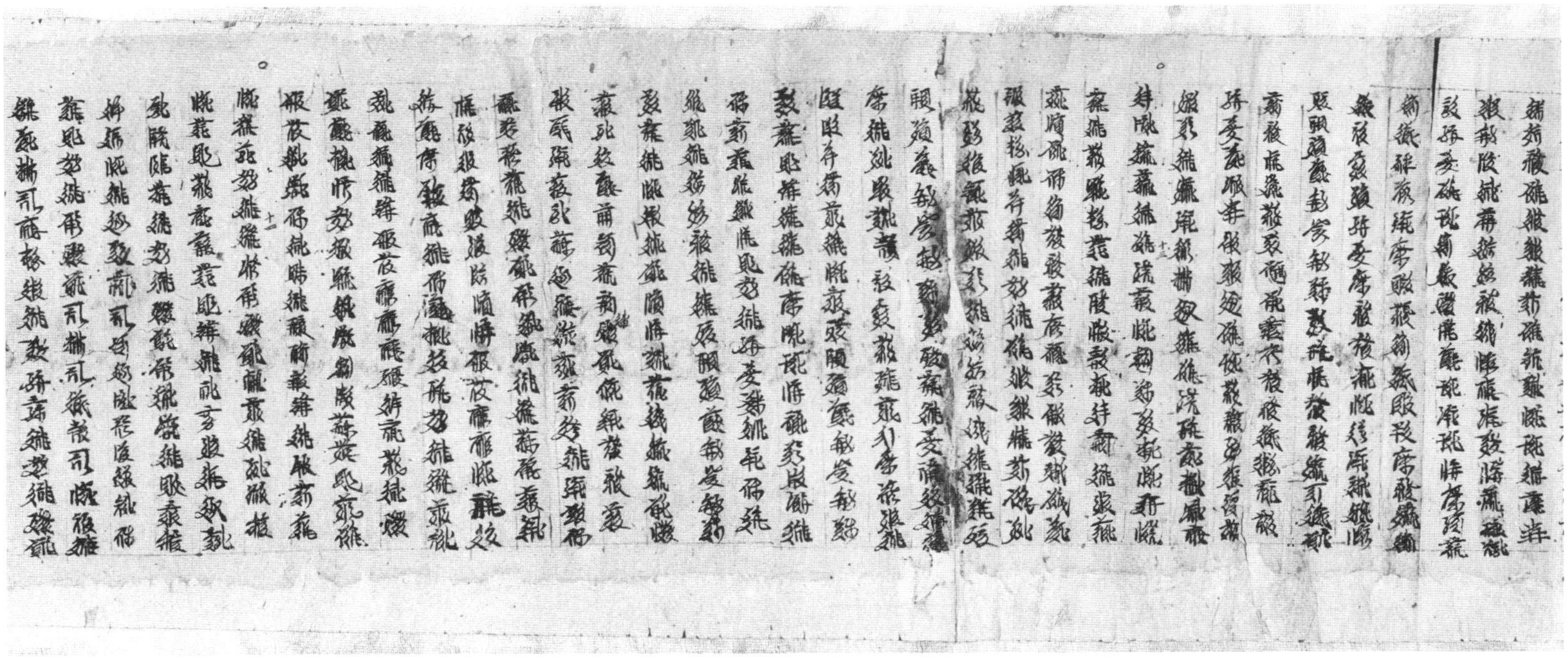

俄 Инв.No.920　大般涅槃經卷第二十九　(16–12)

俄 Инв.No.920　大般涅槃經卷第二十九　　　(16-13)

俄 Инв.No.920　大般涅槃經卷第二十九　　　(16-14)

俄 Инв.No.920　大般涅槃經卷第二十九　　　(16-15)

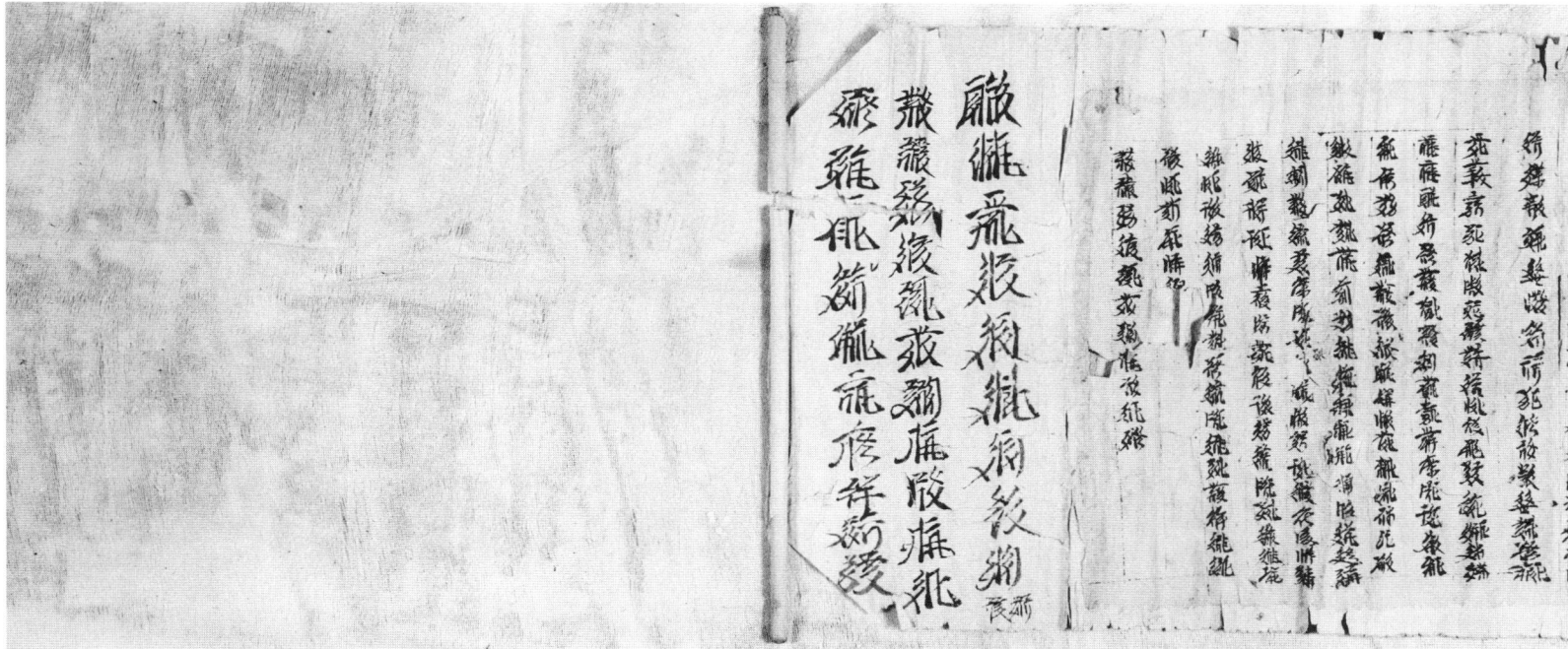

俄 Инв.No.920 　大般涅槃經卷第二十九 　　　(16-16)

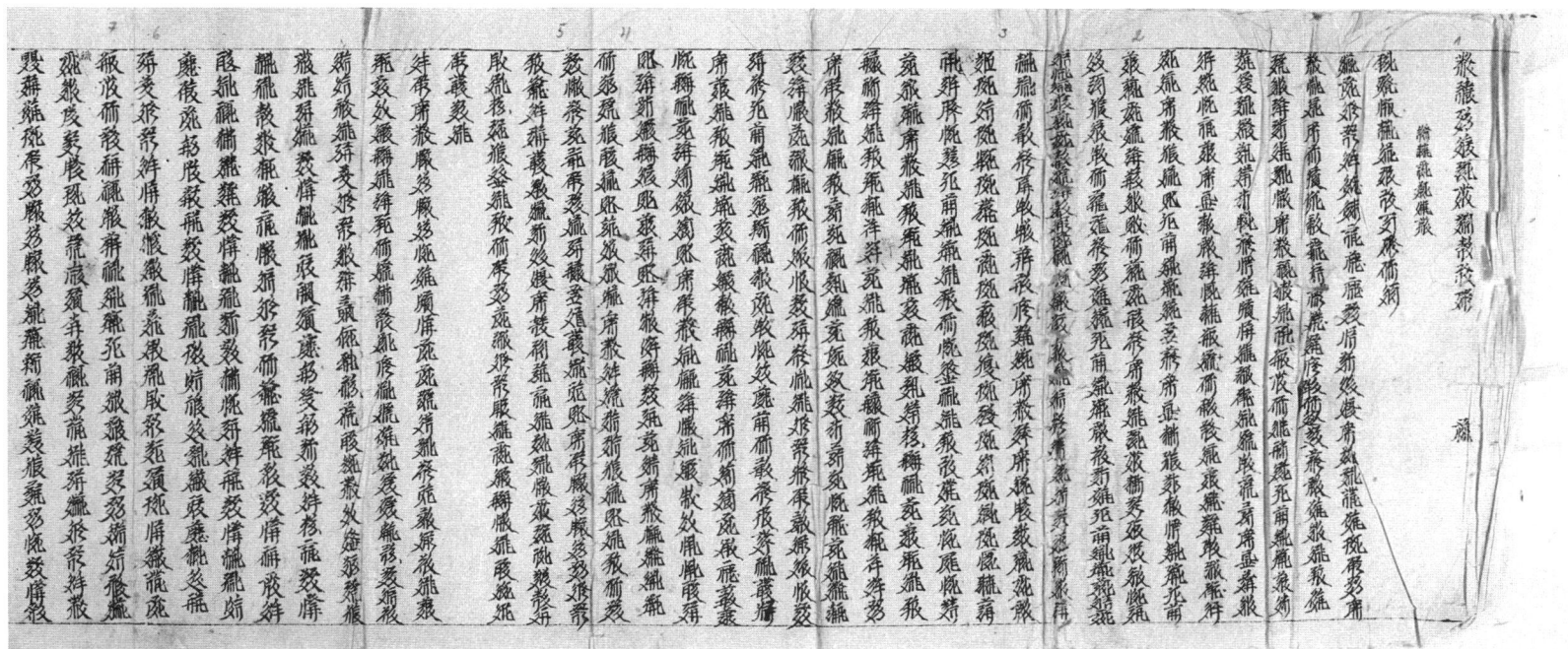

俄 Инв.No.426 　大般涅槃經卷第三十 　　　(11-1)

俄 Инв.No.426 　大般涅槃經卷第三十 　　　(11-2)

俄 **И**нв.No.426　　大般涅槃經卷第三十　　　（11-3）

俄 **И**нв.No.426　　大般涅槃經卷第三十　　　（11-4）

俄 **И**нв.No.426　　大般涅槃經卷第三十　　　（11-5）

俄 Инв.No.426　大般涅槃經卷第三十　　　（11-7）

俄 Инв.No.426　大般涅槃經卷第三十　　　（11-8）

俄 **И**нв.No.426　大般涅槃經卷第三十　　　（11-9）

俄 **И**нв.No.426　大般涅槃經卷第三十　　　（11-10）

俄 **И**нв.No.426　大般涅槃經卷第三十　　　（11-11）

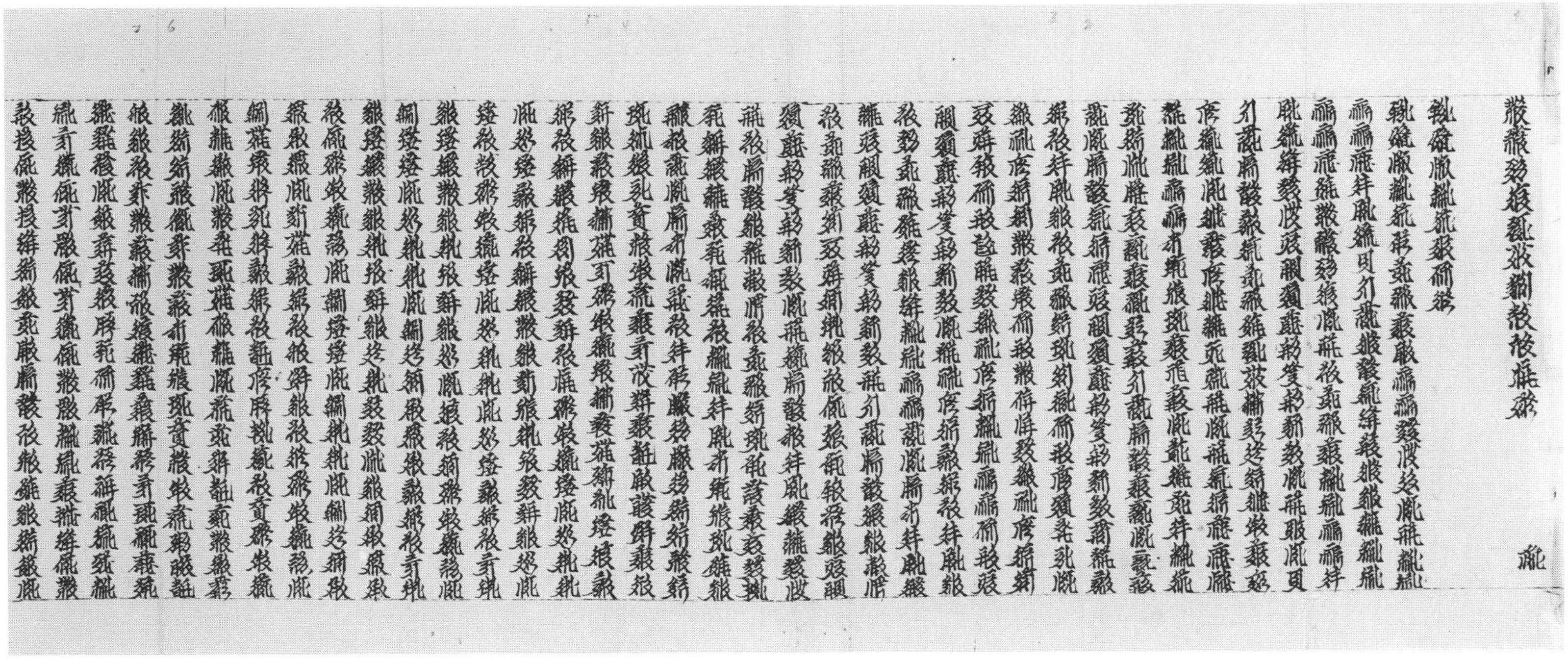

俄 Инв.No.1982　大般涅槃經卷第三十二　(13–1)

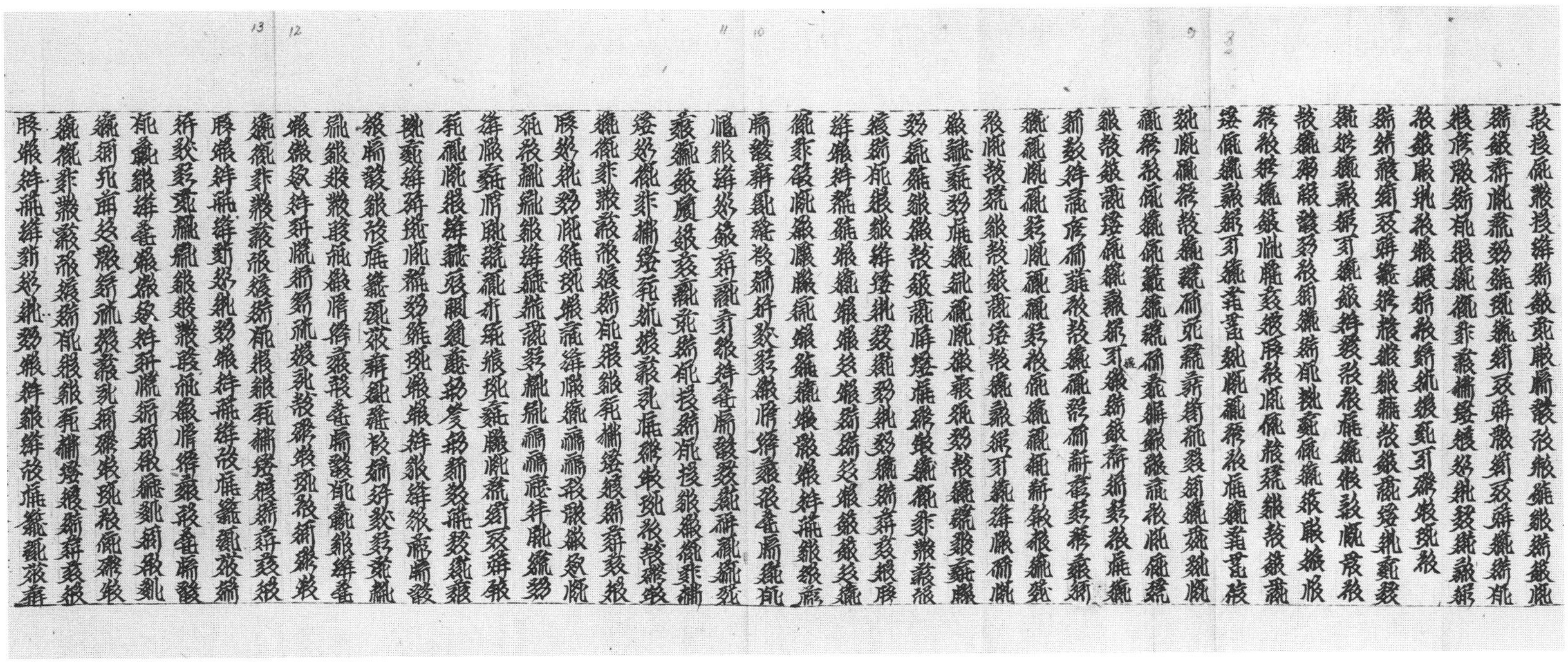

俄 Инв.No.1982　大般涅槃經卷第三十二　(13–2)

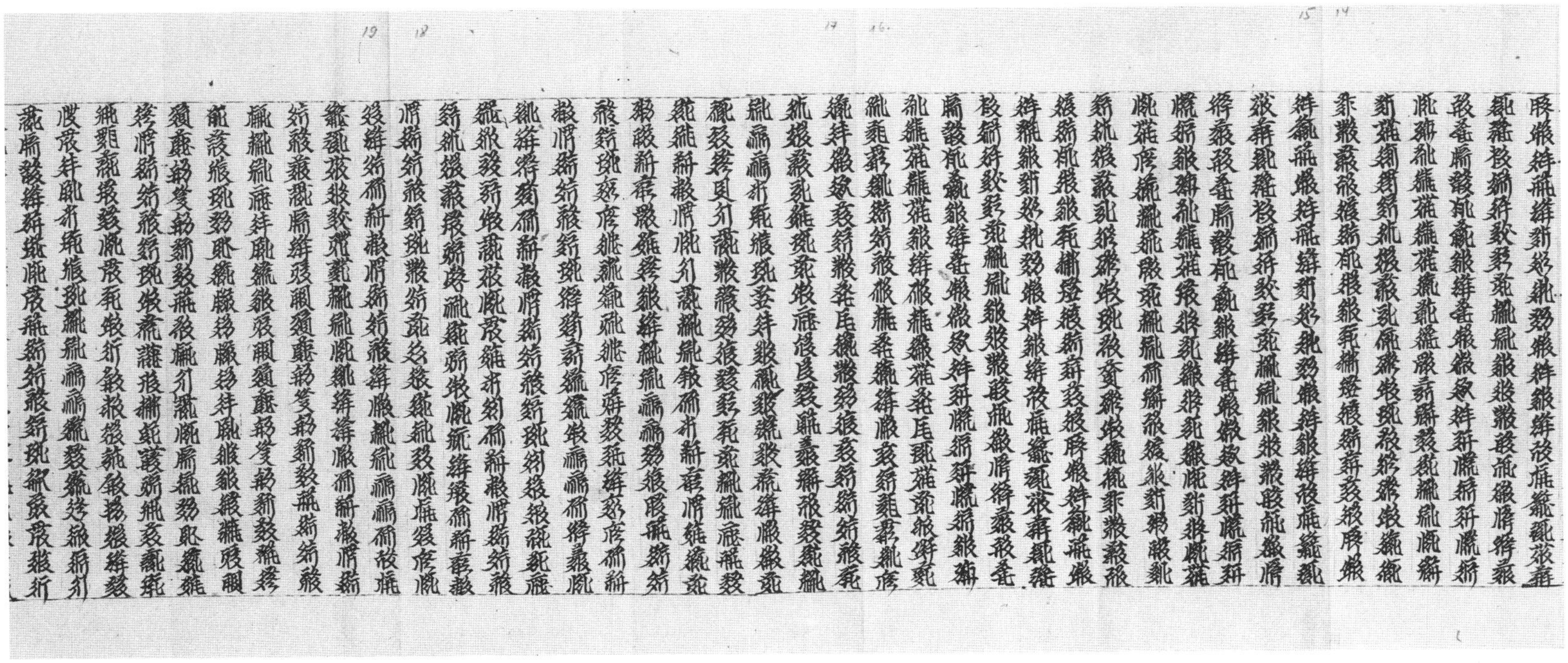

俄 Инв.No.1982　大般涅槃經卷第三十二　(13–3)

俄 **И**нв.No.1982　大般涅槃經卷第三十二　　　(13-4)

俄 **И**нв.No.1982　大般涅槃經卷第三十二　　　(13-5)

俄 **И**нв.No.1982　大般涅槃經卷第三十二　　　(13-6)

俄**И**нв.No.1982　大般涅槃經卷第三十二　　(13-7)

俄**И**нв.No.1982　大般涅槃經卷第三十二　　(13-8)

俄**И**нв.No.1982　大般涅槃經卷第三十二　　(13-9)

俄 **И**нв.No.1982　大般涅槃經卷第三十二　　　(13-10)

俄 **И**нв.No.1982　大般涅槃經卷第三十二　　　(13-11)

俄 **И**нв.No.1982　大般涅槃經卷第三十二　　　(13-12)

俄 **И**нв.No.1982　大般涅槃經卷第三十二　　　(13-13)

俄 **И**нв.No.1983　大般涅槃經卷第三十三　　　(8-1)

俄 **И**нв.No.1983　大般涅槃經卷第三十三　　　(8-2)

俄 Инв.No.1983　大般涅槃經卷第三十三　　　(8-3)

俄 Инв.No.1983　大般涅槃經卷第三十三　　　(8-4)

俄 Инв.No.1983　大般涅槃經卷第三十三　　　(8-5)

俄 Инв.No.1983 大般涅槃經卷第三十三 (8-6)

俄 Инв.No.1983 大般涅槃經卷第三十三 (8-7)

俄 Инв.No.1983 大般涅槃經卷第三十三 (8-8)

俄 Инв.No.5138 大般涅槃經卷第三十三

俄 Инв.No.471 大般涅槃經卷第三十四 （12-1）

俄 Инв.No.471 大般涅槃經卷第三十四 （12-2）

俄Инв.No.471　大般涅槃經卷第三十四　　(12-3)

俄Инв.No.471　大般涅槃經卷第三十四　　(12-4)

俄Инв.No.471　大般涅槃經卷第三十四　　(12-5)

俄 Инв.No.471　大般涅槃經卷第三十四　(12-6)

俄 Инв.No.471　大般涅槃經卷第三十四　(12-7)

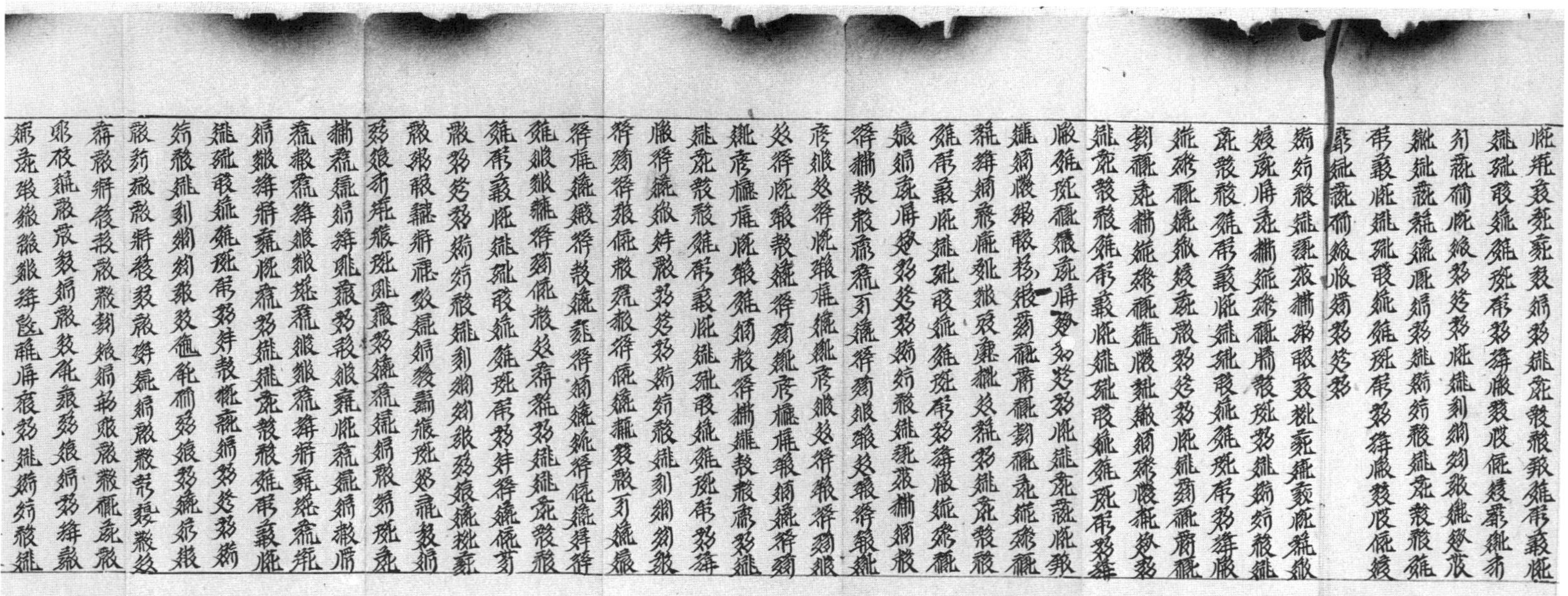

俄 Инв.No.471　大般涅槃經卷第三十四　(12-8)

俄Инв.No.471　大般涅槃經卷第三十四　　　(12-9)

俄Инв.No.471　大般涅槃經卷第三十四　　　(12-10)

俄Инв.No.471　大般涅槃經卷第三十四　　　(12-11)

俄 ИнВ.No.471　大般涅槃經卷第三十四　　（12-12）

俄 ИнВ.No.470　大般涅槃經卷第三十五　　（10-1）

俄 ИнВ.No.470　大般涅槃經卷第三十五　　（10-2）

俄Инв.No.470　大般涅槃經卷第三十五　　　（10-3）

俄Инв.No.470　大般涅槃經卷第三十五　　　（10-4）

俄Инв.No.470　大般涅槃經卷第三十五　　　（10-5）

俄 Инв.No.470　　大般涅槃經卷第三十五　　　　(10-6)

俄 Инв.No.470　　大般涅槃經卷第三十五　　　　(10-7)

俄 Инв.No.470　　大般涅槃經卷第三十五　　　　(10-8)

俄 **Инв**.No.470　大般涅槃經卷第三十五　　　(10-9)

俄 **Инв**.No.470　大般涅槃經卷第三十五　　　(10-10)

俄 **Инв**.No.963　大般涅槃經卷第三十六　　　(16-1)

俄 **И**нв.No.963 大般涅槃經卷第三十六 (16-2)

俄 **И**нв.No.963 大般涅槃經卷第三十六 (16-3)

俄 **И**нв.No.963 大般涅槃經卷第三十六 (16-4)

俄Инв.No.963　大般涅槃經卷第三十六　　　(16-5)

俄Инв.No.963　大般涅槃經卷第三十六　　　(16-6)

俄Инв.No.963　大般涅槃經卷第三十六　　　(16-7)

俄 **И**нв.No.963　大般涅槃經卷第三十六　　　(16-8)

俄 **И**нв.No.963　大般涅槃經卷第三十六　　　(16-9)

俄 **И**нв.No.963　大般涅槃經卷第三十六　　　(16-10)

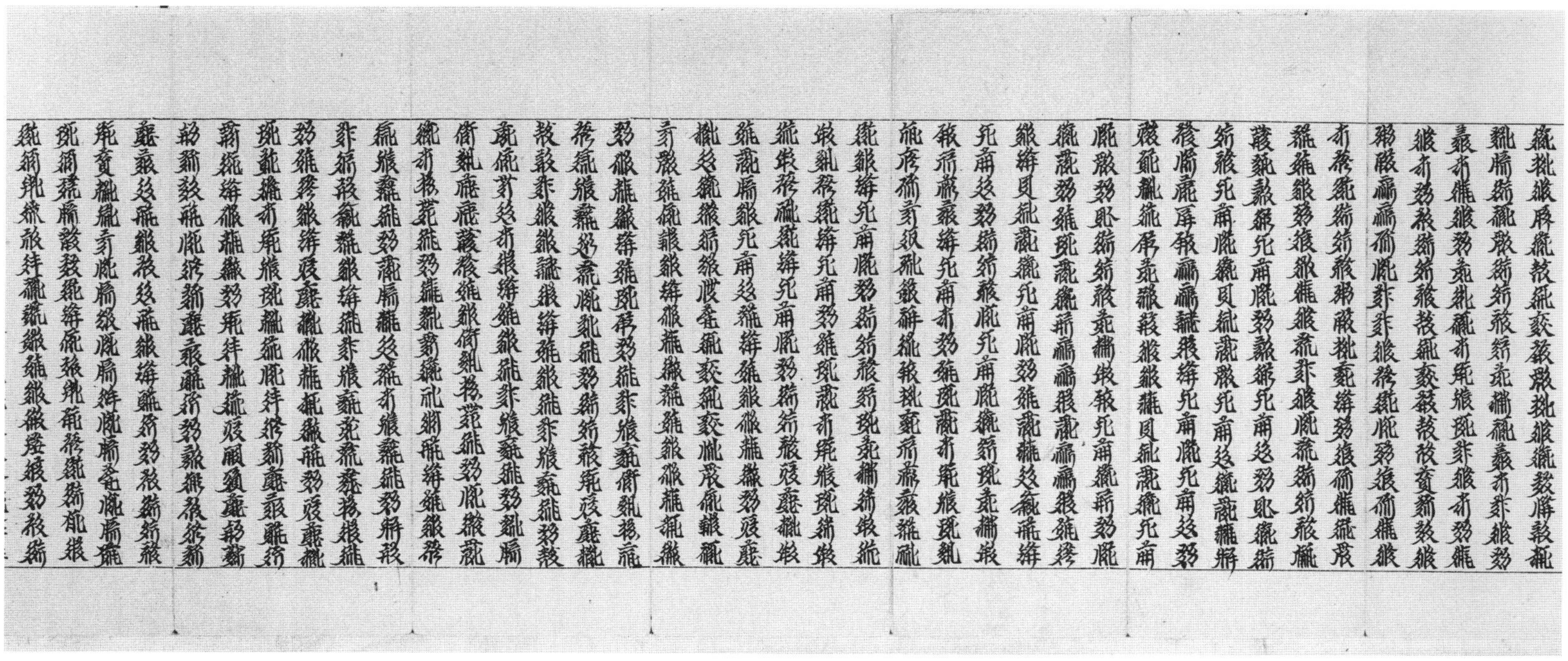

俄 Инв.No.963　大般涅槃經卷第三十六　(16-14)

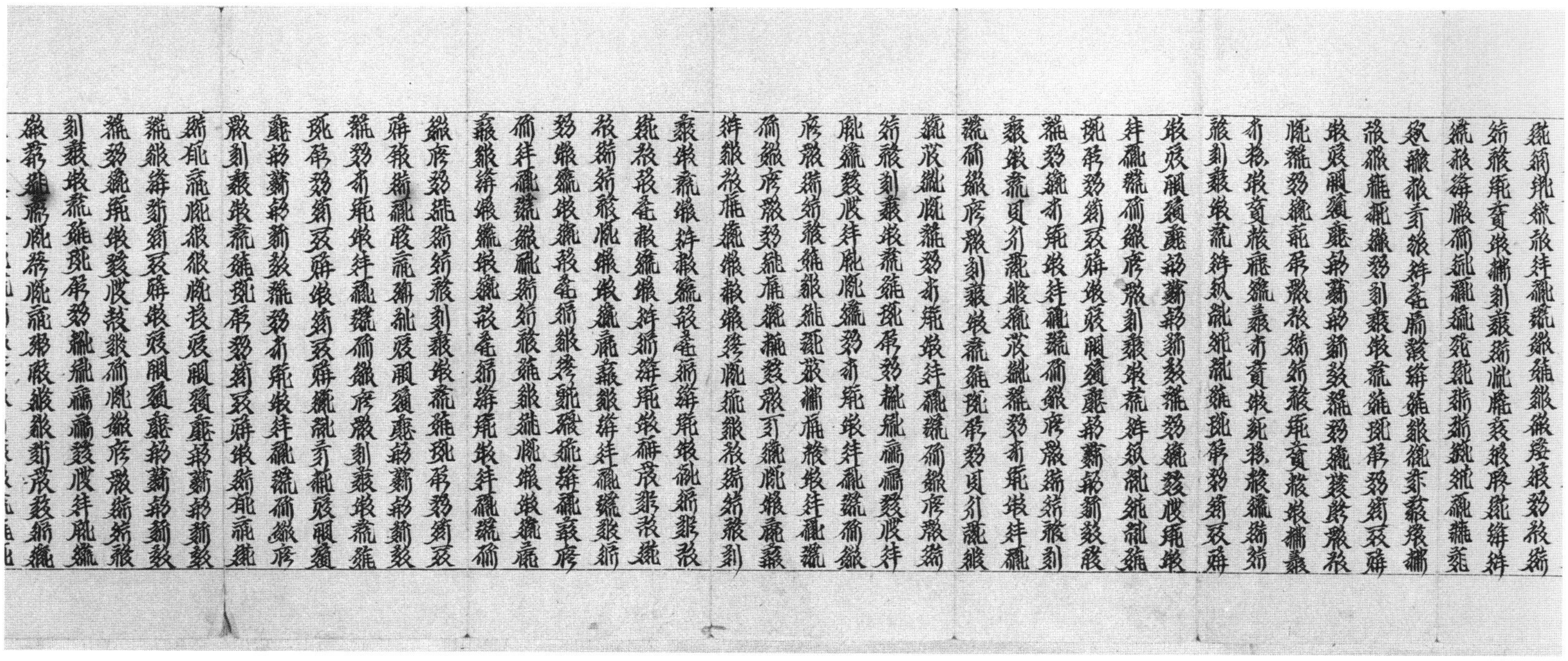

俄 Инв.No.963　大般涅槃經卷第三十六　(16-15)

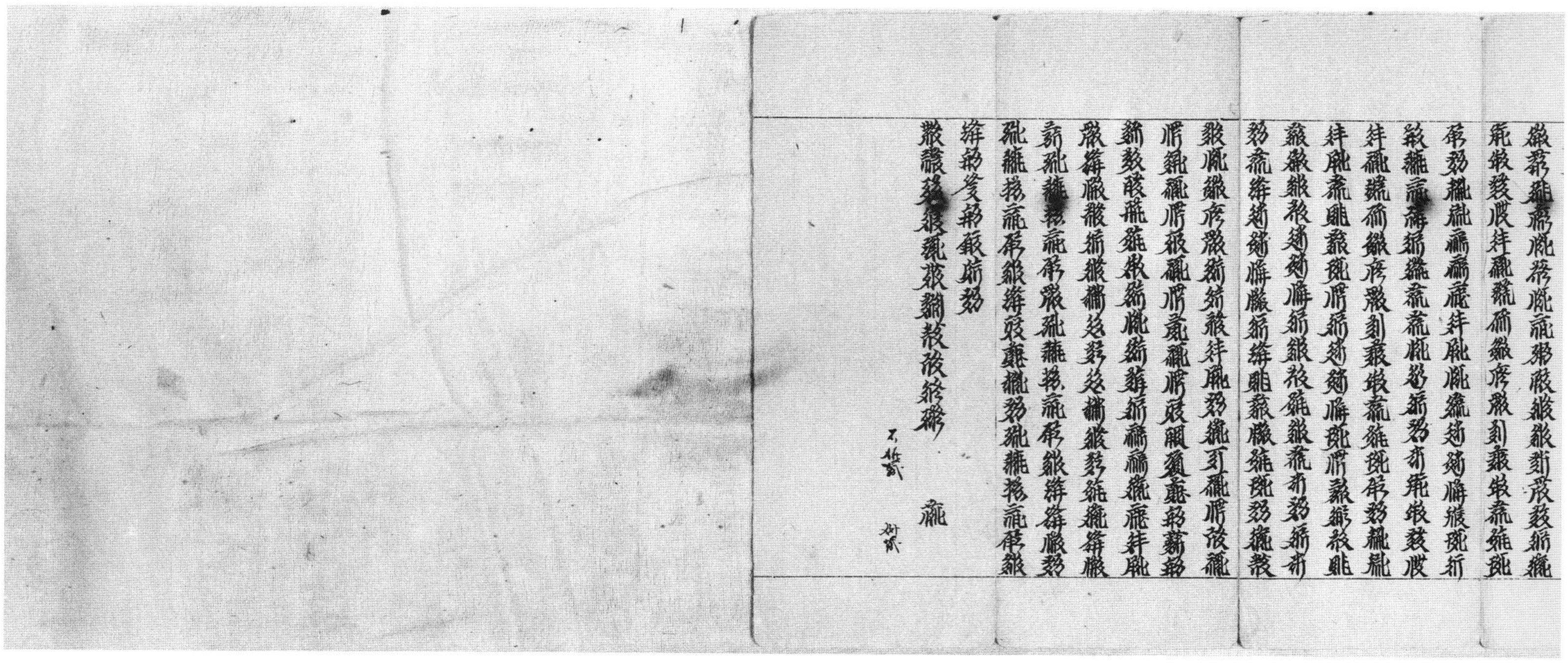

俄 Инв.No.963　大般涅槃經卷第三十六　(16-16)

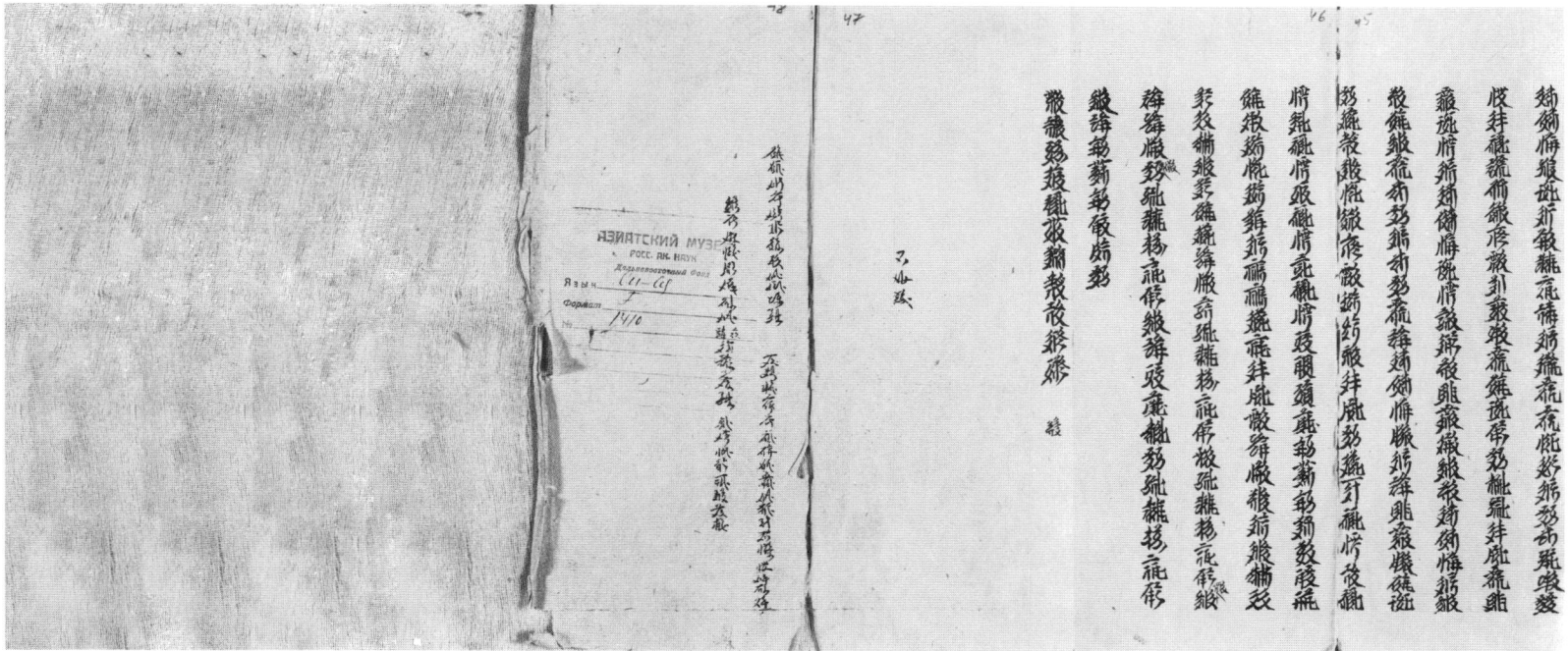

俄 Инв.No.469　大般涅槃經卷第三十六

俄 Инв.No.3543+467　大般涅槃經卷第三十七　　　(14-1)

俄 Инв.No.3543+467　大般涅槃經卷第三十七　　　(14-2)

俄 Инв.No.3543+467　大般涅槃經卷第三十七　　(14-3)

俄 Инв.No.3543+467　大般涅槃經卷第三十七　　(14-4)

俄 Инв.No.3543+467　大般涅槃經卷第三十七　　(14-5)

俄 **И**нв.No.3543+467　　大般涅槃經卷第三十七　　　　(14-6)

俄 **И**нв.No.3543+467　　大般涅槃經卷第三十七　　　　(14-7)

俄 **И**нв.No.3543+467　　大般涅槃經卷第三十七　　　　(14-8)

俄 **Инв**.No.3543+467　　大般涅槃經卷第三十七　　　　(14-9)

俄 **Инв**.No.3543+467　　大般涅槃經卷第三十七　　　　(14-10)

俄 **Инв**.No.3543+467　　大般涅槃經卷第三十七　　　　(14-11)

133

俄 Инв.No.3543+467 大般涅槃經卷第三十七 (14–12)

俄 Инв.No.3543+467 大般涅槃經卷第三十七 (14–13)

俄 Инв.No.3543+467 大般涅槃經卷第三十七 (14–14)

俄 **Инв**.No.468　大般涅槃經卷第三十八　　　(10-1)

俄 **Инв**.No.468　大般涅槃經卷第三十八　　　(10-2)

俄 **Инв**.No.468　大般涅槃經卷第三十八　　　(10-3)

俄 **И**нв.No.468　大般涅槃經卷第三十八　　　(10-4)

俄 **И**нв.No.468　大般涅槃經卷第三十八　　　(10-5)

俄 **И**нв.No.468　大般涅槃經卷第三十八　　　(10-6)

俄Инв.No.468　大般涅槃經卷第三十八　　　（10-7）

俄Инв.No.468　大般涅槃經卷第三十八　　　（10-8）

俄Инв.No.468　大般涅槃經卷第三十八　　　（10-9）

俄Инв.No.468　大般涅槃經卷第三十八　　　　(10-10)

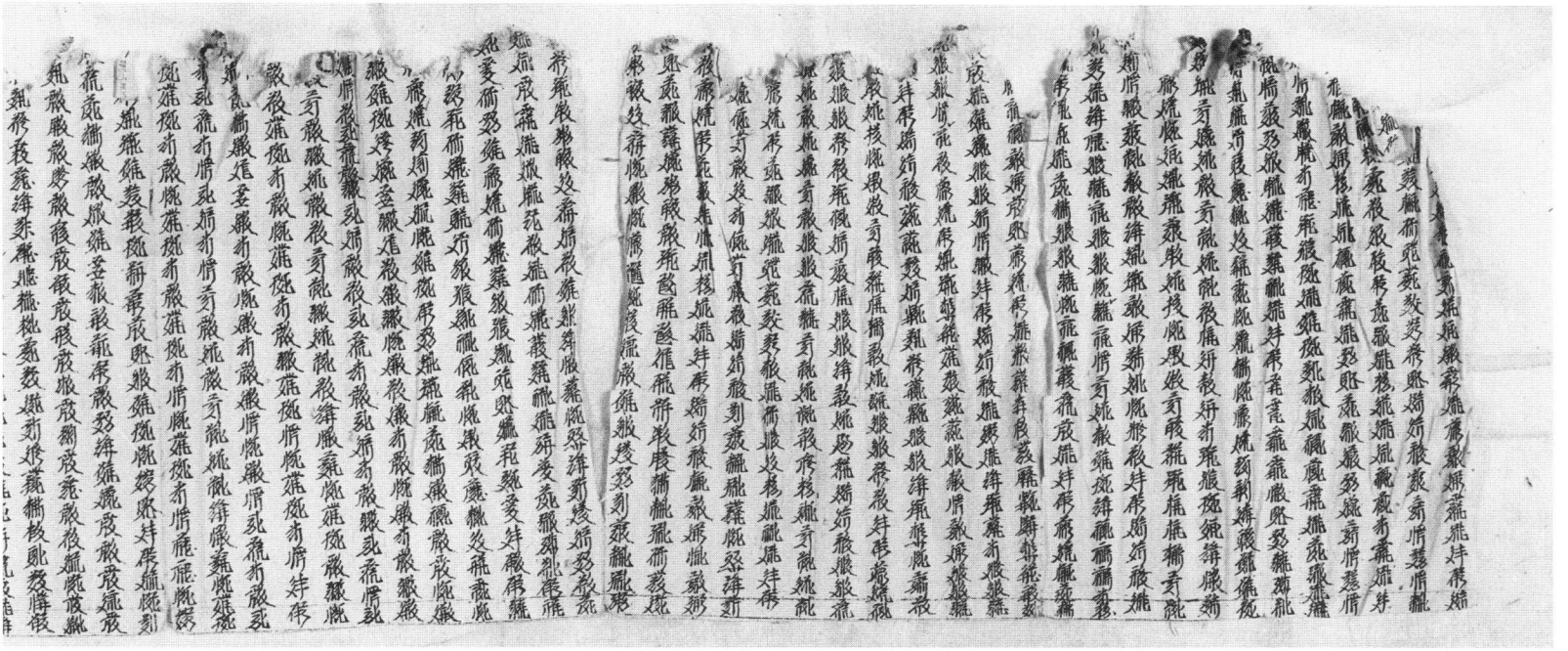

俄Инв.No.7574　大般涅槃經卷第三十九　　　(2-1)

俄Инв.No.7574　大般涅槃經卷第三十九　　　(2-2)

俄 **И**нв.No.970　大般涅槃經卷第四十　　(13-1)

俄 **И**нв.No.970　大般涅槃經卷第四十　　(13-2)

俄 **И**нв.No.970　大般涅槃經卷第四十　　(13-3)

俄 Инв.No.970　大般涅槃經卷第四十　　　(13-4)

俄 Инв.No.970　大般涅槃經卷第四十　　　(13-5)

俄 Инв.No.970　大般涅槃經卷第四十　　　(13-6)

俄 **И**нв.No.970　大般涅槃經卷第四十　　　(13-7)

俄 **И**нв.No.970　大般涅槃經卷第四十　　　(13-8)

俄 **И**нв.No.970　大般涅槃經卷第四十　　　(13-9)

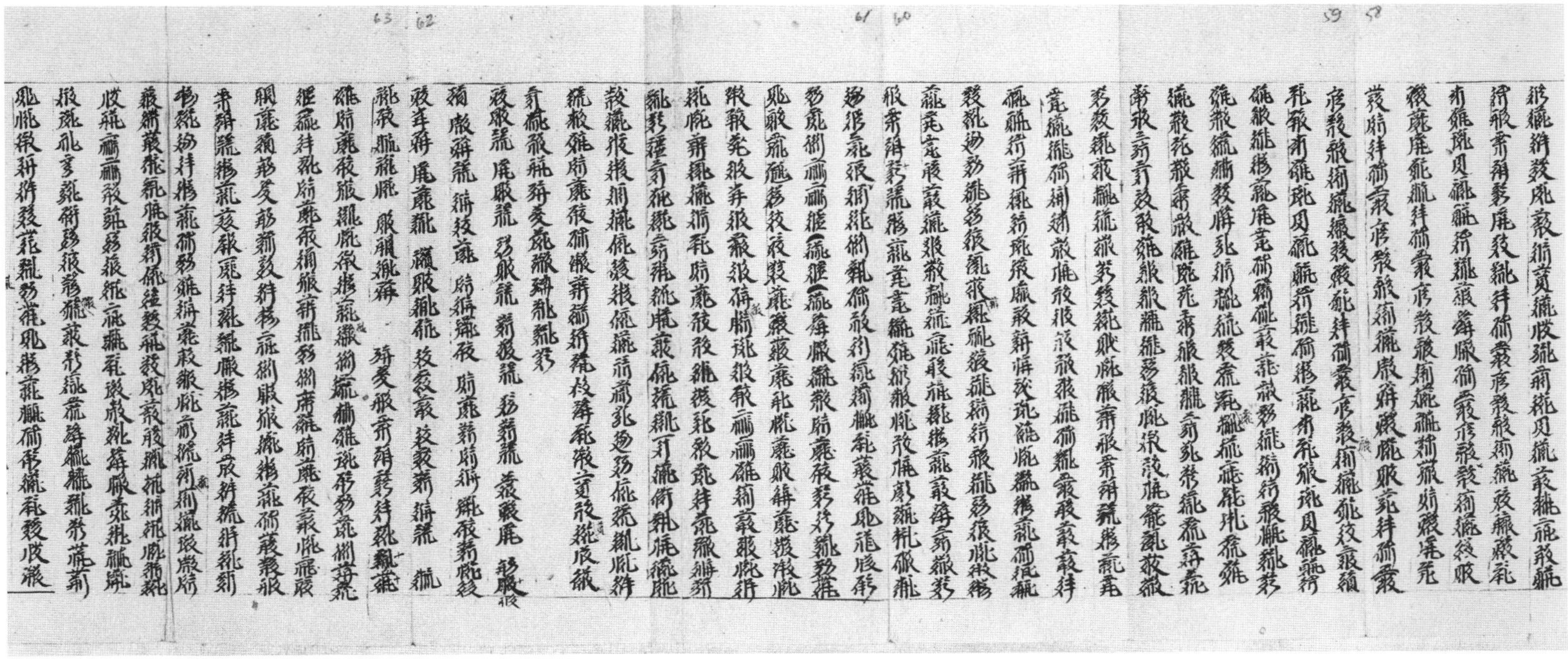

俄 Инв.No.970　大般涅槃經卷第四十　(13–10)

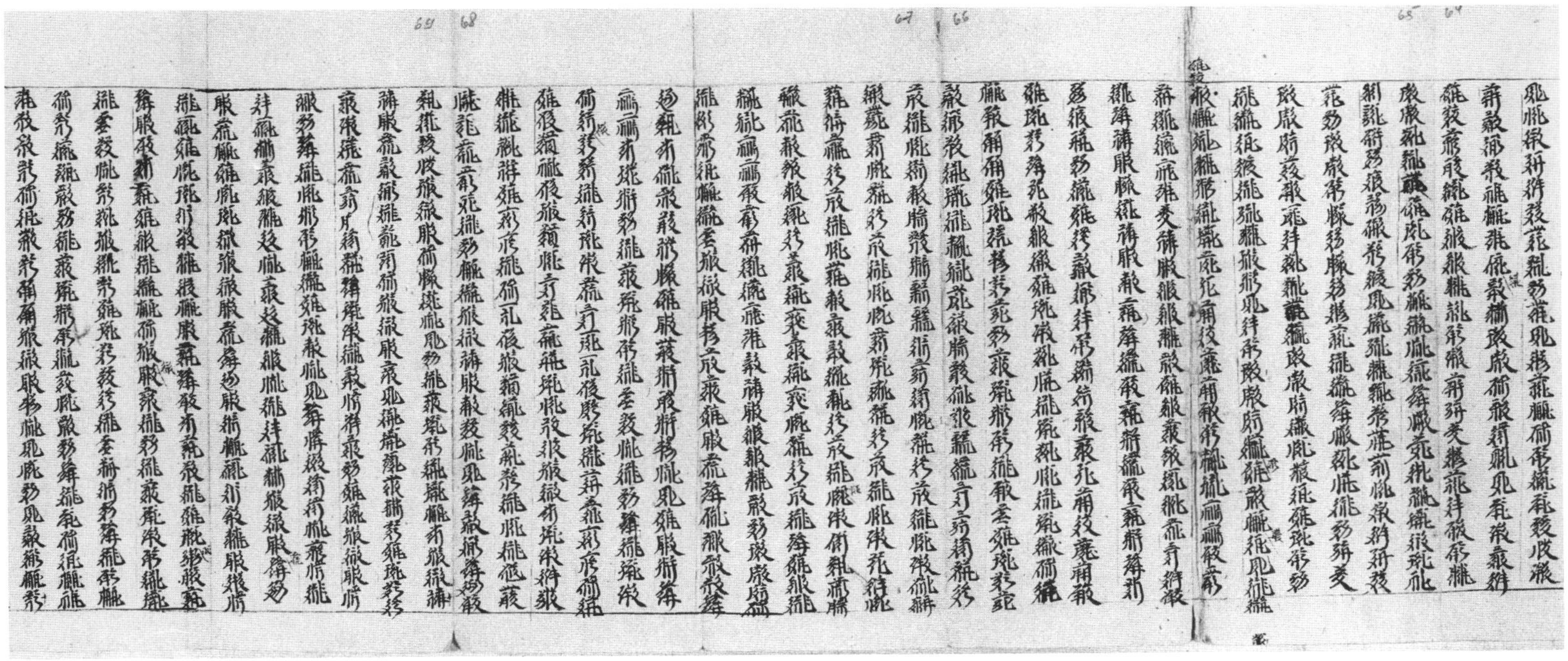

俄 Инв.No.970　大般涅槃經卷第四十　(13–11)

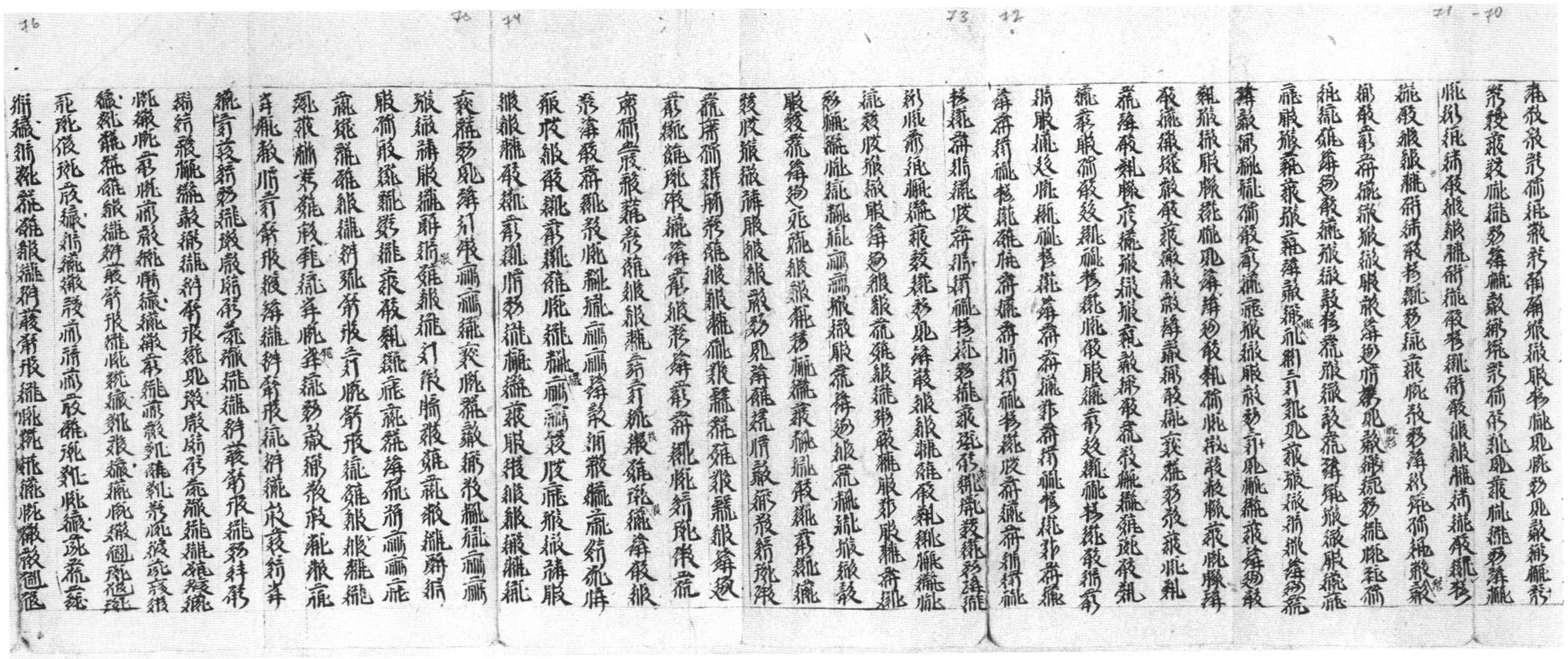

俄 Инв.No.970　大般涅槃經卷第四十　(13–12)

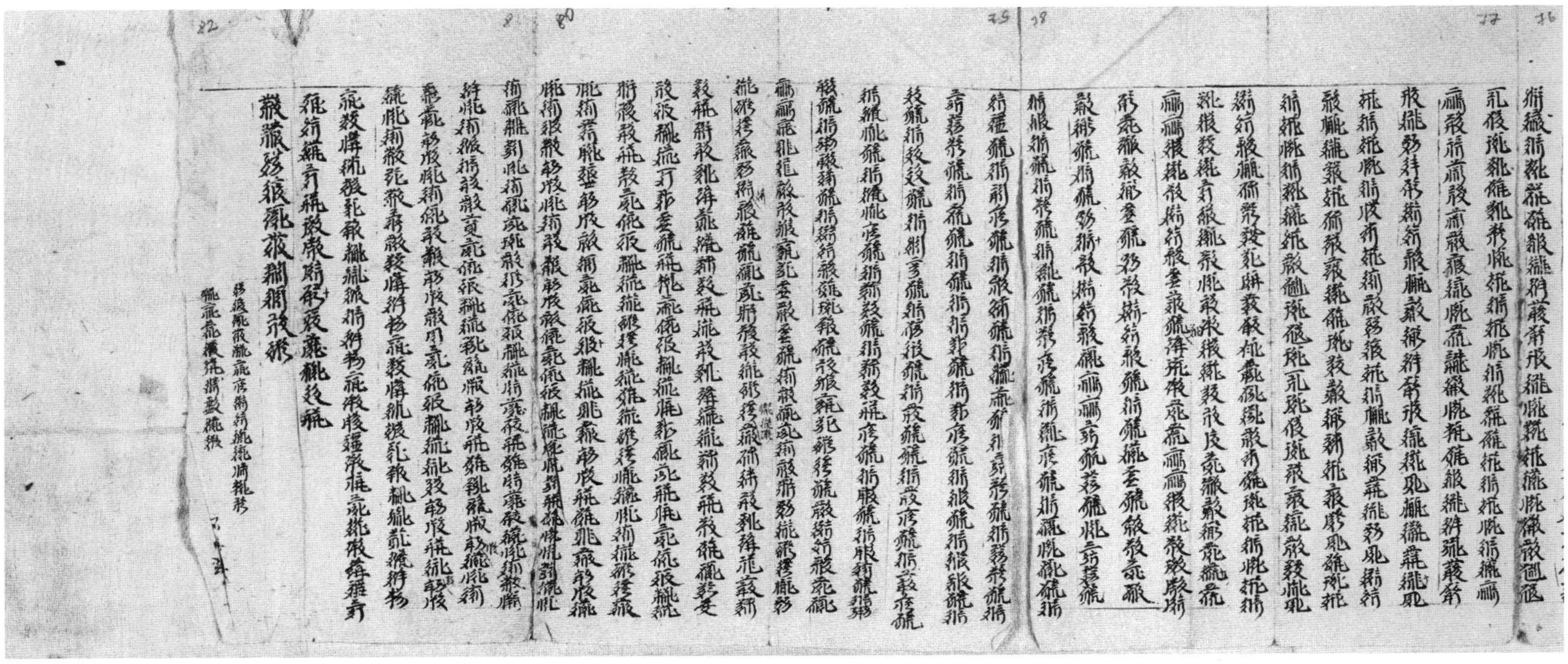

俄 Инв.No.970 大般涅槃經卷第四十 (13–13)

俄 Инв.No.6331　大般涅槃經卷第一　　　(20-1)

俄 Инв.No.6331　大般涅槃經卷第一　　　(20-2)

俄 Инв.No.6331　大般涅槃經卷第一　　　(20-3)

俄 Инв.No.6331　大般涅槃經卷第一　　　(20-4)

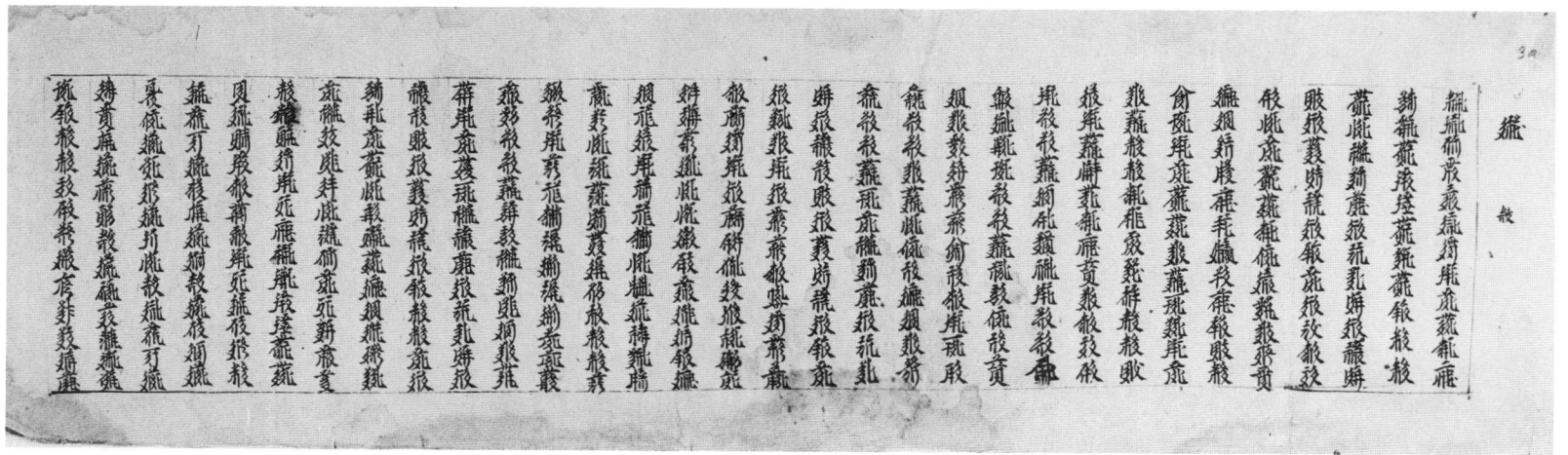

俄 **И**нв.No.6331　大般涅槃經卷第一　　　(20-5)

俄 **И**нв.No.6331　大般涅槃經卷第一　　　(20-6)

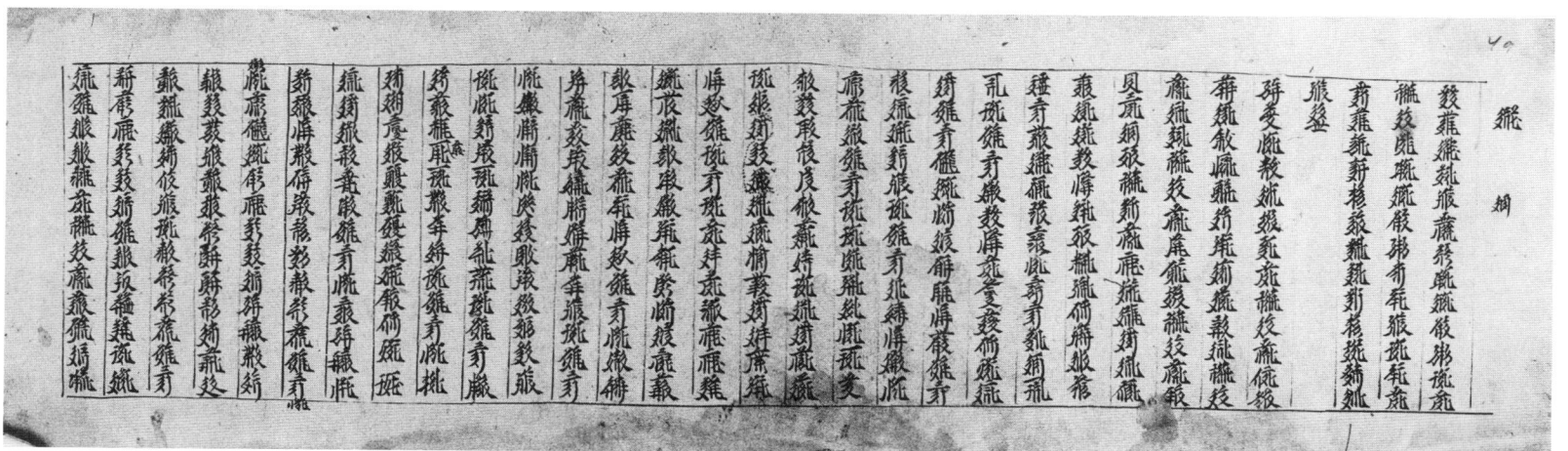

俄 **И**нв.No.6331　大般涅槃經卷第一　　　(20-7)

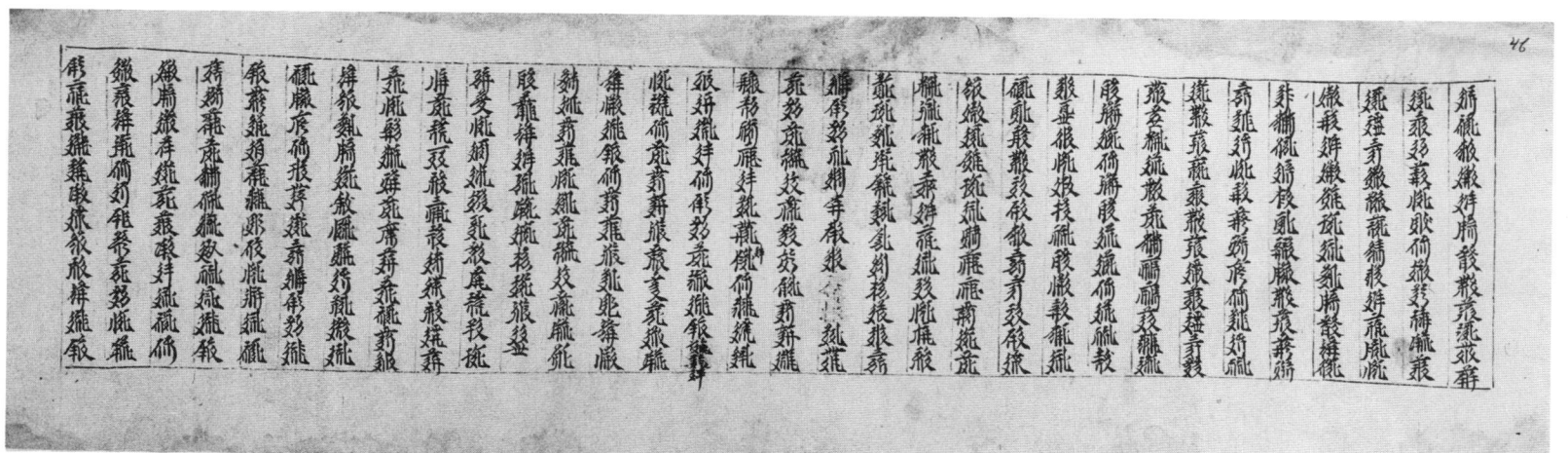

俄 **И**нв.No.6331　大般涅槃經卷第一　　　(20-8)

俄 **И**нв.No.6331　大般涅槃經卷第一　　　(20-9)

俄 **И**нв.No.6331　大般涅槃經卷第一　　　(20-10)

俄 **И**нв.No.6331　大般涅槃經卷第一　　　(20-11)

俄 **И**нв.No.6331　大般涅槃經卷第一　　　(20-12)

俄 **И**нв.No.6331　大般涅槃經卷第一　　　(20-13)

俄 **И**нв.No.6331　大般涅槃經卷第一　　　(20-14)

俄 **И**нв.No.6331　大般涅槃經卷第一　　　(20-15)

俄 **И**нв.No.6331　大般涅槃經卷第一　　　(20-16)

俄ИНВ.No.6331　大般涅槃經卷第一　　（20-17）

俄ИНВ.No.6331　大般涅槃經卷第一　　（20-18）

俄ИНВ.No.6331　大般涅槃經卷第一　　（20-19）

俄ИНВ.No.6331　大般涅槃經卷第一　　（20-20）

俄 Инв.No.6331　大般涅槃經卷第二　　　(9-1)

俄 Инв.No.6331　大般涅槃經卷第二　　　(9-2)

俄 Инв.No.6331　大般涅槃經卷第二　　　(9-3)

俄 Инв.No.6331　大般涅槃經卷第二　　　(9-4)

俄 ИНВ.No.6331　大般涅槃經卷第二　　　(9-5)

俄 ИНВ.No.6331　大般涅槃經卷第二　　　(9-6)

俄 ИНВ.No.6331　大般涅槃經卷第二　　　(9-7)

俄 ИНВ.No.6331　大般涅槃經卷第二　　　(9-8)

俄 **И**нв.No.6331　大般涅槃經卷第二　　　(9-9)

俄 **И**нв.No.6331　大般涅槃經卷第三　　　(24-1)

俄 **И**нв.No.6331　大般涅槃經卷第三　　　(24-2)

俄 **И**нв.No.6331　大般涅槃經卷第三　　　(24-3)

俄 ИНВ.No.6331　大般涅槃經卷第三　　(24-4)

俄 ИНВ.No.6331　大般涅槃經卷第三　　(24-5)

俄 ИНВ.No.6331　大般涅槃經卷第三　　(24-6)

俄 ИНВ.No.6331　大般涅槃經卷第三　　(24-7)

俄 **И**нв.No.6331　大般涅槃經卷第三　　　(24-8)

俄 **И**нв.No.6331　大般涅槃經卷第三　　　(24-9)

俄 **И**нв.No.6331　大般涅槃經卷第三　　　(24-10)

俄 **И**нв.No.6331　大般涅槃經卷第三　　　(24-11)

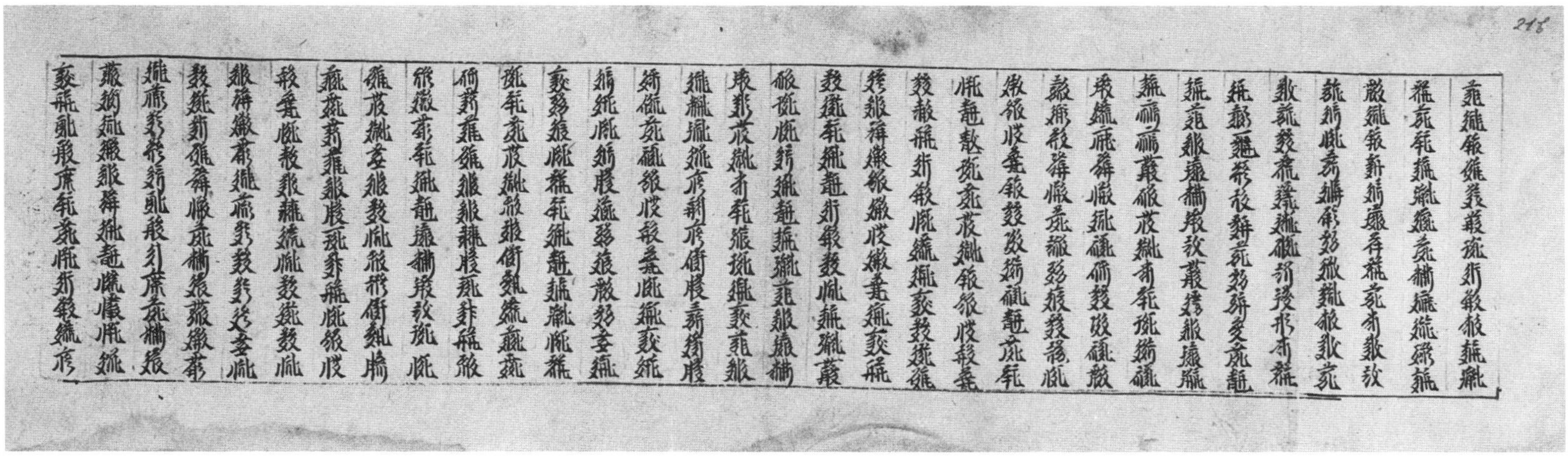

俄 Инв.No.6331　大般涅槃經卷第三　(24–12)

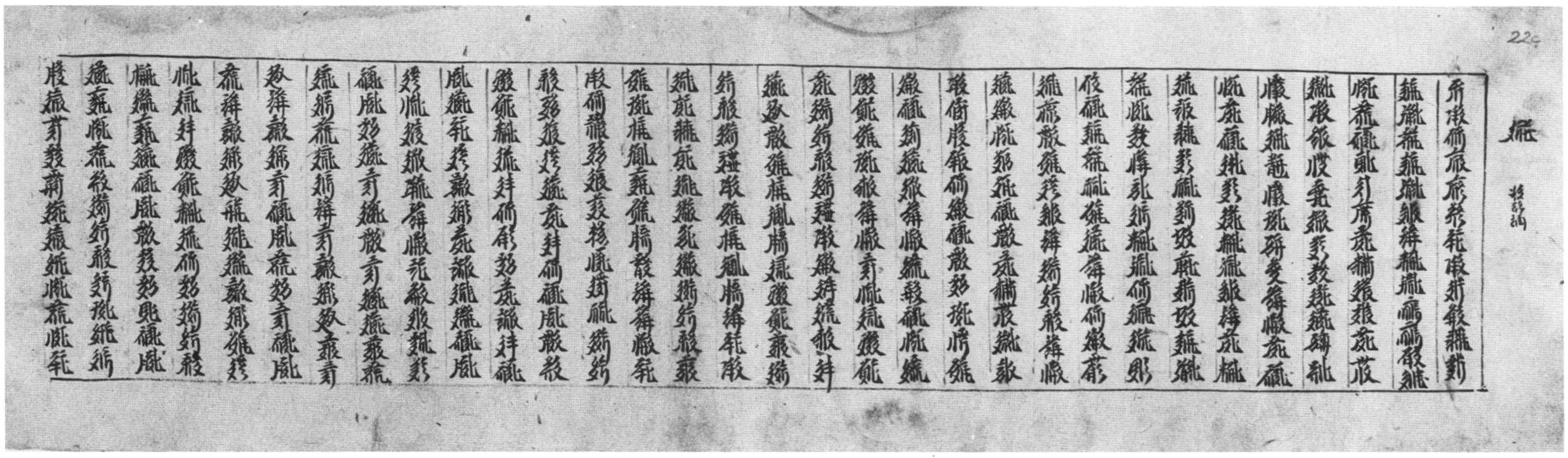

俄 Инв.No.6331　大般涅槃經卷第三　(24–13)

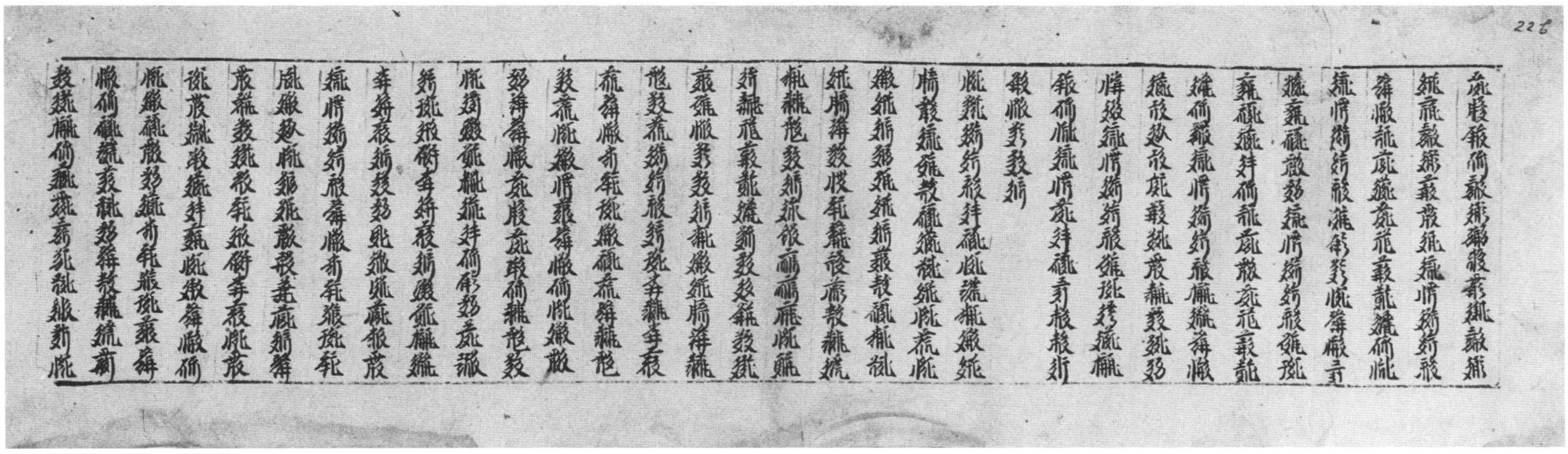

俄 Инв.No.6331　大般涅槃經卷第三　(24–14)

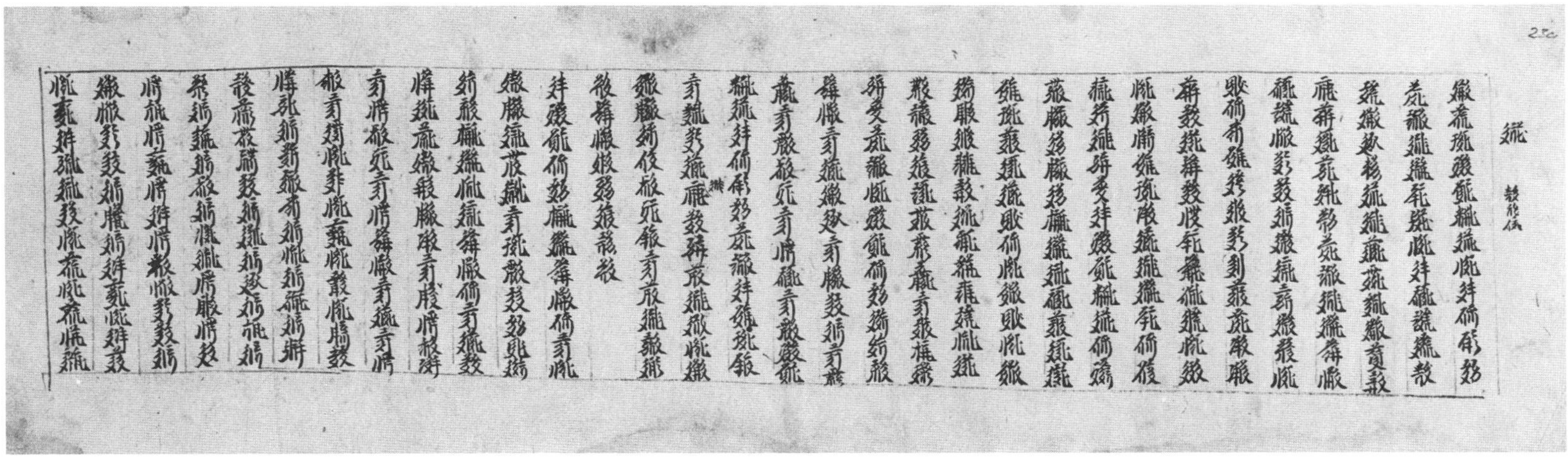

俄 Инв.No.6331　大般涅槃經卷第三　(24–15)

俄 **И**нв.No.6331　大般涅槃經卷第三　　　(24-16)

俄 **И**нв.No.6331　大般涅槃經卷第三　　　(24-17)

俄 **И**нв.No.6331　大般涅槃經卷第三　　　(24-18)

俄 **И**нв.No.6331　大般涅槃經卷第三　　　(24-19)

俄 **И**нв.No.6331 大般涅槃經卷第三 (24-20)

俄 **И**нв.No.6331 大般涅槃經卷第三 (24-21)

俄 **И**нв.No.6331 大般涅槃經卷第三 (24-22)

俄 **И**нв.No.6331 大般涅槃經卷第三 (24-23)

俄 **Инв**.No.6331　　大般涅槃經卷第三　　　　(24-24)

俄 **Инв**.No.6331　　大般涅槃經卷第四　　　　(20-1)

俄 **Инв**.No.6331　　大般涅槃經卷第四　　　　(20-2)

俄 **Инв**.No.6331　　大般涅槃經卷第四　　　　(20-3)

俄 **И**нв.No.6331　大般涅槃經卷第四　　　(20-4)

俄 **И**нв.No.6331　大般涅槃經卷第四　　　(20-5)

俄 **И**нв.No.6331　大般涅槃經卷第四　　　(20-6)

俄 **И**нв.No.6331　大般涅槃經卷第四　　　(20-7)

俄 **И**нв.No.6331　　大般涅槃經卷第四　　　　(20-8)

俄 **И**нв.No.6331　　大般涅槃經卷第四　　　　(20-9)

俄 **И**нв.No.6331　　大般涅槃經卷第四　　　　(20-10)

俄 **И**нв.No.6331　　大般涅槃經卷第四　　　　(20-11)

俄 **И**нв.No.6331　大般涅槃經卷第四　　　(20-12)

俄 **И**нв.No.6331　大般涅槃經卷第四　　　(20-13)

俄 **И**нв.No.6331　大般涅槃經卷第四　　　(20-14)

俄 **И**нв.No.6331　大般涅槃經卷第四　　　(20-15)

俄 **И**нв.No.6331　大般涅槃經卷第四　　　(20-16)

俄 **И**нв.No.6331　大般涅槃經卷第四　　　(20-17)

俄 **И**нв.No.6331　大般涅槃經卷第四　　　(20-18)

俄 **И**нв.No.6331　大般涅槃經卷第四　　　(20-19)

俄 ИНВ.No.6331　大般涅槃經卷第四　　　(20-20)

俄 ИНВ.No.6331　大般涅槃經卷第五　　　(26-1)

俄 ИНВ.No.6331　大般涅槃經卷第五　　　(26-2)

俄 ИНВ.No.6331　大般涅槃經卷第五　　　(26-3)

俄 Инв.No.6331　大般涅槃經卷第五　　(26-4)

俄 Инв.No.6331　大般涅槃經卷第五　　(26-5)

俄 Инв.No.6331　大般涅槃經卷第五　　(26-6)

俄 Инв.No.6331　大般涅槃經卷第五　　(26-7)

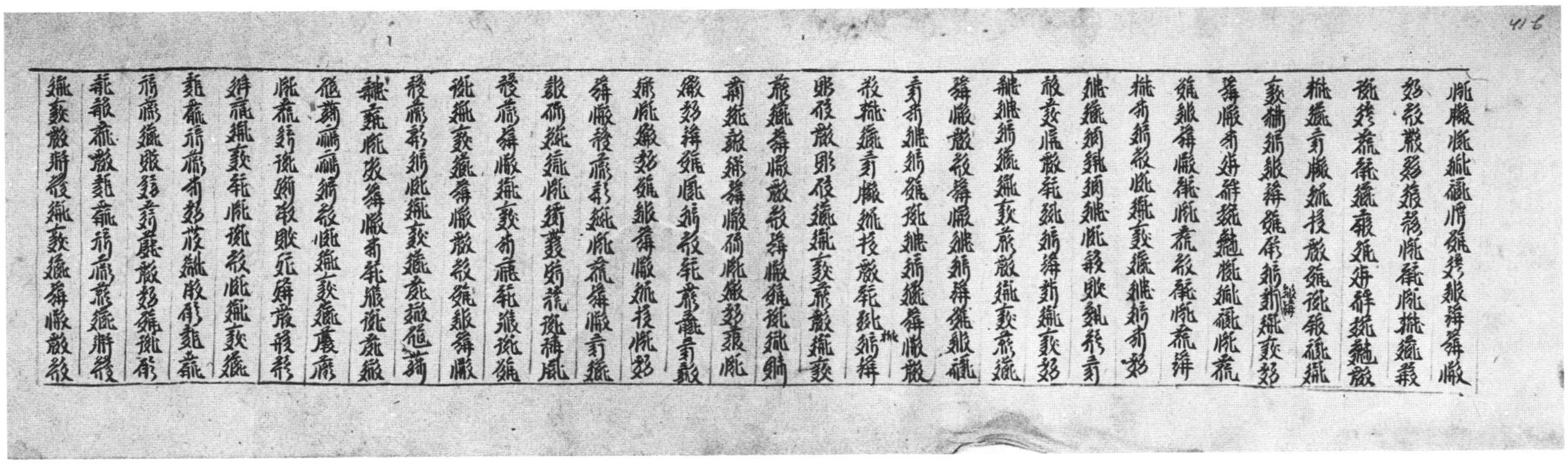

俄 Инв.No.6331　大般涅槃經卷第五　(26–8)

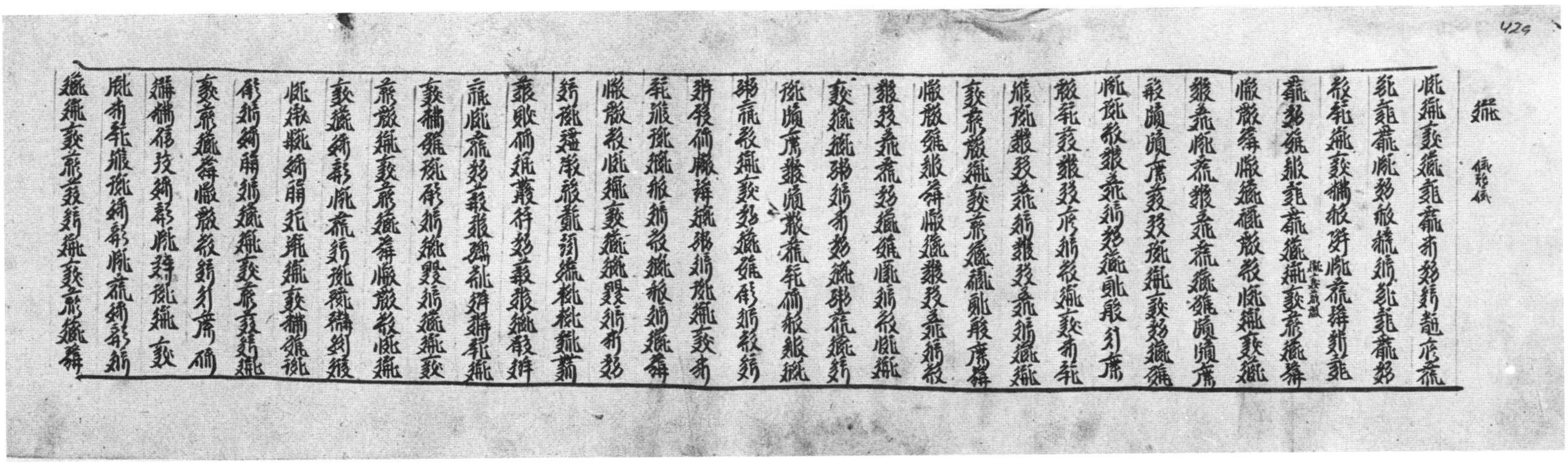

俄 Инв.No.6331　大般涅槃經卷第五　(26–9)

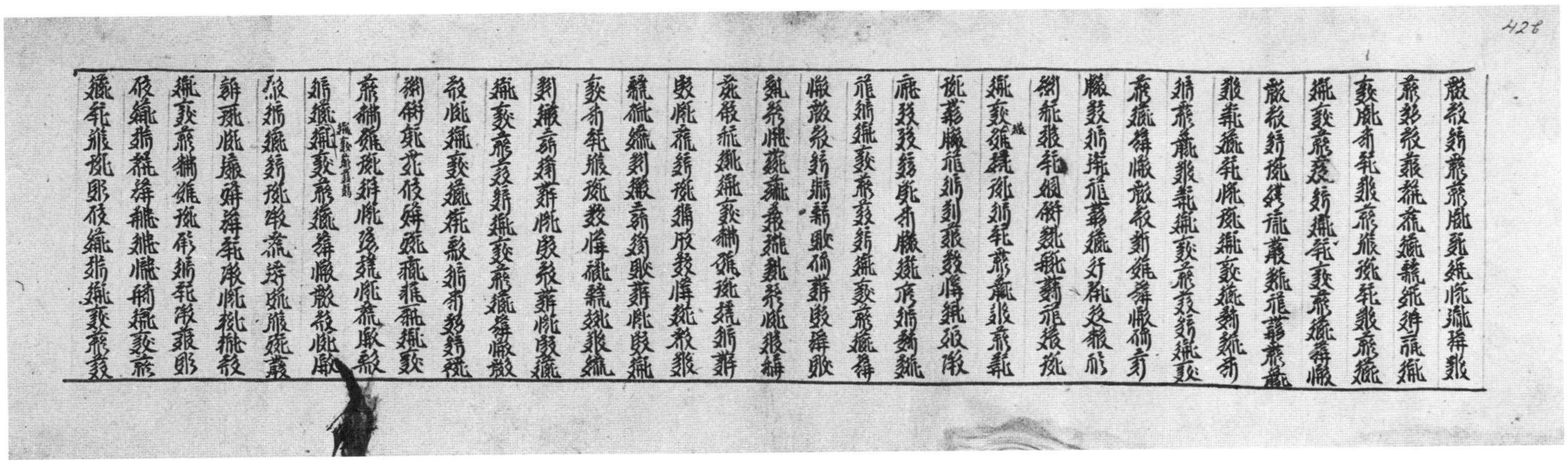

俄 Инв.No.6331　大般涅槃經卷第五　(26–10)

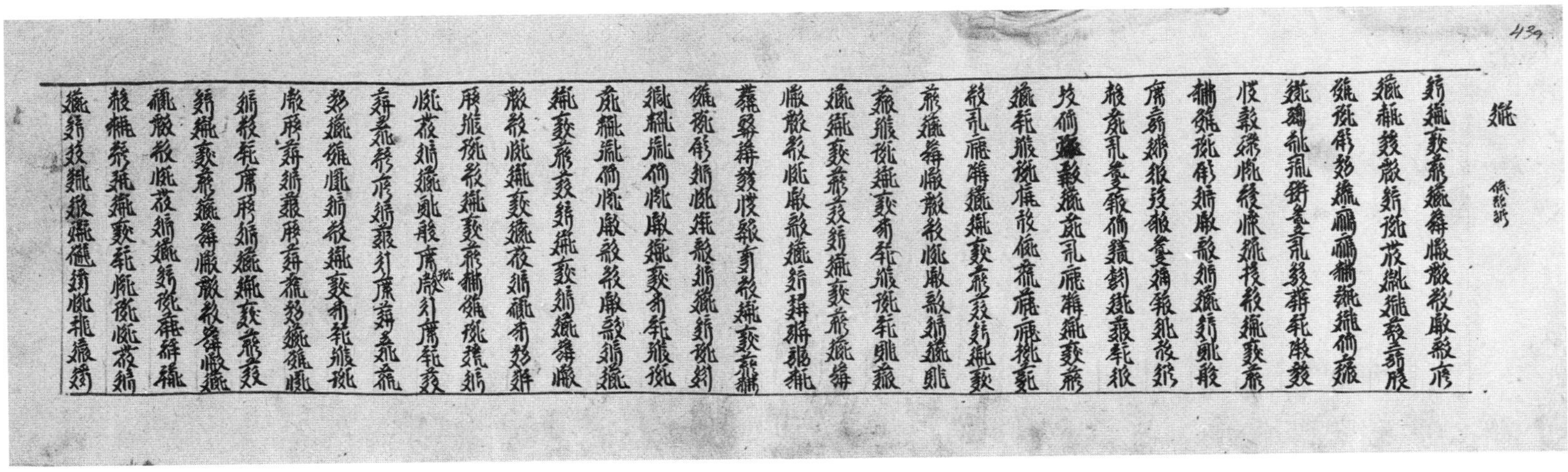

俄 Инв.No.6331　大般涅槃經卷第五　(26–11)

俄 Инв.No.6331 大般涅槃經卷第五 (26-12)

俄 Инв.No.6331 大般涅槃經卷第五 (26-13)

俄 Инв.No.6331 大般涅槃經卷第五 (26-14)

俄 Инв.No.6331 大般涅槃經卷第五 (26-15)

456

俄Инв.No.6331　大般涅槃經卷第五　　　(26-16)

467

俄Инв.No.6331　大般涅槃經卷第五　　　(26-17)

468

俄Инв.No.6331　大般涅槃經卷第五　　　(26-18)

470

俄Инв.No.6331　大般涅槃經卷第五　　　(26-19)

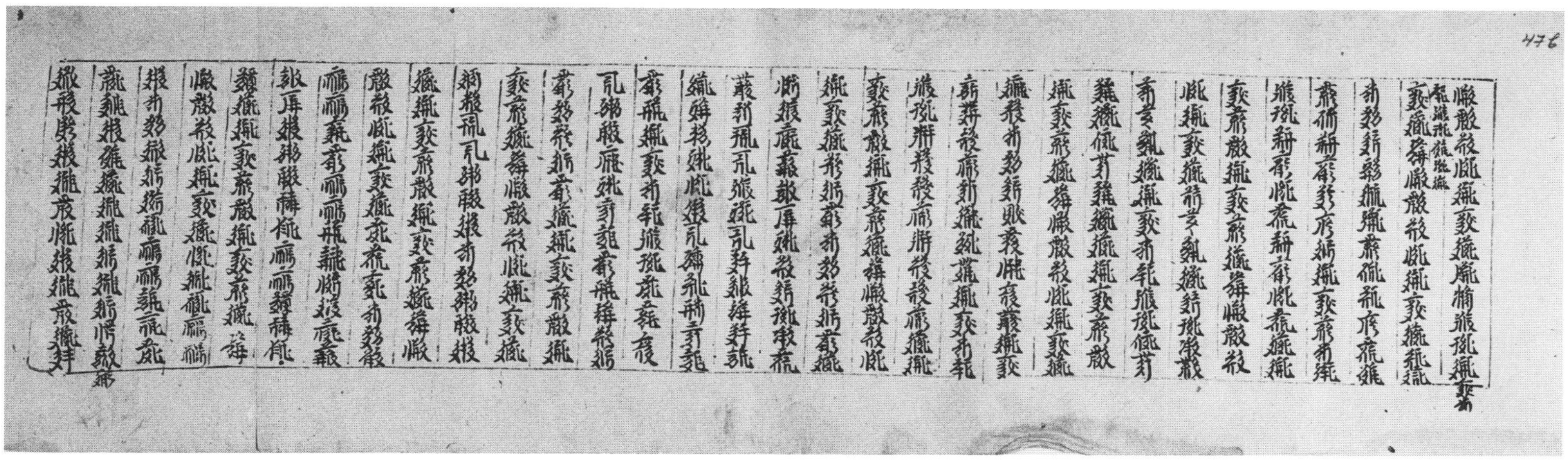

俄 Инв.No.6331　大般涅槃經卷第五　(26-20)

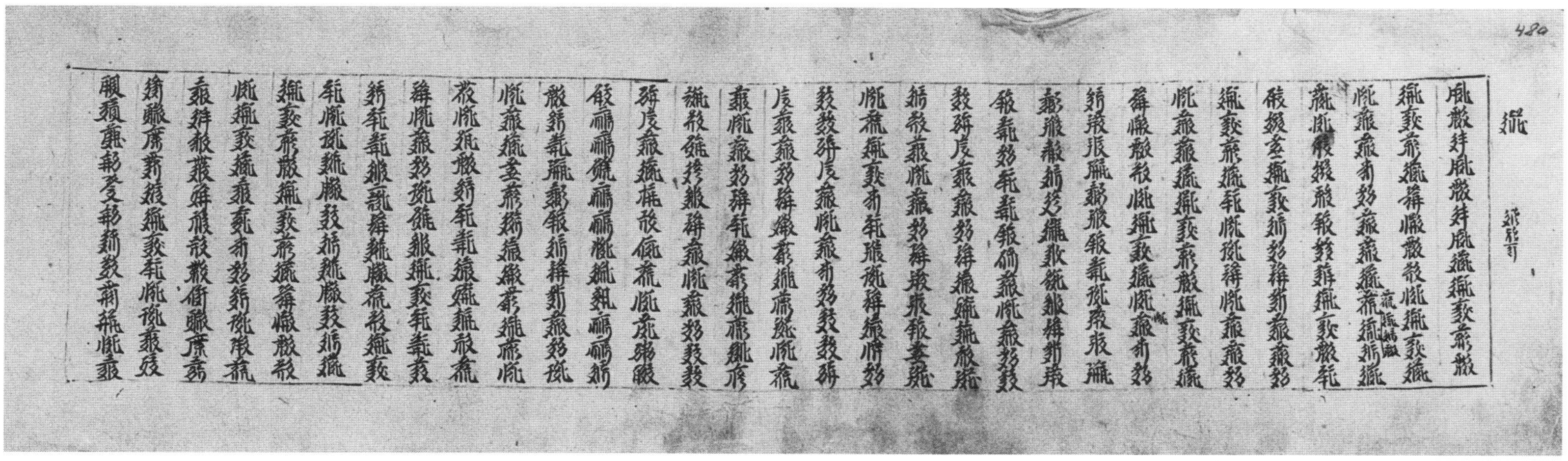

俄 Инв.No.6331　大般涅槃經卷第五　(26-21)

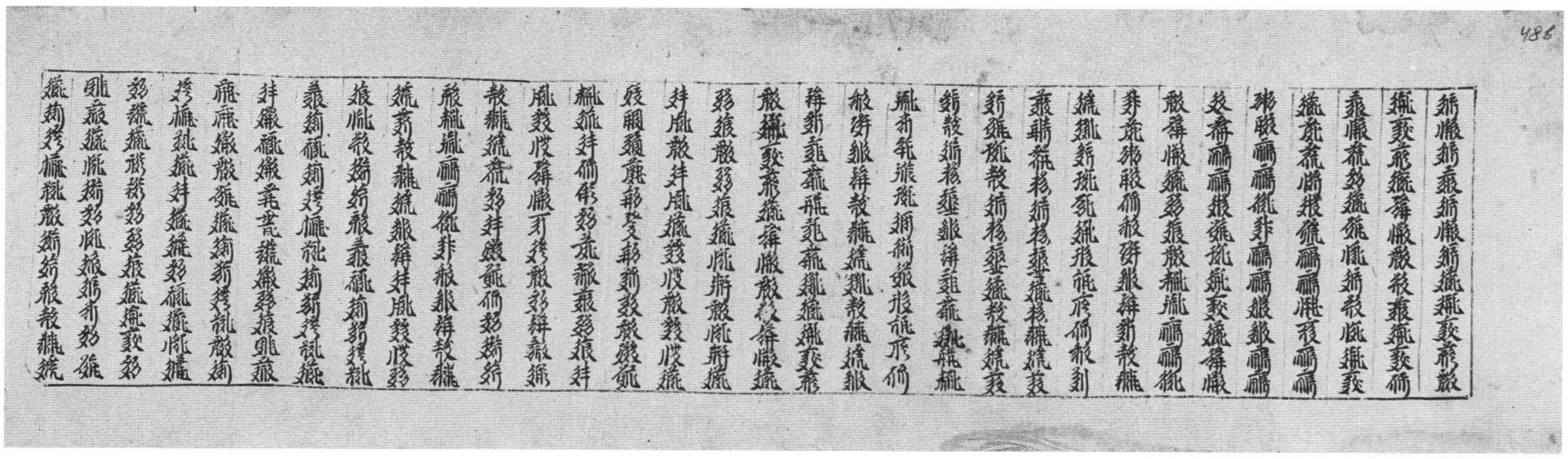

俄 Инв.No.6331　大般涅槃經卷第五　(26-22)

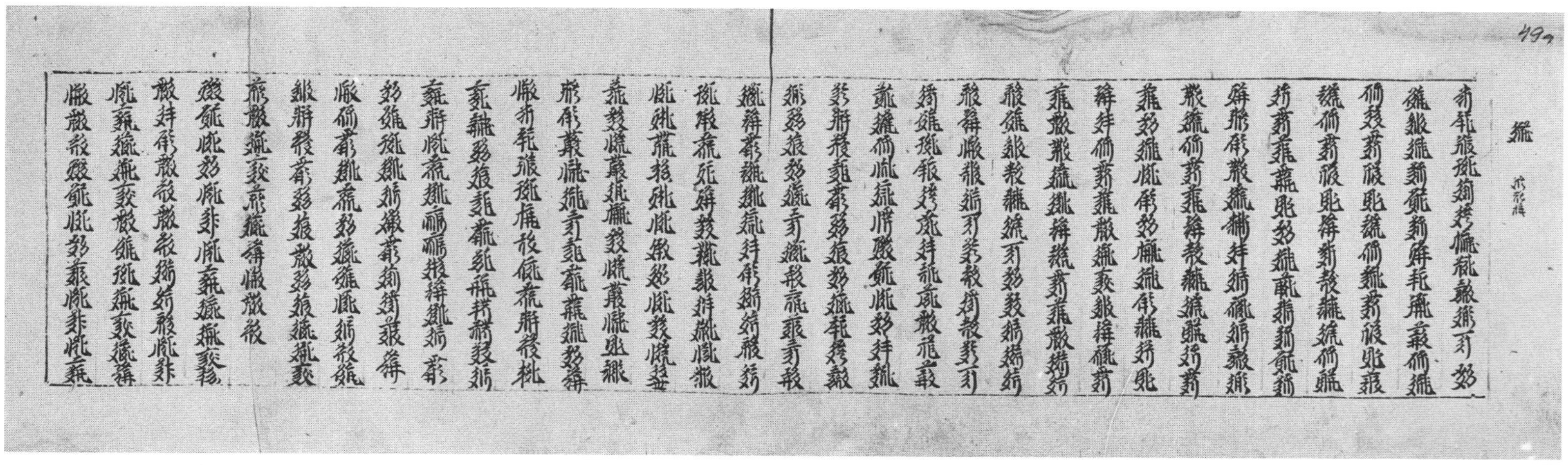

俄 Инв.No.6331　大般涅槃經卷第五　(26-23)

俄ИНВ.No.6331 大般涅槃經卷第五 (26-24)

俄ИНВ.No.6331 大般涅槃經卷第五 (26-25)

俄ИНВ.No.6331 大般涅槃經卷第五 (26-26)

俄ИНВ.No.6331 大般涅槃經卷第六 (21-1)

俄 **И**нв.No.6331 　大般涅槃經卷第六 　　(21-2)

俄 **И**нв.No.6331 　大般涅槃經卷第六 　　(21-3)

俄 **И**нв.No.6331 　大般涅槃經卷第六 　　(21-4)

俄 **И**нв.No.6331 　大般涅槃經卷第六 　　(21-5)

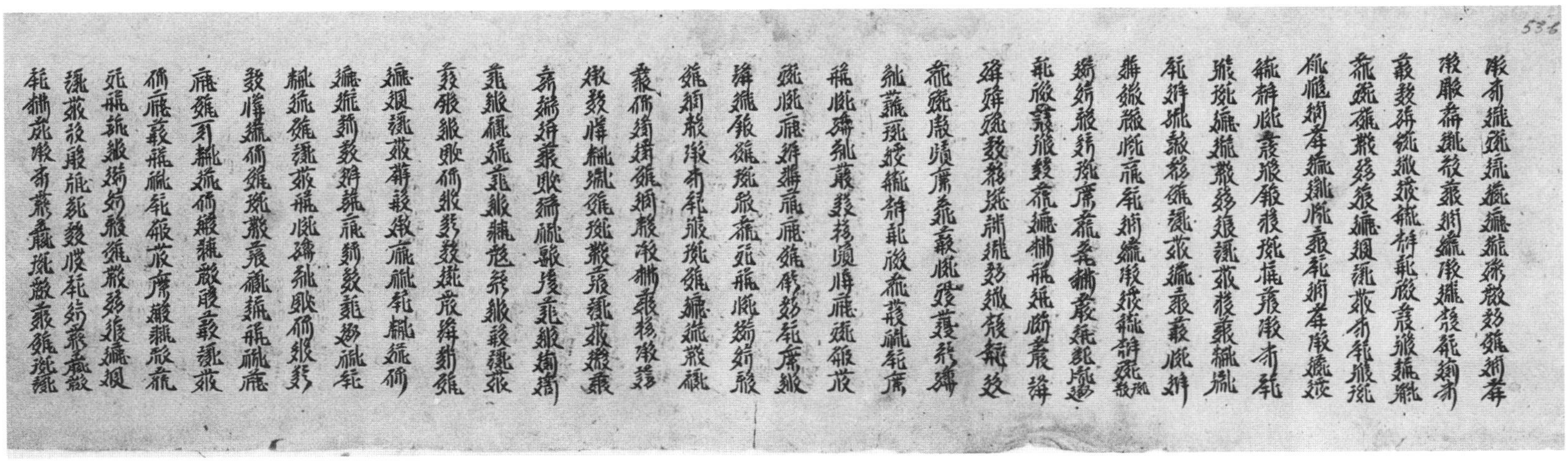

俄 Инв.No.6331　大般涅槃經卷第六　(21–6)

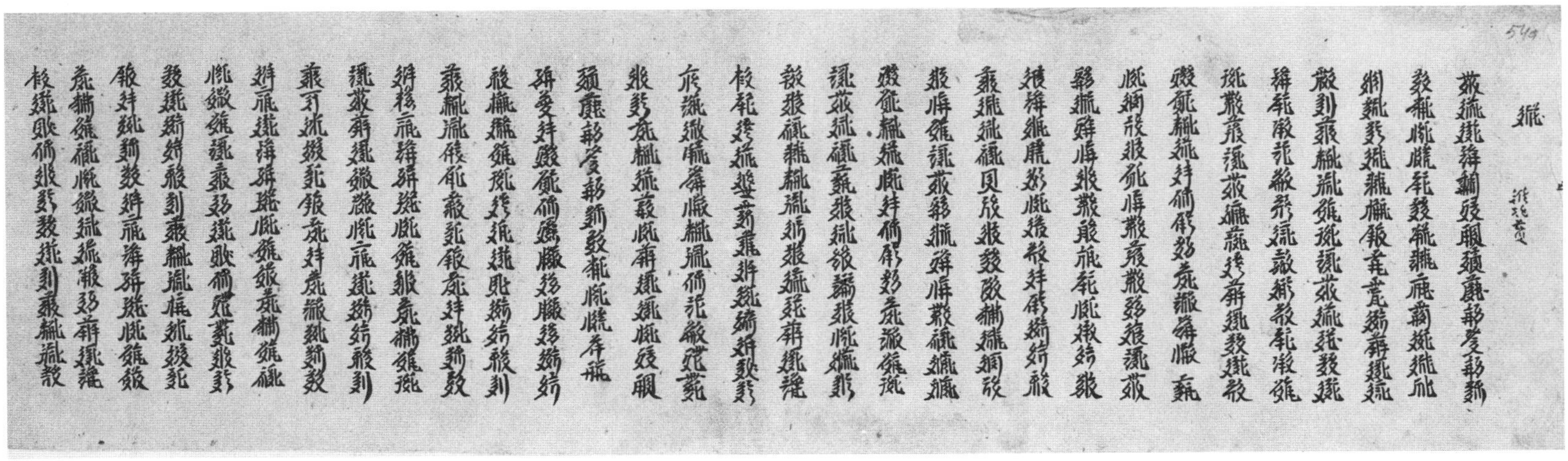

俄 Инв.No.6331　大般涅槃經卷第六　(21–7)

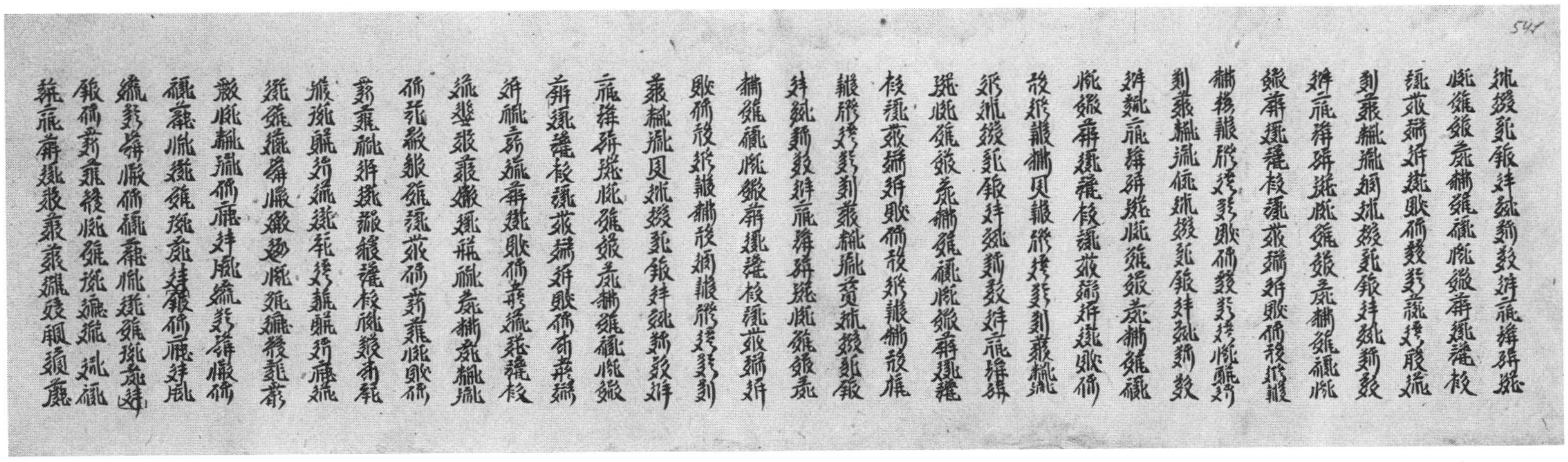

俄 Инв.No.6331　大般涅槃經卷第六　(21–8)

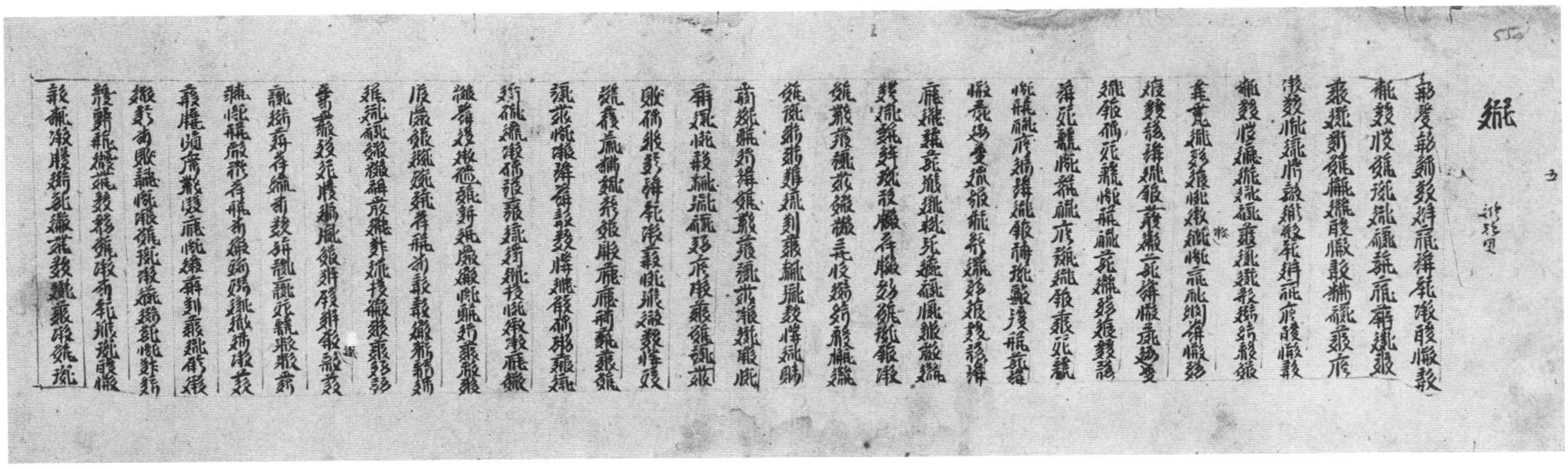

俄 Инв.No.6331　大般涅槃經卷第六　(21–9)

俄 Инв.No.6331　大般涅槃經卷第六　　　(21-10)

俄 Инв.No.6331　大般涅槃經卷第六　　　(21-11)

俄 Инв.No.6331　大般涅槃經卷第六　　　(21-12)

俄 Инв.No.6331　大般涅槃經卷第六　　　(21-13)

俄 Инв.No.6331　大般涅槃經卷第六　　(21-14)

俄 Инв.No.6331　大般涅槃經卷第六　　(21-15)

俄 Инв.No.6331　大般涅槃經卷第六　　(21-16)

俄 Инв.No.6331　大般涅槃經卷第六　　(21-17)

俄 **И**нв.No.6331　大般涅槃經卷第六　　　(21-18)

俄 **И**нв.No.6331　大般涅槃經卷第六　　　(21-19)

俄 **И**нв.No.6331　大般涅槃經卷第六　　　(21-20)

俄 **И**нв.No.6331　大般涅槃經卷第六　　　(21-21)

俄Инв.No.6331　大般涅槃經卷第七　　　（24-1）

俄Инв.No.6331　大般涅槃經卷第七　　　（24-2）

俄Инв.No.6331　大般涅槃經卷第七　　　（24-3）

俄Инв.No.6331　大般涅槃經卷第七　　　（24-4）

俄 **И**нв.No.6331　大般涅槃經卷第七　　(24-5)

俄 **И**нв.No.6331　大般涅槃經卷第七　　(24-6)

俄 **И**нв.No.6331　大般涅槃經卷第七　　(24-7)

俄 **И**нв.No.6331　大般涅槃經卷第七　　(24-8)

俄 ИнВ.No.6331　大般涅槃經卷第七　　　(24-9)

俄 ИнВ.No.6331　大般涅槃經卷第七　　　(24-10)

俄 ИнВ.No.6331　大般涅槃經卷第七　　　(24-11)

俄 ИнВ.No.6331　大般涅槃經卷第七　　　(24-12)

俄 Инв.No.6331　大般涅槃經卷第七　　　(24-13)

俄 Инв.No.6331　大般涅槃經卷第七　　　(24-14)

俄 Инв.No.6331　大般涅槃經卷第七　　　(24-15)

俄 Инв.No.6331　大般涅槃經卷第七　　　(24-16)

俄 **И**нв.No.6331　大般涅槃經卷第七　　　(24-17)

俄 **И**нв.No.6331　大般涅槃經卷第七　　　(24-18)

俄 **И**нв.No.6331　大般涅槃經卷第七　　　(24-19)

俄 **И**нв.No.6331　大般涅槃經卷第七　　　(24-20)

俄 **И**нв.No.6331　大般涅槃經卷第七　　　(24-21)

俄 **И**нв.No.6331　大般涅槃經卷第七　　　(24-22)

俄 **И**нв.No.6331　大般涅槃經卷第七　　　(24-23)

俄 **И**нв.No.6331　大般涅槃經卷第七　　　(24-24)

俄 **И**нв.No.6331　大般涅槃經卷第八　　(22-1)

俄 **И**нв.No.6331　大般涅槃經卷第八　　(22-2)

俄 **И**нв.No.6331　大般涅槃經卷第八　　(22-3)

俄 **И**нв.No.6331　大般涅槃經卷第八　　(22-4)

俄 **И**нв.No.6331　　大般涅槃經卷第八　　(22-5)

俄 **И**нв.No.6331　　大般涅槃經卷第八　　(22-6)

俄 **И**нв.No.6331　　大般涅槃經卷第八　　(22-7)

俄 **И**нв.No.6331　　大般涅槃經卷第八　　(22-8)

俄 Инв.No.6331　大般涅槃經卷第八　　(22-9)

俄 Инв.No.6331　大般涅槃經卷第八　　(22-10)

俄 Инв.No.6331　大般涅槃經卷第八　　(22-11)

俄 Инв.No.6331　大般涅槃經卷第八　　(22-12)

俄 **И**нв.№.6331　大般涅槃經卷第八　　　　(22-13)

俄 **И**нв.№.6331　大般涅槃經卷第八　　　　(22-14)

俄 **И**нв.№.6331　大般涅槃經卷第八　　　　(22-15)

俄 **И**нв.№.6331　大般涅槃經卷第八　　　　(22-16)

俄 Инв.No.6331 大般涅槃經卷第八 (22-17)

俄 Инв.No.6331 大般涅槃經卷第八 (22-18)

俄 Инв.No.6331 大般涅槃經卷第八 (22-19)

俄 Инв.No.6331 大般涅槃經卷第八 (22-20)

俄 **И**нв.No.6331　大般涅槃經卷第八　　　(22-21)

俄 **И**нв.No.6331　大般涅槃經卷第八　　　(22-22)

俄 **И**нв.No.6331　大般涅槃經卷第九　　　(16-1)

俄 **И**нв.No.6331　大般涅槃經卷第九　　　(16-2)

俄 ИНВ.No.6331　大般涅槃經卷第九　　　（16-3）

俄 ИНВ.No.6331　大般涅槃經卷第九　　　（16-4）

俄 ИНВ.No.6331　大般涅槃經卷第九　　　（16-5）

俄 ИНВ.No.6331　大般涅槃經卷第九　　　（16-6）

俄 Инв.No.6331　大般涅槃經卷第九　　　(16-7)

俄 Инв.No.6331　大般涅槃經卷第九　　　(16-8)

俄 Инв.No.6331　大般涅槃經卷第九　　　(16-9)

俄 Инв.No.6331　大般涅槃經卷第九　　　(16-10)

俄Инв.No.6331　大般涅槃經卷第九　　　(16-11)

俄Инв.No.6331　大般涅槃經卷第九　　　(16-12)

俄Инв.No.6331　大般涅槃經卷第九　　　(16-13)

俄Инв.No.6331　大般涅槃經卷第九　　　(16-14)

俄 **И**нв.No.6331　　大般涅槃經卷第九　　　　(16-15)

俄 **И**нв.No.6331　　大般涅槃經卷第九　　　　(16-16)

俄 **И**нв.No.6331　　大般涅槃經卷第十　　　　(19-1)

俄 **И**нв.No.6331　　大般涅槃經卷第十　　　　(19-2)

俄 Инв.No.6331　大般涅槃經卷第十　　　(19-3)

俄 Инв.No.6331　大般涅槃經卷第十　　　(19-4)

俄 Инв.No.6331　大般涅槃經卷第十　　　(19-5)

俄 Инв.No.6331　大般涅槃經卷第十　　　(19-6)

俄 **Инв**.No.6331　大般涅槃經卷第十　　　(19-7)

俄 **Инв**.No.6331　大般涅槃經卷第十　　　(19-8)

俄 **Инв**.No.6331　大般涅槃經卷第十　　　(19-9)

俄 **Инв**.No.6331　大般涅槃經卷第十　　　(19-10)

俄 **И**нв.No.6331　大般涅槃經卷第十　　　(19-11)

俄 **И**нв.No.6331　大般涅槃經卷第十　　　(19-12)

俄 **И**нв.No.6331　大般涅槃經卷第十　　　(19-13)

俄 **И**нв.No.6331　大般涅槃經卷第十　　　(19-14)

俄 Инв.No.6331　大般涅槃經卷第十　　(19-15)

俄 Инв.No.6331　大般涅槃經卷第十　　(19-16)

俄 Инв.No.6331　大般涅槃經卷第十　　(19-17)

俄 Инв.No.6331　大般涅槃經卷第十　　(19-18)

俄 Инв.No.6331　大般涅槃經卷第十　　（19-19）

俄 Инв.No.6331　大般涅槃經卷第十一　　（20-1）

俄 Инв.No.6331　大般涅槃經卷第十一　　（20-2）

俄 Инв.No.6331　大般涅槃經卷第十一　　（20-3）

俄 **И**нв.No.6331　大般涅槃經卷第十一　　　(20-4)

俄 **И**нв.No.6331　大般涅槃經卷第十一　　　(20-5)

俄 **И**нв.No.6331　大般涅槃經卷第十一　　　(20-6)

俄 **И**нв.No.6331　大般涅槃經卷第十一　　　(20-7)

俄 Инв.No.6331　大般涅槃經卷第十一　　　(20-8)

俄 Инв.No.6331　大般涅槃經卷第十一　　　(20-9)

俄 Инв.No.6331　大般涅槃經卷第十一　　　(20-10)

俄 Инв.No.6331　大般涅槃經卷第十一　　　(20-11)

俄 Инв.No.6331　大般涅槃經卷第十一　　　(20-12)

俄 Инв.No.6331　大般涅槃經卷第十一　　　(20-13)

俄 Инв.No.6331　大般涅槃經卷第十一　　　(20-14)

俄 Инв.No.6331　大般涅槃經卷第十一　　　(20-15)

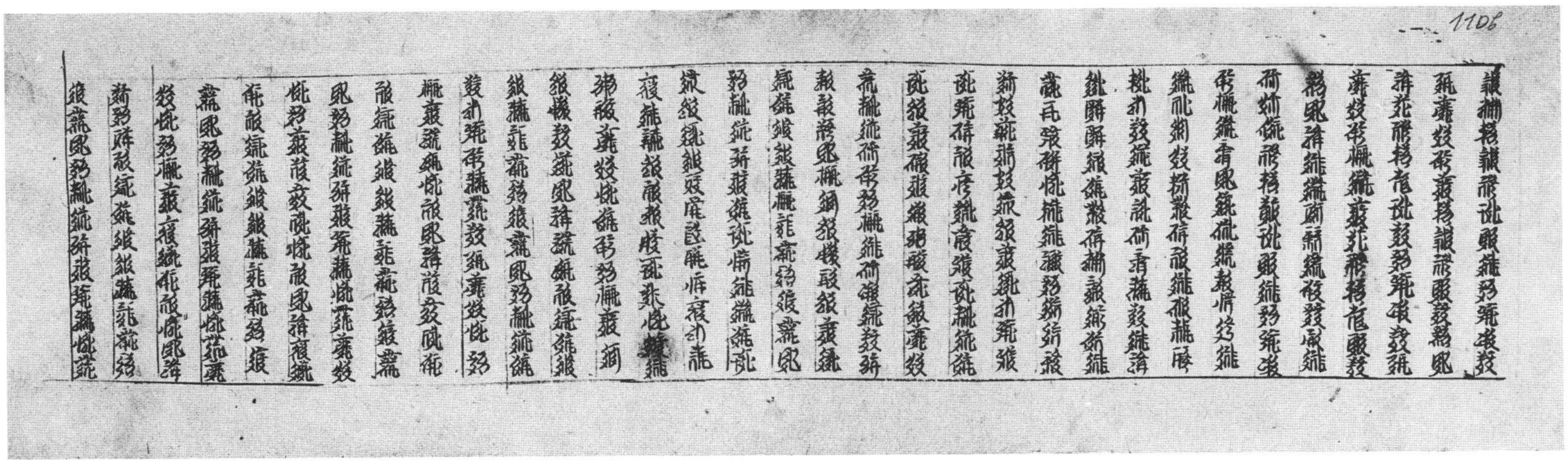

俄 Инв.No.6331　大般涅槃經卷第十一　(20–16)

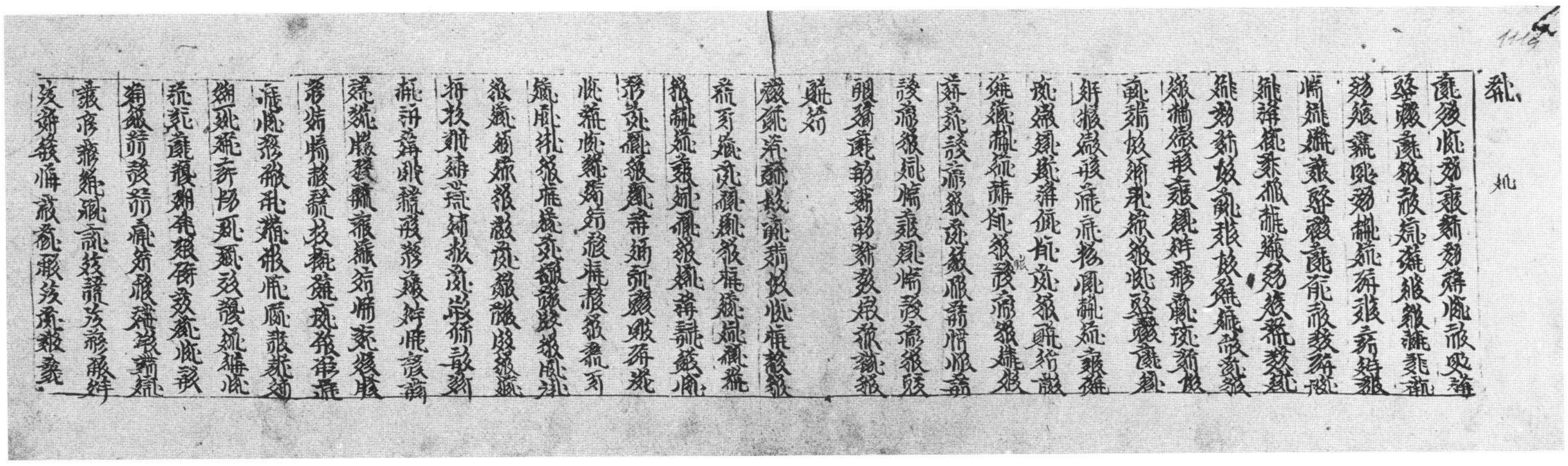

俄 Инв.No.6331　大般涅槃經卷第十一　(20–17)

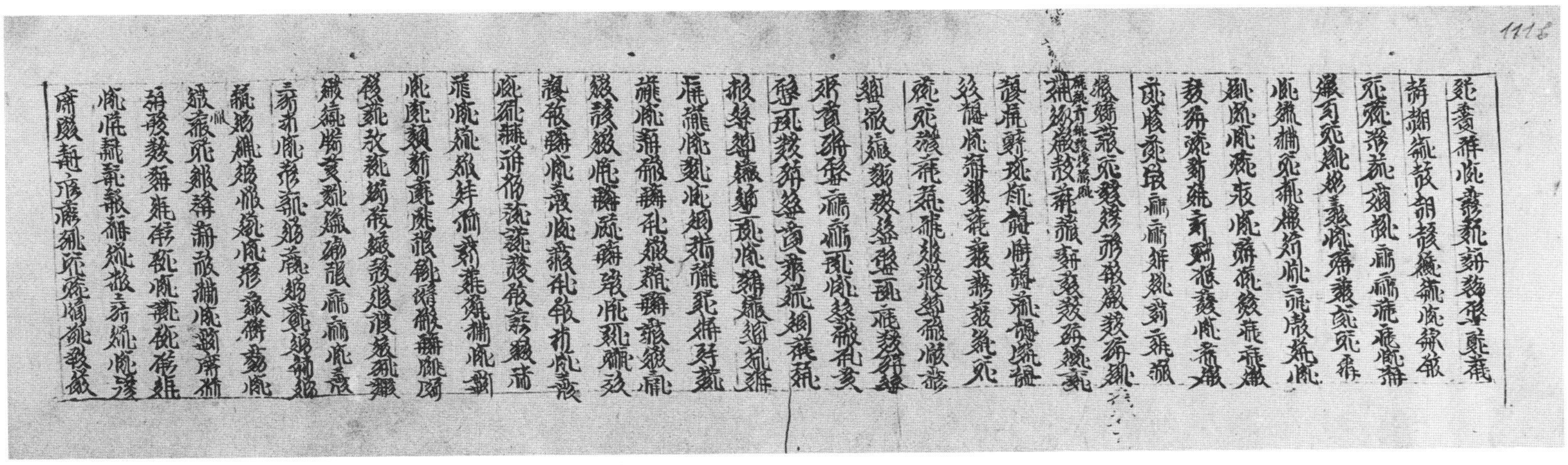

俄 Инв.No.6331　大般涅槃經卷第十一　(20–18)

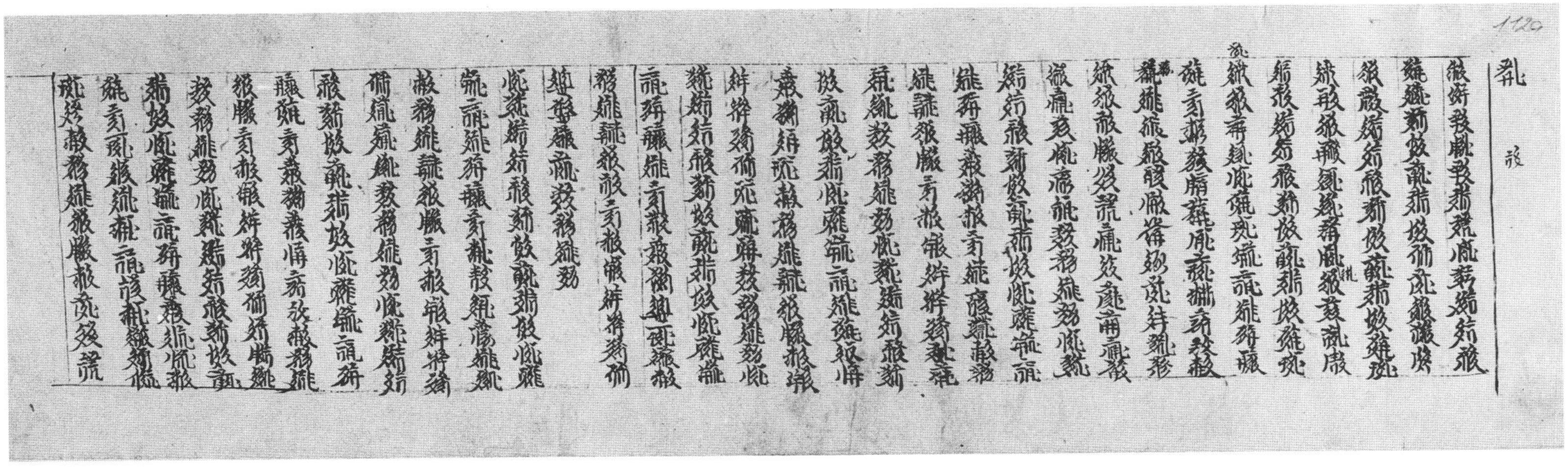

俄 Инв.No.6331　大般涅槃經卷第十一　(20–19)

俄 **И**нв.No.6331　大般涅槃經卷第十一　　　(20–20)

俄 **И**нв.No.6331　大般涅槃經卷第十二　　　(26–1)

俄 **И**нв.No.6331　大般涅槃經卷第十二　　　(26–2)

俄 **И**нв.No.6331　大般涅槃經卷第十二　　　(26–3)

俄 Инв.No.6331　大般涅槃經卷第十二　　　(26-4)

俄 Инв.No.6331　大般涅槃經卷第十二　　　(26-5)

俄 Инв.No.6331　大般涅槃經卷第十二　　　(26-6)

俄 Инв.No.6331　大般涅槃經卷第十二　　　(26-7)

俄 Инв.No.6331　大般涅槃經卷第十二　　　(26-8)

俄 Инв.No.6331　大般涅槃經卷第十二　　　(26-9)

俄 Инв.No.6331　大般涅槃經卷第十二　　　(26-10)

俄 Инв.No.6331　大般涅槃經卷第十二　　　(26-11)

俄 Инв.No.6331　大般涅槃經卷第十二　　(26-12)

俄 Инв.No.6331　大般涅槃經卷第十二　　(26-13)

俄 Инв.No.6331　大般涅槃經卷第十二　　(26-14)

俄 Инв.No.6331　大般涅槃經卷第十二　　(26-15)

俄 Инв.No.6331　大般涅槃經卷第十二　　　(26-16)

俄 Инв.No.6331　大般涅槃經卷第十二　　　(26-17)

俄 Инв.No.6331　大般涅槃經卷第十二　　　(26-18)

俄 Инв.No.6331　大般涅槃經卷第十二　　　(26-19)

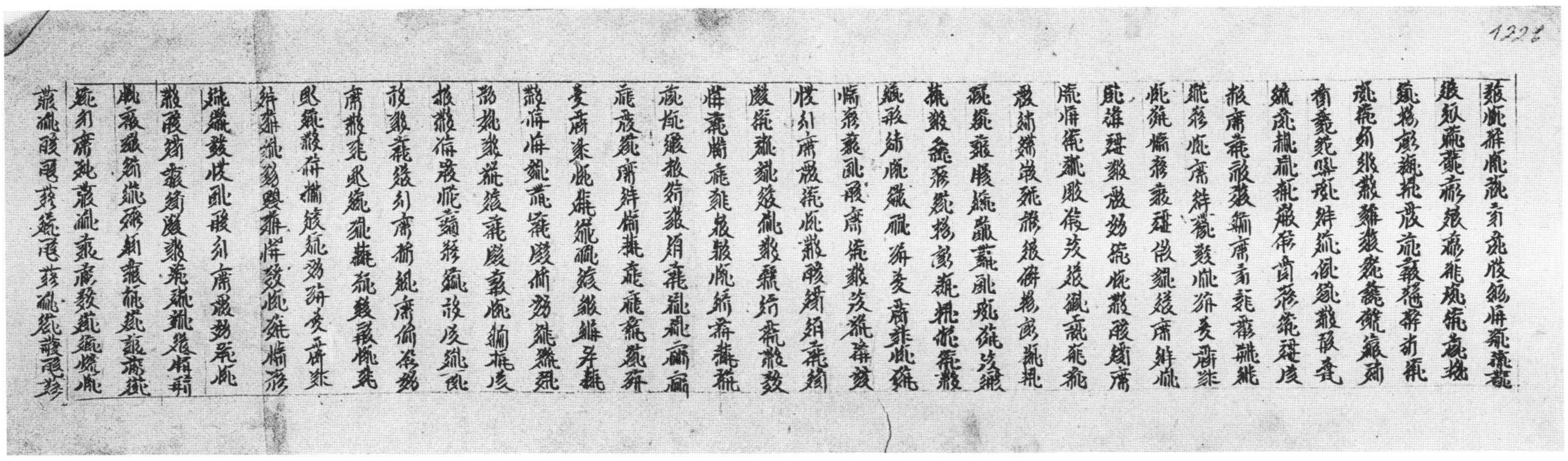

俄 Инв.No.6331　大般涅槃經卷第十二　　(26–20)

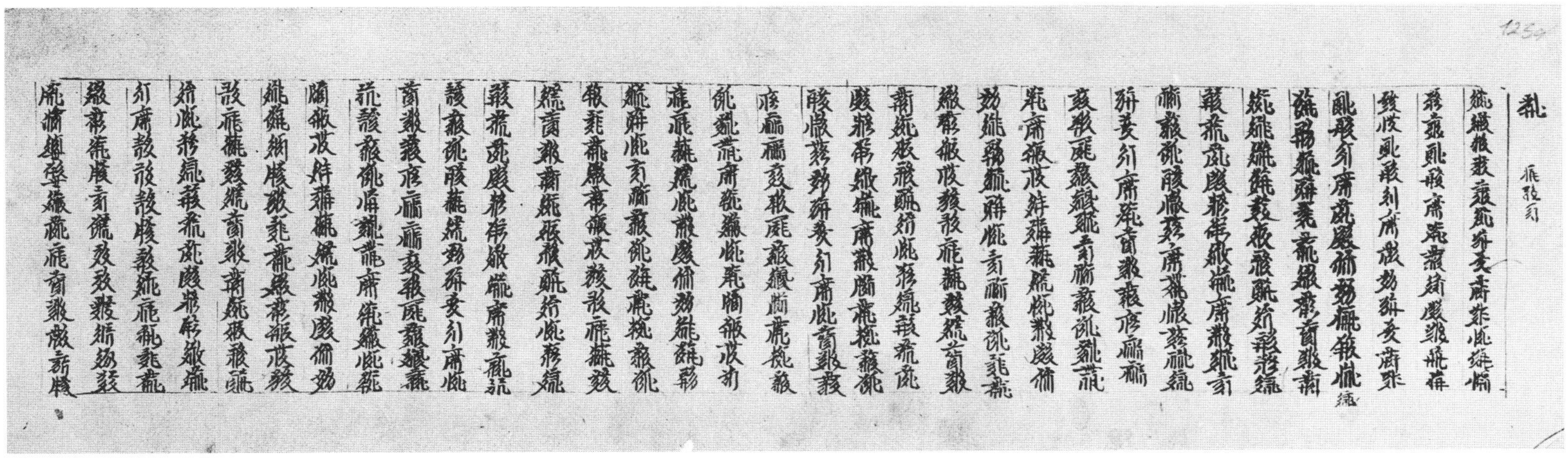

俄 Инв.No.6331　大般涅槃經卷第十二　　(26–21)

俄 Инв.No.6331　大般涅槃經卷第十二　　(26–22)

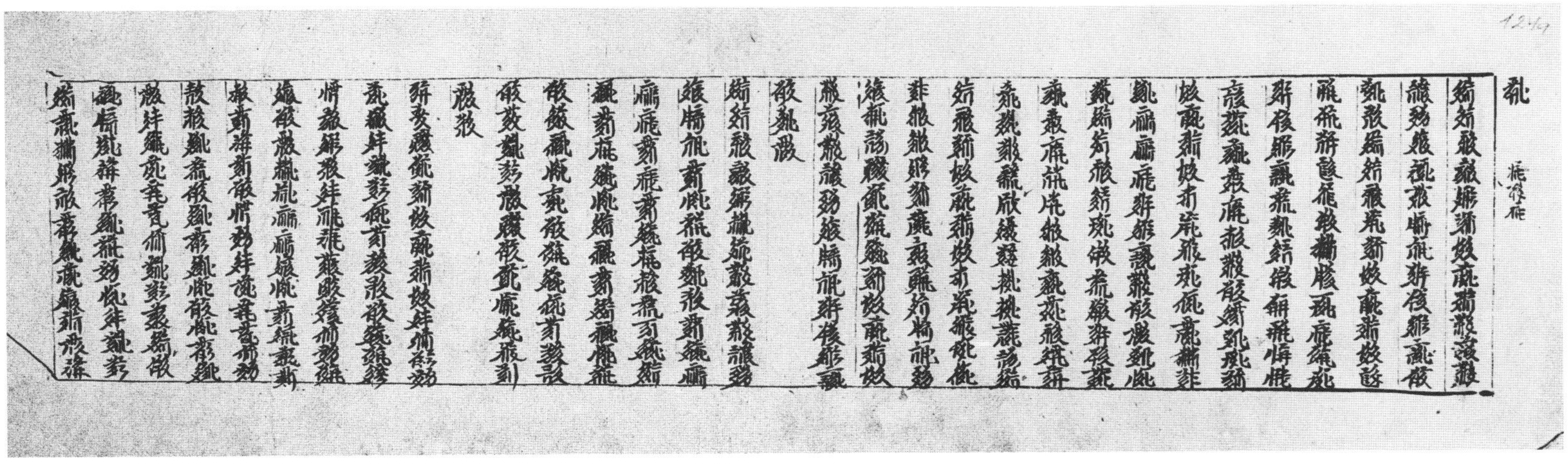

俄 Инв.No.6331　大般涅槃經卷第十二　　(26–23)

俄 **И**нв.No.6331　大般涅槃經卷第十二　　　(26-24)

俄 **И**нв.No.6331　大般涅槃經卷第十二　　　(26-25)

俄 **И**нв.No.6331　大般涅槃經卷第十二　　　(26-26)

俄 **И**нв.No.6331　大般涅槃經卷第十三　　　(22-1)

俄Инв.No.6331　大般涅槃經卷第十三　　　(22-2)

俄Инв.No.6331　大般涅槃經卷第十三　　　(22-3)

俄Инв.No.6331　大般涅槃經卷第十三　　　(22-4)

俄Инв.No.6331　大般涅槃經卷第十三　　　(22-5)

俄 Инв.No.6331　大般涅槃經卷第十三　　(22-6)

俄 Инв.No.6331　大般涅槃經卷第十三　　(22-7)

俄 Инв.No.6331　大般涅槃經卷第十三　　(22-8)

俄 Инв.No.6331　大般涅槃經卷第十三　　(22-9)

俄 Инв.No.6331　大般涅槃經卷第十三　　(22-10)

俄 Инв.No.6331　大般涅槃經卷第十三　　(22-11)

俄 Инв.No.6331　大般涅槃經卷第十三　　(22-12)

俄 Инв.No.6331　大般涅槃經卷第十三　　(22-13)

俄 Инв.No.6331　大般涅槃經卷第十三　　　(22-14)

俄 Инв.No.6331　大般涅槃經卷第十三　　　(22-15)

俄 Инв.No.6331　大般涅槃經卷第十三　　　(22-16)

俄 Инв.No.6331　大般涅槃經卷第十三　　　(22-17)

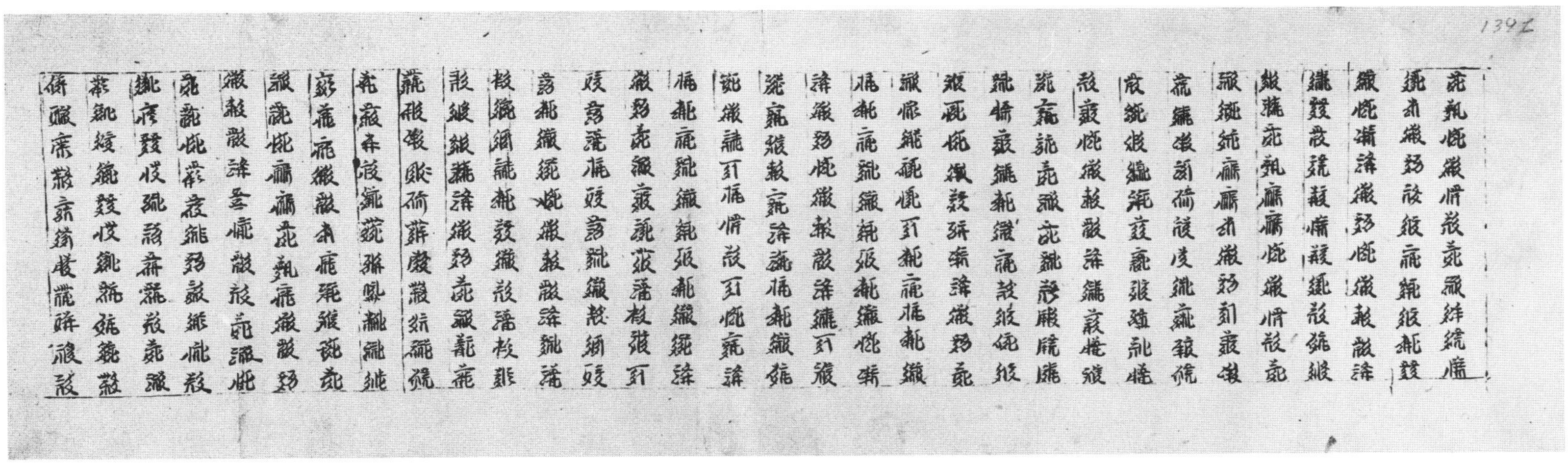

俄 Инв.No.6331　大般涅槃經卷第十三　(22–18)

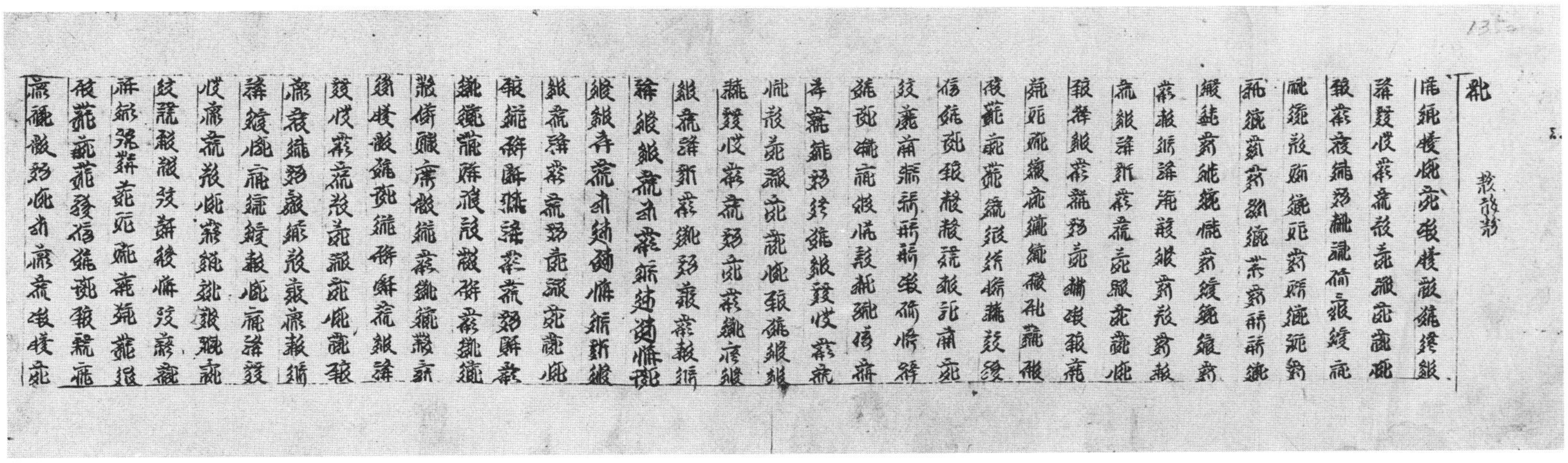

俄 Инв.No.6331　大般涅槃經卷第十三　(22–19)

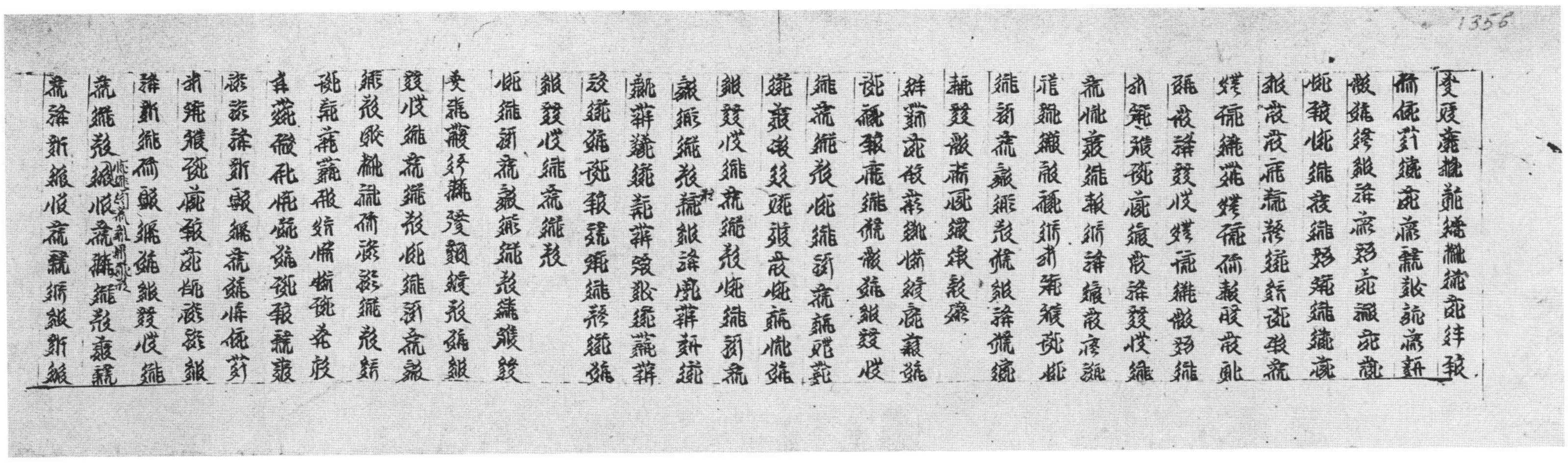

俄 Инв.No.6331　大般涅槃經卷第十三　(22–20)

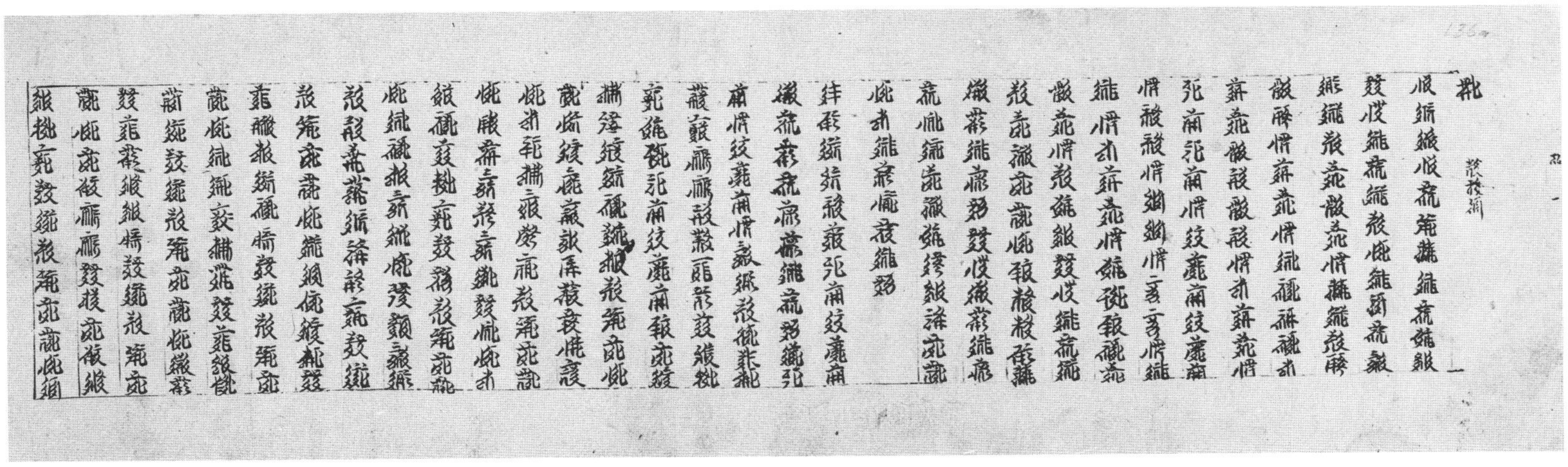

俄 Инв.No.6331　大般涅槃經卷第十三　(22–21)

俄 Инв.No.6331　大般涅槃經卷第十三　　　(22-22)

俄 Инв.No.6331　大般涅槃經卷第十四　　　(23-1)

俄 Инв.No.6331　大般涅槃經卷第十四　　　(23-2)

俄 Инв.No.6331　大般涅槃經卷第十四　　　(23-3)

俄 ИНВ.No.6331　大般涅槃經卷第十四　　　(23-4)

俄 ИНВ.No.6331　大般涅槃經卷第十四　　　(23-5)

俄 ИНВ.No.6331　大般涅槃經卷第十四　　　(23-6)

俄 ИНВ.No.6331　大般涅槃經卷第十四　　　(23-7)

俄**И**нв.No.6331　大般涅槃經卷第十四　　(23-8)

俄**И**нв.No.6331　大般涅槃經卷第十四　　(23-9)

俄**И**нв.No.6331　大般涅槃經卷第十四　　(23-10)

俄**И**нв.No.6331　大般涅槃經卷第十四　　(23-11)

俄 **И**нв.No.6331　大般涅槃經卷第十四　　　(23-12)

俄 **И**нв.No.6331　大般涅槃經卷第十四　　　(23-13)

俄 **И**нв.No.6331　大般涅槃經卷第十四　　　(23-14)

俄 **И**нв.No.6331　大般涅槃經卷第十四　　　(23-15)

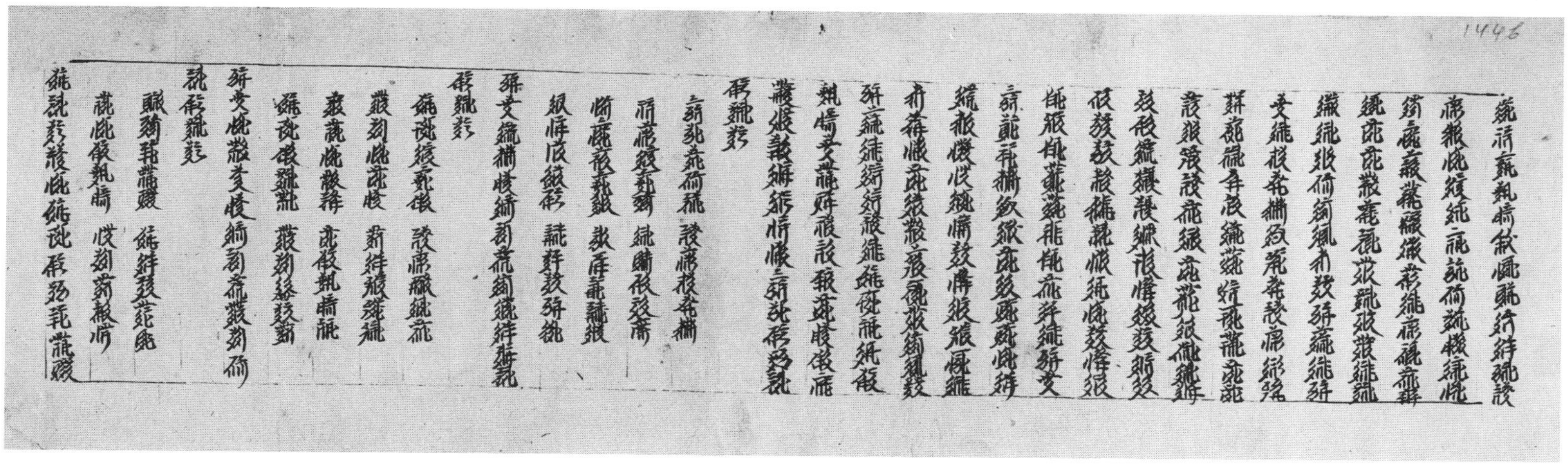

俄 Инв.No.6331 大般涅槃經卷第十四 (23-16)

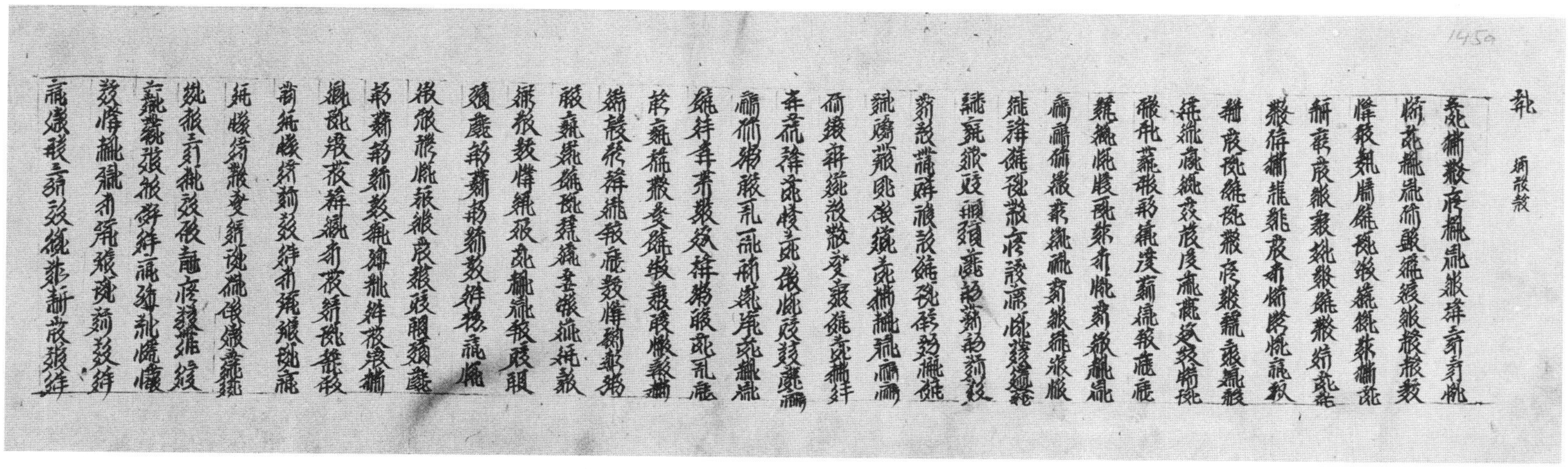

俄 Инв.No.6331 大般涅槃經卷第十四 (23-17)

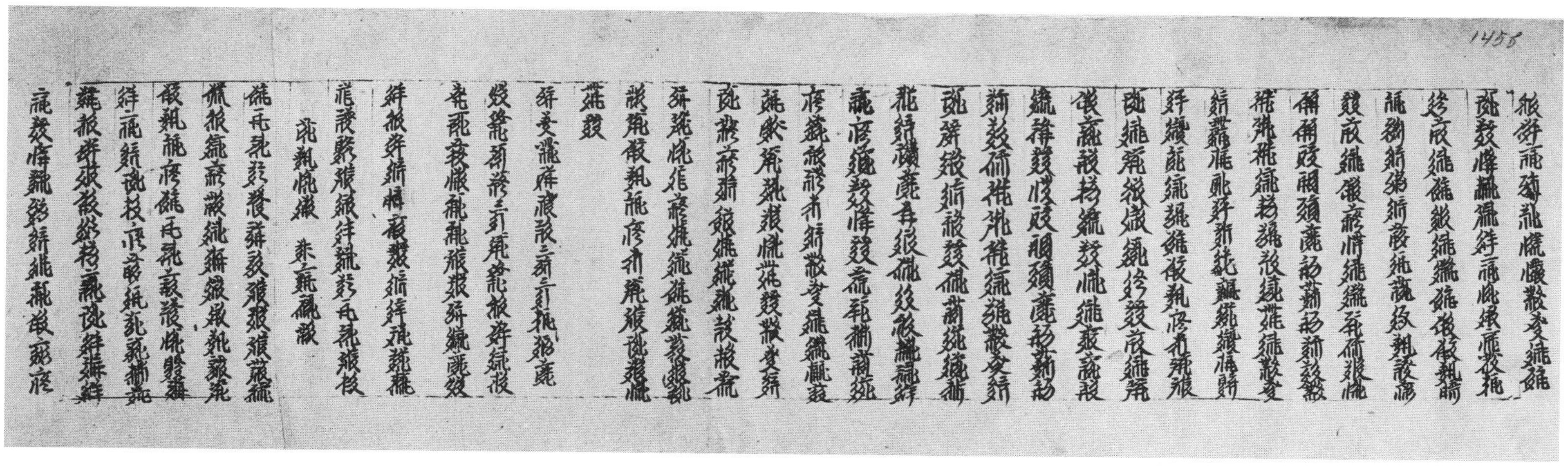

俄 Инв.No.6331 大般涅槃經卷第十四 (23-18)

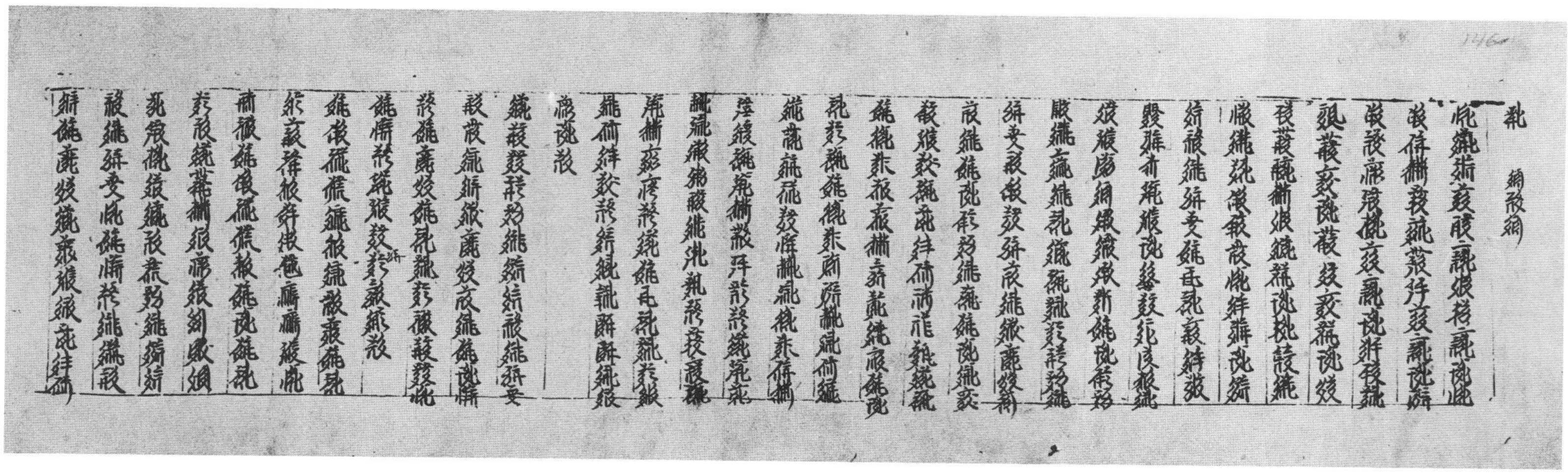

俄 Инв.No.6331 大般涅槃經卷第十四 (23-19)

俄 **И**нв.No.6331　大般涅槃經卷第十四　　　(23-20)

俄 **И**нв.No.6331　大般涅槃經卷第十四　　　(23-21)

俄 **И**нв.No.6331　大般涅槃經卷第十四　　　(23-22)

俄 **И**нв.No.6331　大般涅槃經卷第十四　　　(23-23)

俄 Инв.No.6331　大般涅槃經卷第十五　　(23-1)

俄 Инв.No.6331　大般涅槃經卷第十五　　(23-2)

俄 Инв.No.6331　大般涅槃經卷第十五　　(23-3)

俄 Инв.No.6331　大般涅槃經卷第十五　　(23-4)

俄 **И**нв.No.6331　大般涅槃經卷第十五　　　(23-5)

俄 **И**нв.No.6331　大般涅槃經卷第十五　　　(23-6)

俄 **И**нв.No.6331　大般涅槃經卷第十五　　　(23-7)

俄 **И**нв.No.6331　大般涅槃經卷第十五　　　(23-8)

俄 Инв.No.6331　大般涅槃經卷第十五　　　(23-9)

俄 Инв.No.6331　大般涅槃經卷第十五　　　(23-10)

俄 Инв.No.6331　大般涅槃經卷第十五　　　(23-11)

俄 Инв.No.6331　大般涅槃經卷第十五　　　(23-12)

俄 Инв.No.6331　大般涅槃經卷第十五　　　(23-13)

俄 Инв.No.6331　大般涅槃經卷第十五　　　(23-14)

俄 Инв.No.6331　大般涅槃經卷第十五　　　(23-15)

俄 Инв.No.6331　大般涅槃經卷第十五　　　(23-16)

俄 Инв.No.6331　大般涅槃經卷第十五　　　(23-17)

俄 Инв.No.6331　大般涅槃經卷第十五　　　(23-18)

俄 Инв.No.6331　大般涅槃經卷第十五　　　(23-19)

俄 Инв.No.6331　大般涅槃經卷第十五　　　(23-20)

俄 **И**нв.No.6331　大般涅槃經卷第十五　　　(23-21)

俄 **И**нв.No.6331　大般涅槃經卷第十五　　　(23-22)

俄 **И**нв.No.6331　大般涅槃經卷第十五　　　(23-23)

俄 **И**нв.No.6331　大般涅槃經卷第二十一

俄 Инв.No.6331　大般涅槃經卷第三十一　　　(22-1)

俄 Инв.No.6331　大般涅槃經卷第三十一　　　(22-2)

俄 Инв.No.6331　大般涅槃經卷第三十一　　　(22-3)

俄 Инв.No.6331　大般涅槃經卷第三十一　　　(22-4)

俄 Инв.No.6331　大般涅槃經卷第三十一　　　(22-5)

俄 Инв.No.6331　大般涅槃經卷第三十一　　　(22-6)

俄 Инв.No.6331　大般涅槃經卷第三十一　　　(22-7)

俄 Инв.No.6331　大般涅槃經卷第三十一　　　(22-8)

俄 **И**нв.No.6331　　大般涅槃經卷第三十一　　　　（22-9）

俄 **И**нв.No.6331　　大般涅槃經卷第三十一　　　　（22-10）

俄 **И**нв.No.6331　　大般涅槃經卷第三十一　　　　（22-11）

俄 **И**нв.No.6331　　大般涅槃經卷第三十一　　　　（22-12）

俄Инв.No.6331　大般涅槃經卷第三十一　　　(22-13)

俄Инв.No.6331　大般涅槃經卷第三十一　　　(22-14)

俄Инв.No.6331　大般涅槃經卷第三十一　　　(22-15)

俄Инв.No.6331　大般涅槃經卷第三十一　　　(22-16)

俄 Инв.No.6331　大般涅槃經卷第三十一　　　(22-17)

俄 Инв.No.6331　大般涅槃經卷第三十一　　　(22-18)

俄 Инв.No.6331　大般涅槃經卷第三十一　　　(22-19)

俄 Инв.No.6331　大般涅槃經卷第三十一　　　(22-20)

俄 **И**нв.No.6331　大般涅槃經卷第三十一　　　（22-21）

俄 **И**нв.No.6331　大般涅槃經卷第三十一　　　（22-22）

俄 **И**нв.No.6331　大般涅槃經卷第三十二　　　（2-1）

俄 **И**нв.No.6331　大般涅槃經卷第三十二　　　（2-2）

俄ИНВ.No.787　妙法蓮華經序

俄ИНВ.No.4631　妙法蓮華經序卷第一

俄ИНВ.No.2436　妙法蓮華經卷第一　　(18-1)

俄 **И**нв.No.2436　妙法蓮華經卷第一　　　(18-2)

俄 **И**нв.No.2436　妙法蓮華經卷第一　　　(18-3)

俄 **И**нв.No.2436　妙法蓮華經卷第一　　　(18-4)

俄 **И**нв.No.2436　妙法蓮華經卷第一　　　(18-5)

俄 **И**нв.No.2436　妙法蓮華經卷第一　　　(18-6)

俄 **И**нв.No.2436　妙法蓮華經卷第一　　　(18-7)

俄 Инв.No.2436　妙法蓮華經卷第一　　　（18-8）

俄 Инв.No.2436　妙法蓮華經卷第一　　　（18-9）

俄 Инв.No.2436　妙法蓮華經卷第一　　　（18-10）

俄 ИНВ.No.2436　妙法蓮華經卷第一　　　(18-11)

俄 ИНВ.No.2436　妙法蓮華經卷第一　　　(18-12)

俄 ИНВ.No.2436　妙法蓮華經卷第一　　　(18-13)

俄 **И**нв.No.2436　妙法蓮華經卷第一　　　(18-14)

俄 **И**нв.No.2436　妙法蓮華經卷第一　　　(18-15)

俄 **И**нв.No.2436　妙法蓮華經卷第一　　　(18-16)

俄 **И**нв.No.2436　妙法蓮華經卷第一　　　(18-17)

俄 **И**нв.No.2436　妙法蓮華經卷第一　　　(18-18)

俄 **И**нв.No.66　妙法蓮華經卷第一　　　(6-1)

俄 **И**нв.No.66　妙法蓮華經卷第一　　　(6-2)

俄 **И**нв.No.66　妙法蓮華經卷第一　　　(6-3)

俄 **И**нв.No.66　妙法蓮華經卷第一　　　(6-4)

俄 **Инв**.No.66　妙法蓮華經卷第一　　　(6-5)

俄 **Инв**.No.66　妙法蓮華經卷第一　　　(6-6)

俄 **Инв**.No.4562　妙法蓮華經卷第二

俄 **И**нв.No.805　妙法蓮華經卷第二　　(9-1)

俄 **И**нв.No.805　妙法蓮華經卷第二　　(9-2)

俄 **И**нв.No.805　妙法蓮華經卷第二　　(9-3)

俄 **И**нв.No.805　妙法蓮華經卷第二　　　(9-4)

俄 **И**нв.No.805　妙法蓮華經卷第二　　　(9-5)

俄 **И**нв.No.805　妙法蓮華經卷第二　　　(9-6)

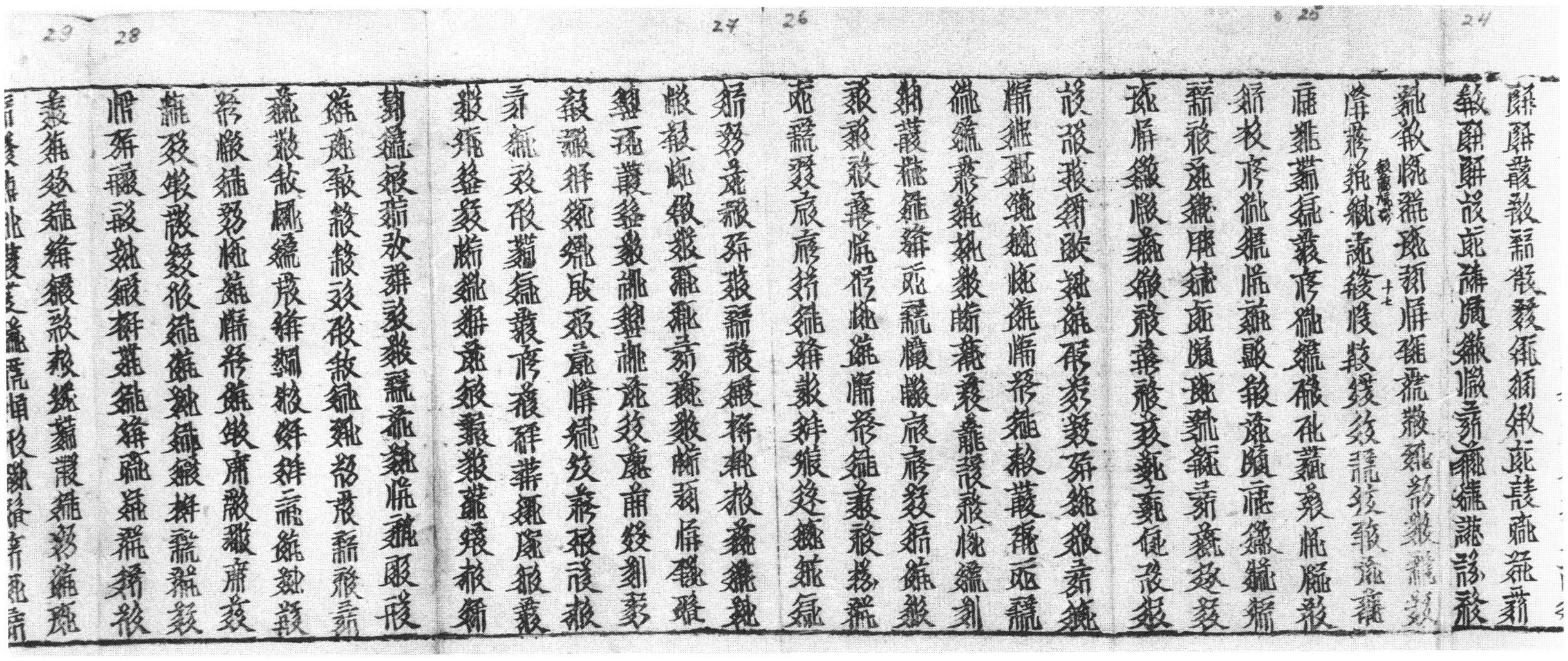

俄 Инв.No.805 妙法蓮華經卷第二 (9–7)

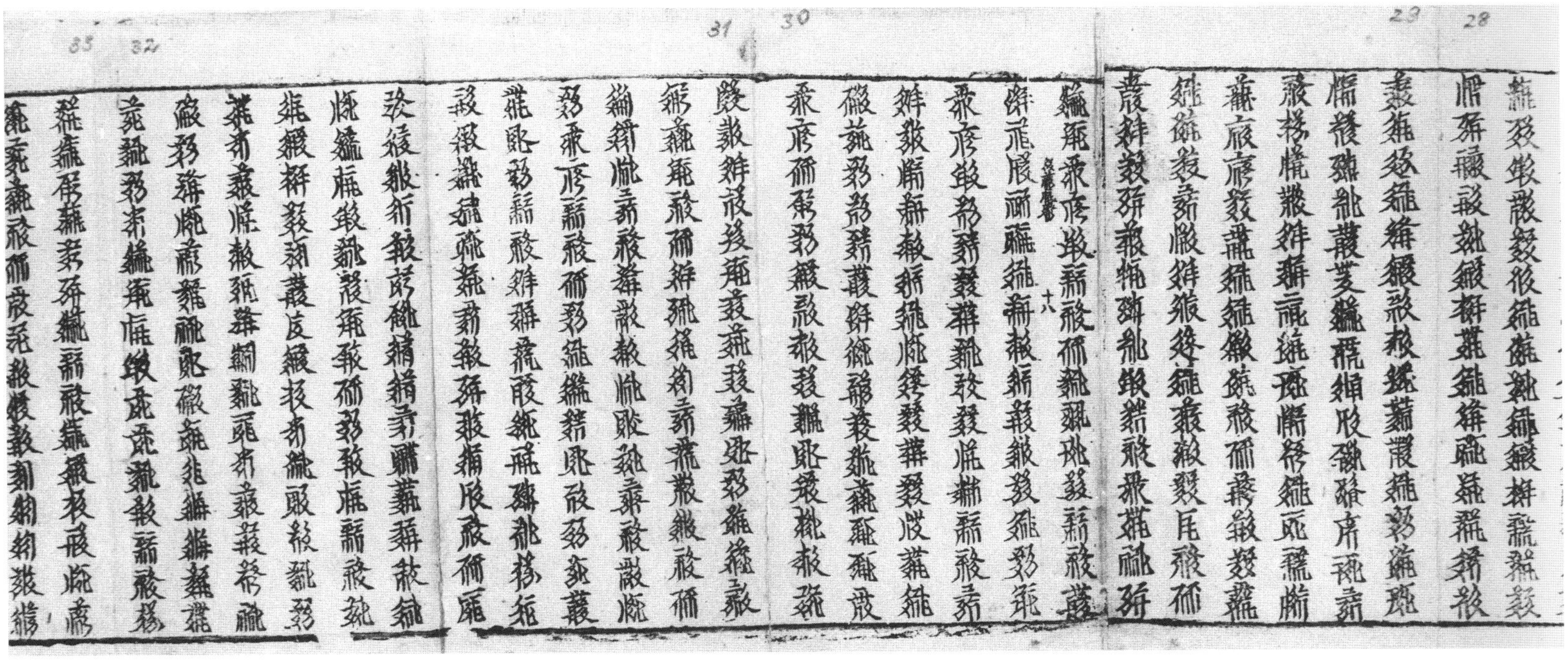

俄 Инв.No.805 妙法蓮華經卷第二 (9–8)

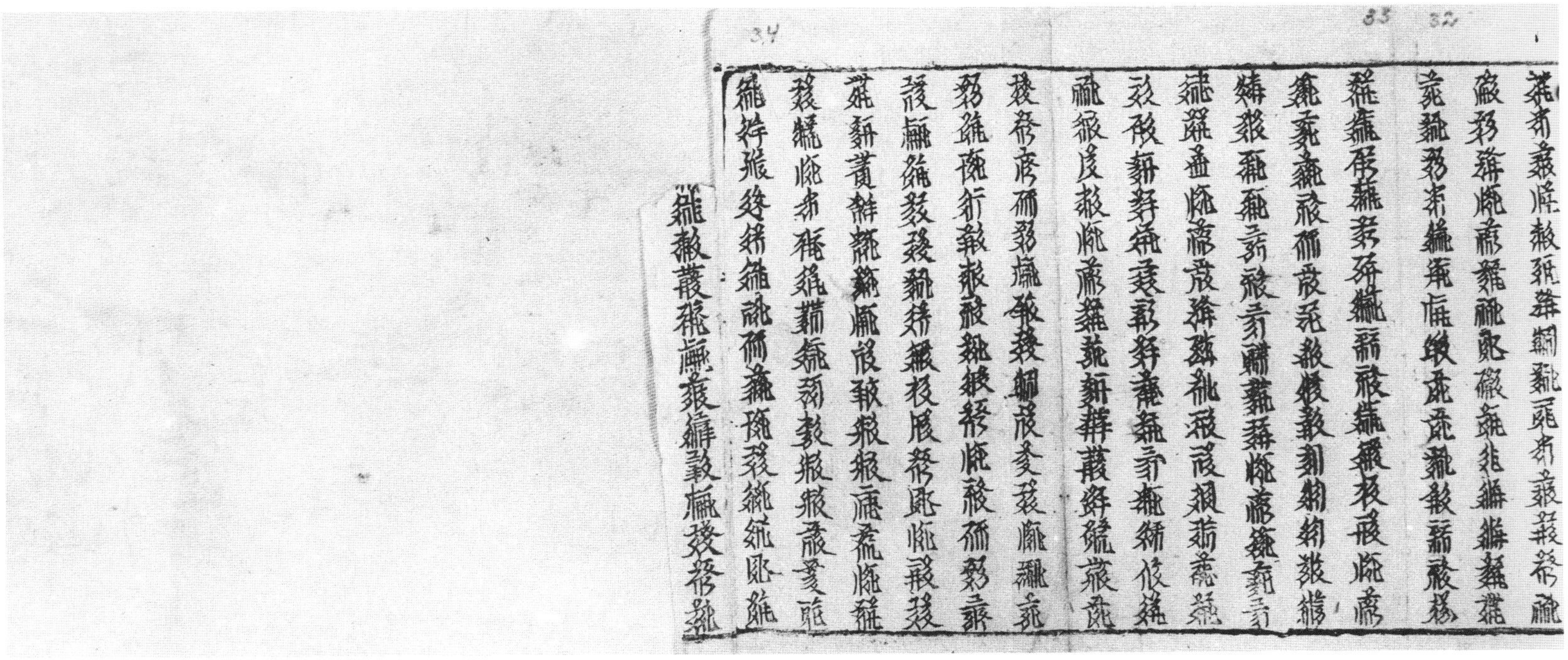

俄 Инв.No.805 妙法蓮華經卷第二 (9–9)

俄 Инв.No.3900　妙法蓮華經卷第二

俄 Инв.No.6310　妙法蓮華經卷第二　　　(2-1)

俄 Инв.No.6310　妙法蓮華經卷第二　　　(2-2)

俄Инв.No.7350a　妙法蓮華經卷第二

俄Инв.No.3900　妙法蓮華經卷第三

俄Инв.No.787　妙法蓮華經卷第三

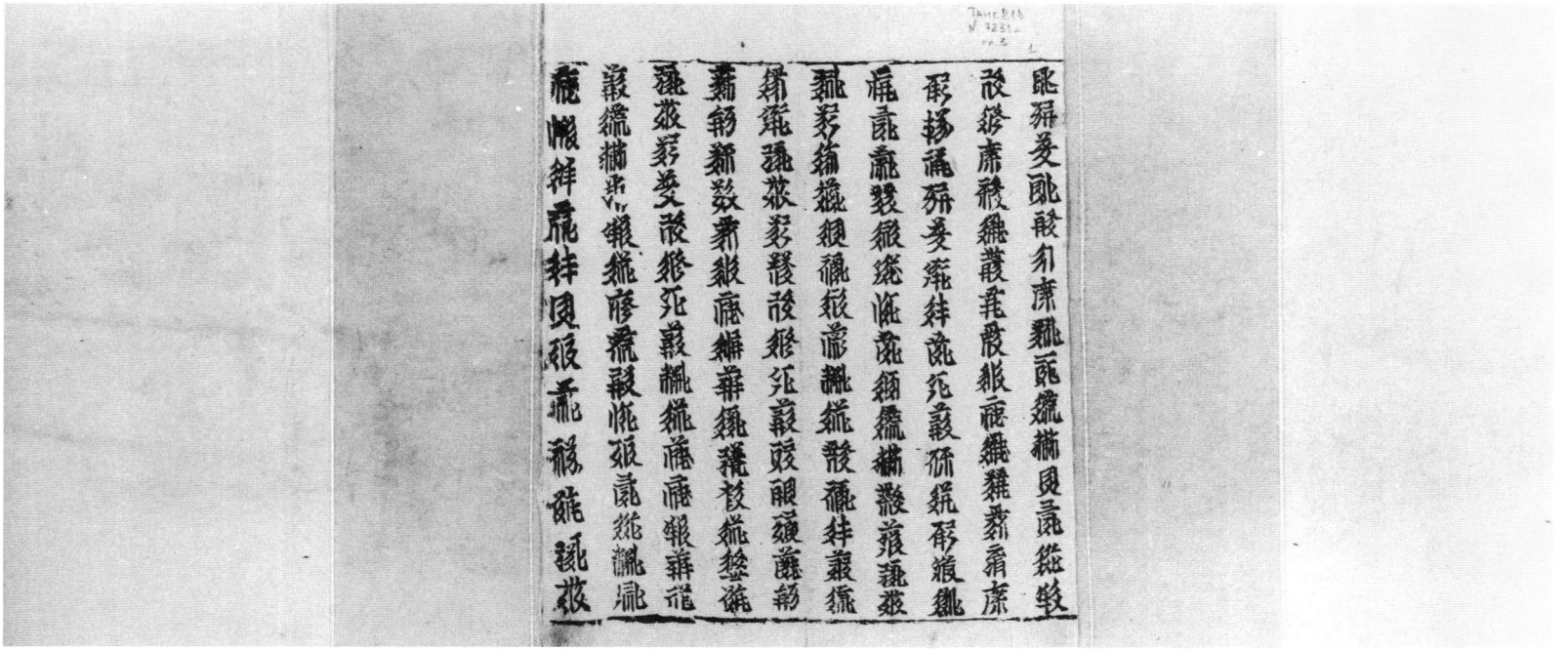

俄**И**нв.No.7231　妙法蓮華經卷第三

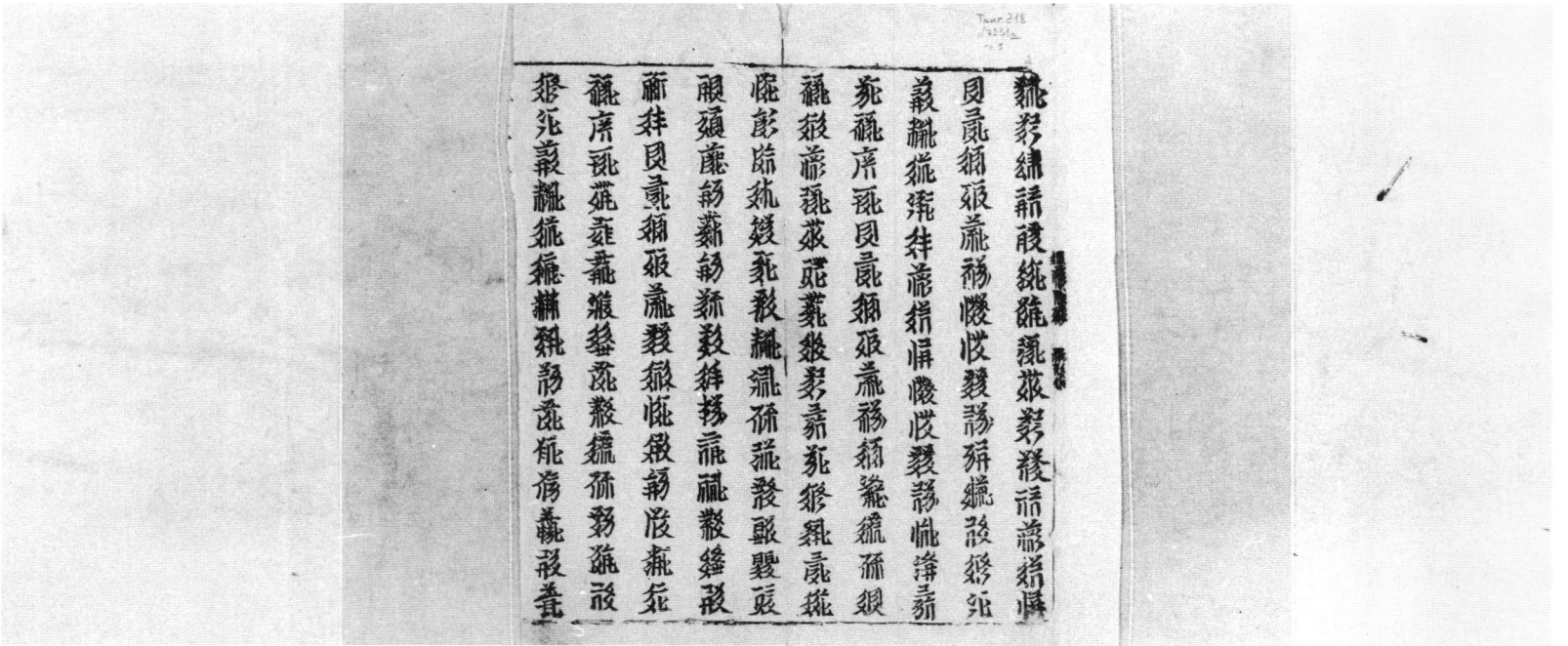

俄**И**нв.No.7231a　妙法蓮華經卷第三

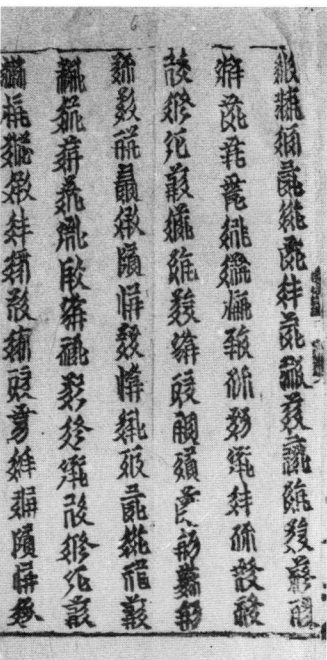

俄**И**нв.No.787　妙法蓮華經卷第三　　　(2-1)

俄 **И**нв.No.787　妙法蓮華經卷第三　　（2-2）

俄 **И**нв.No.2317　妙法蓮華經卷第四　　（18-1）

俄 **И**нв.No.2317　妙法蓮華經卷第四　　（18-2）

俄Инв.No.2317　妙法蓮華經卷第四　　　(18-3)

俄Инв.No.2317　妙法蓮華經卷第四　　　(18-4)

俄Инв.No.2317　妙法蓮華經卷第四　　　(18-5)

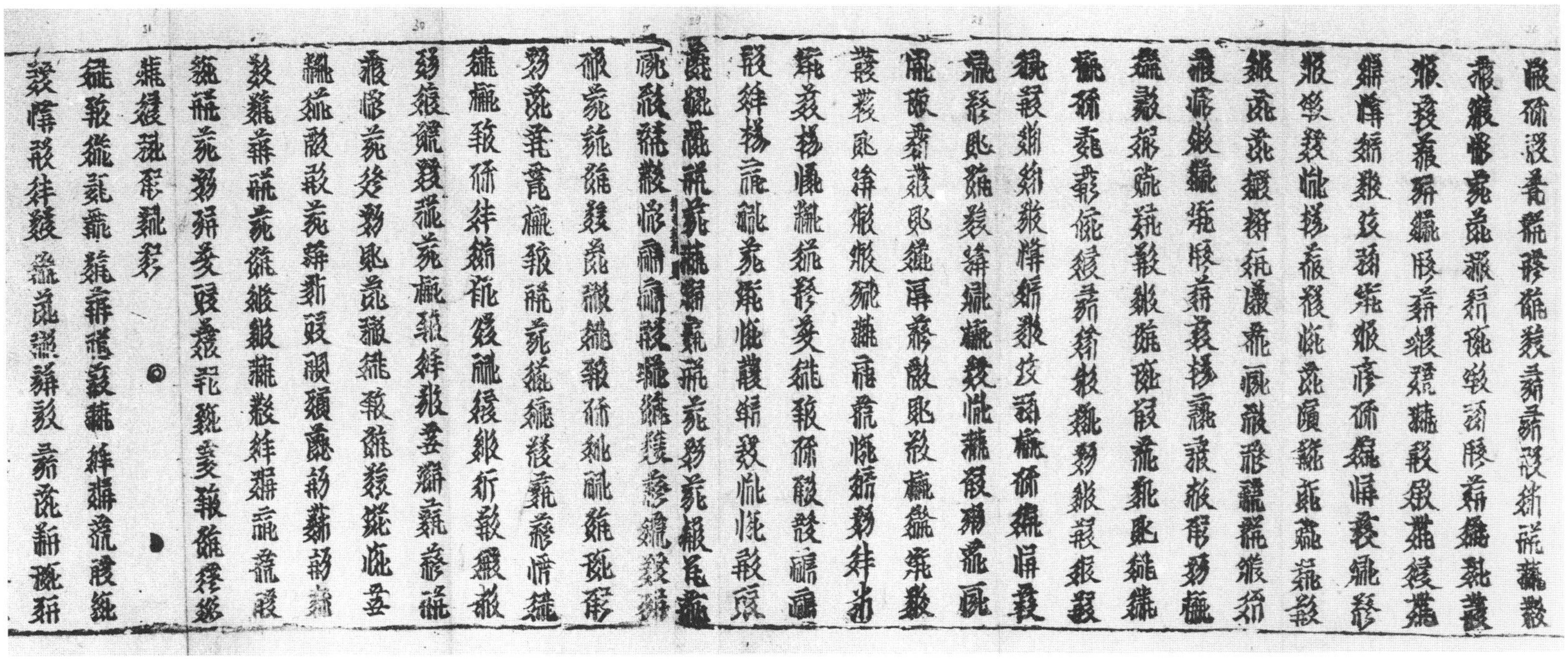

俄 Инв.No.2317　妙法蓮華經卷第四　(18–6)

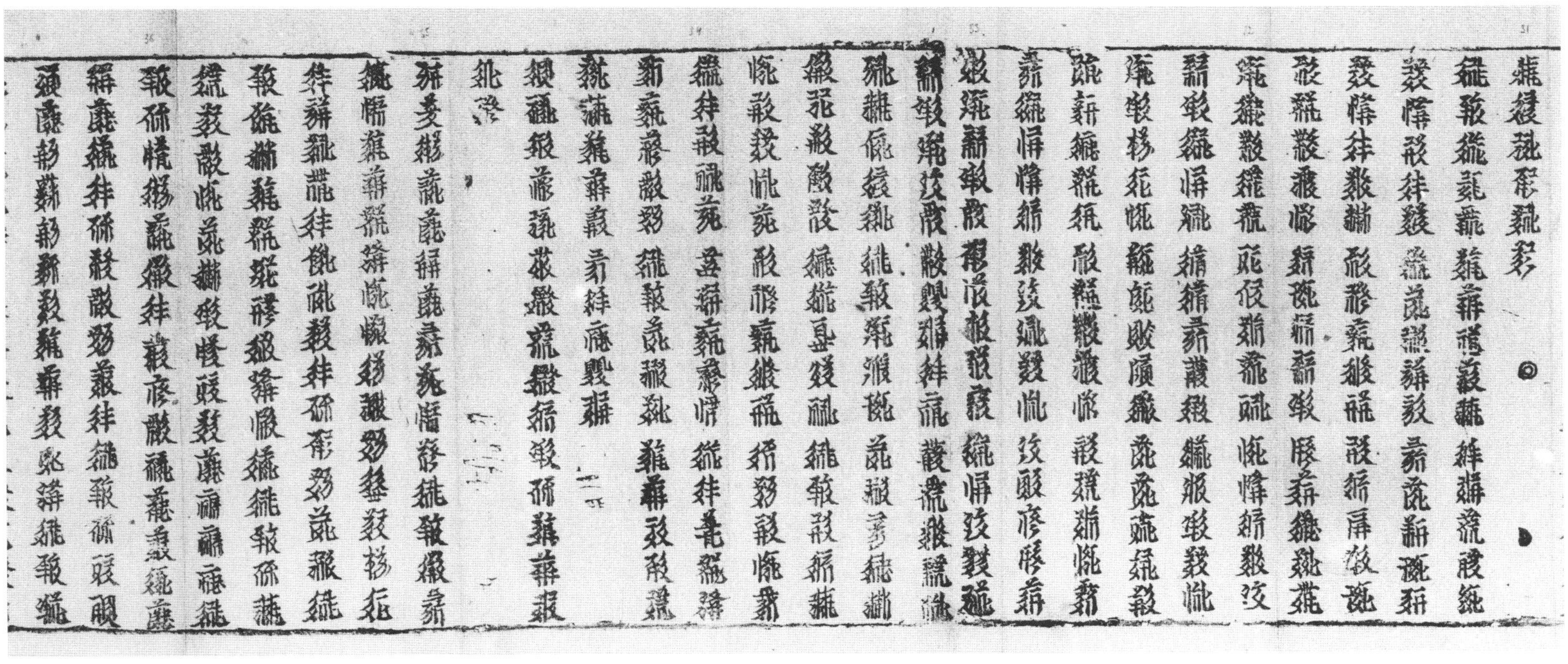

俄 Инв.No.2317　妙法蓮華經卷第四　(18–7)

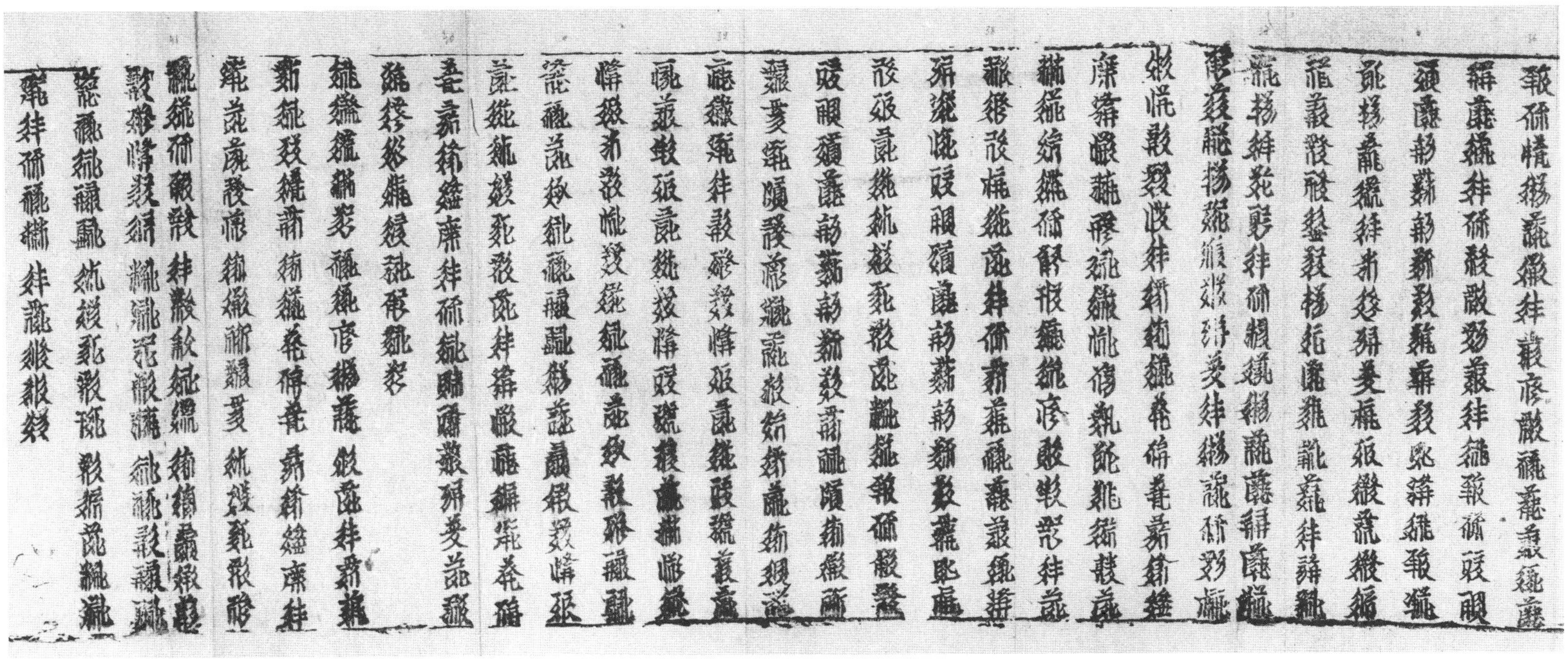

俄 Инв.No.2317　妙法蓮華經卷第四　(18–8)

俄 Инв.No.2317　妙法蓮華經卷第四　　(18-9)

俄 Инв.No.2317　妙法蓮華經卷第四　　(18-10)

俄 Инв.No.2317　妙法蓮華經卷第四　　(18-11)

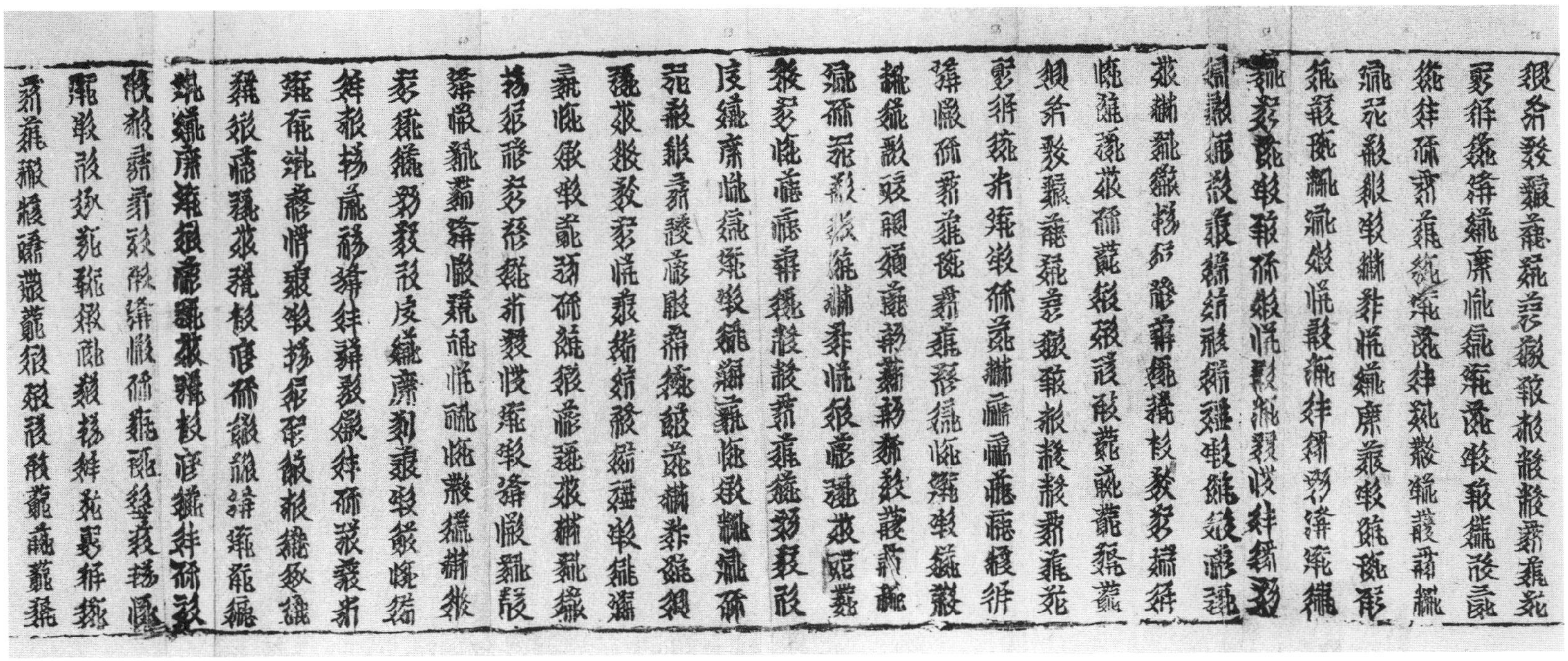

俄 Инв.No.2317　妙法蓮華經卷第四　(18–12)

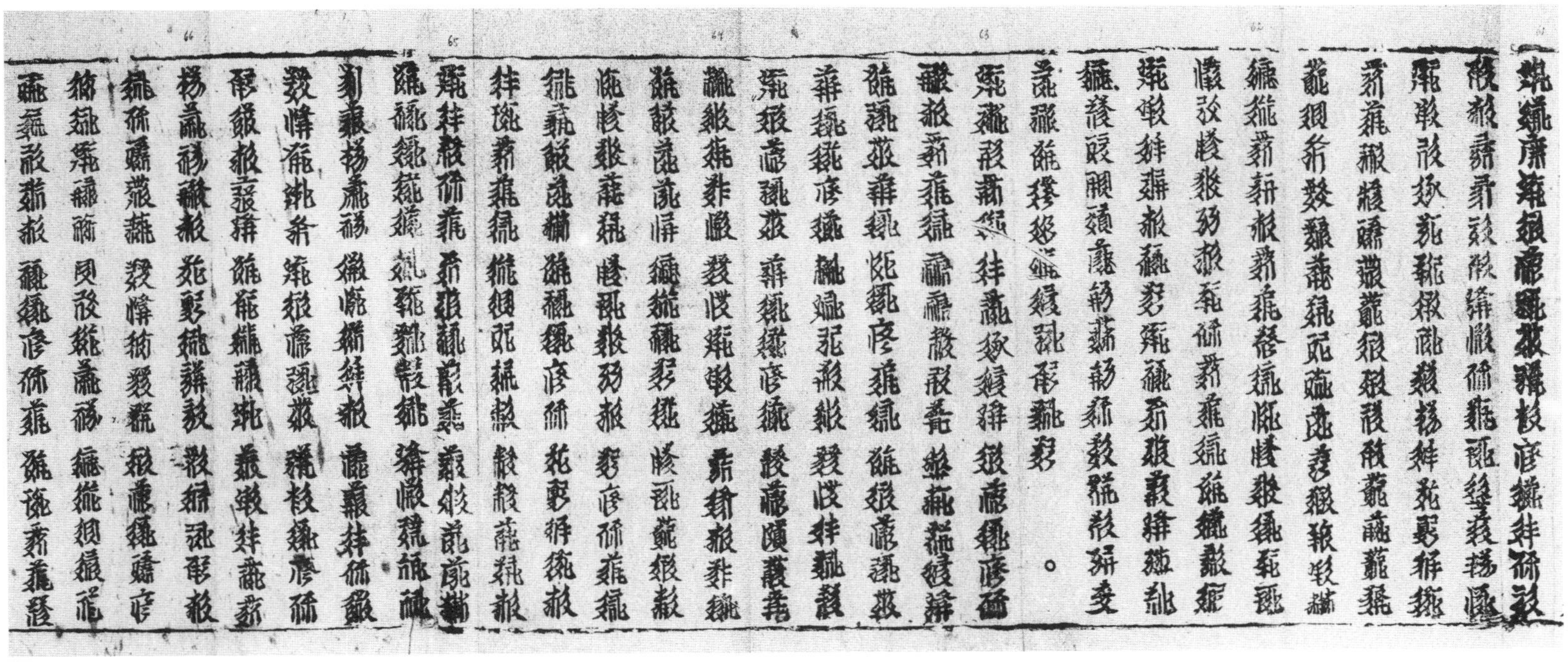

俄 Инв.No.2317　妙法蓮華經卷第四　(18–13)

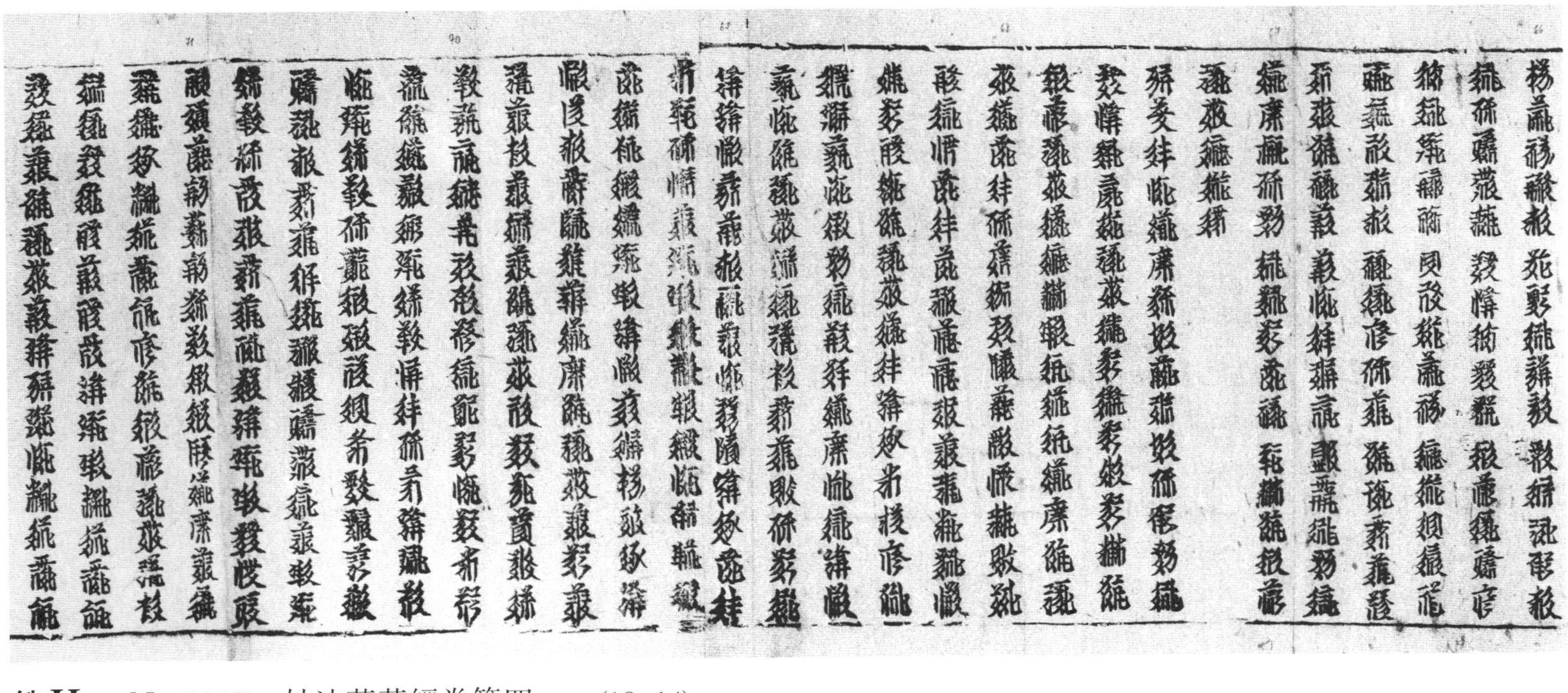

俄 Инв.No.2317　妙法蓮華經卷第四　(18–14)

俄 Инв.No.2317　妙法蓮華經卷第四　　　(18-18)

俄 Инв.No.3900　妙法蓮華經卷第四　　　(2-1)

俄 Инв.No.3900　妙法蓮華經卷第四　　　(2-2)

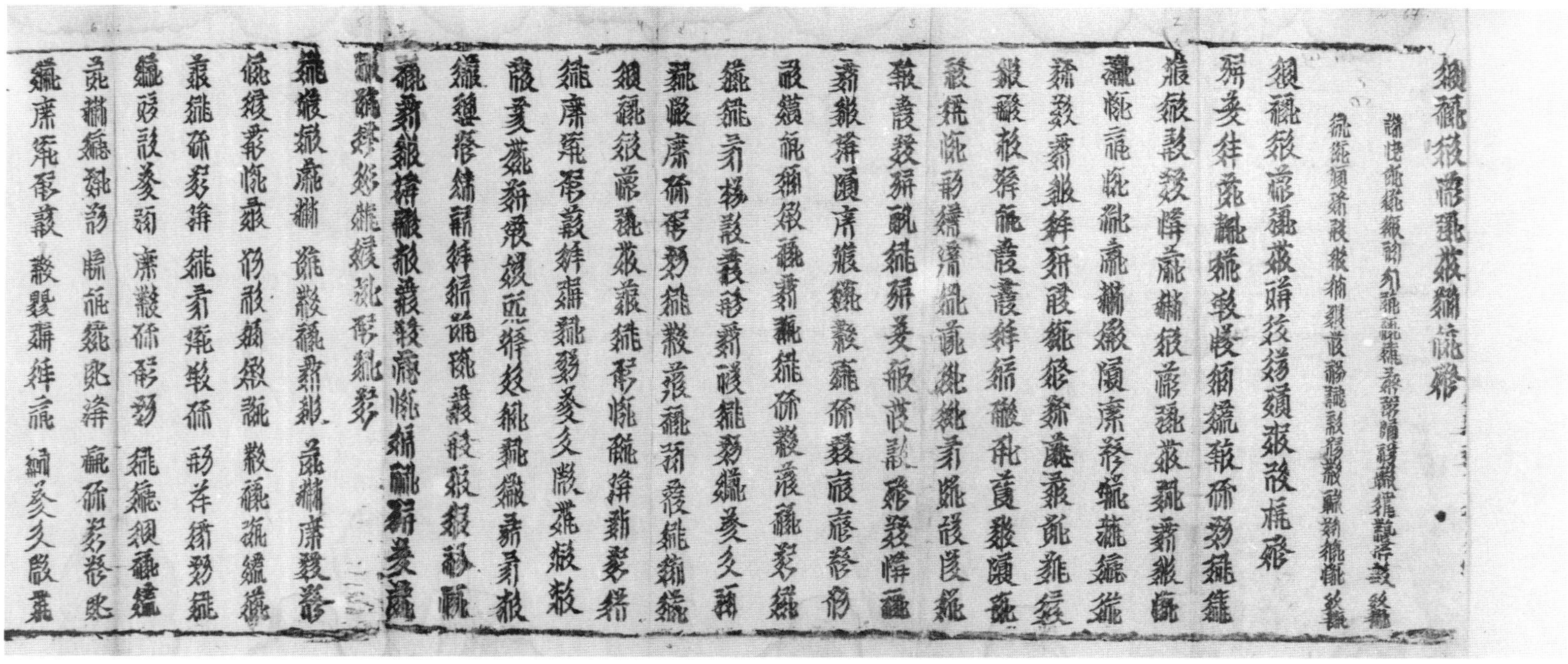

俄 Инв.No.67　妙法蓮華經卷第五　(26-1)

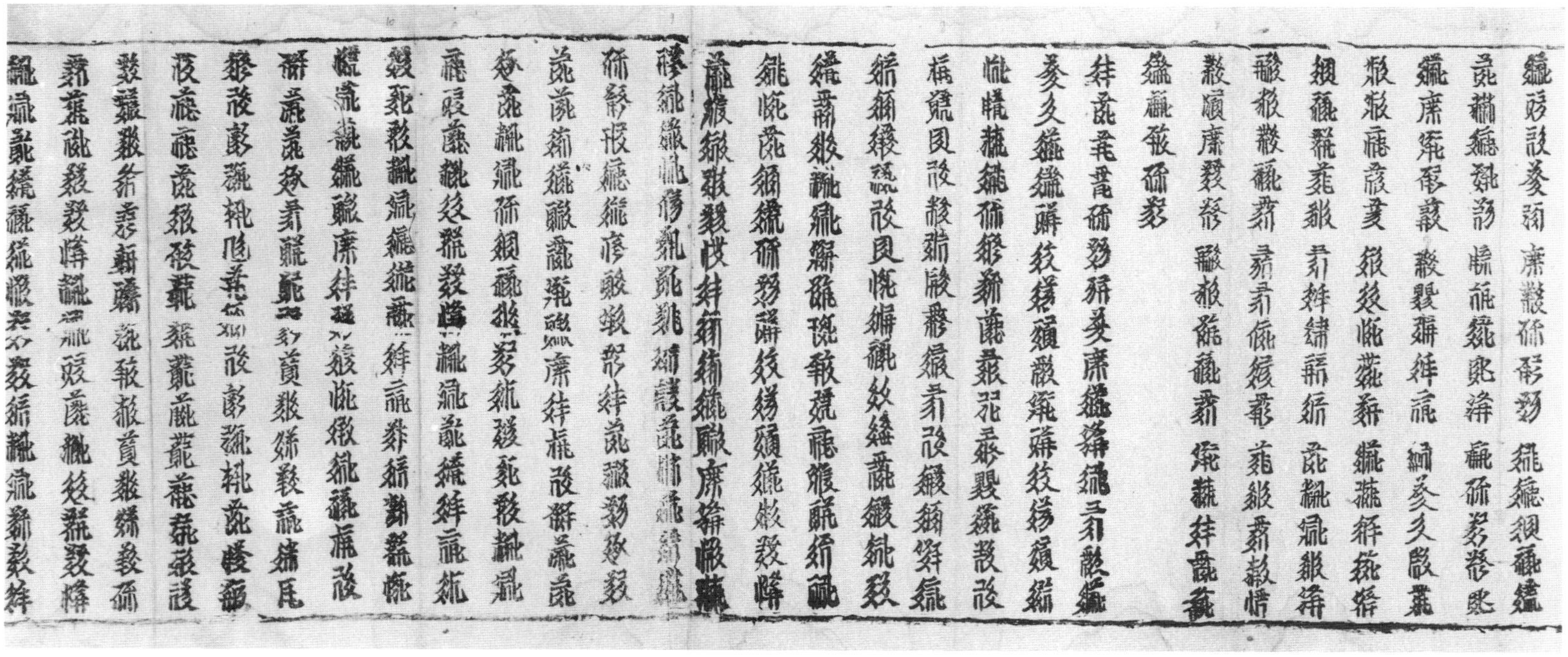

俄 Инв.No.67　妙法蓮華經卷第五　(26-2)

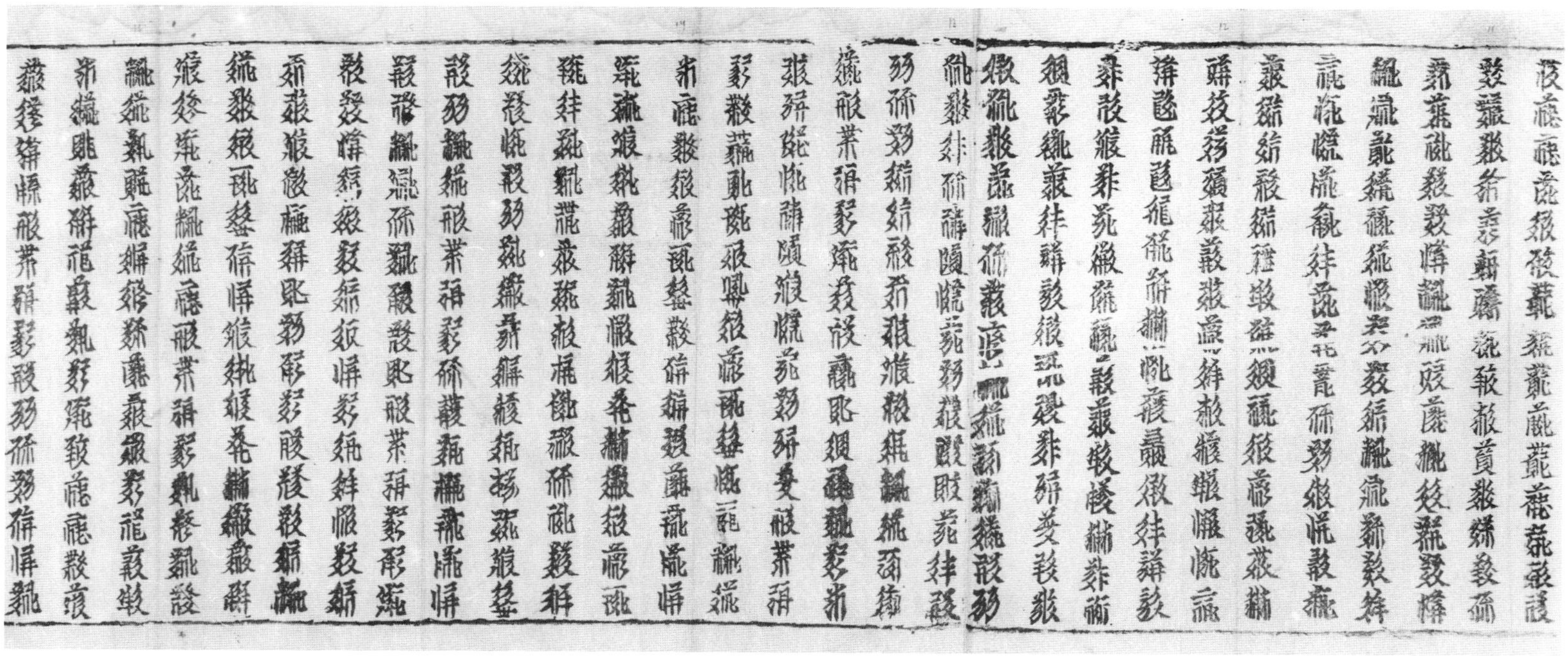

俄 Инв.No.67　妙法蓮華經卷第五　(26-3)

俄 **И**нв.No.67　妙法蓮華經卷第五　　　　(26-4)

俄 **И**нв.No.67　妙法蓮華經卷第五　　　　(26-5)

俄 **И**нв.No.67　妙法蓮華經卷第五　　　　(26-6)

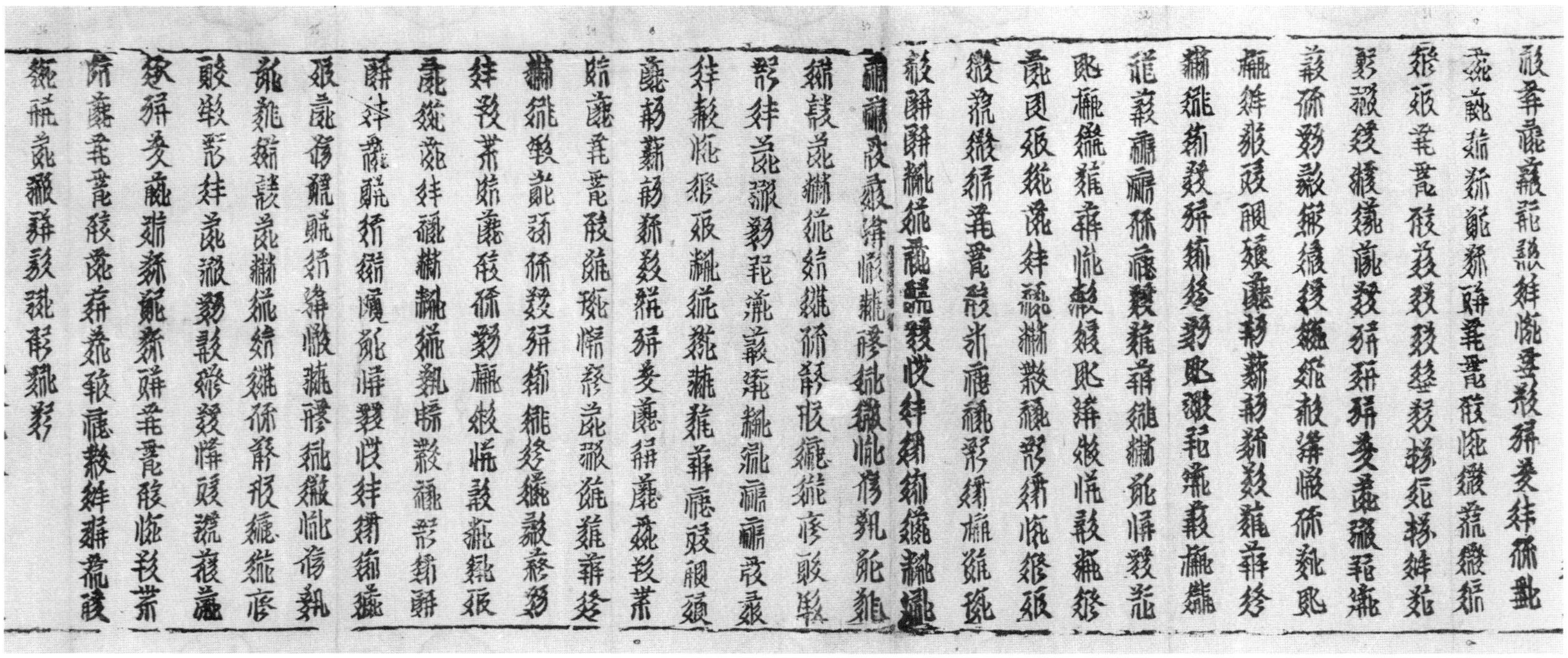

俄 Инв.No.67　妙法蓮華經卷第五　(26-7)

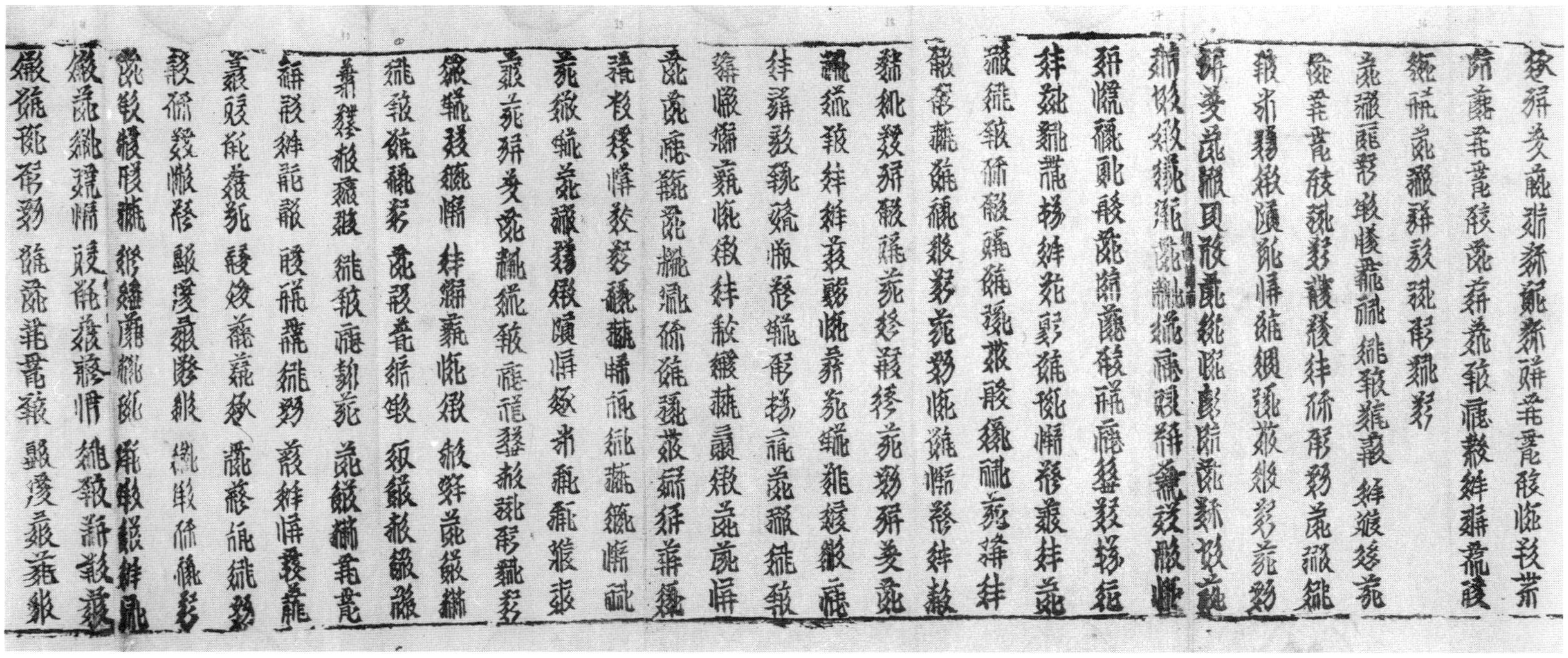

俄 Инв.No.67　妙法蓮華經卷第五　(26-8)

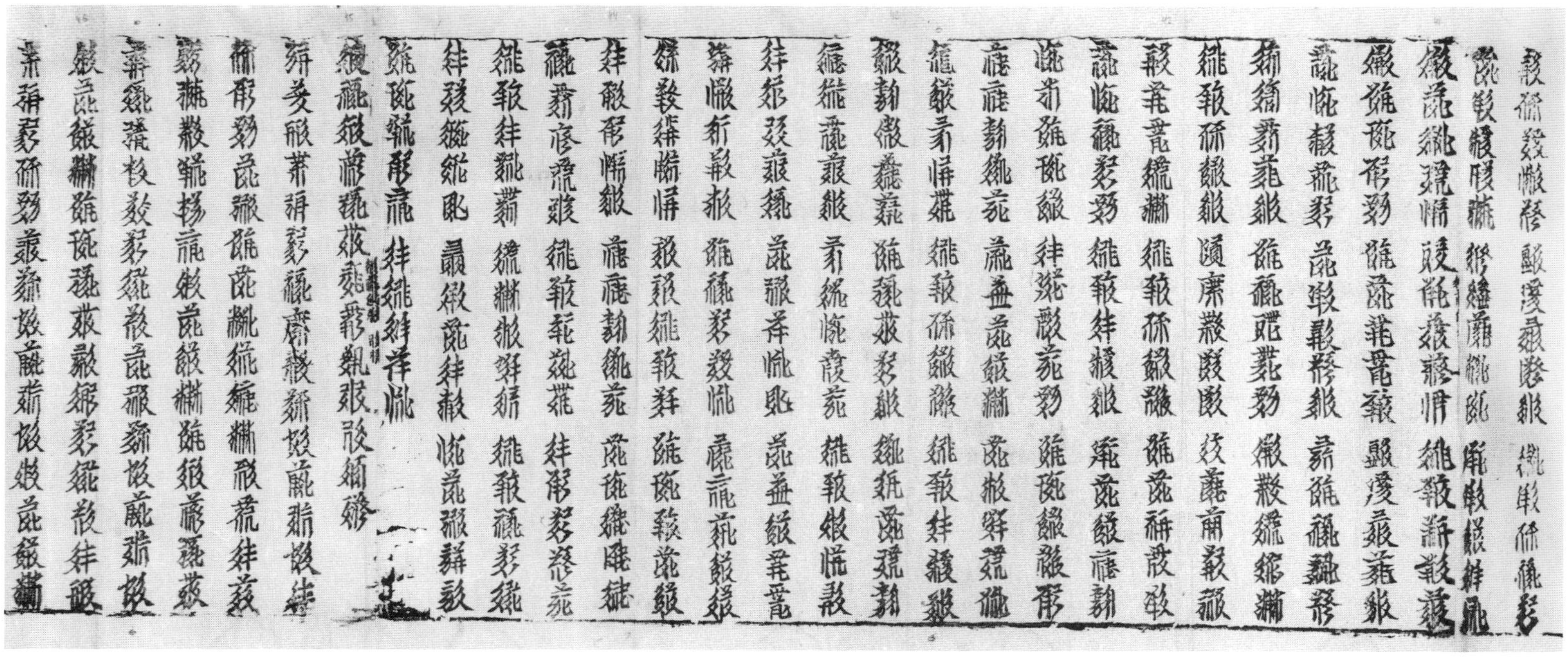

俄 Инв.No.67　妙法蓮華經卷第五　(26-9)

俄Инв.No.67　妙法蓮華經卷第五　　　　（26-10）

俄Инв.No.67　妙法蓮華經卷第五　　　　（26-11）

俄Инв.No.67　妙法蓮華經卷第五　　　　（26-12）

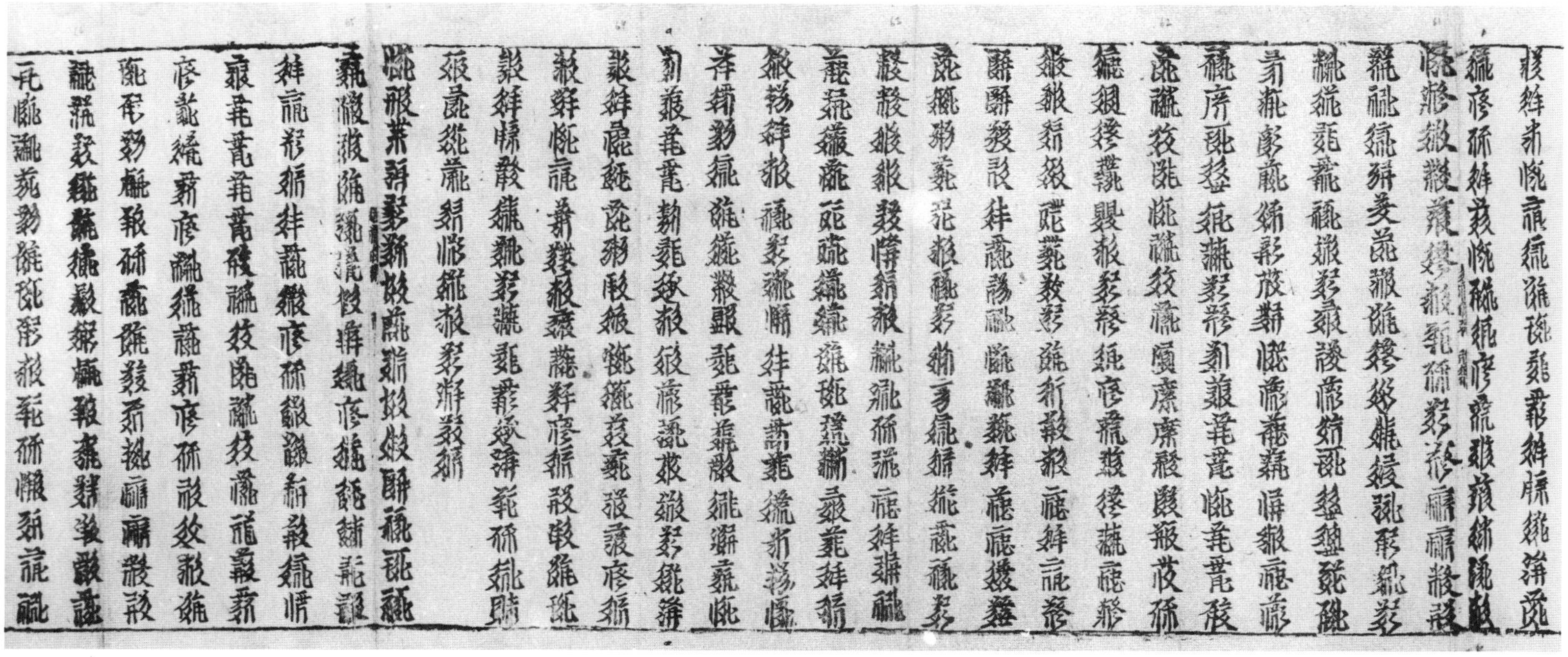

俄 Инв.No.67　妙法蓮華經卷第五　　(26-13)

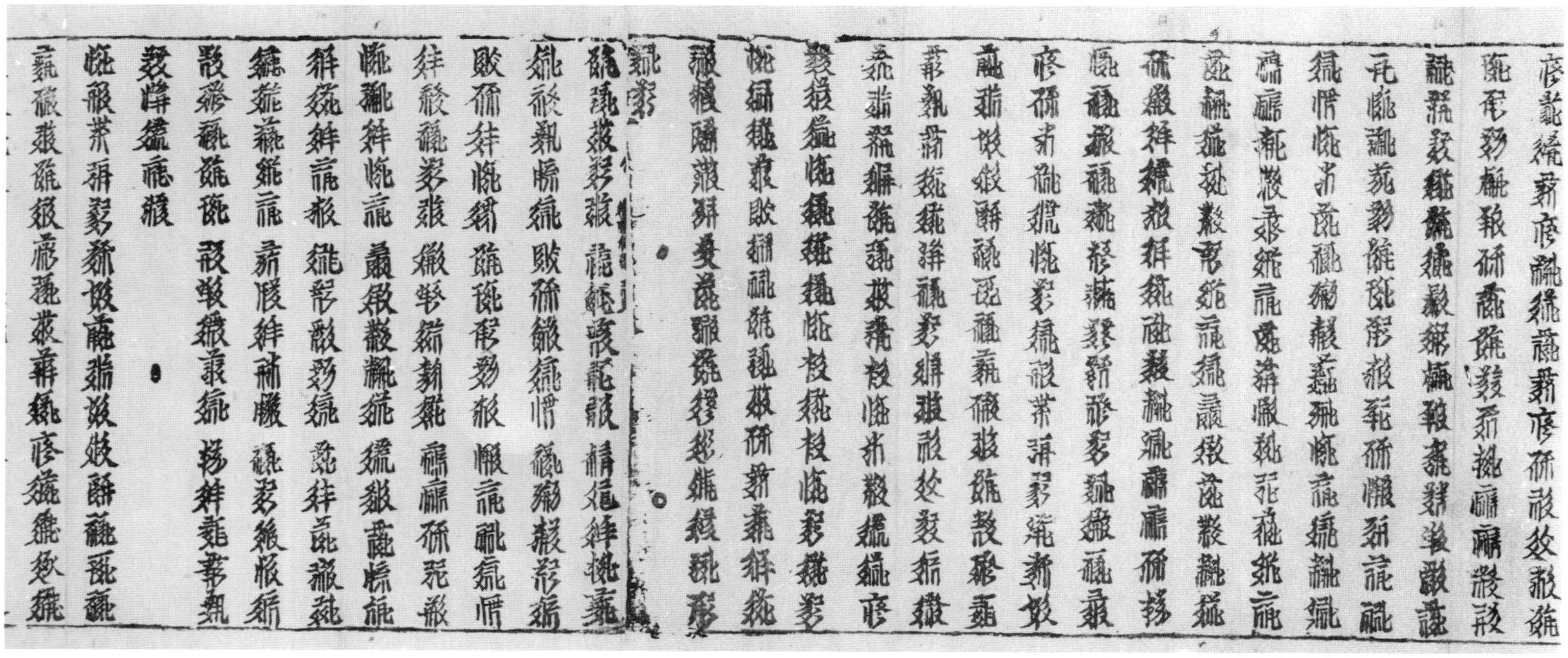

俄 Инв.No.67　妙法蓮華經卷第五　　(26-14)

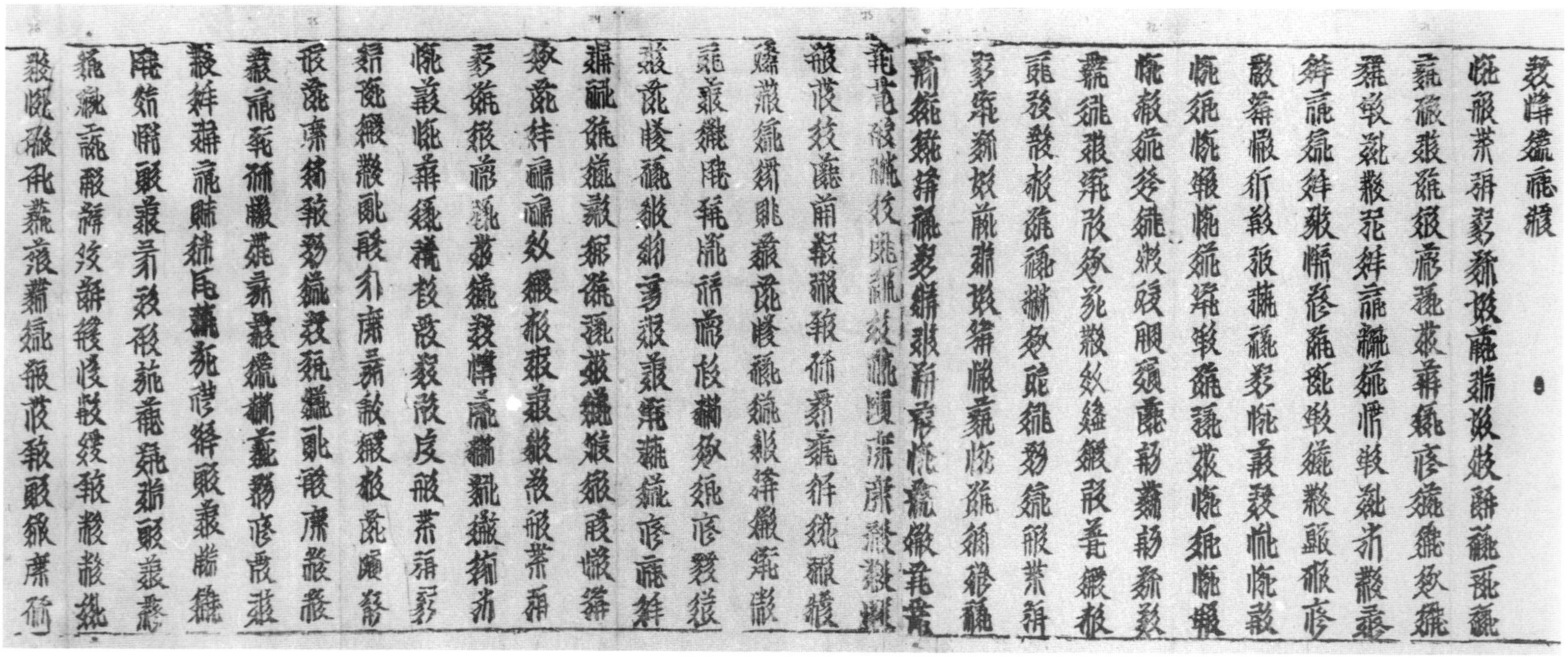

俄 Инв.No.67　妙法蓮華經卷第五　　(26-15)

俄 **И**нв.No.67 妙法蓮華經卷第五 (26-16)

俄 **И**нв.No.67 妙法蓮華經卷第五 (26-17)

俄 **И**нв.No.67 妙法蓮華經卷第五 (26-18)

俄 Инв.No.67　妙法蓮華經卷第五　　　(26-19)

俄 Инв.No.67　妙法蓮華經卷第五　　　(26-20)

俄 Инв.No.67　妙法蓮華經卷第五　　　(26-21)

俄 Инв.No.67　妙法蓮華經卷第五　　　(26-22)

俄 Инв.No.67　妙法蓮華經卷第五　　　(26-23)

俄 Инв.No.67　妙法蓮華經卷第五　　　(26-24)

俄 **И**нв.No.67　妙法蓮華經卷第五　　　(26-25)

俄 **И**нв.No.67　妙法蓮華經卷第五　　　(26-26)

俄 **И**нв.No.782　妙法蓮華經卷第六　　　(26-1)

俄 Инв.No.782　妙法蓮華經卷第六　　　(26-2)

俄 Инв.No.782　妙法蓮華經卷第六　　　(26-3)

俄 Инв.No.782　妙法蓮華經卷第六　　　(26-4)

俄Инв.No.782 妙法蓮華經卷第六 （26-5）

俄Инв.No.782 妙法蓮華經卷第六 （26-6）

俄Инв.No.782 妙法蓮華經卷第六 （26-7）

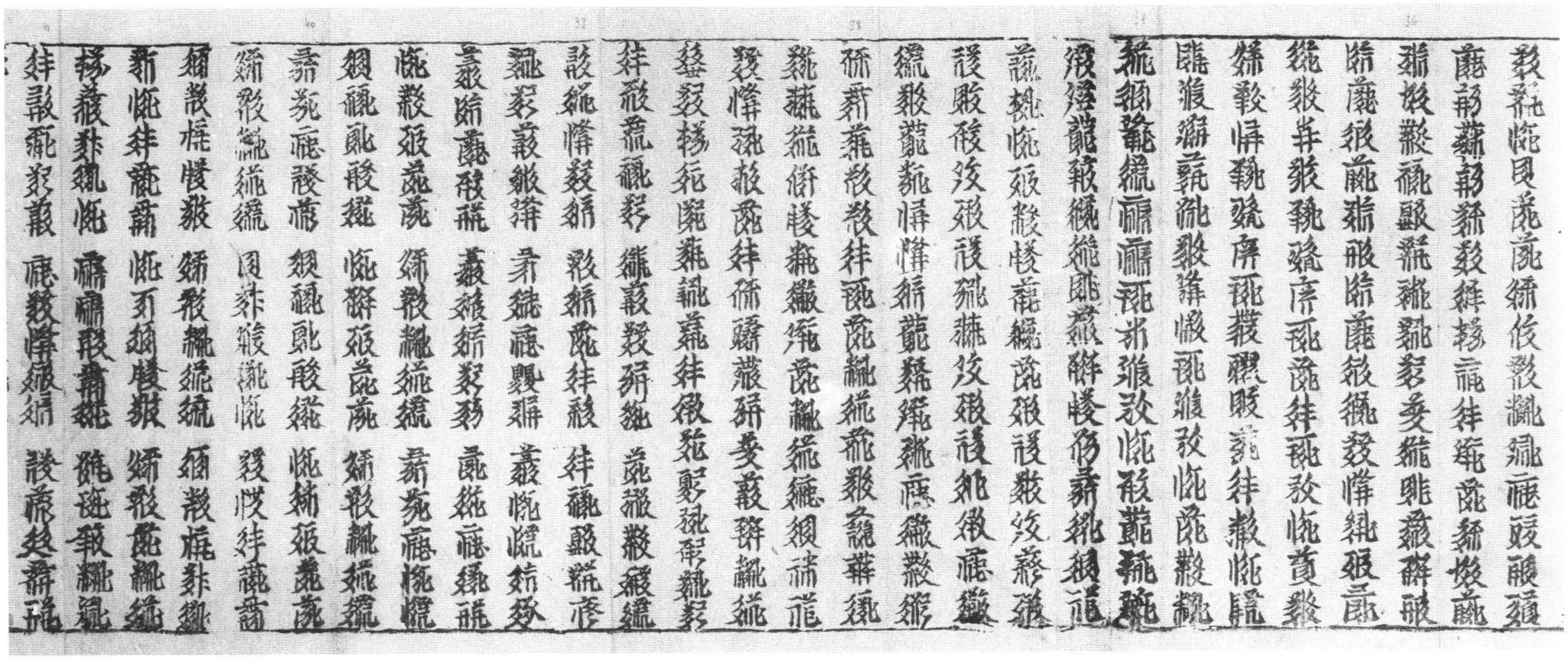

俄 Инв.No.782　妙法蓮華經卷第六　　(26–8)

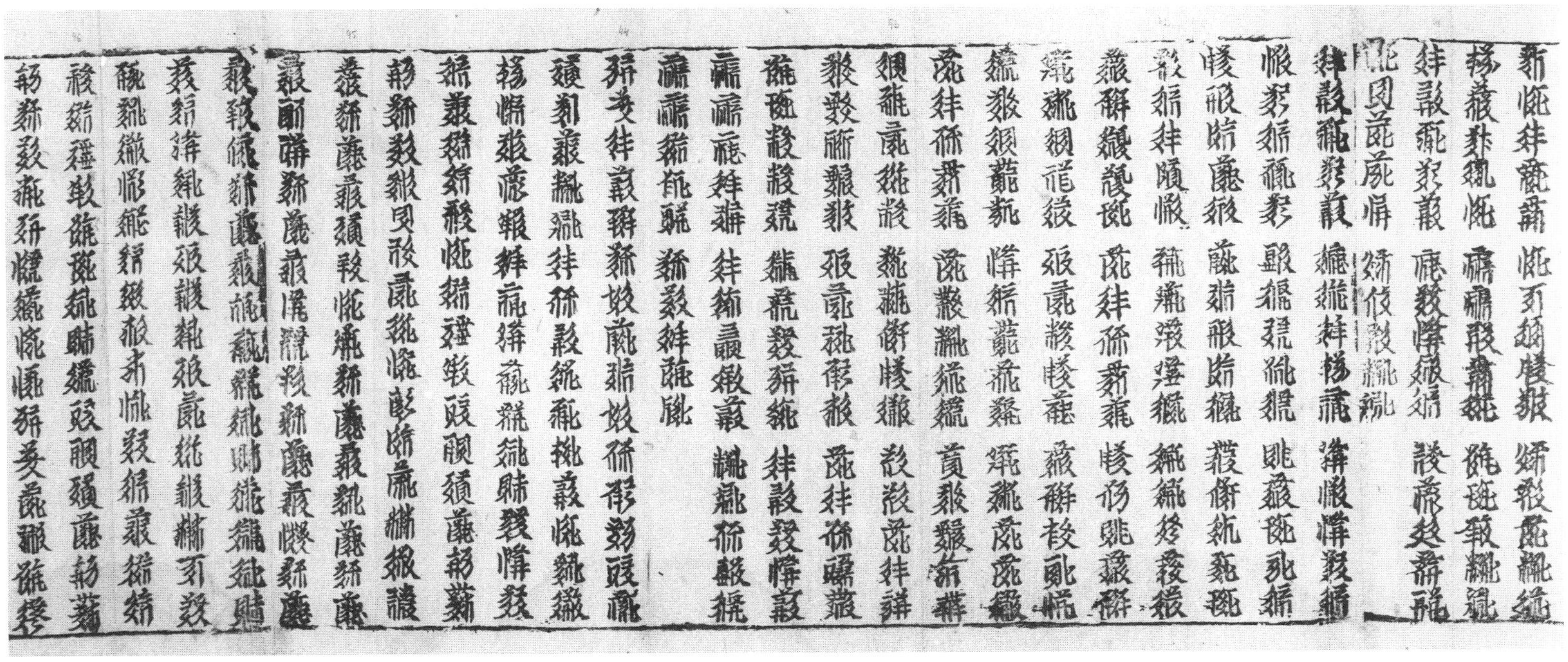

俄 Инв.No.782　妙法蓮華經卷第六　　(26–9)

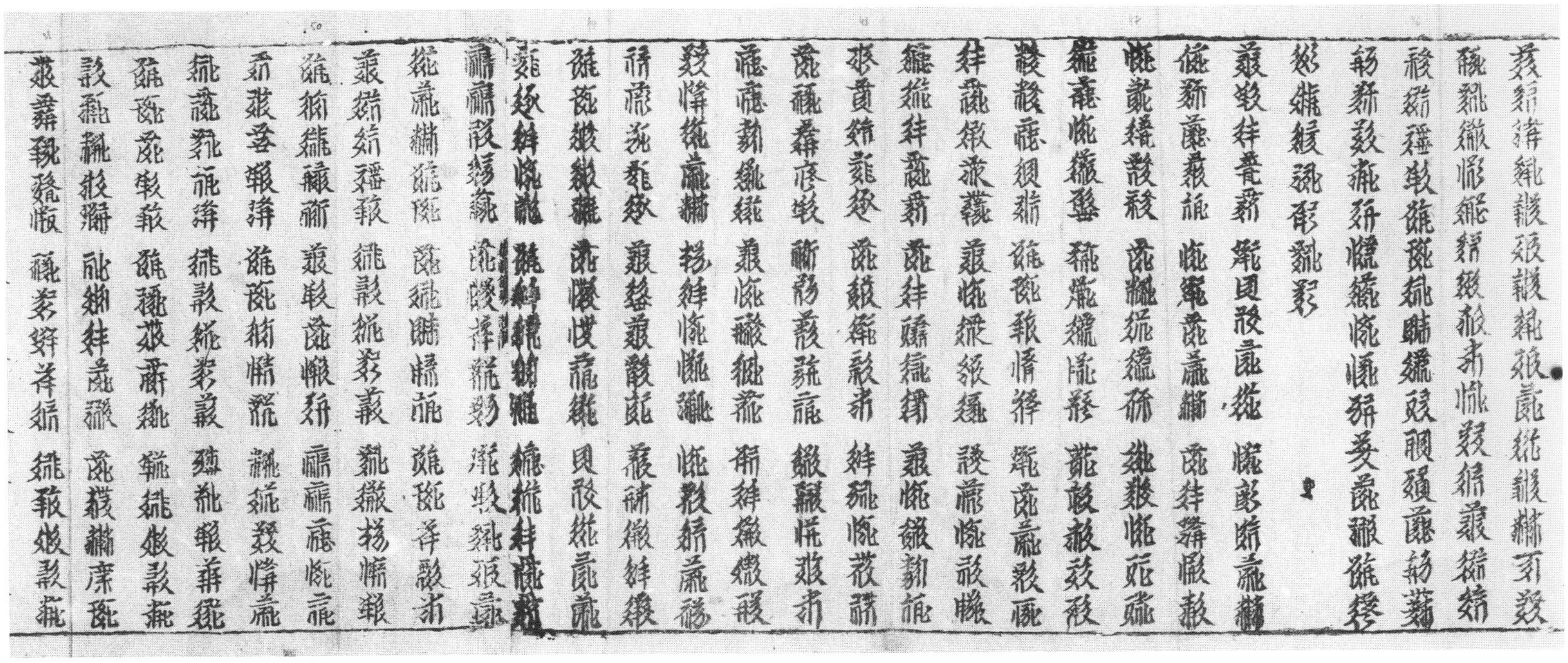

俄 Инв.No.782　妙法蓮華經卷第六　　(26–10)

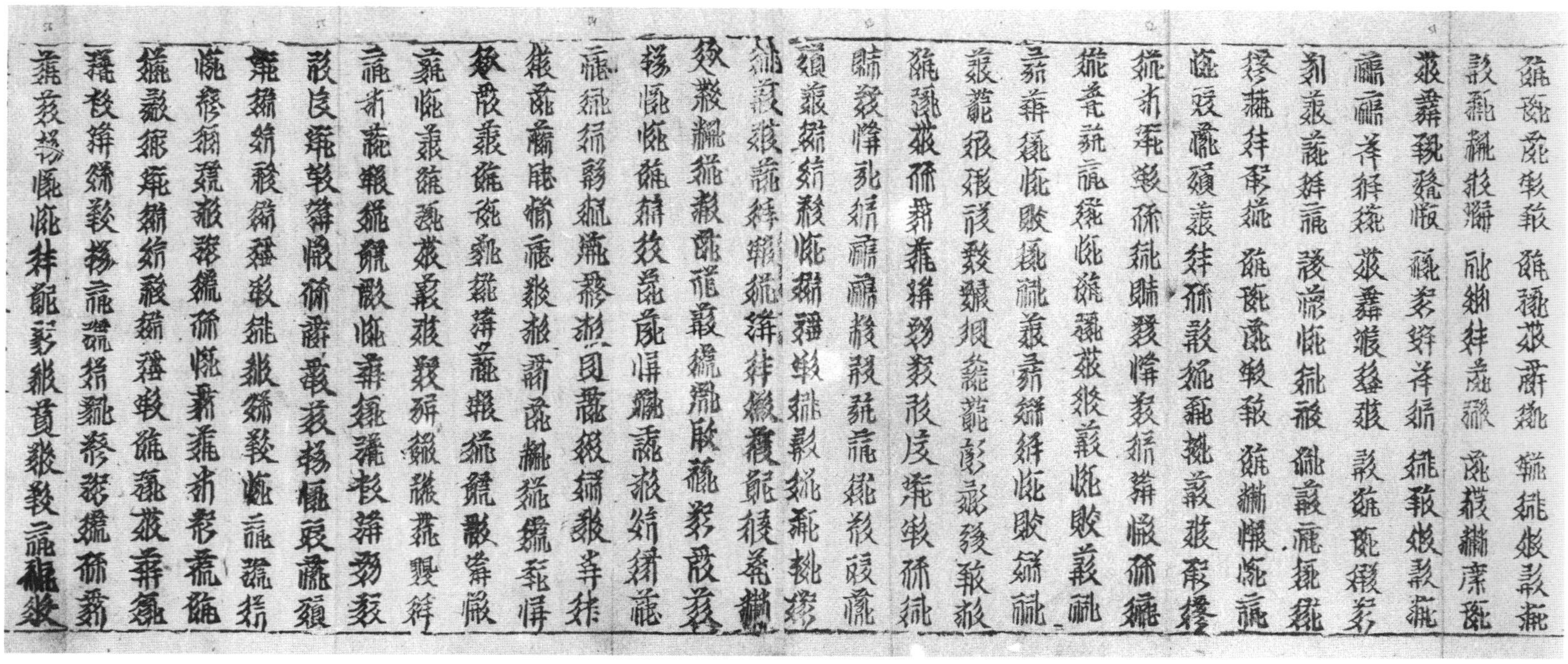

俄 Инв.No.782　妙法蓮華經卷第六　(26–11)

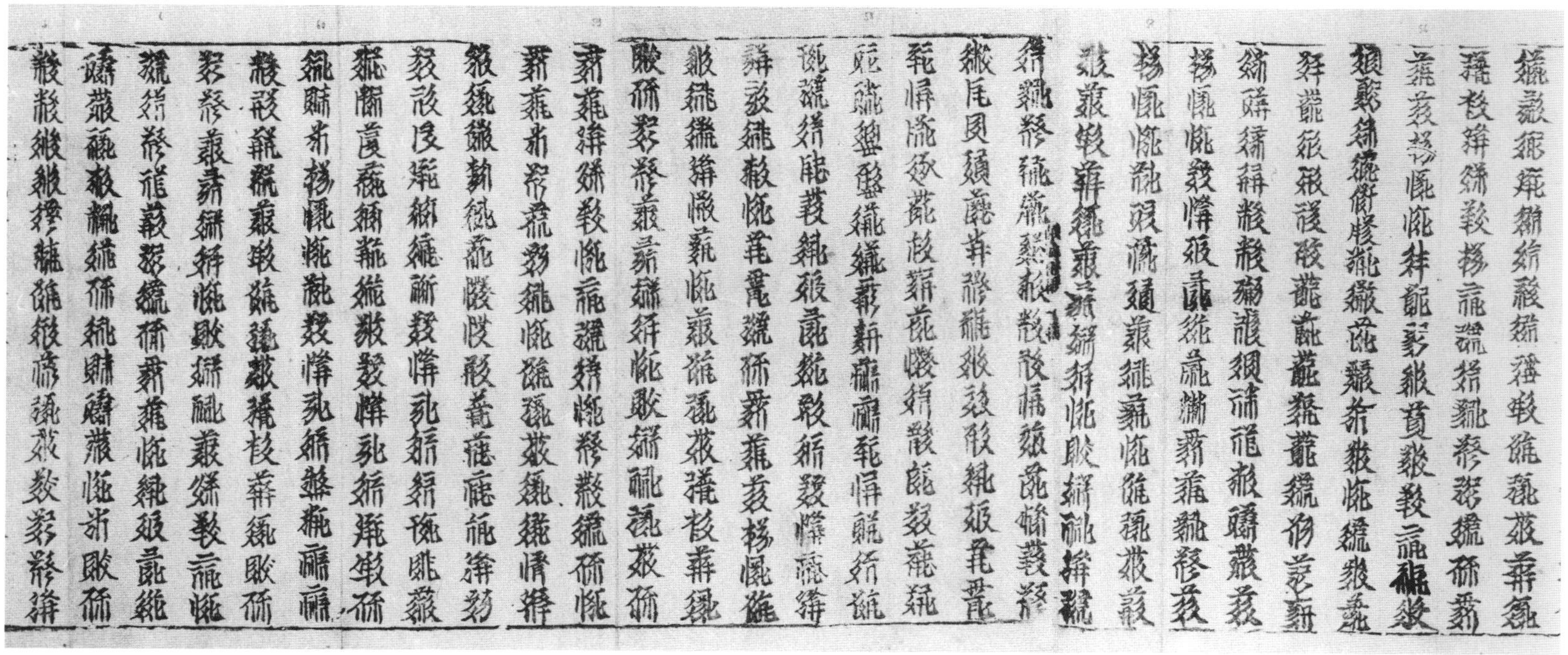

俄 Инв.No.782　妙法蓮華經卷第六　(26–12)

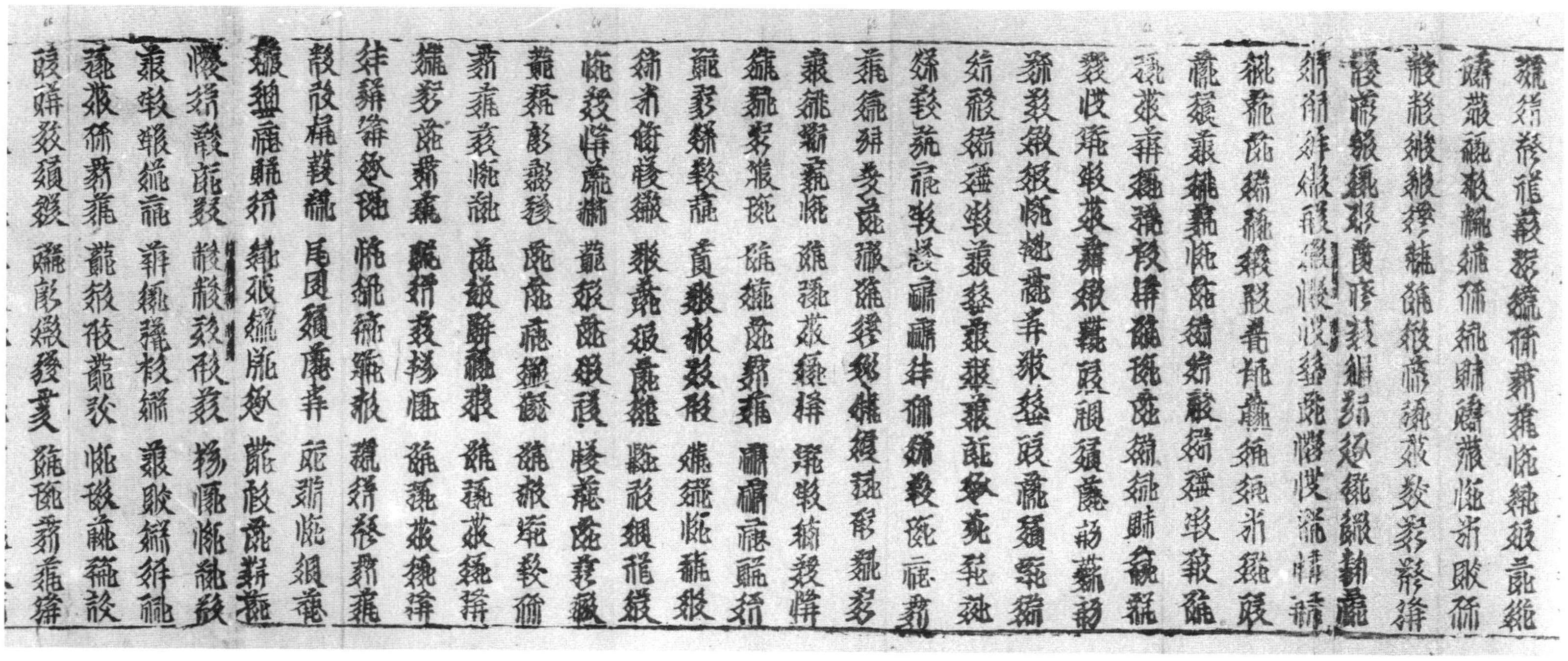

俄 Инв.No.782　妙法蓮華經卷第六　(26–13)

俄 **Инв**.No.782　妙法蓮華經卷第六　　　(26-14)

俄 **Инв**.No.782　妙法蓮華經卷第六　　　(26-15)

俄 **Инв**.No.782　妙法蓮華經卷第六　　　(26-16)

俄Инв.No.782　妙法蓮華經卷第六　　　(26-17)

俄Инв.No.782　妙法蓮華經卷第六　　　(26-18)

俄Инв.No.782　妙法蓮華經卷第六　　　(26-19)

俄 Инв.No.782　妙法蓮華經卷第六　　　(26-20)

俄 Инв.No.782　妙法蓮華經卷第六　　　(26-21)

俄 Инв.No.782　妙法蓮華經卷第六　　　(26-22)

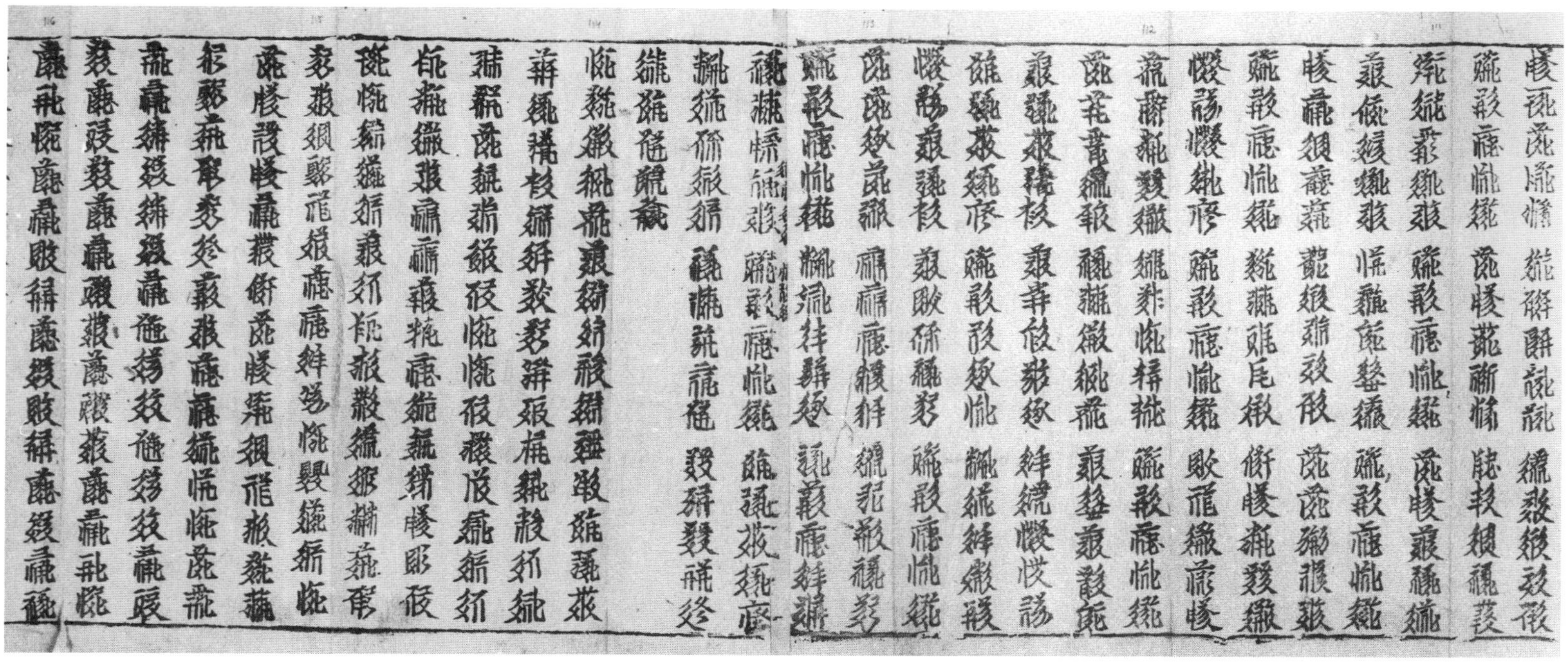

俄 Инв.No.782　妙法蓮華經卷第六　(26–23)

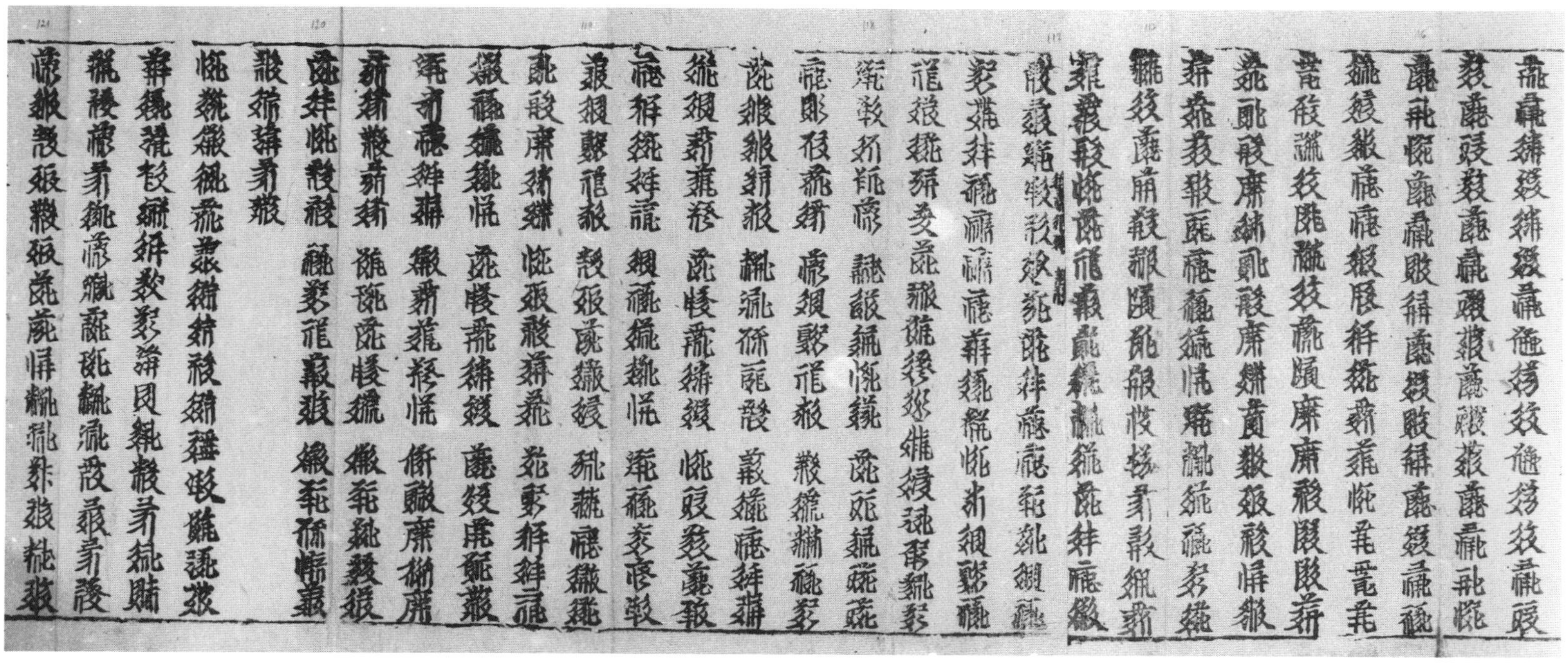

俄 Инв.No.782　妙法蓮華經卷第六　(26–24)

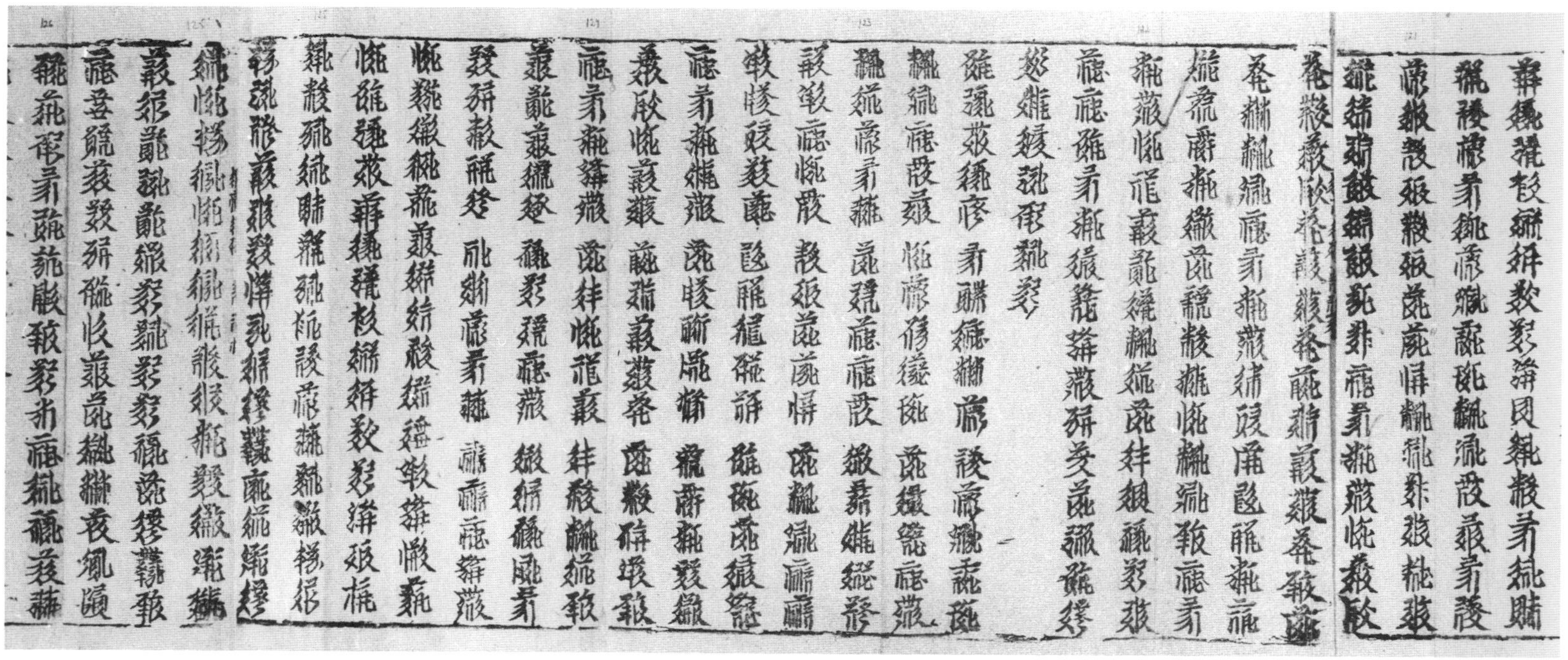

俄 Инв.No.782　妙法蓮華經卷第六　(26–25)

俄 Инв.No.782　妙法蓮華經卷第六　　　(26-26)

俄 Инв.No.7231　妙法蓮華經卷第六

俄 Инв.No.6452a　妙法蓮華經卷第六　　　(6-1)

俄 Инв.No.6452a　妙法蓮華經卷第六　　　　(6-2)

俄 Инв.No.6452a　妙法蓮華經卷第六　　　　(6-3)

俄 Инв.No.6452a　妙法蓮華經卷第六　　　　(6-4)

俄 **И**нв.No.6452a　妙法蓮華經卷第六　　(6-5)

俄 **И**нв.No.6452a　妙法蓮華經卷第六　　(6-6)

俄 **И**нв.No.6452б　妙法蓮華經卷第七　　(23-1)

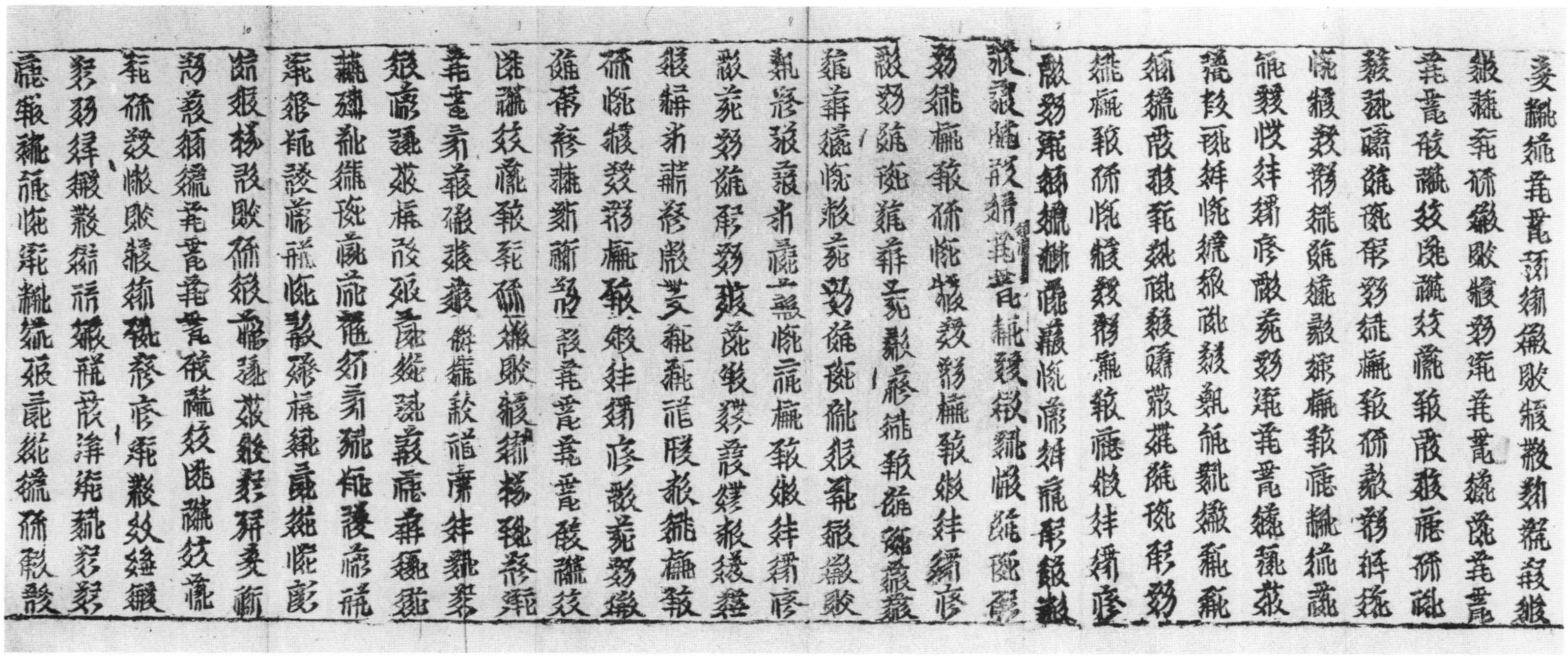

俄 Инв.No.6452б　妙法蓮華經卷第七　　(23-2)

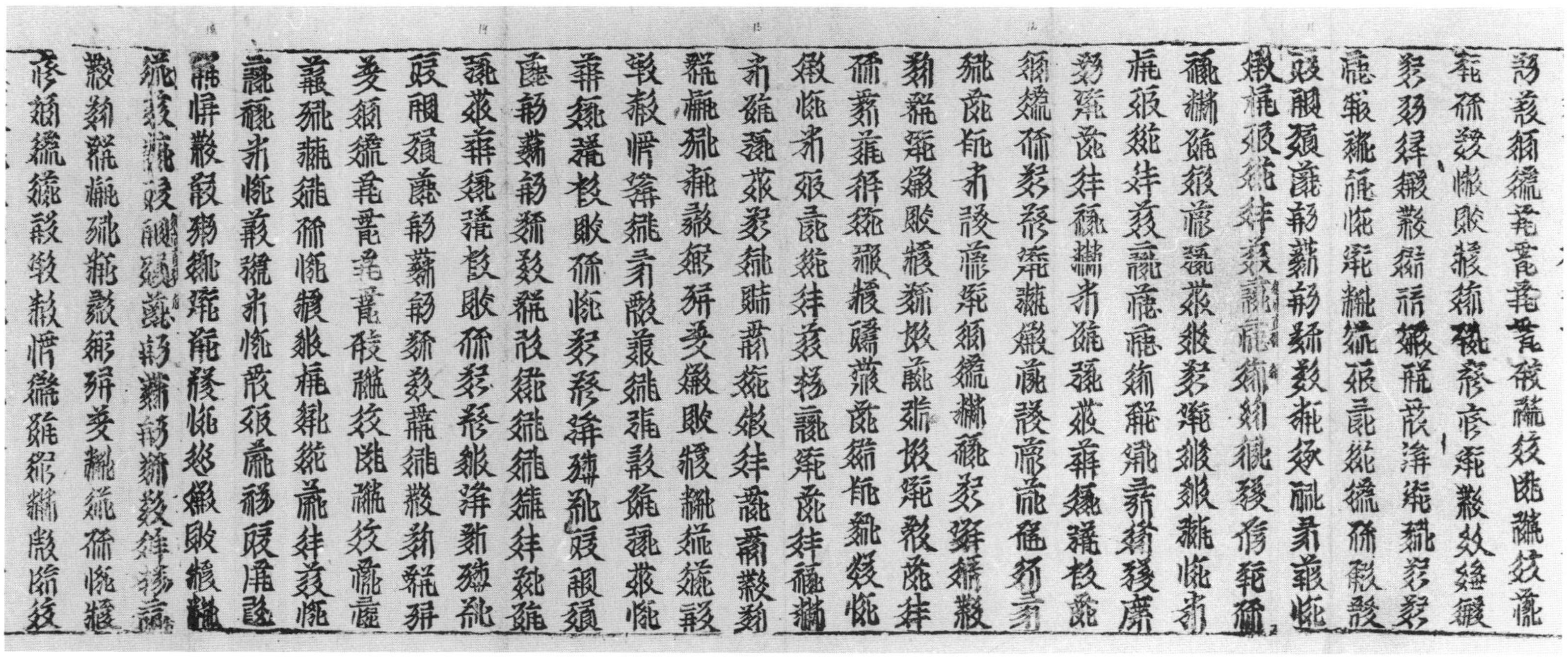

俄 Инв.No.6452б　妙法蓮華經卷第七　　(23-3)

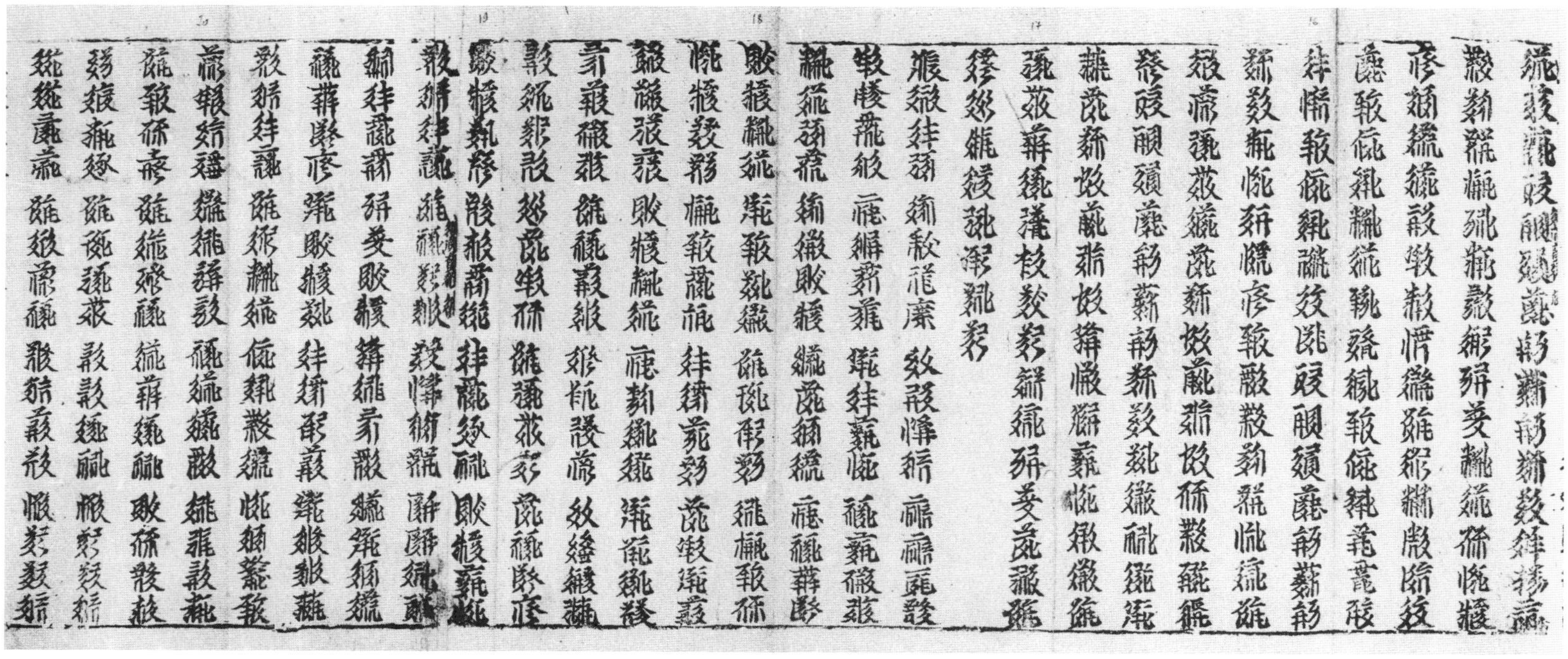

俄 Инв.No.6452б　妙法蓮華經卷第七　　(23-4)

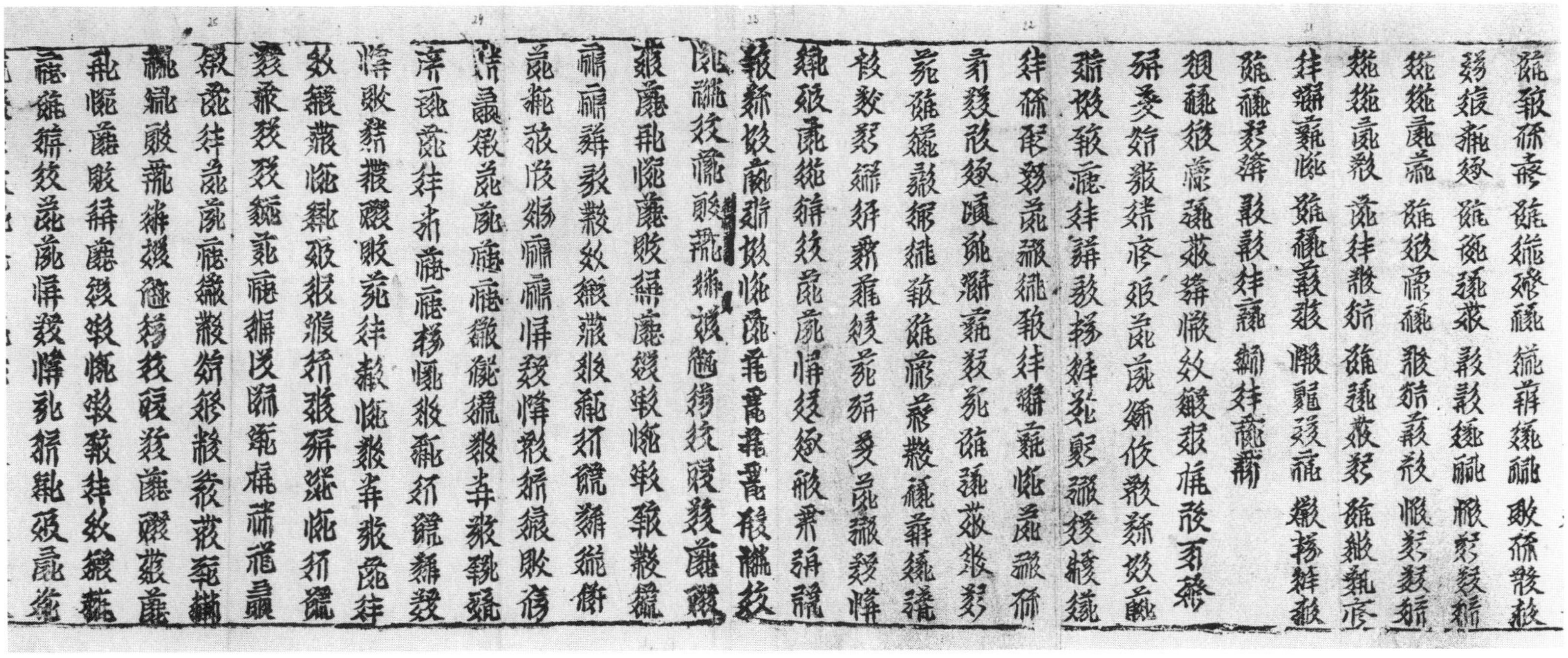

俄 Инв.No.6452б 妙法蓮華經卷第七 (23-5)

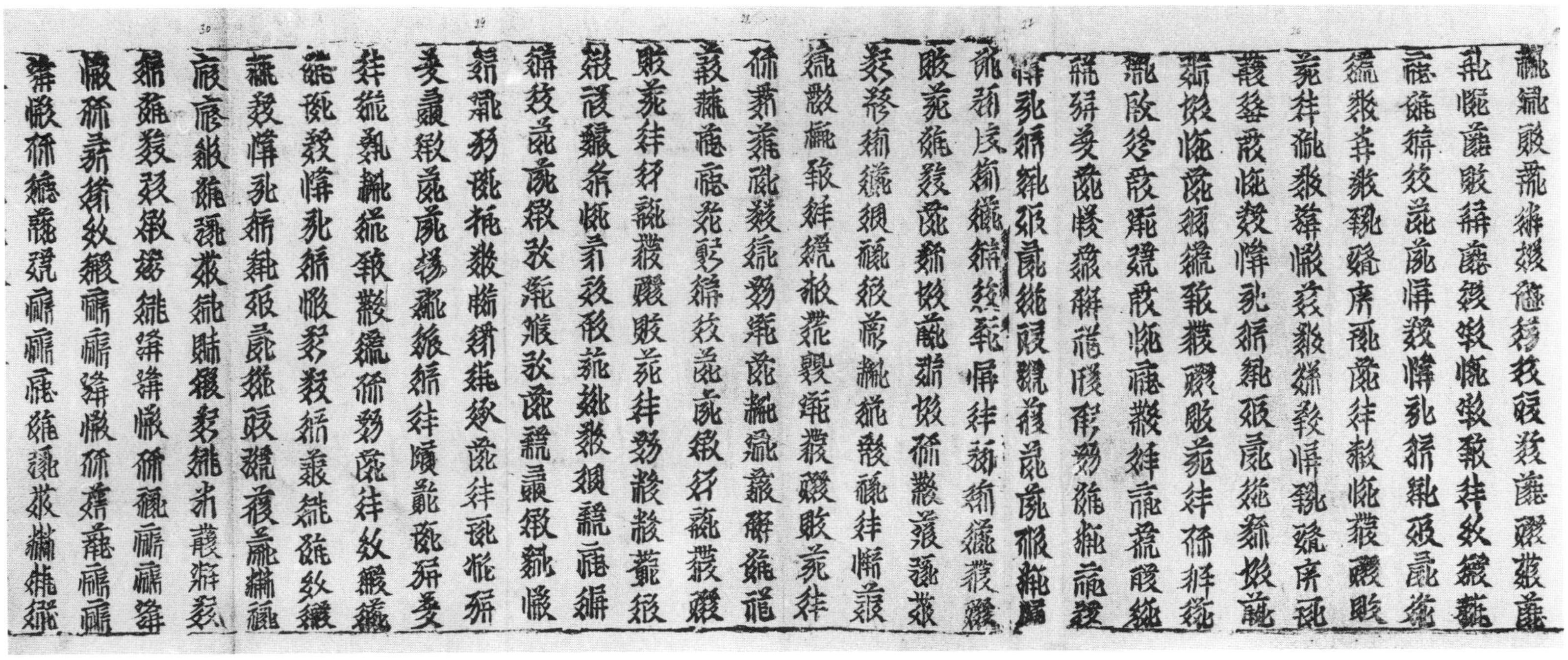

俄 Инв.No.6452б 妙法蓮華經卷第七 (23-6)

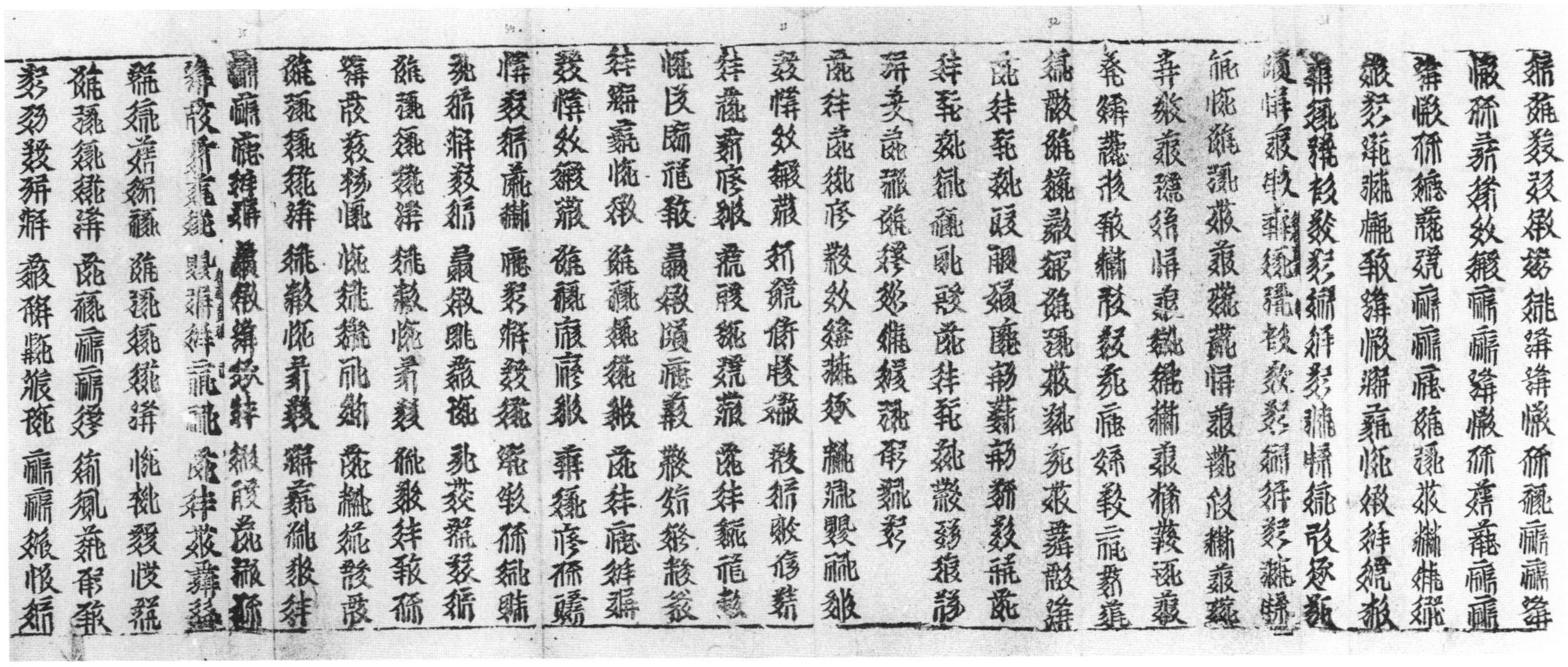

俄 Инв.No.6452б 妙法蓮華經卷第七 (23-7)

俄 Инв.No.6452б 妙法蓮華經卷第七 (23-8)

俄 Инв.No.6452б 妙法蓮華經卷第七 (23-9)

俄 Инв.No.6452б 妙法蓮華經卷第七 (23-10)

俄 **Инв**.No.64526　妙法蓮華經卷第七　　（23-11）

俄 **Инв**.No.64526　妙法蓮華經卷第七　　（23-12）

俄 **Инв**.No.64526　妙法蓮華經卷第七　　（23-13）

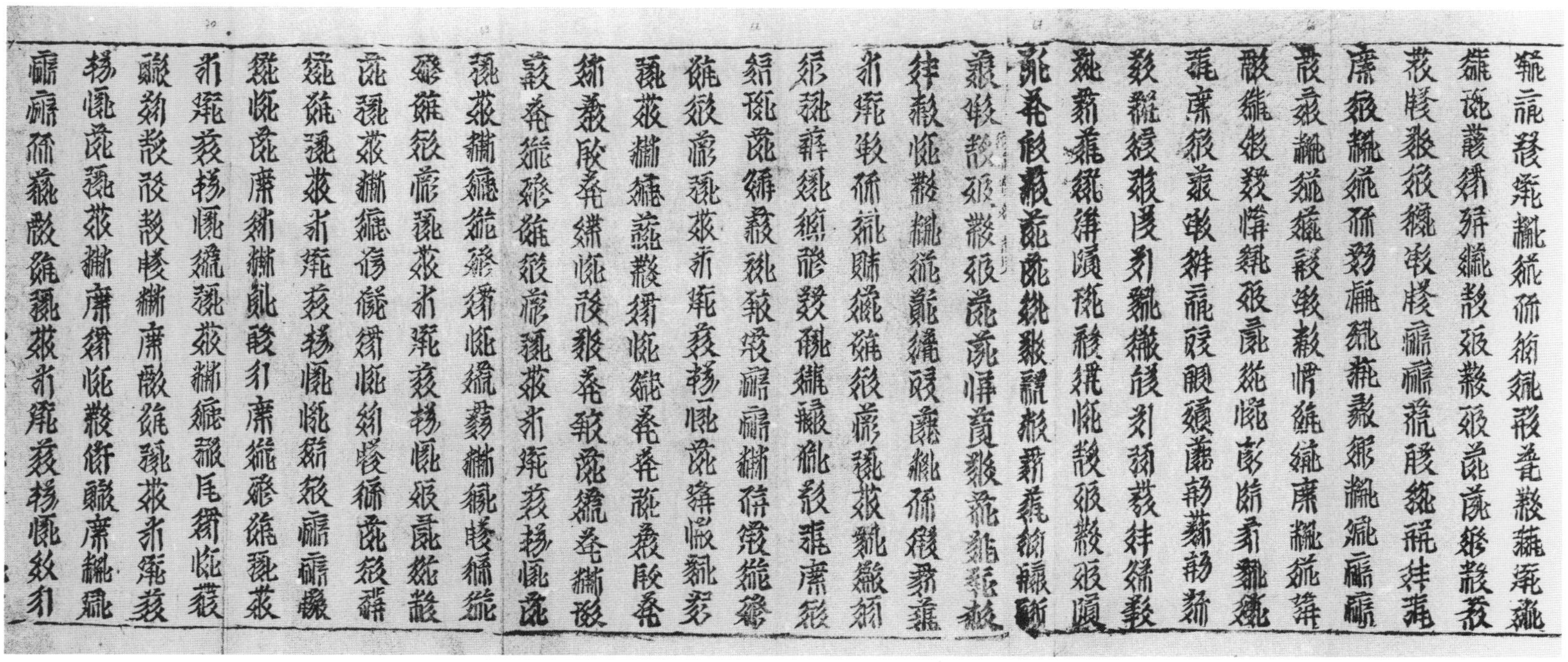

俄 Инв.No.6452б　妙法蓮華經卷第七　(23-14)

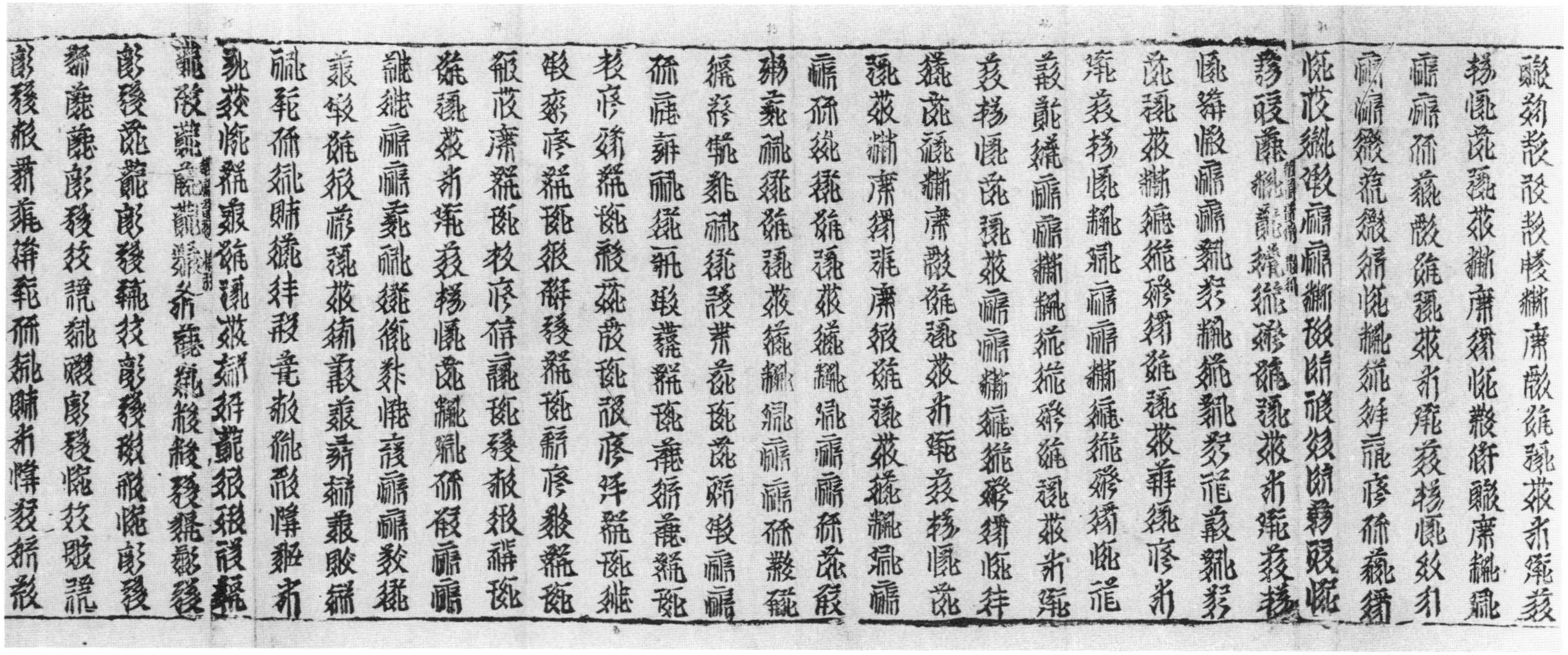

俄 Инв.No.6452б　妙法蓮華經卷第七　(23-15)

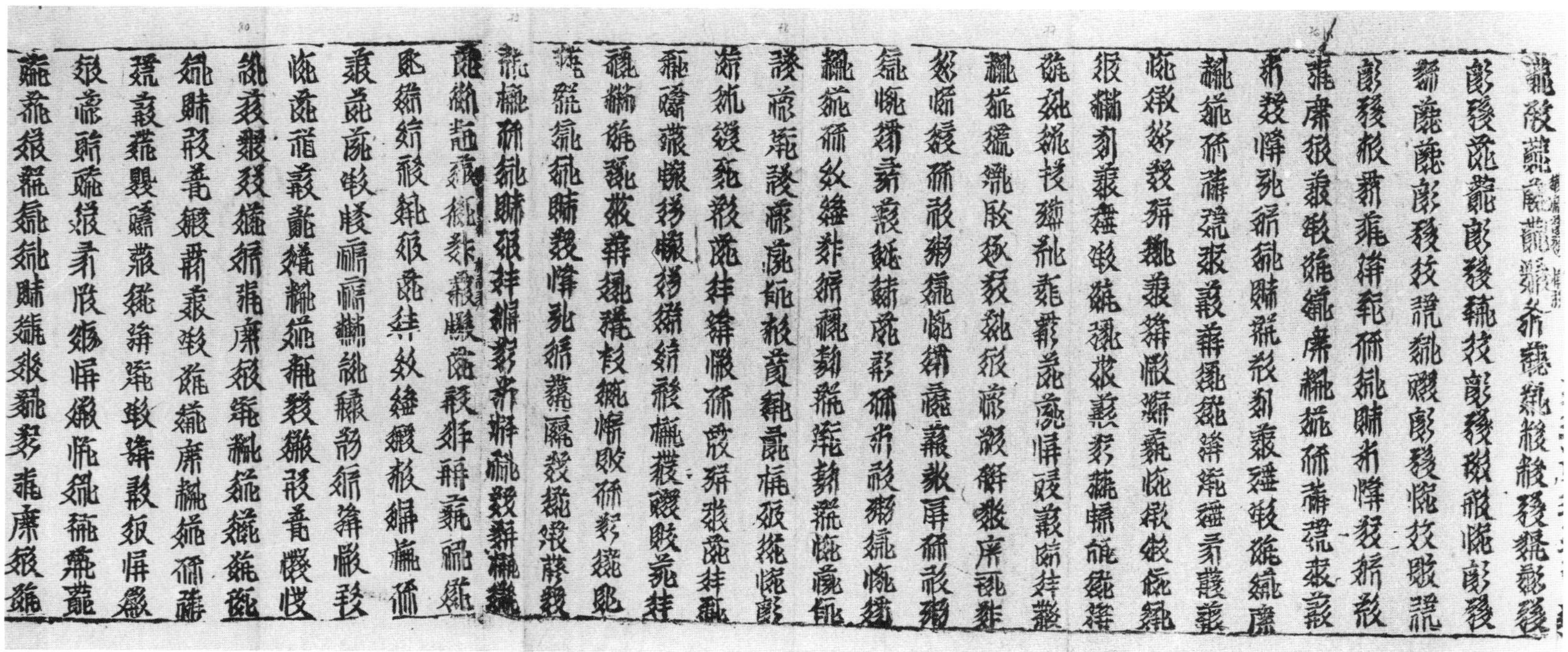

俄 Инв.No.6452б　妙法蓮華經卷第七　(23-16)

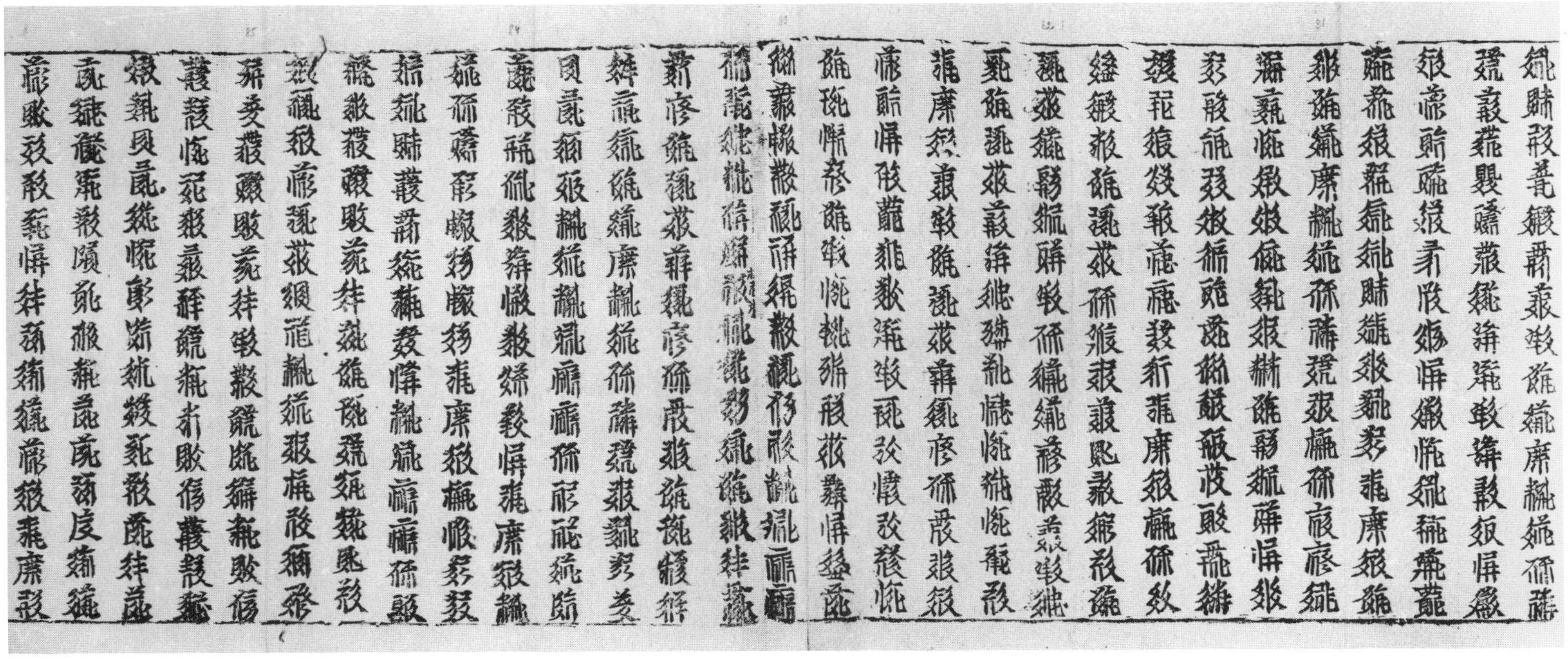

俄 Инв.No.6452б　妙法蓮華經卷第七　(23–17)

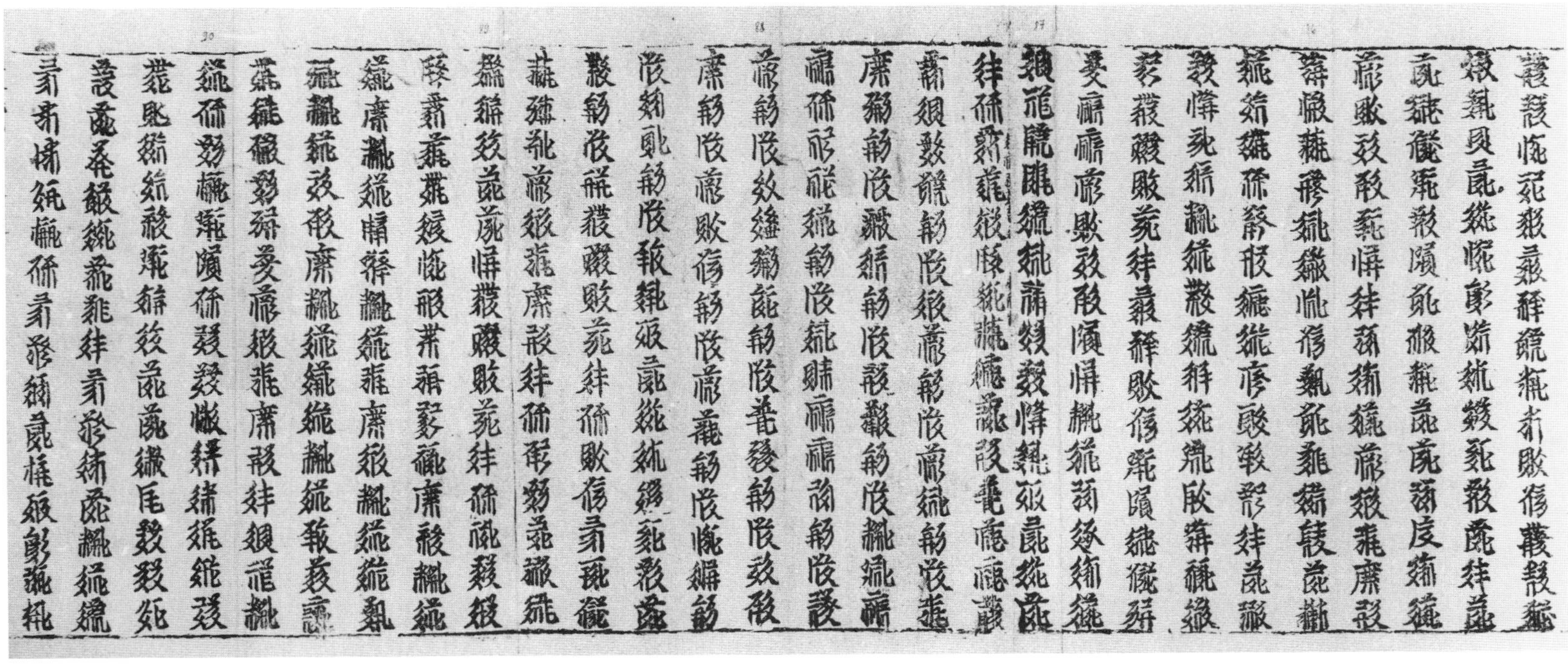

俄 Инв.No.6452б　妙法蓮華經卷第七　(23–18)

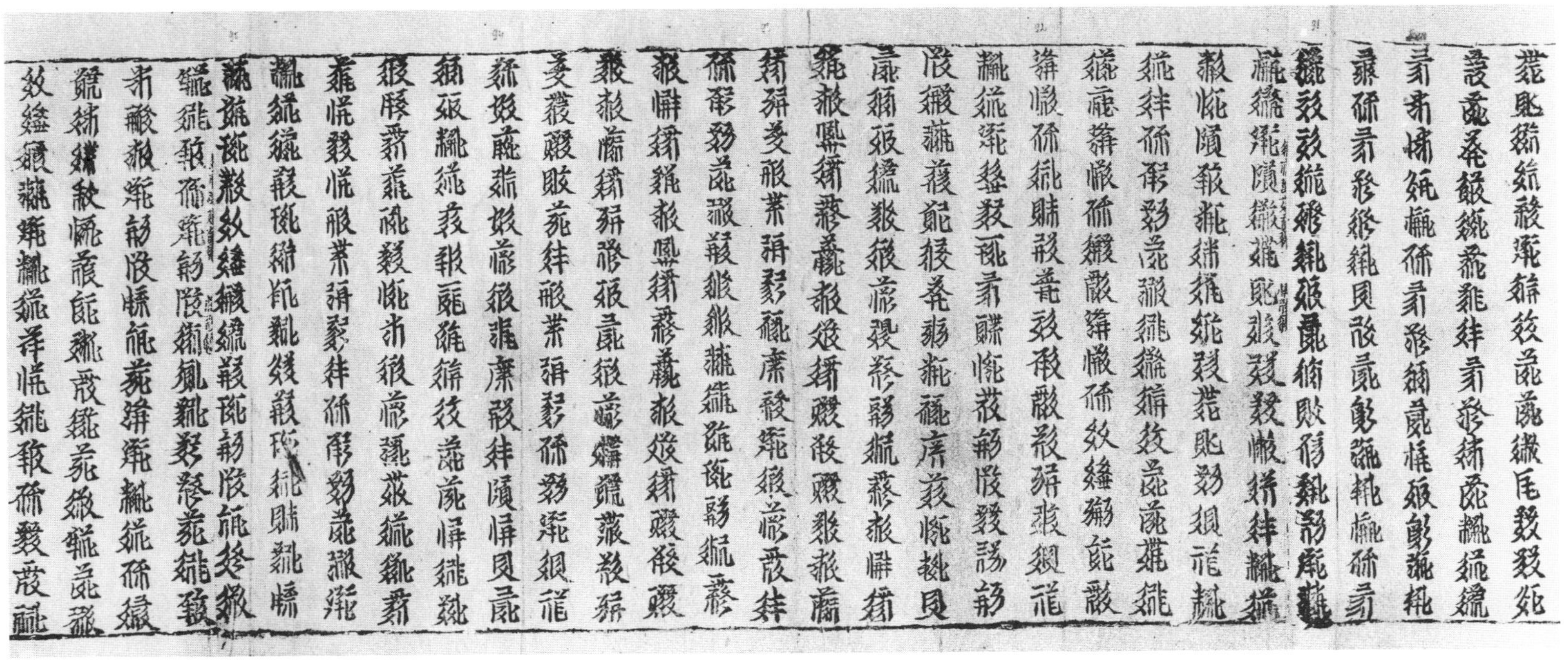

俄 Инв.No.6452б　妙法蓮華經卷第七　(23–19)

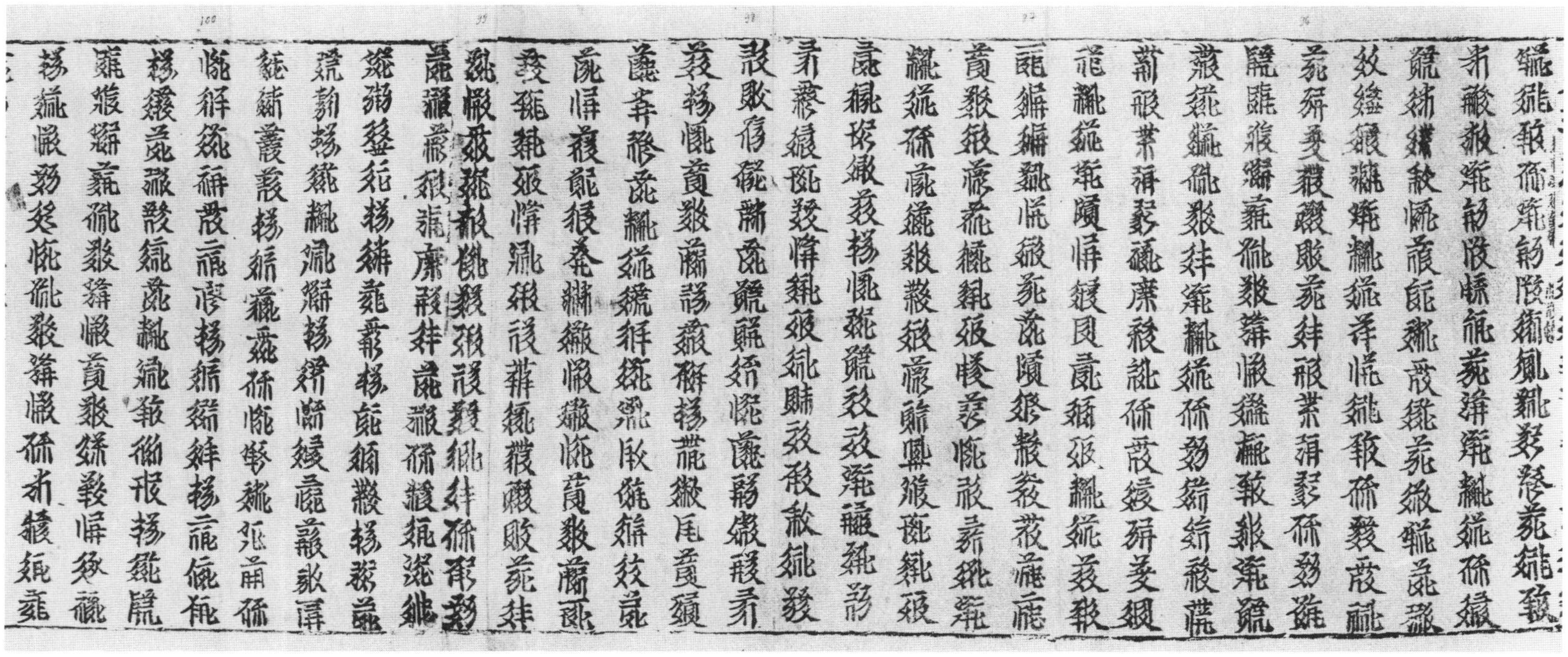

俄 Инв.No.6452б　妙法蓮華經卷第七　　(23-20)

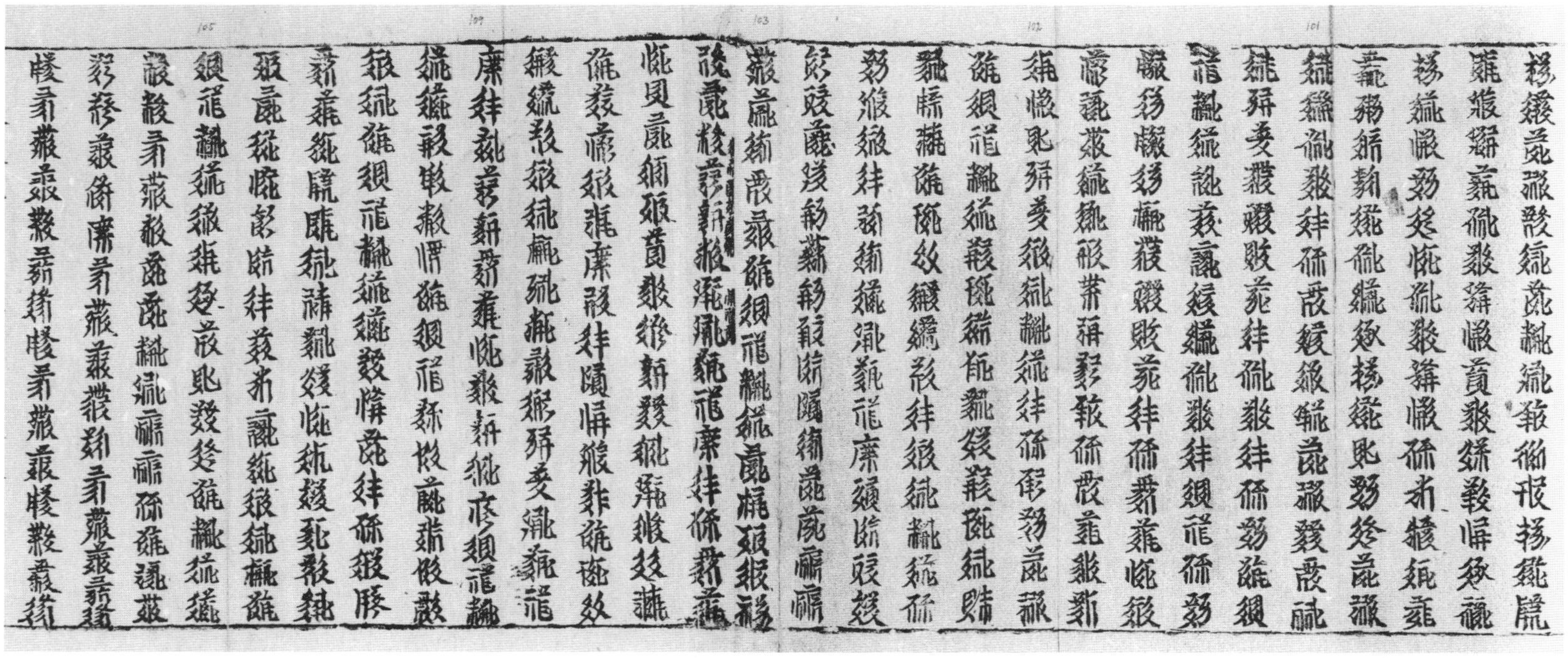

俄 Инв.No.6452б　妙法蓮華經卷第七　　(23-21)

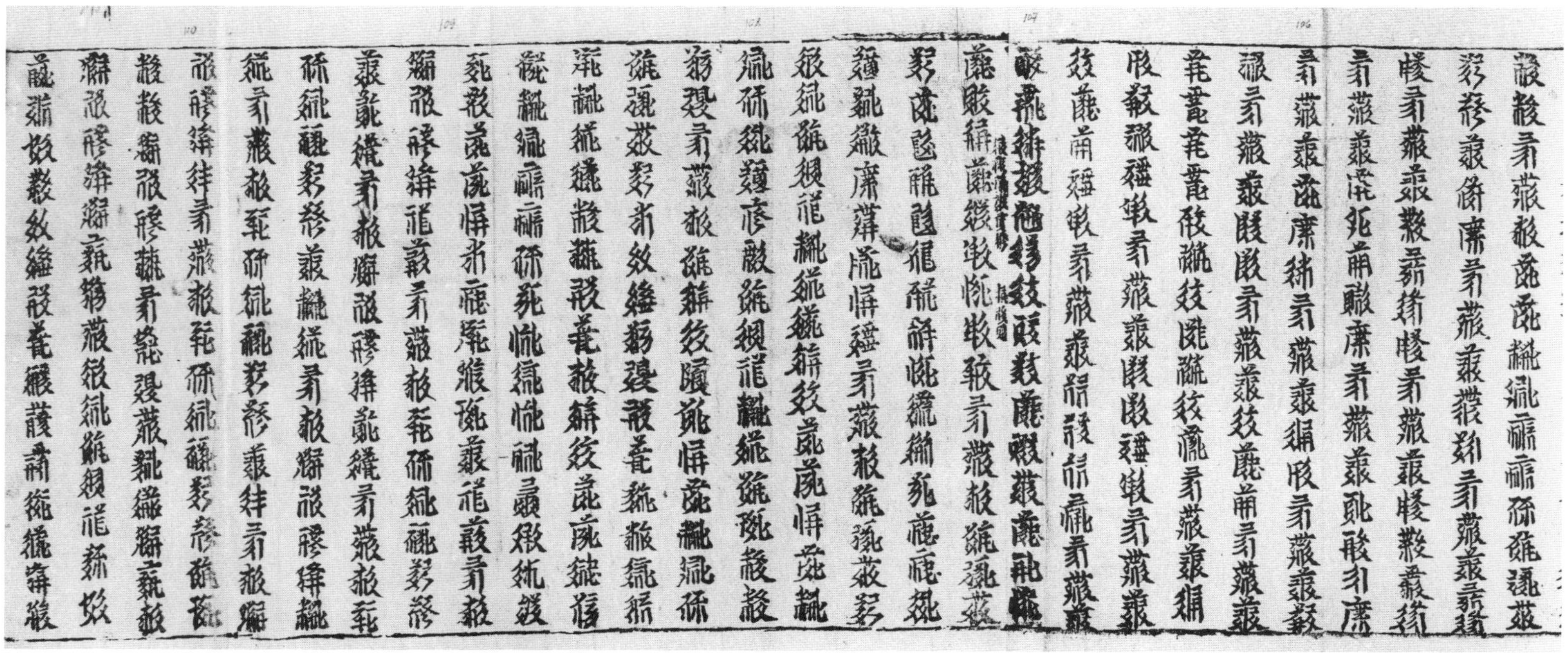

俄 Инв.No.6452б　妙法蓮華經卷第七　　(23-22)

俄 Инв.No.6452б　妙法蓮華經卷第七　　　(23-23)

俄 Инв.No.7350a　妙法蓮華經卷第七

俄 Инв.No.2436　妙法蓮華經卷第七

俄 **Инв**.No.3901　妙法蓮華經卷第八

俄 **Инв**.No.7178　妙法蓮華經卷第八

俄 **Инв**.No.6452　妙法蓮華經卷第八　　　(18−1)

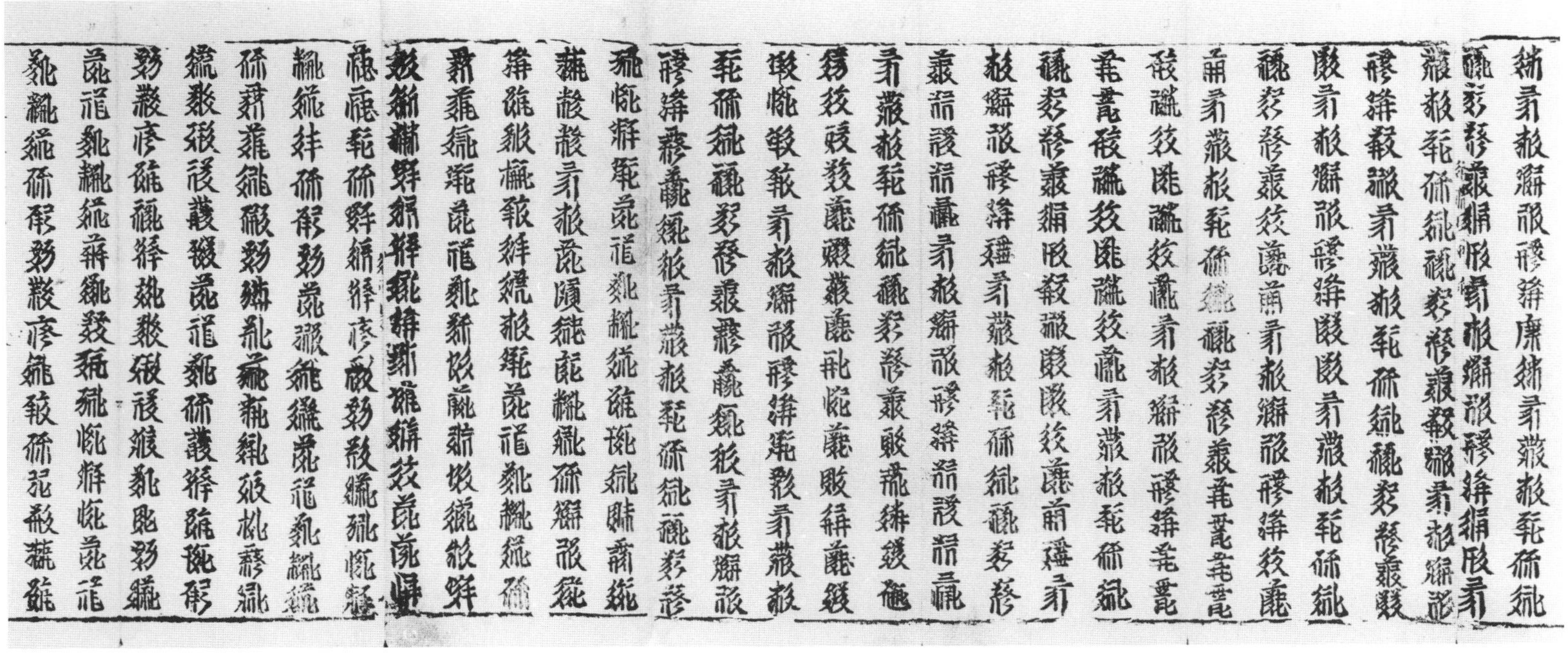

俄 Инв.No.6452 妙法蓮華經卷第八 (18–2)

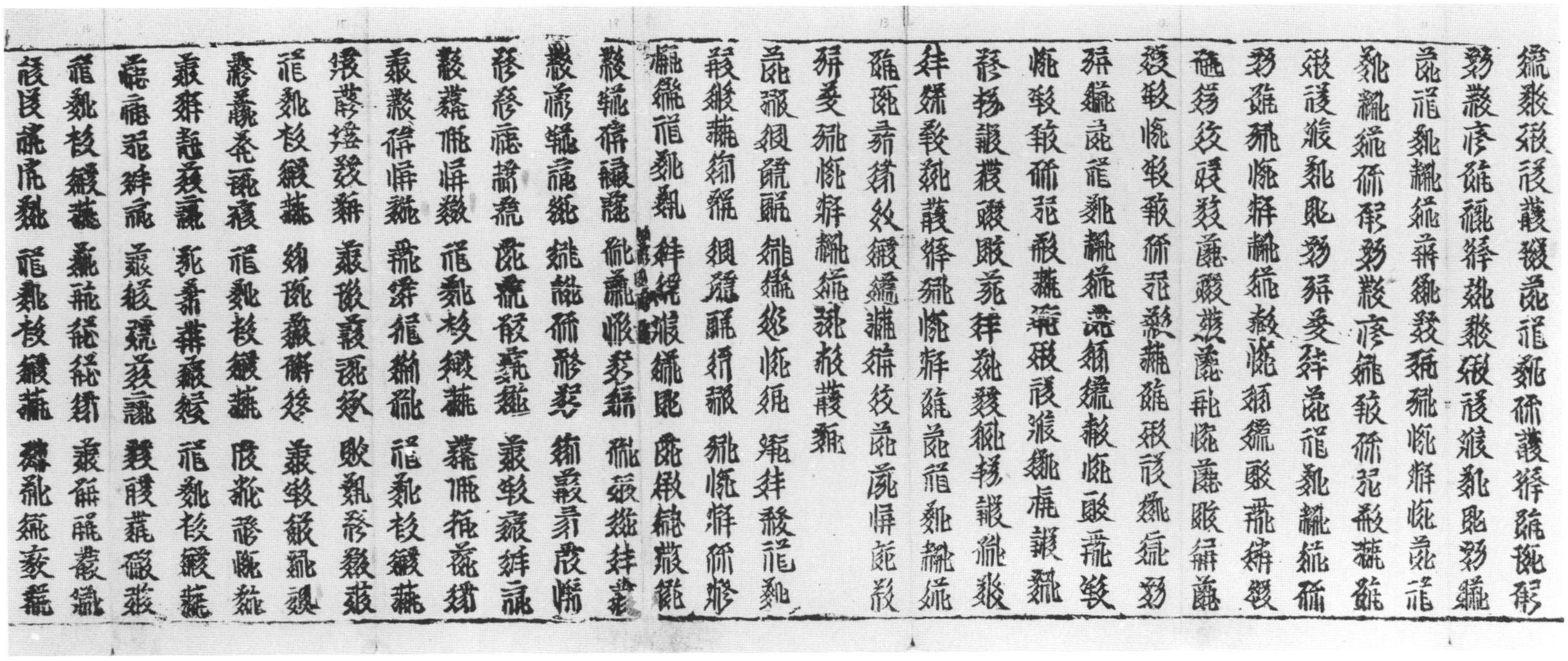

俄 Инв.No.6452 妙法蓮華經卷第八 (18–3)

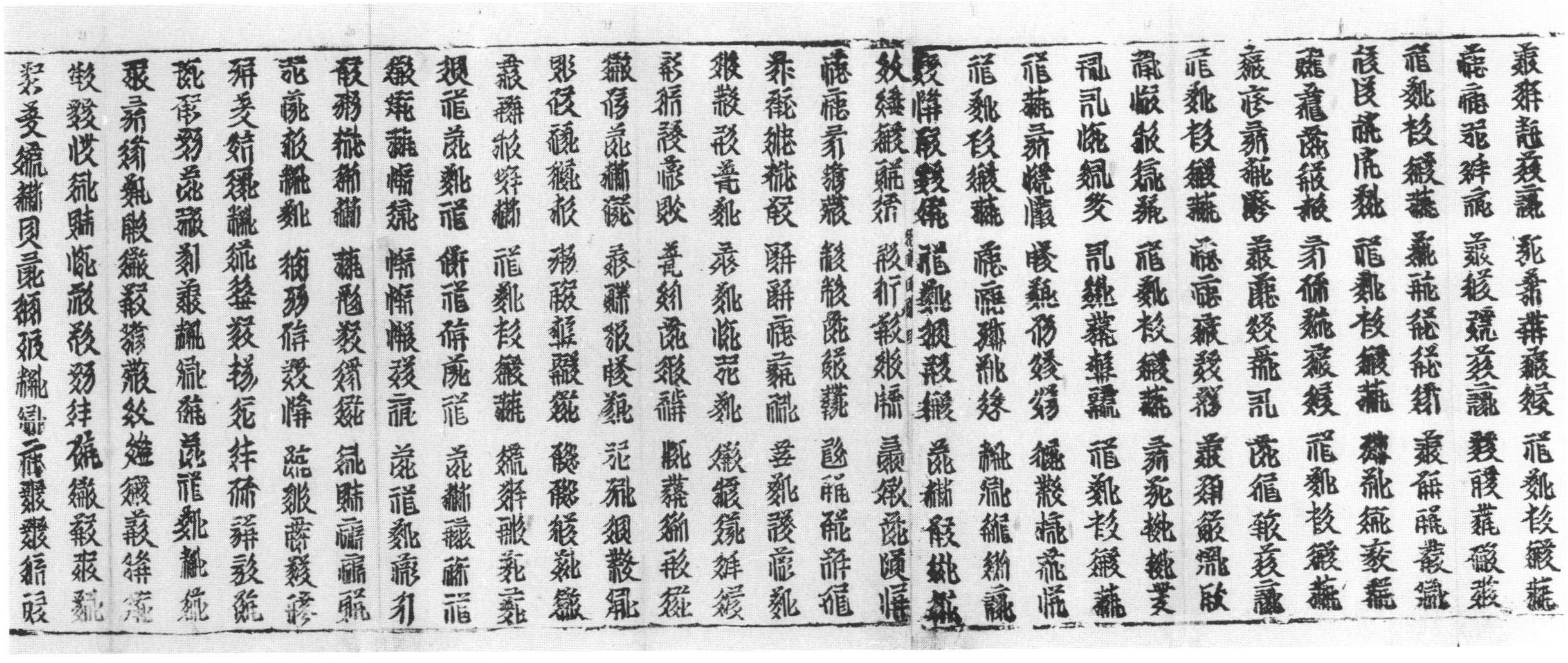

俄 Инв.No.6452 妙法蓮華經卷第八 (18–4)

俄 Инв.No.6452 妙法蓮華經卷第八 (18-5)

俄 Инв.No.6452 妙法蓮華經卷第八 (18-6)

俄 Инв.No.6452 妙法蓮華經卷第八 (18-7)

俄 Инв.No.6452　妙法蓮華經卷第八　　　(18-8)

俄 Инв.No.6452　妙法蓮華經卷第八　　　(18-9)

俄 Инв.No.6452　妙法蓮華經卷第八　　　(18-10)

俄 Инв.No.6452 妙法蓮華經卷第八 (18-11)

俄 Инв.No.6452 妙法蓮華經卷第八 (18-12)

俄 Инв.No.6452 妙法蓮華經卷第八 (18-13)

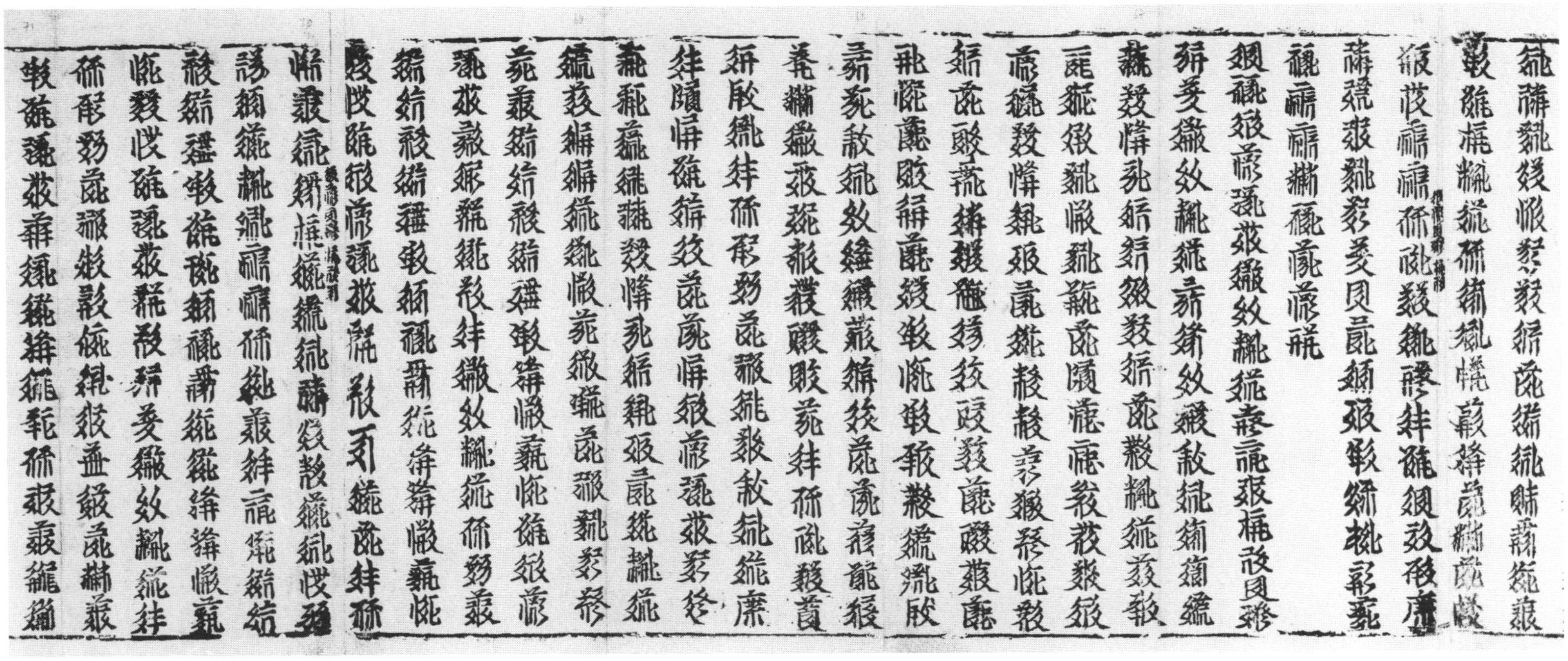

俄 Инв.No.6452　妙法蓮華經卷第八　(18–14)

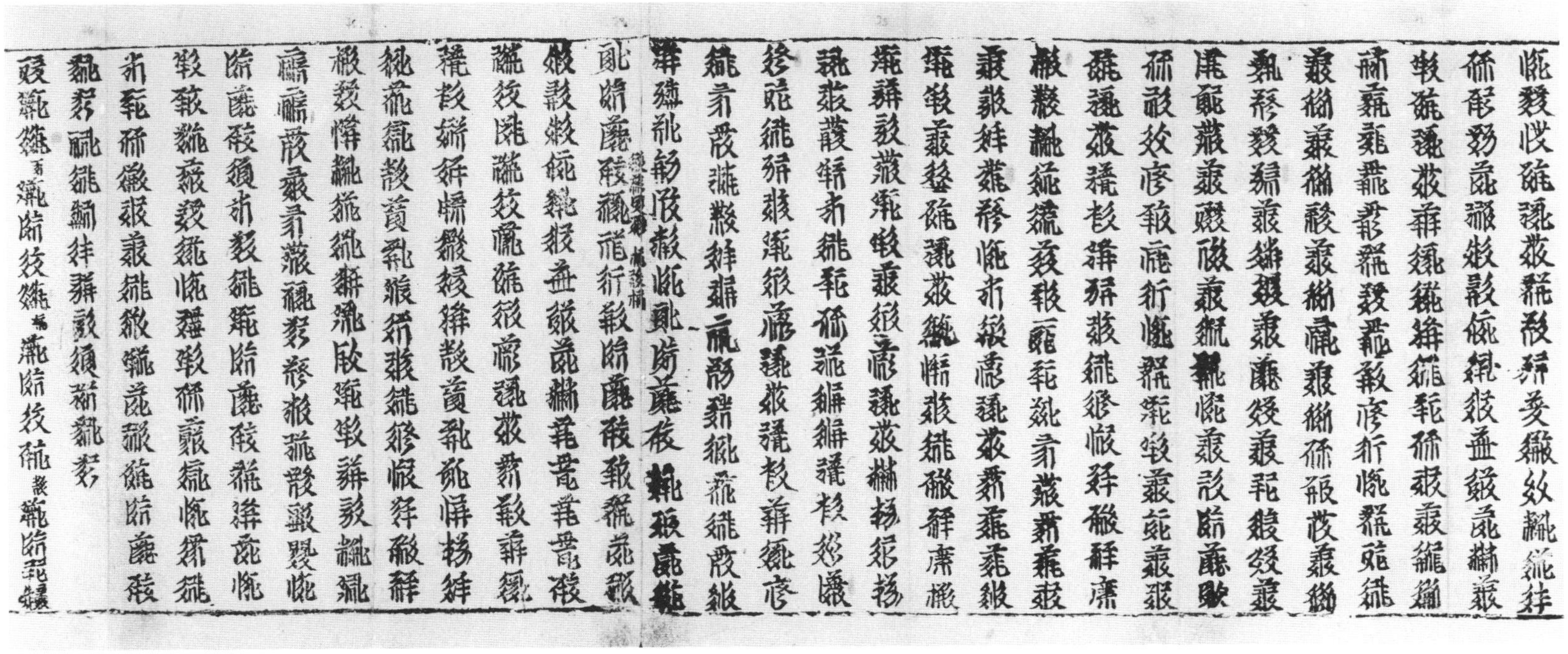

俄 Инв.No.6452　妙法蓮華經卷第八　(18–15)

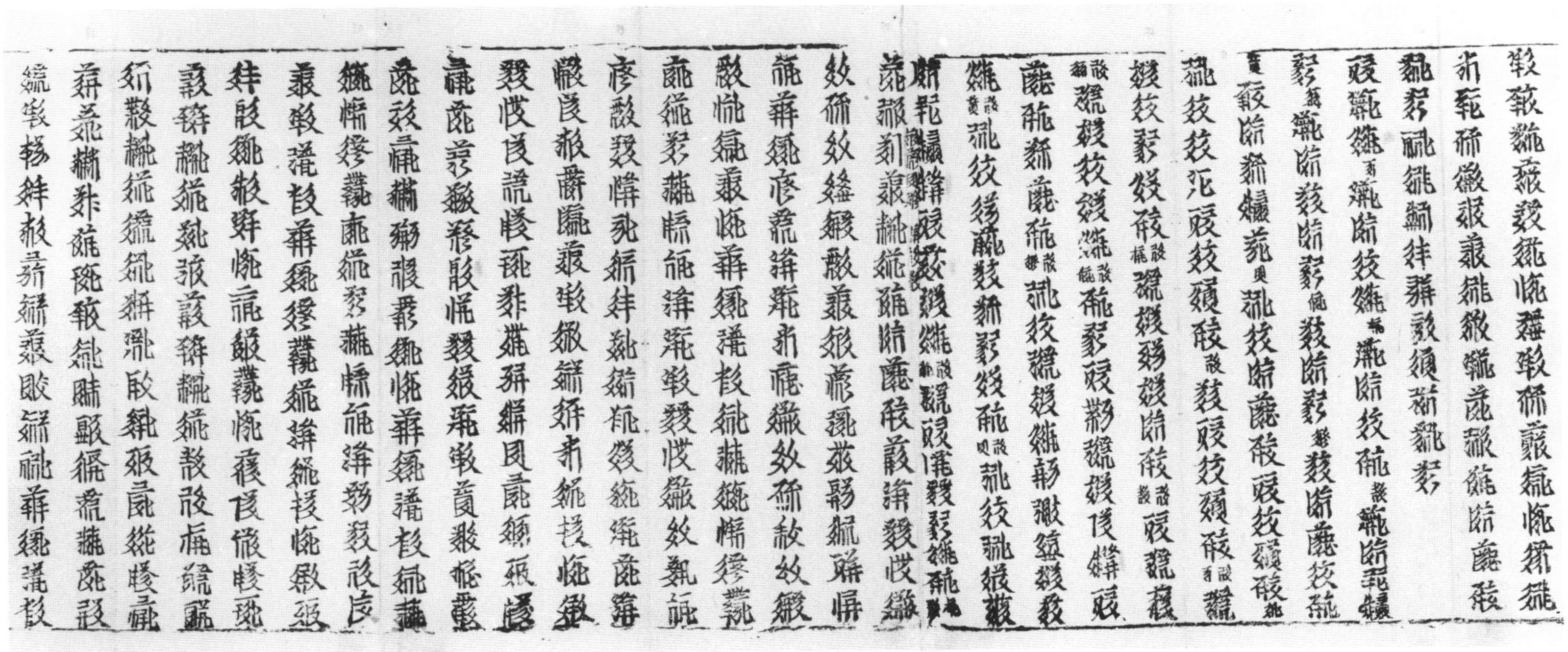

俄 Инв.No.6452　妙法蓮華經卷第八　(18–16)

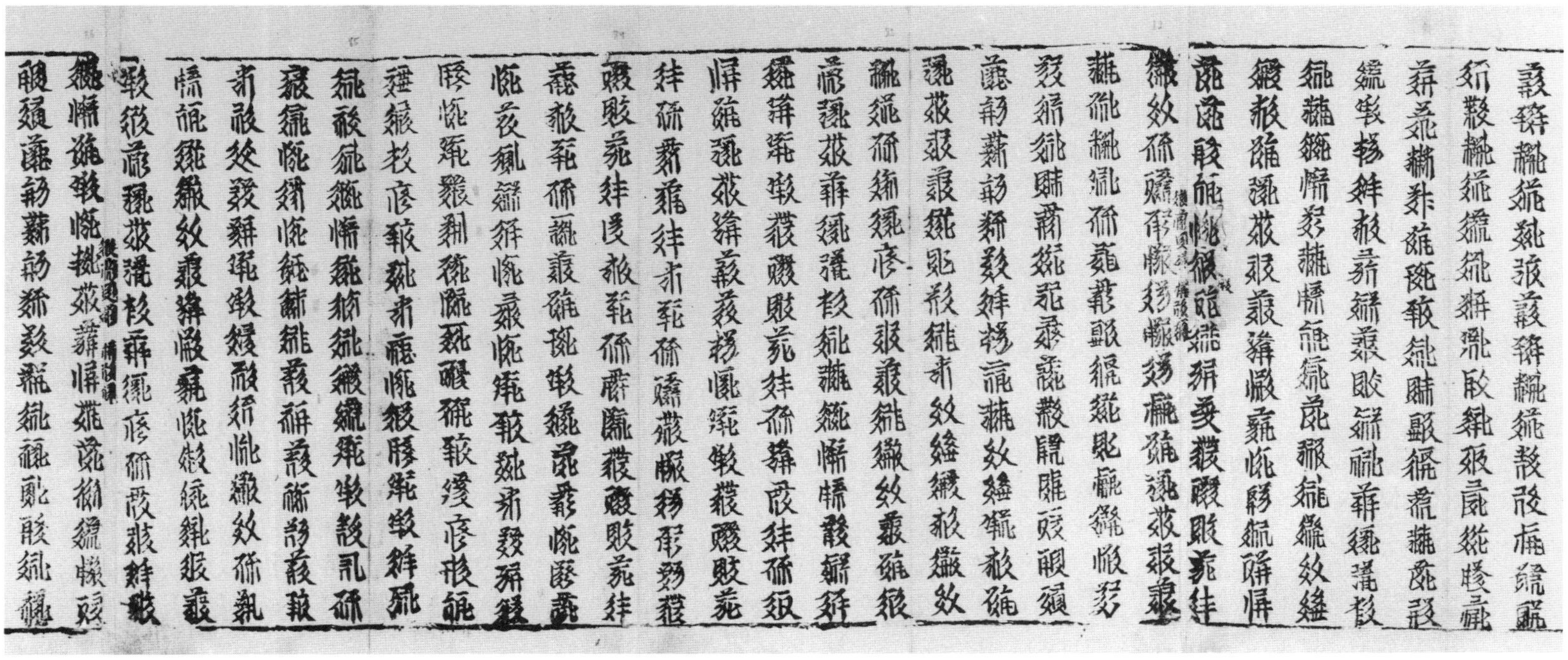

俄 Инв.No.6452　妙法蓮華經卷第八　(18–17)

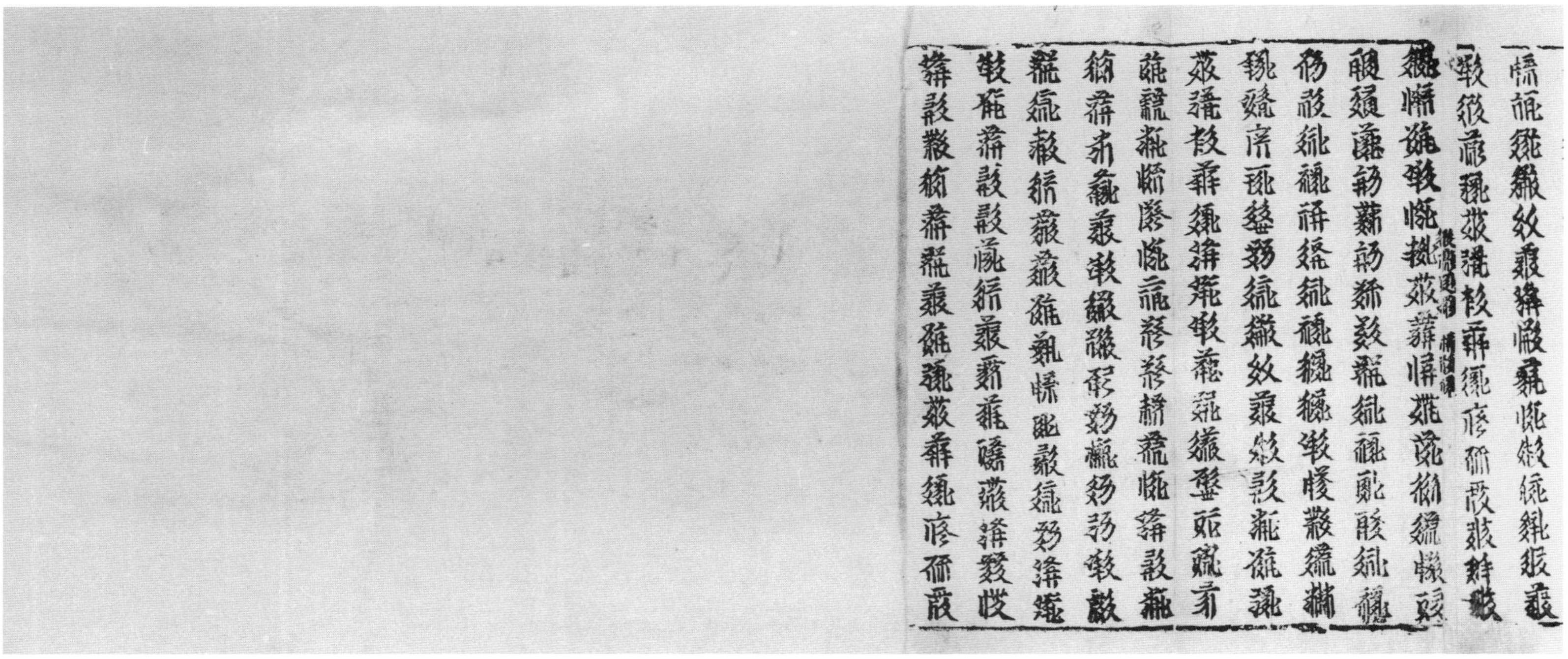

俄 Инв.No.6452　妙法蓮華經卷第八　(18–18)

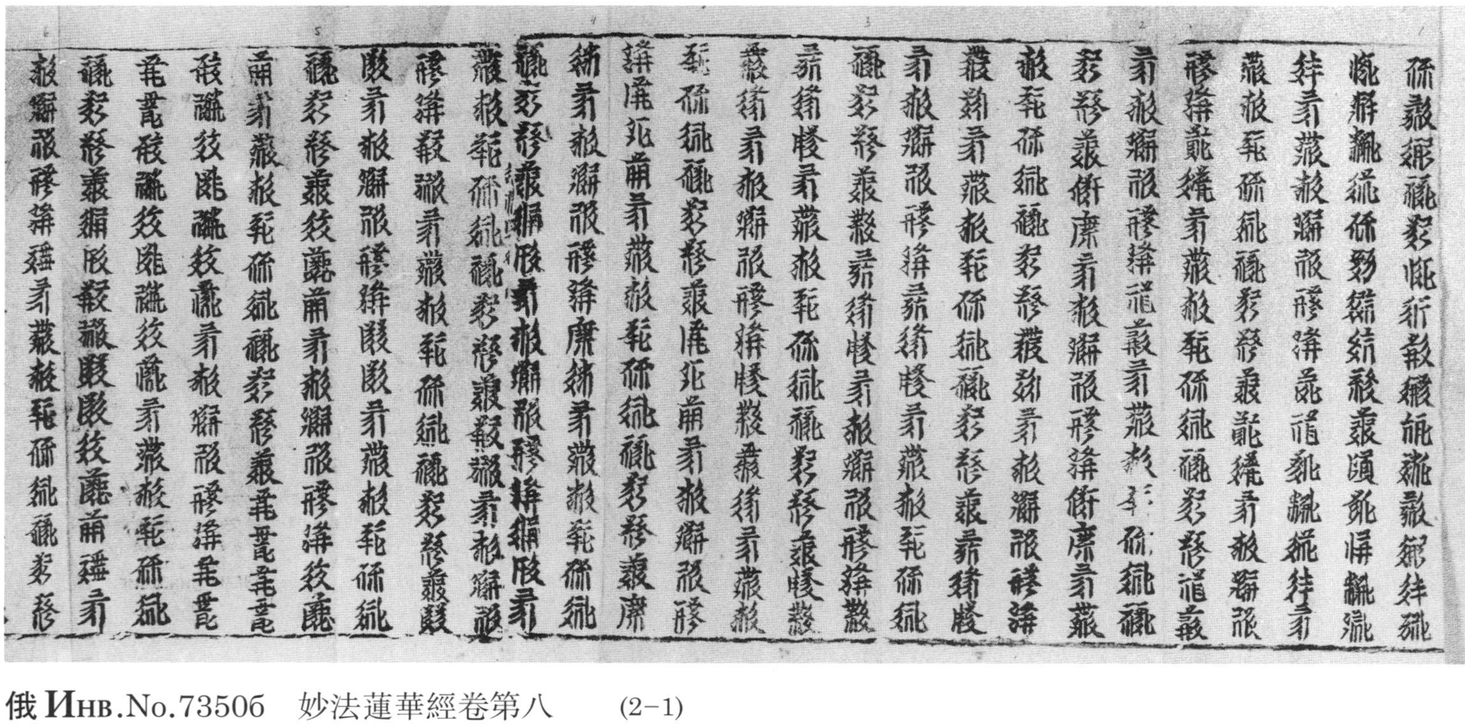

俄 Инв.No.7350б　妙法蓮華經卷第八　(2–1)

俄 Инв.No.7350б　妙法蓮華經卷第八　　　(2-2)

俄 Инв.No.3900　妙法蓮華經卷第八

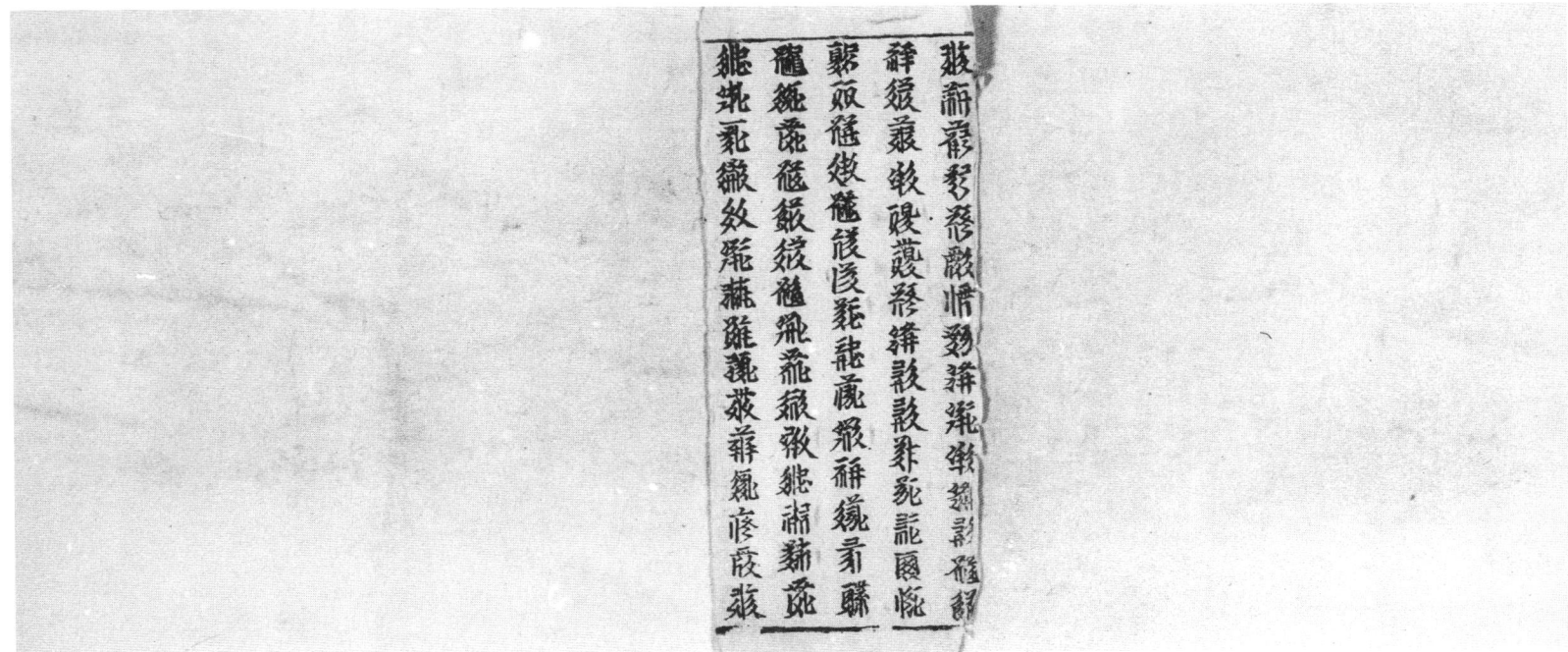

俄 Инв.No.7350a　妙法蓮華經卷第八

俄 **И**нв.No.7178　妙法蓮華經卷第八

俄 **И**нв.No.7231　妙法蓮華經卷第八

俄 **И**нв.No.3259　妙法蓮華經卷第三　　　(4-1)

俄 Инв.No.3259　妙法蓮華經卷第三　　　(4-2)

俄 Инв.No.3259　妙法蓮華經卷第三　　　(4-3)

俄 Инв.No.3259　妙法蓮華經卷第三　　　(4-4)

俄Инв.No.64　妙法蓮華經卷第四　　(11-1)

俄Инв.No.64　妙法蓮華經卷第四　　(11-2)

俄Инв.No.64　妙法蓮華經卷第四　　(11-3)

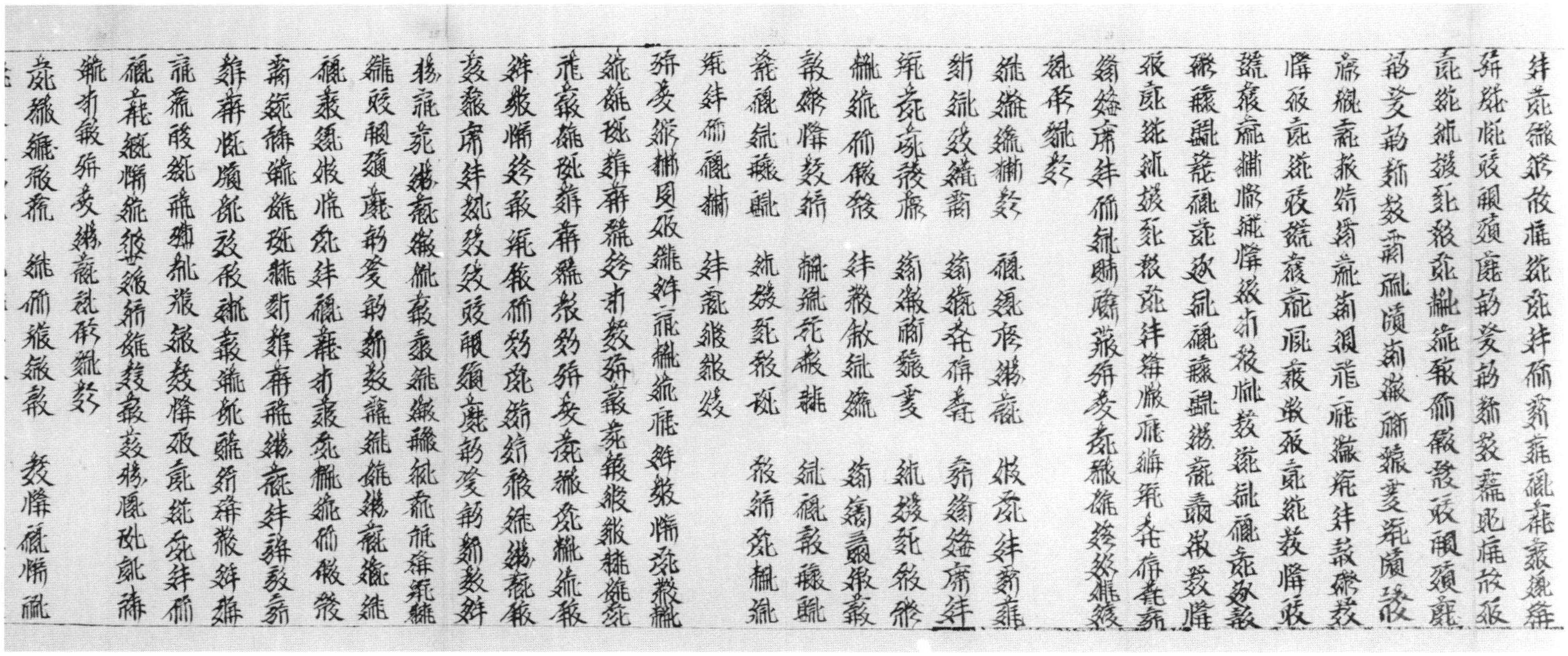

俄 Инв.No.64　妙法蓮華經卷第四　(11–7)

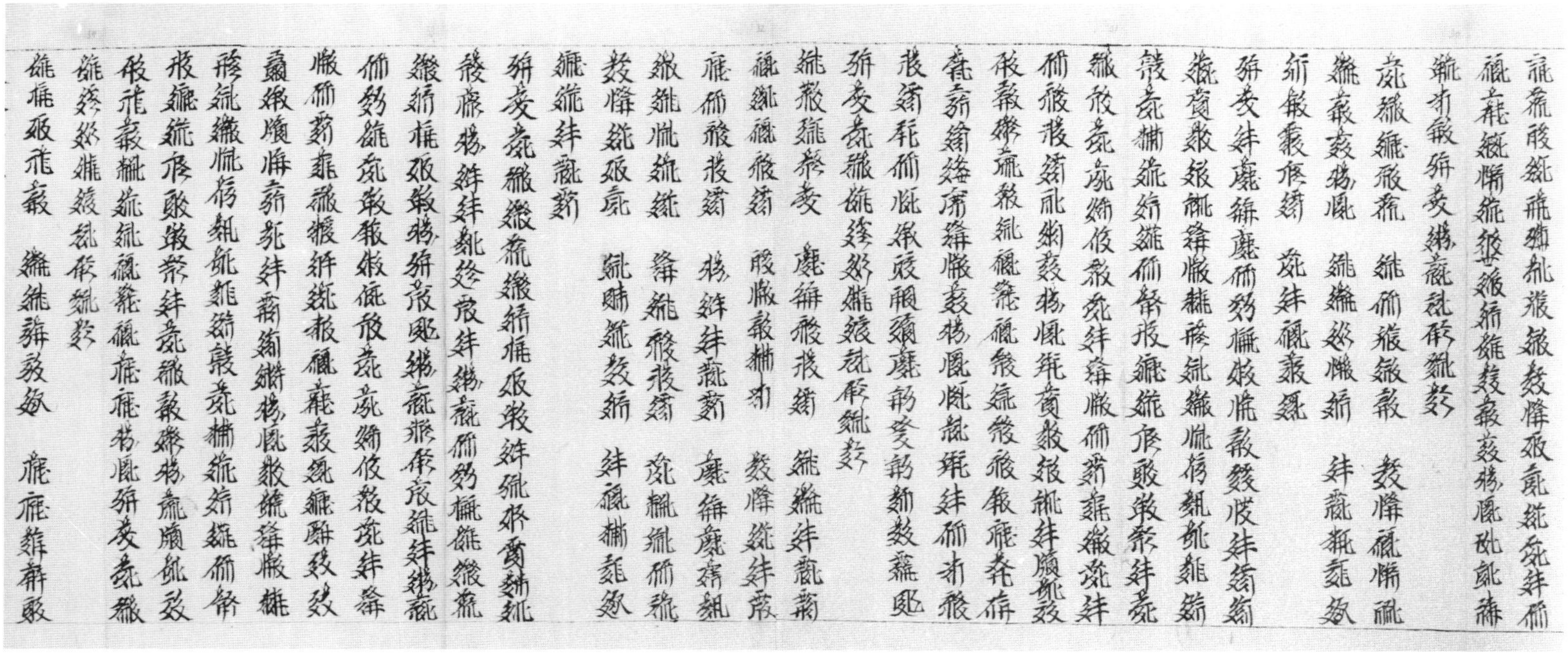

俄 Инв.No.64　妙法蓮華經卷第四　(11–8)

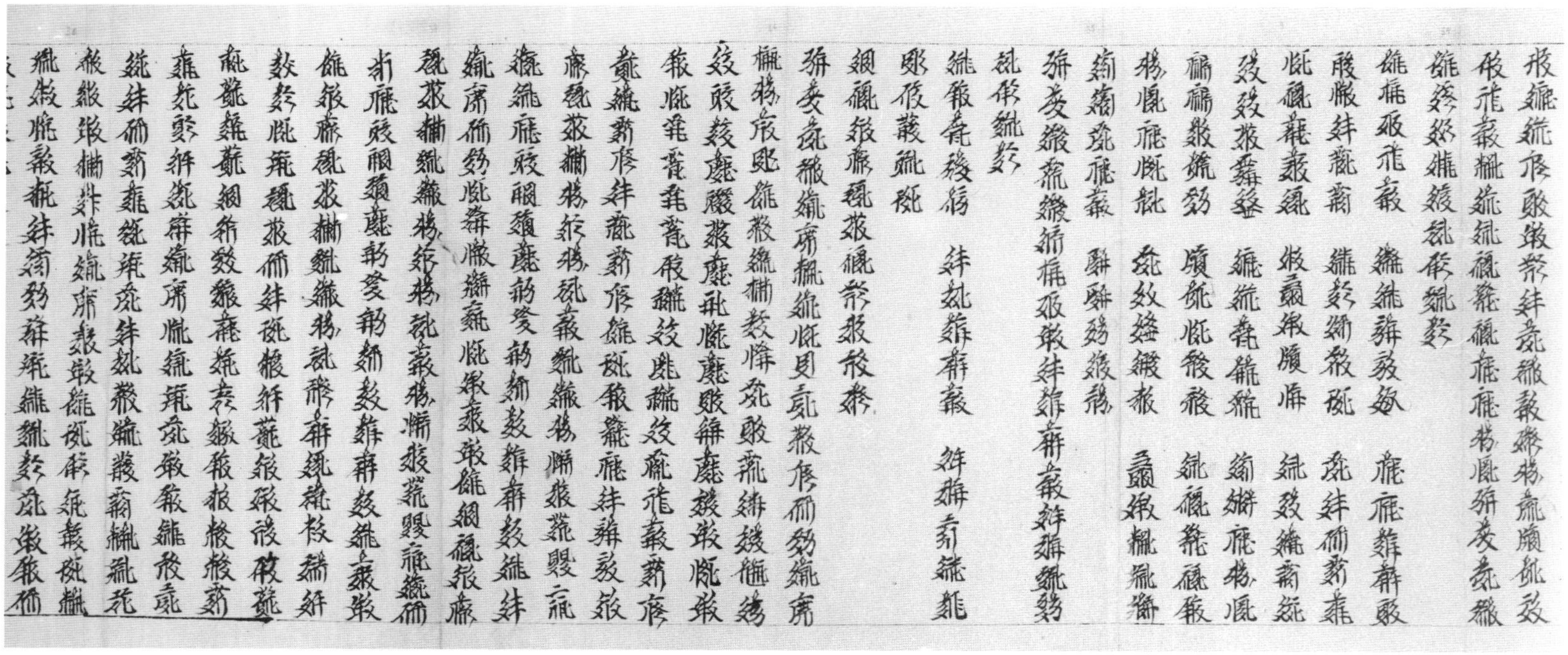

俄 Инв.No.64　妙法蓮華經卷第四　(11–9)

俄 Инв.No.64　妙法蓮華經卷第四　　　（11-10）

俄 Инв.No.64　妙法蓮華經卷第四　　　（11-11）

俄 Инв.No.63　妙法蓮華經卷第四　　　（8-1）

俄ИнВ.No.63　妙法蓮華經卷第四　　(8-2)

俄ИнВ.No.63　妙法蓮華經卷第四　　(8-3)

俄ИнВ.No.63　妙法蓮華經卷第四　　(8-4)

俄 **И**нв.No.63　妙法蓮華經卷第四　　　(8-5)

俄 **И**нв.No.63　妙法蓮華經卷第四　　　(8-6)

俄 **И**нв.No.63　妙法蓮華經卷第四　　　(8-7)

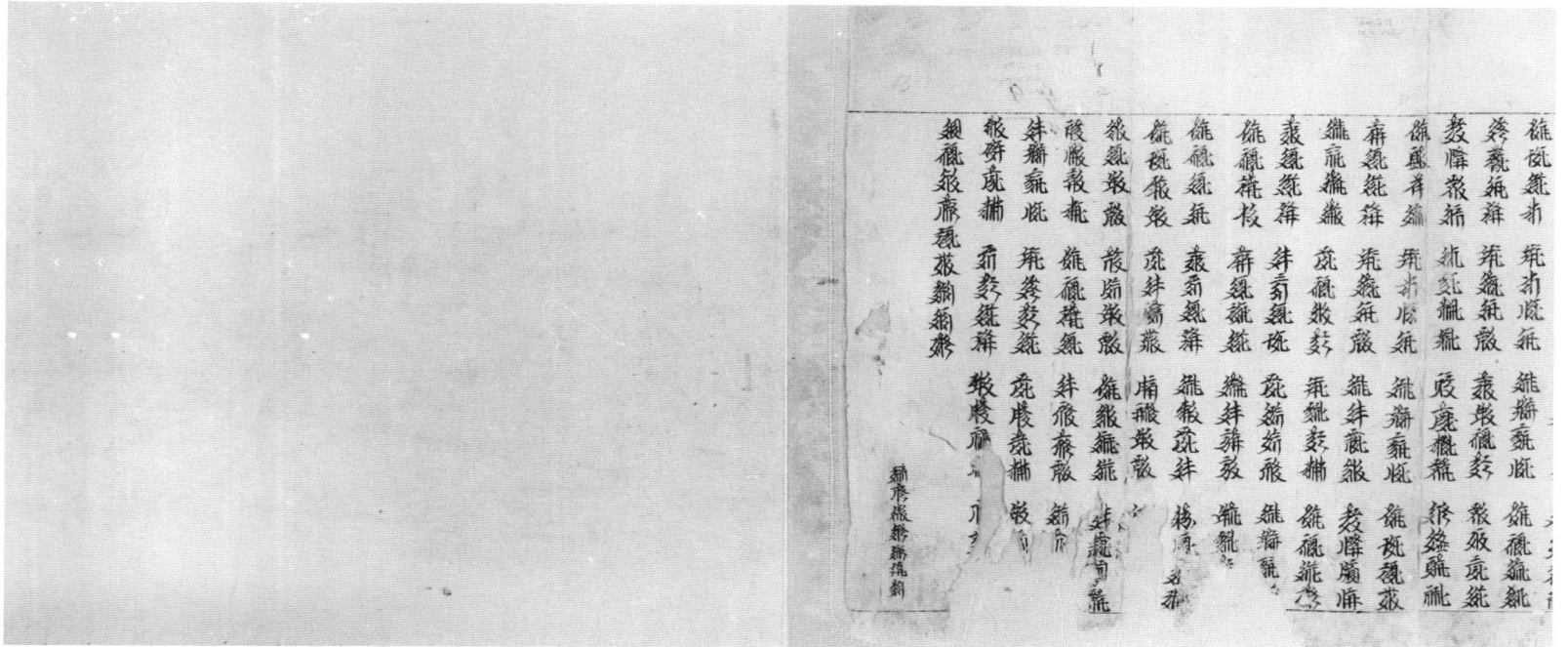

俄 **Инв**.No.63　妙法蓮華經卷第四　　　　(8-8)

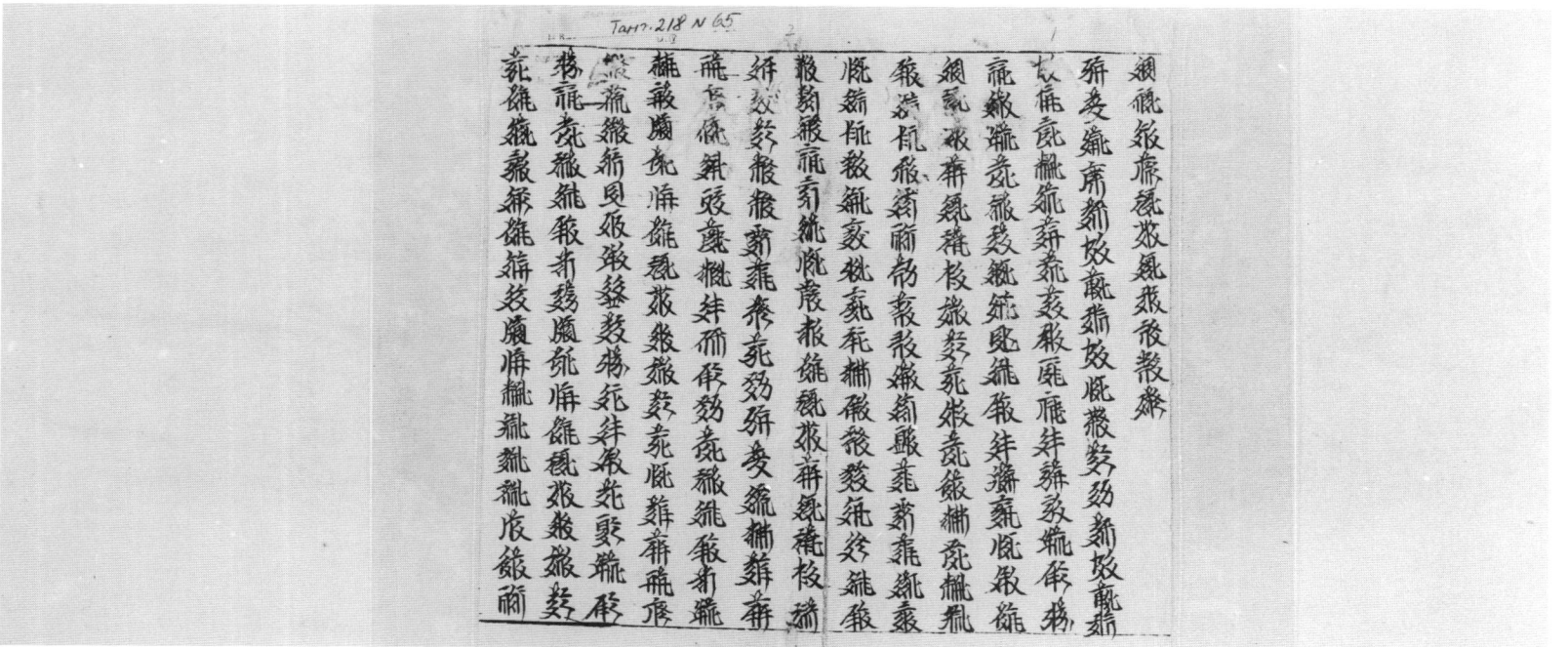

俄 **Инв**.No.65　妙法蓮華經卷第四

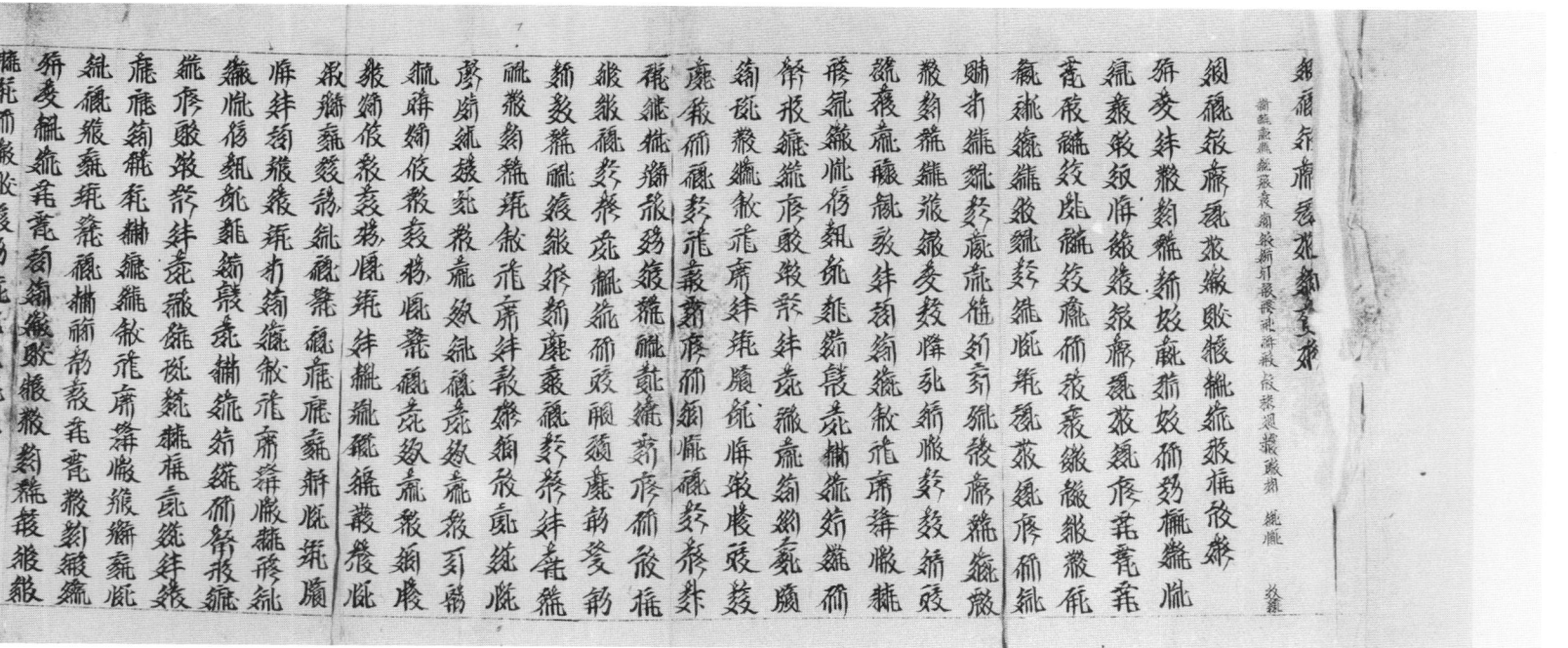

俄 **Инв**.No.68　妙法蓮華經卷第七　　　　(17-1)

俄 Инв.No.68　妙法蓮華經卷第七　　　(17-2)

俄 Инв.No.68　妙法蓮華經卷第七　　　(17-3)

俄 Инв.No.68　妙法蓮華經卷第七　　　(17-4)

俄 **Инв.**No.68　妙法蓮華經卷第七　　　(17-5)

俄 **Инв.**No.68　妙法蓮華經卷第七　　　(17-6)

俄 **Инв.**No.68　妙法蓮華經卷第七　　　(17-7)

俄 **И**нв.No.68　妙法蓮華經卷第七　　　(17-8)

俄 **И**нв.No.68　妙法蓮華經卷第七　　　(17-9)

俄 **И**нв.No.68　妙法蓮華經卷第七　　　(17-10)

俄 **И**нв.No.68　妙法蓮華經卷第七　　　(17-11)

俄 **И**нв.No.68　妙法蓮華經卷第七　　　(17-12)

俄 **И**нв.No.68　妙法蓮華經卷第七　　　(17-13)

俄 ИНВ.No.68　妙法蓮華經卷第七　　　(17-14)

俄 ИНВ.No.68　妙法蓮華經卷第七　　　(17-15)

俄 ИНВ.No.68　妙法蓮華經卷第七　　　(17-16)

俄Инв.No.68　妙法蓮華經卷第七　　　　(17-17)

俄Инв.No.940　妙法蓮華經觀世音菩薩普門品　　　(2-1)

俄Инв.No.940　妙法蓮華經觀世音菩薩普門品　　　(2-2)

俄 **И**нв.No.586　妙法蓮華經觀世音菩薩普門品

俄 **И**нв.No.221　妙法蓮華經觀世音菩薩普門品　　　(5-1)

俄 **И**нв.No.221　妙法蓮華經觀世音菩薩普門品　　　(5-2)

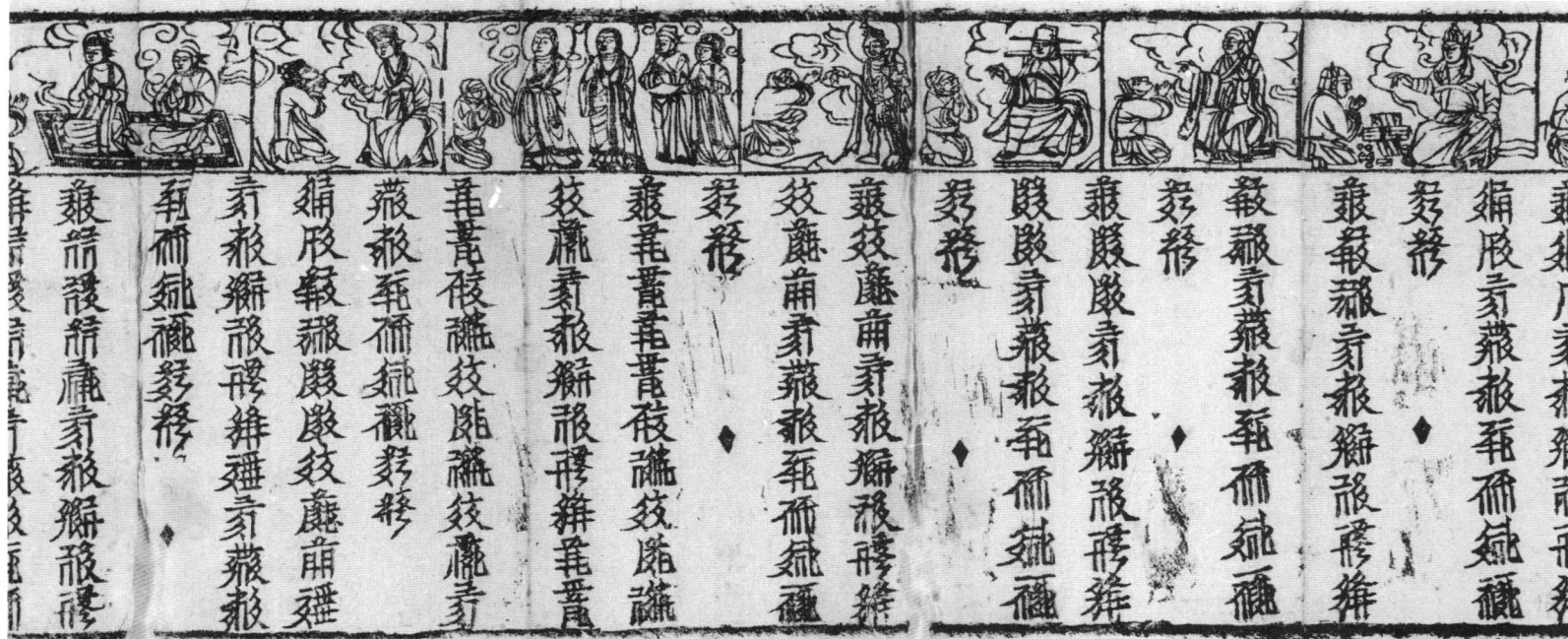

俄 ИНВ.No.221　妙法蓮華經觀世音菩薩普門品　　　(5-3)

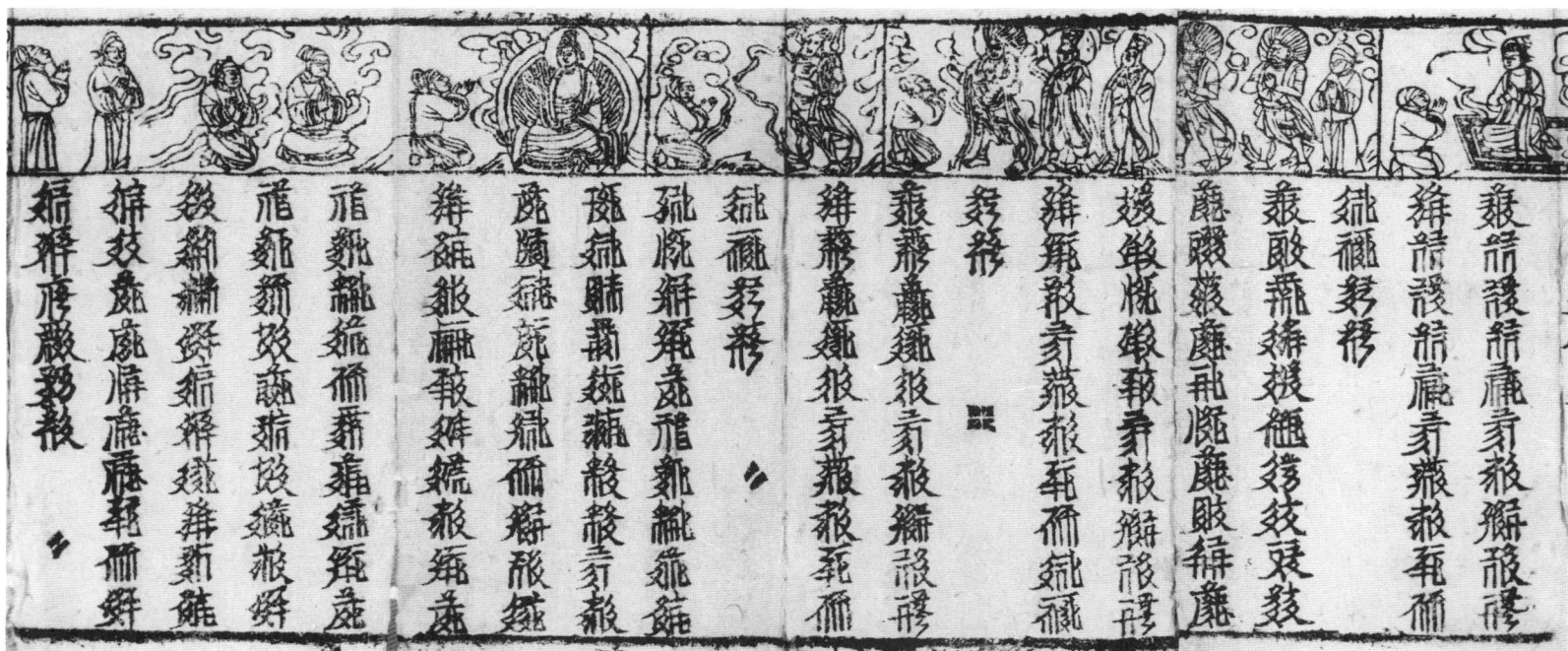

俄 ИНВ.No.221　妙法蓮華經觀世音菩薩普門品　　　(5-4)

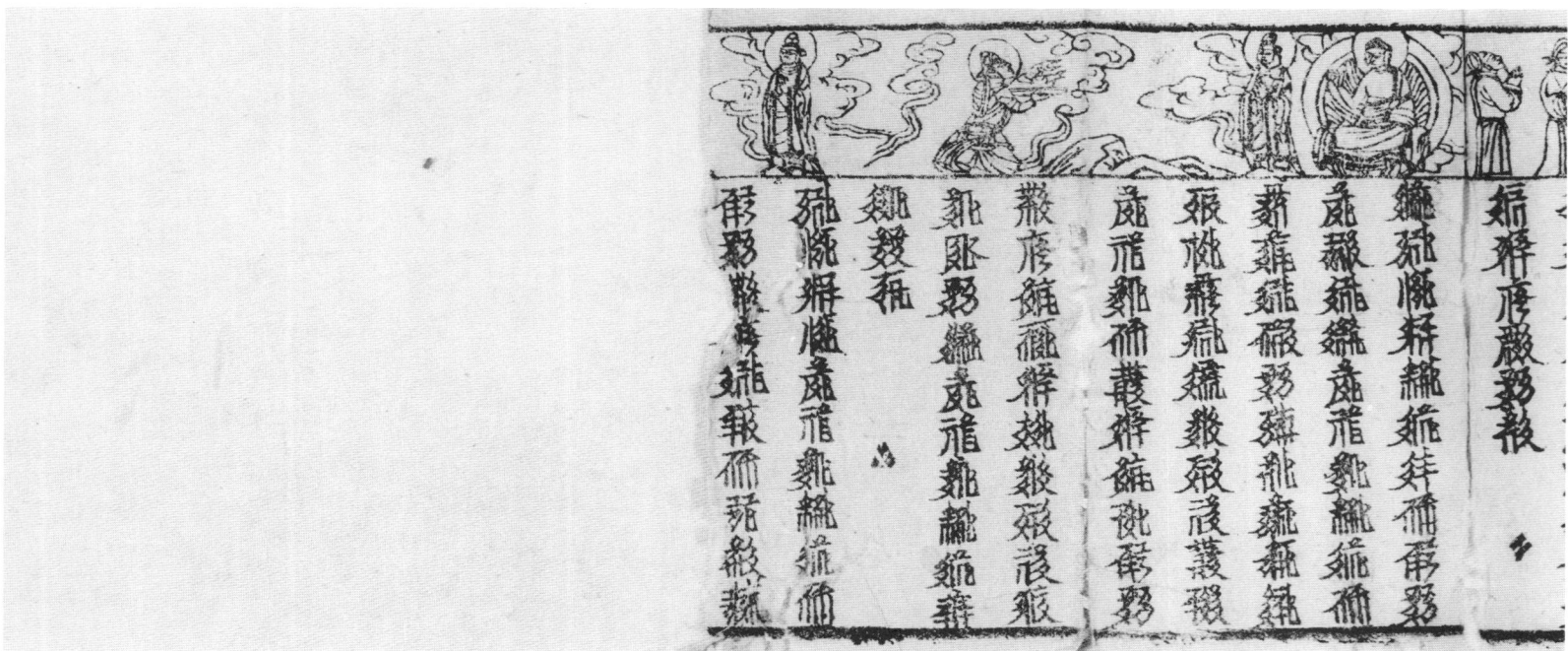

俄 ИНВ.No.221　妙法蓮華經觀世音菩薩普門品　　　(5-5)

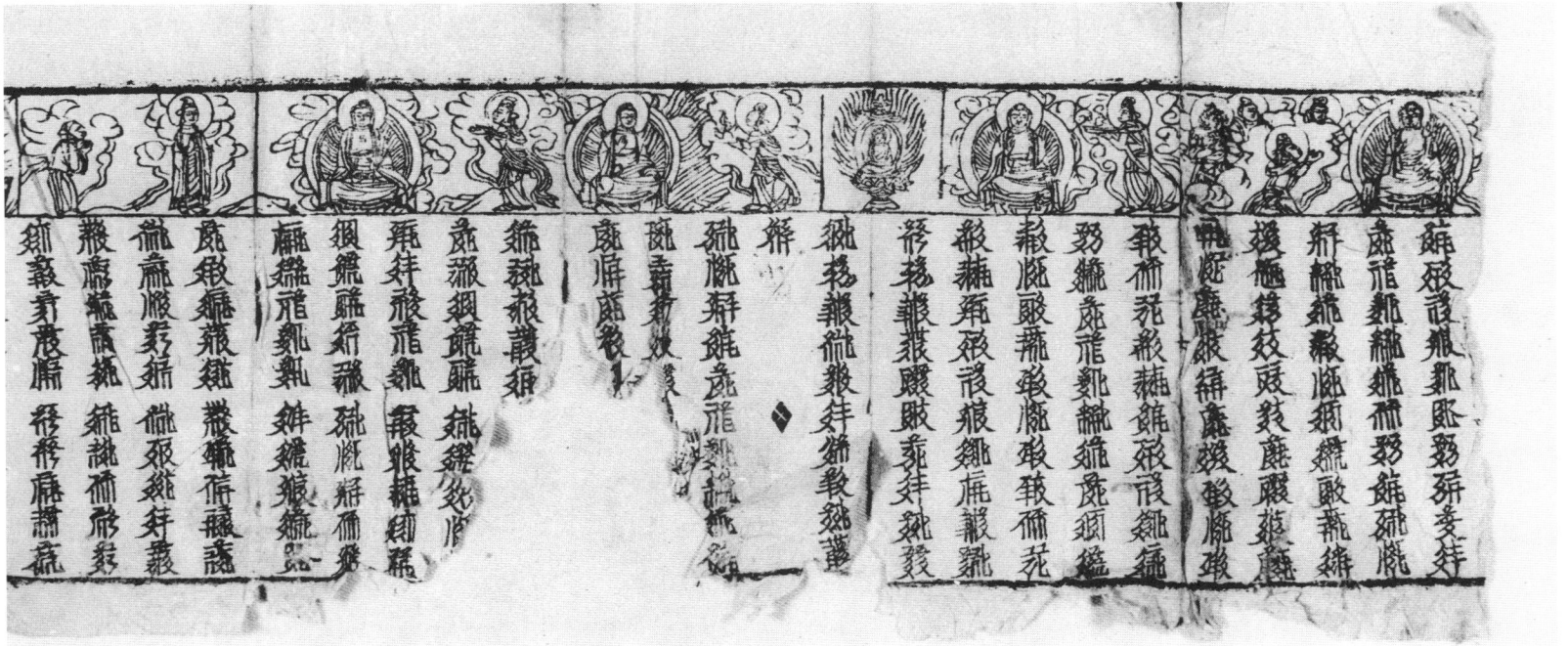

俄 **И**нв.No.4160　妙法蓮華經觀世音菩薩普門品　　　(2-1)

俄 **И**нв.No.4160　妙法蓮華經觀世音菩薩普門品　　　(2-2)

俄 **И**нв.No.6544　妙法蓮華經觀世音菩薩普門品

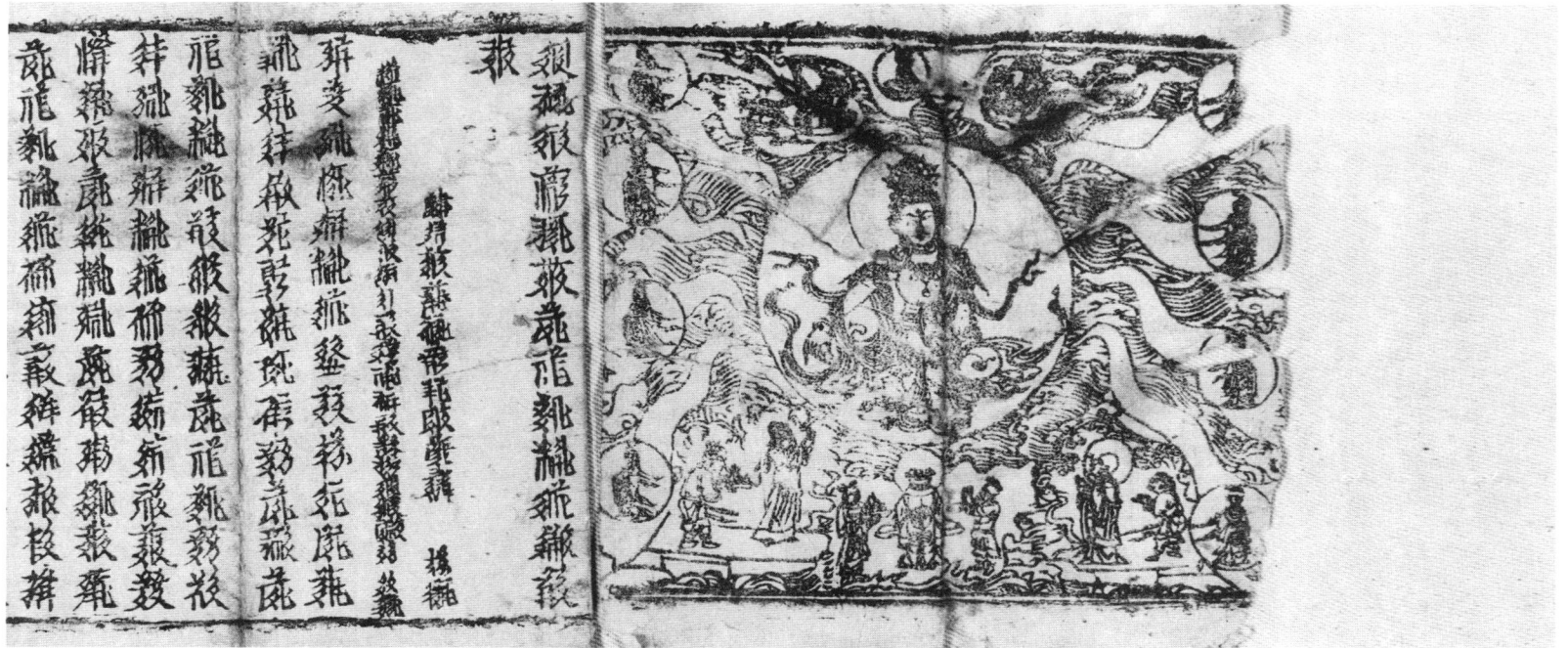

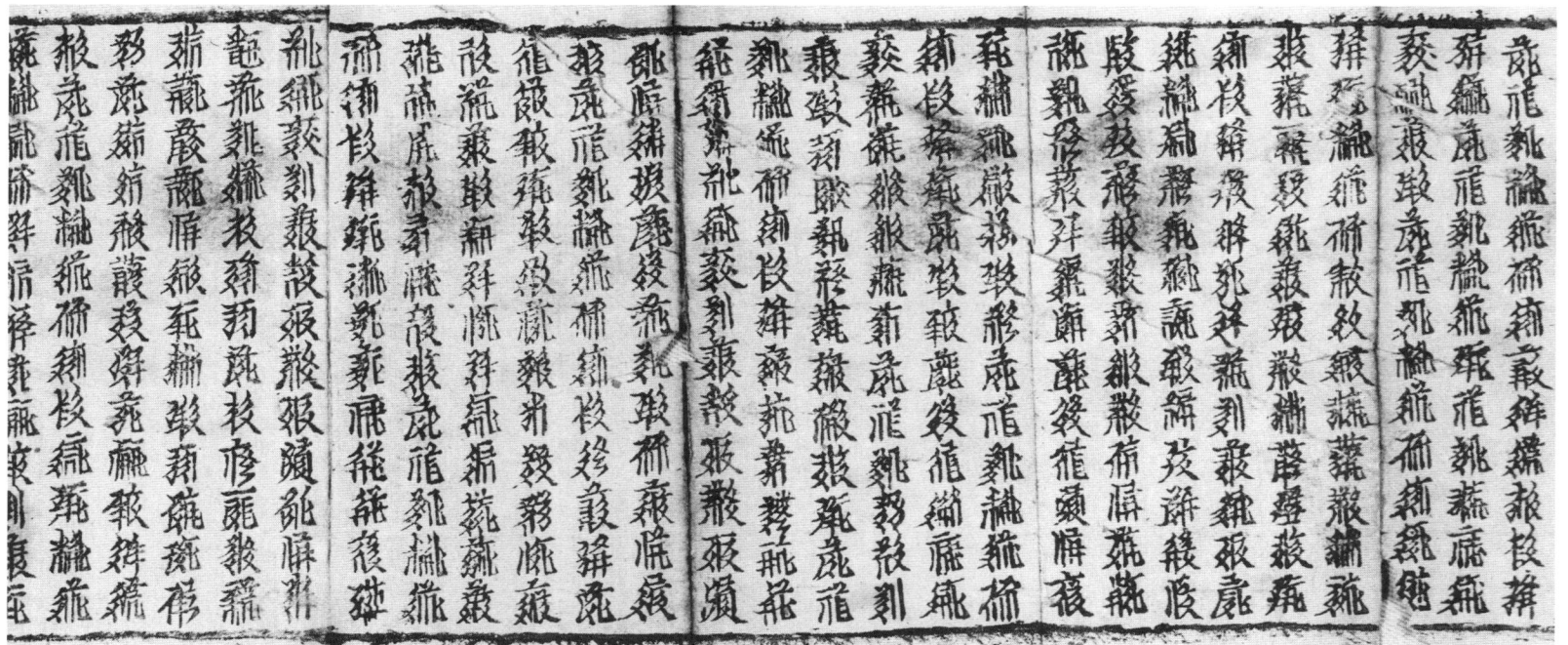

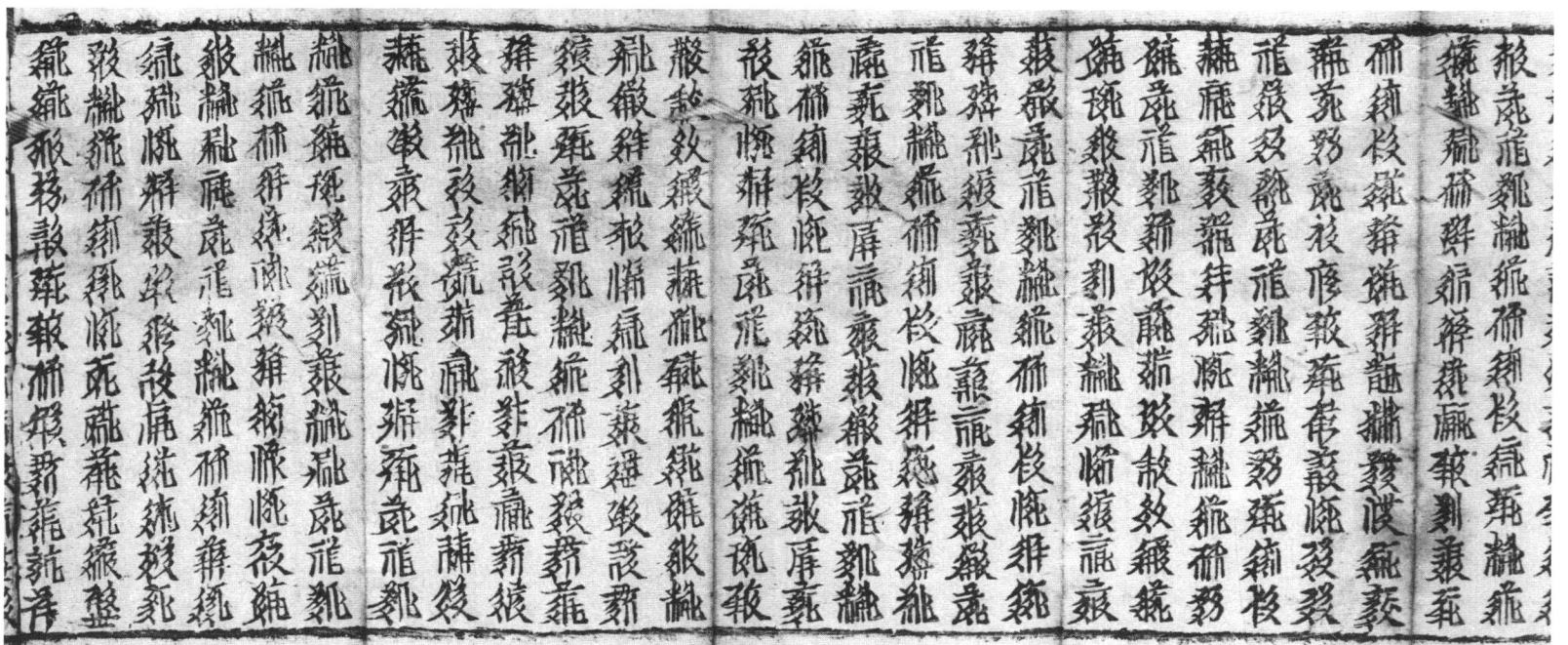

俄 **И**нв.No.574　　妙法蓮華經觀世音菩薩普門品　　　　(10-4)

俄 **И**нв.No.574　　妙法蓮華經觀世音菩薩普門品　　　　(10-5)

俄 **И**нв.No.574　　妙法蓮華經觀世音菩薩普門品　　　　(10-6)

俄 **И**нв.No.574　妙法蓮華經觀世音菩薩普門品　　　(10-7)

俄 **И**нв.No.574　妙法蓮華經觀世音菩薩普門品　　　(10-8)

俄 **И**нв.No.574　妙法蓮華經觀世音菩薩普門品　　　(10-9)

俄 **И**нв.No.574　妙法蓮華經觀世音菩薩普門品　　　(10-10)

俄 **И**нв.No.760　妙法蓮華經觀世音菩薩普門品

俄 **И**нв.No.757　妙法蓮華經觀世音菩薩普門品　　　(3-1)

俄 **Инв.**No.757　妙法蓮華經觀世音菩薩普門品　　　(3-2)

俄 **Инв.**No.757　妙法蓮華經觀世音菩薩普門品　　　(3-3)

俄 **Инв.**No.758　妙法蓮華經觀世音菩薩普門品

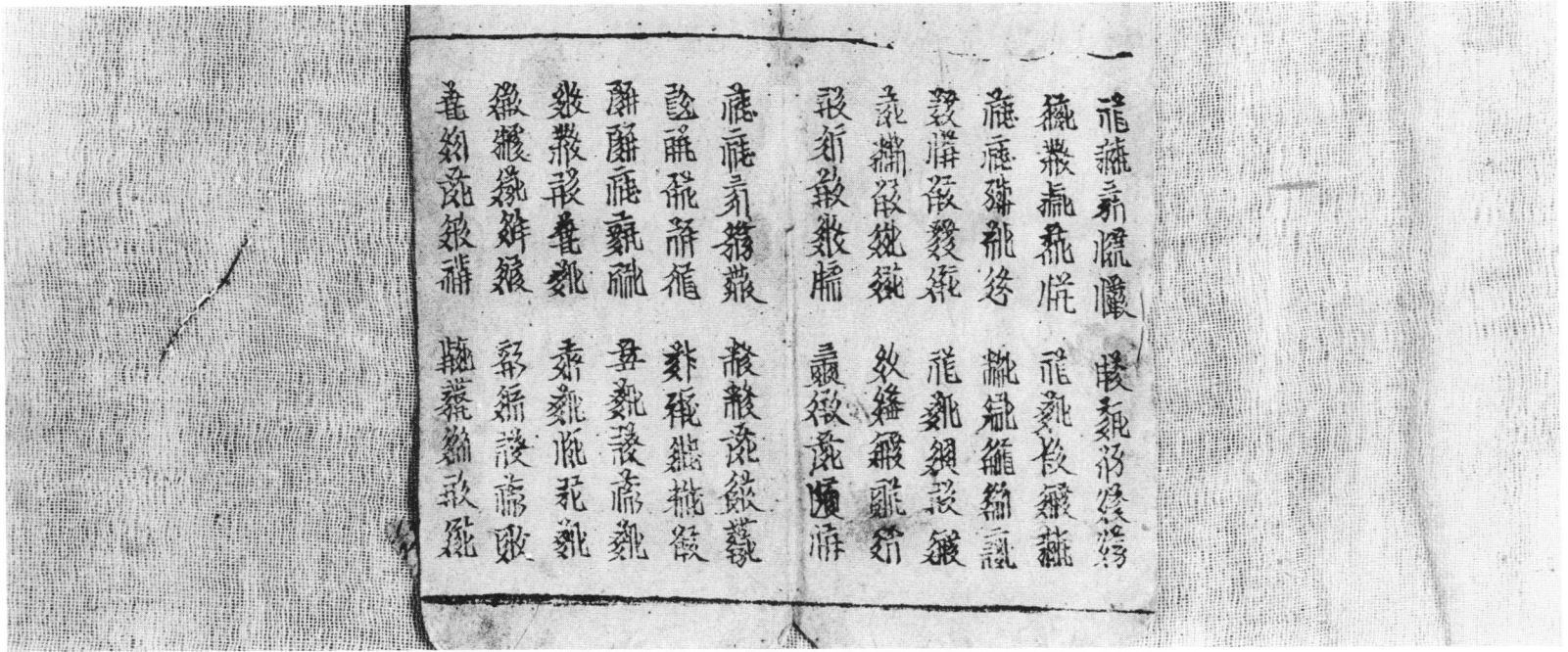

俄 **И**нв.No.7593　　妙法蓮華經觀世音菩薩普門品

俄 **И**нв.No.2864　　妙法蓮華經觀世音菩薩普門品　　　　(19-1)

俄 **И**нв.No.2864　　妙法蓮華經觀世音菩薩普門品　　　　(19-2)

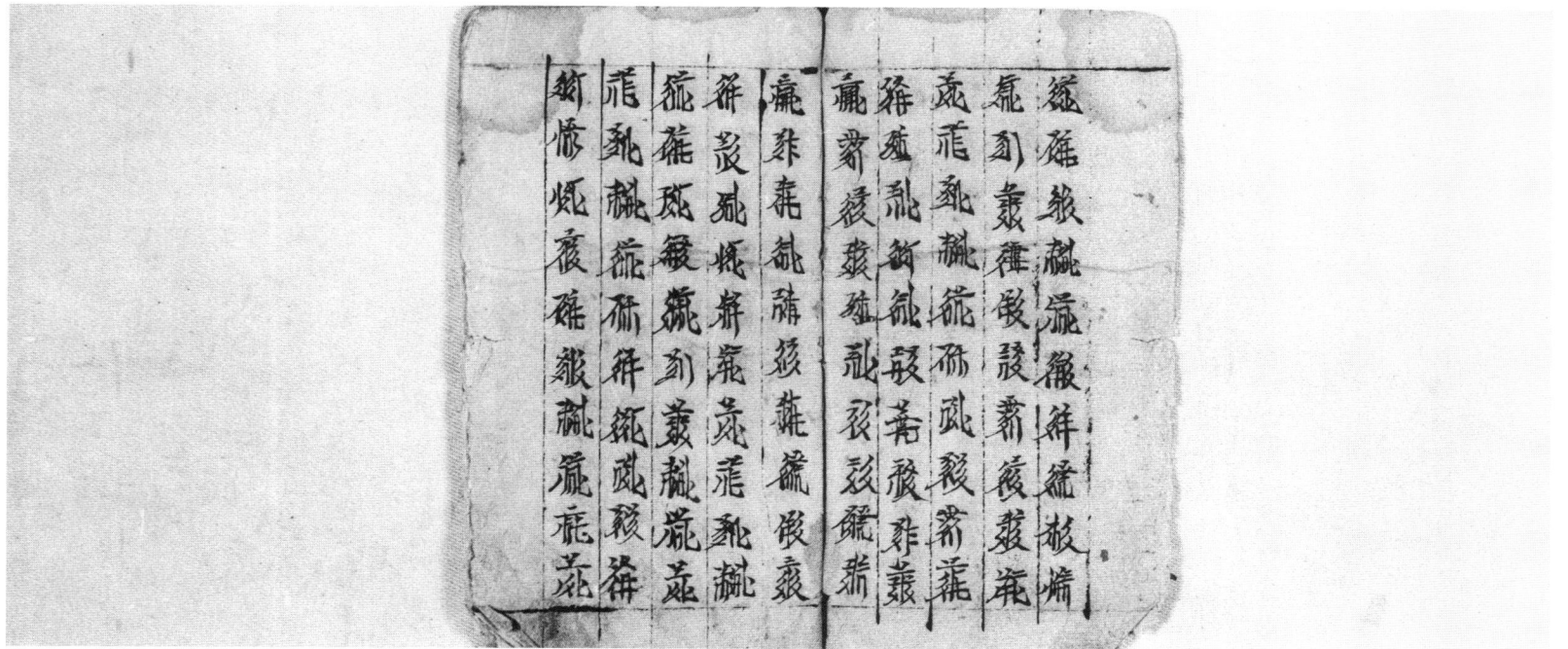

俄 **Инв**.No.2864　妙法蓮華經觀世音菩薩普門品　　（19-3）

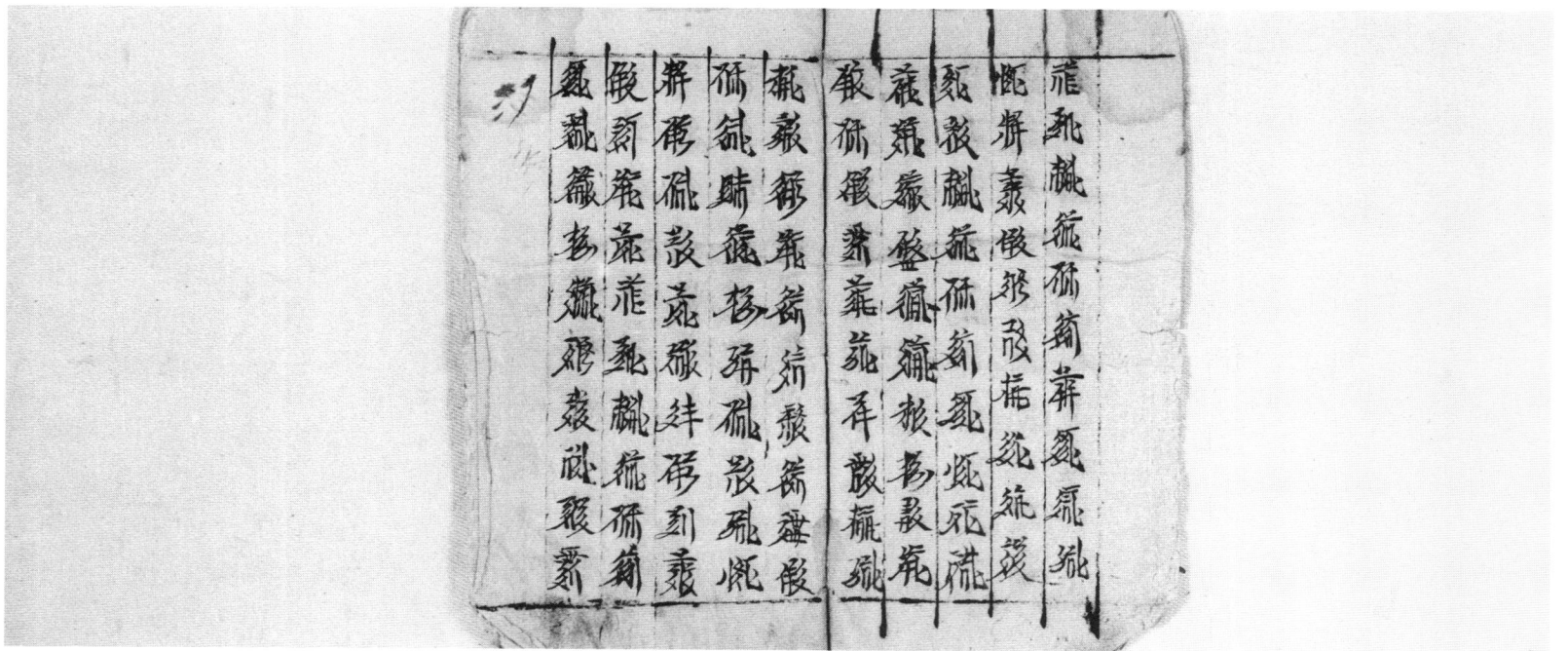

俄 **Инв**.No.2864　妙法蓮華經觀世音菩薩普門品　　（19-4）

俄 **Инв**.No.2864　妙法蓮華經觀世音菩薩普門品　　（19-5）

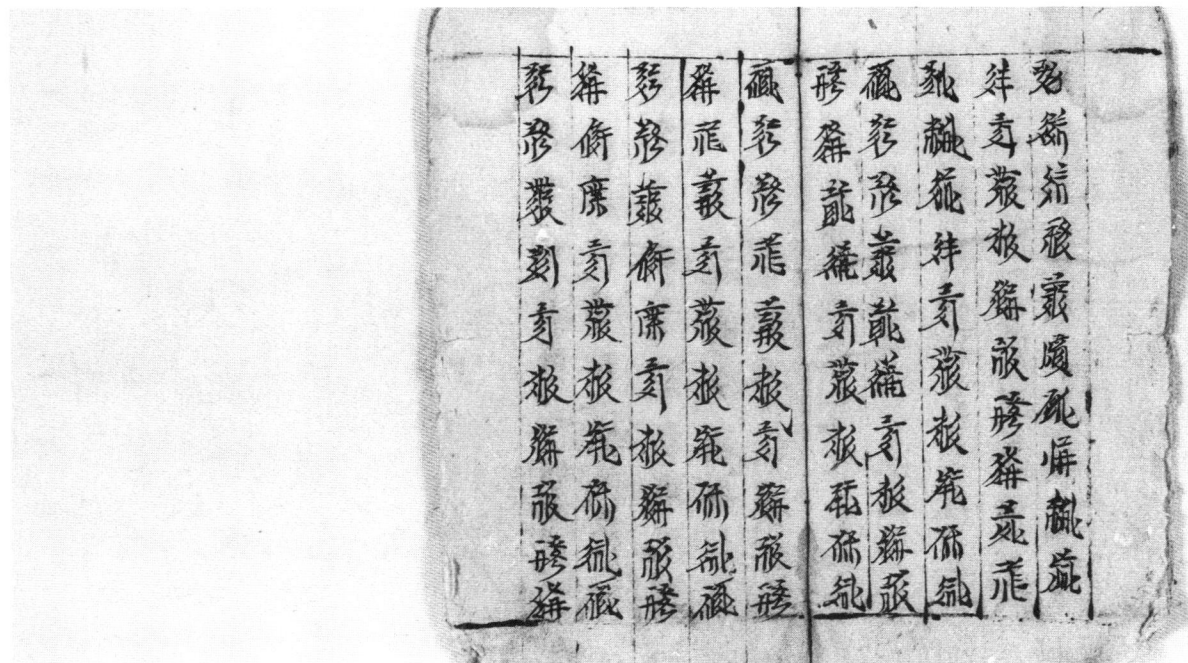

俄 **И**нв.No.2864　妙法蓮華經觀世音菩薩普門品　　　(19-6)

俄 **И**нв.No.2864　妙法蓮華經觀世音菩薩普門品　　　(19-7)

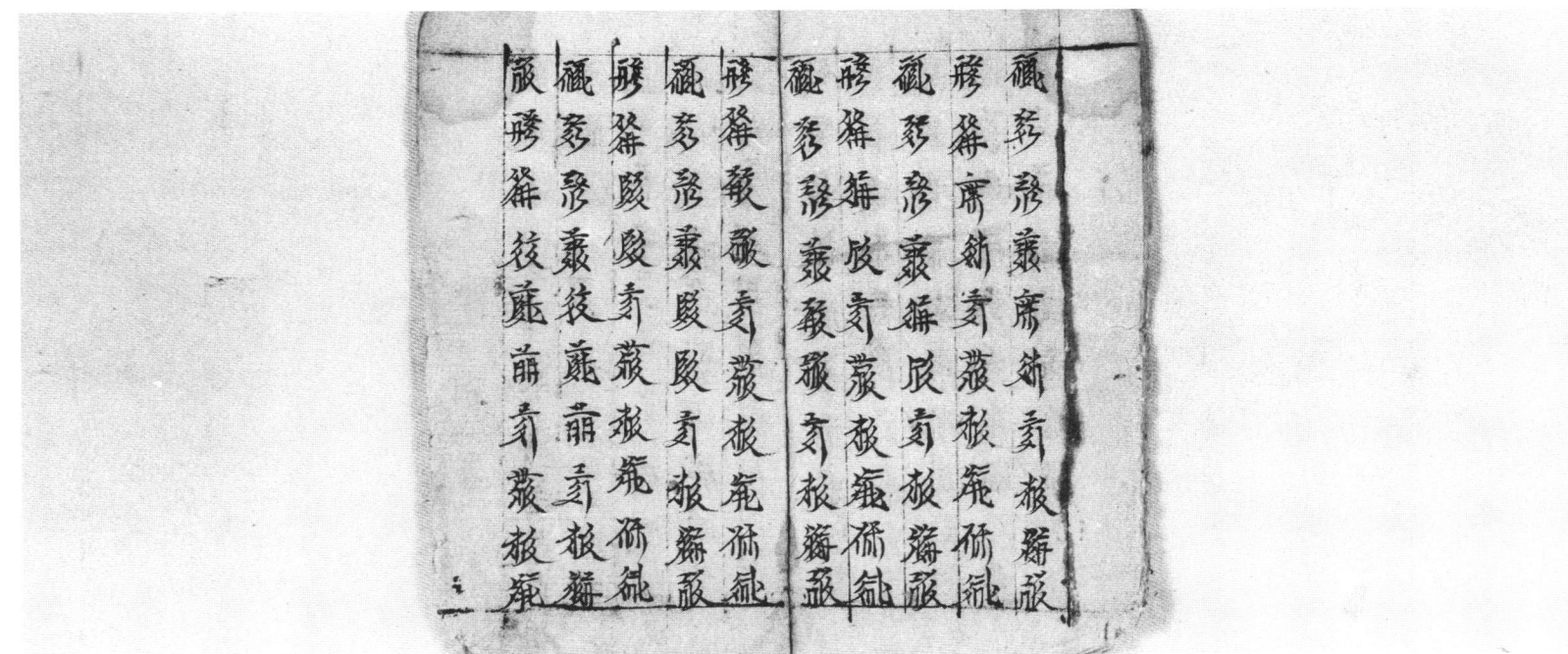

俄 **И**нв.No.2864　妙法蓮華經觀世音菩薩普門品　　　(19-8)

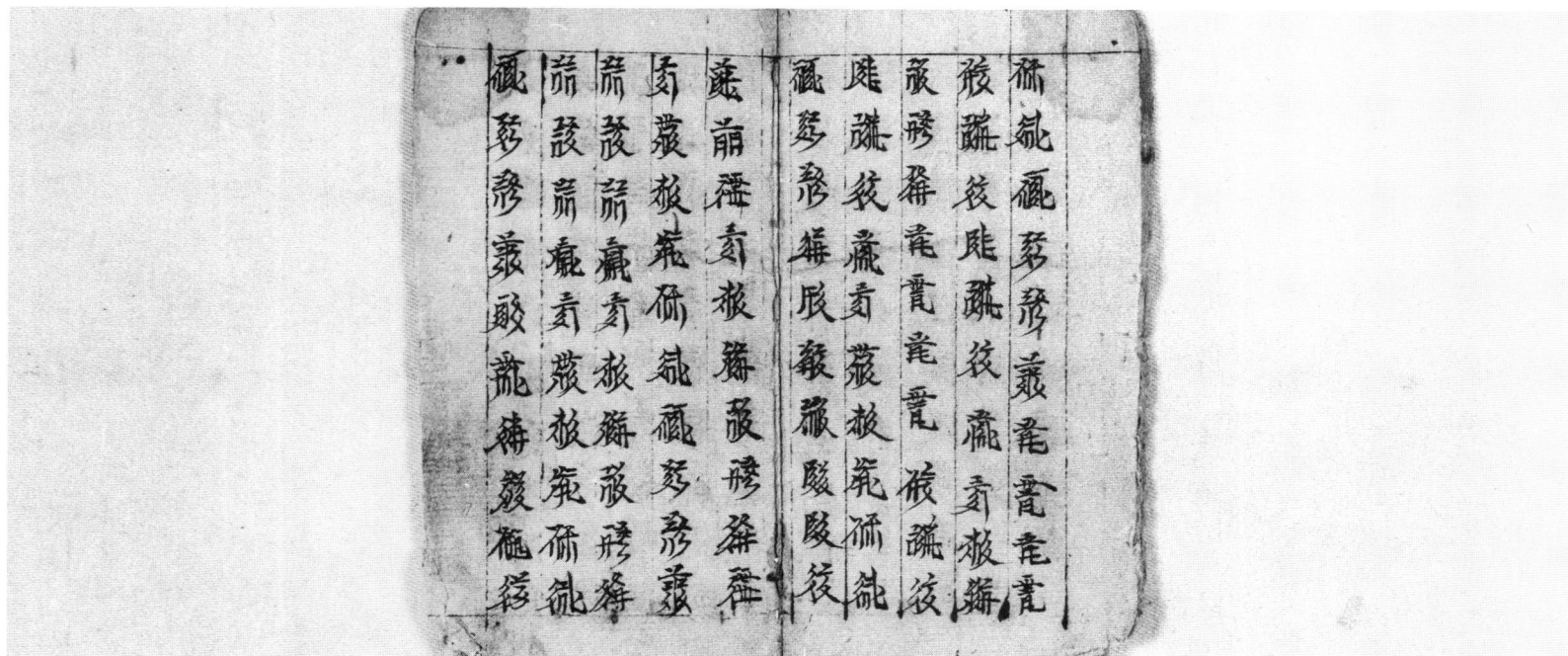

俄 **И**нв.No.2864　妙法蓮華經觀世音菩薩普門品　　　(19-9)

俄 **И**нв.No.2864　妙法蓮華經觀世音菩薩普門品　　　(19-10)

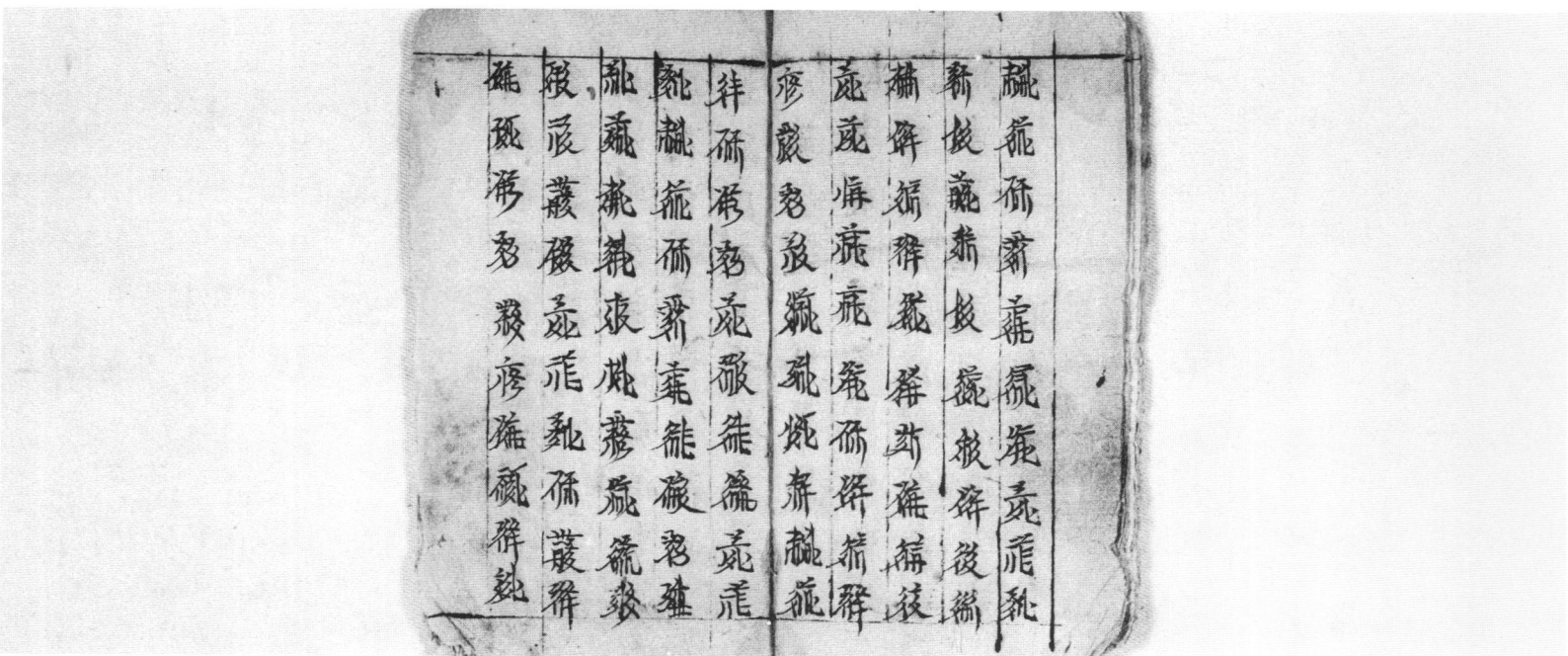

俄 **И**нв.No.2864　妙法蓮華經觀世音菩薩普門品　　　(19-11)

313

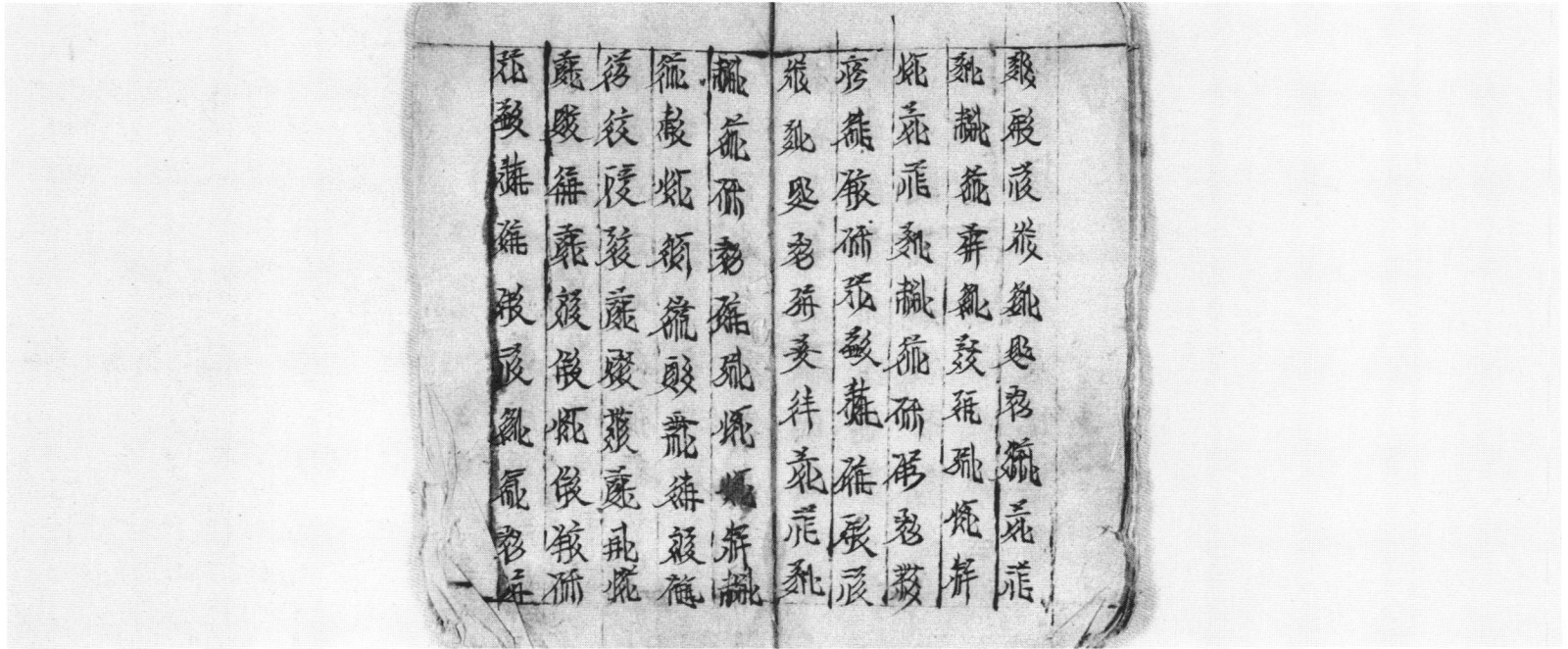

俄 **И**нв.No.2864　　妙法蓮華經觀世音菩薩普門品　　　　（19-12）

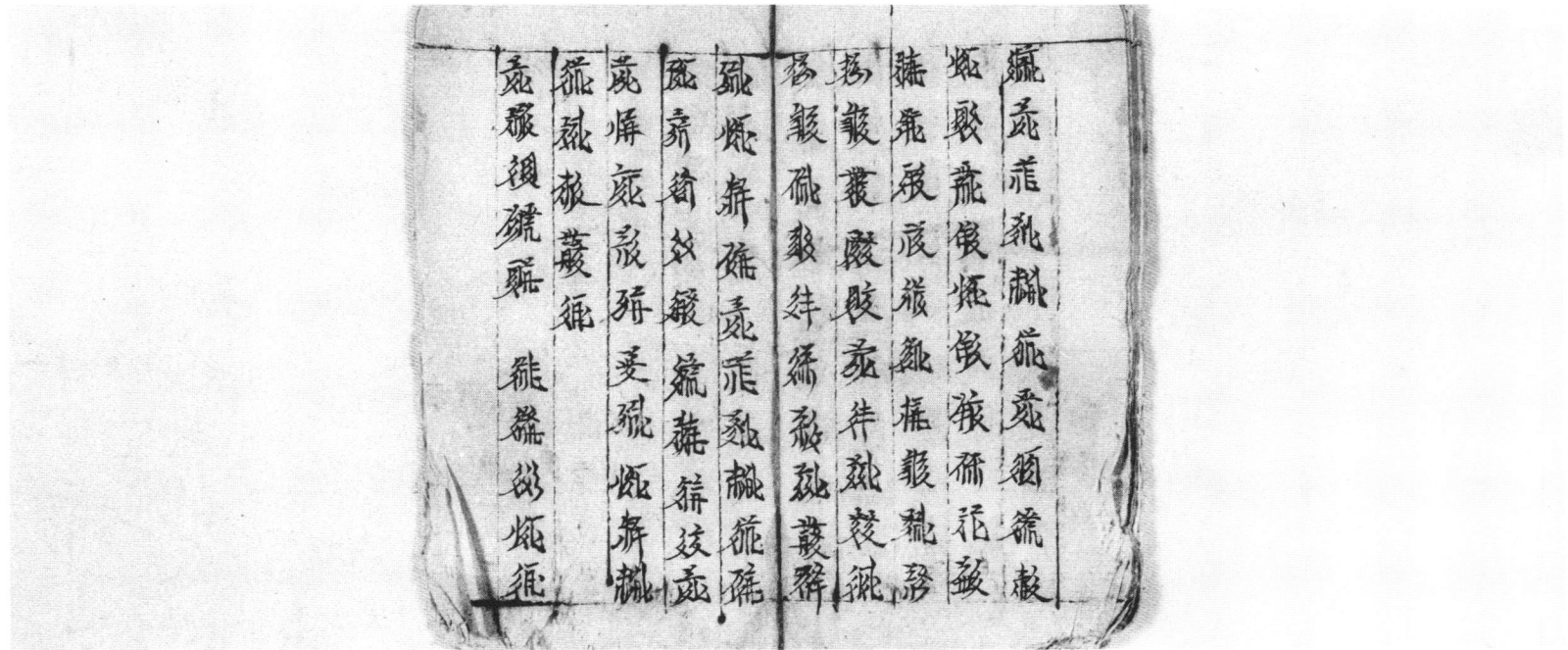

俄 **И**нв.No.2864　　妙法蓮華經觀世音菩薩普門品　　　　（19-13）

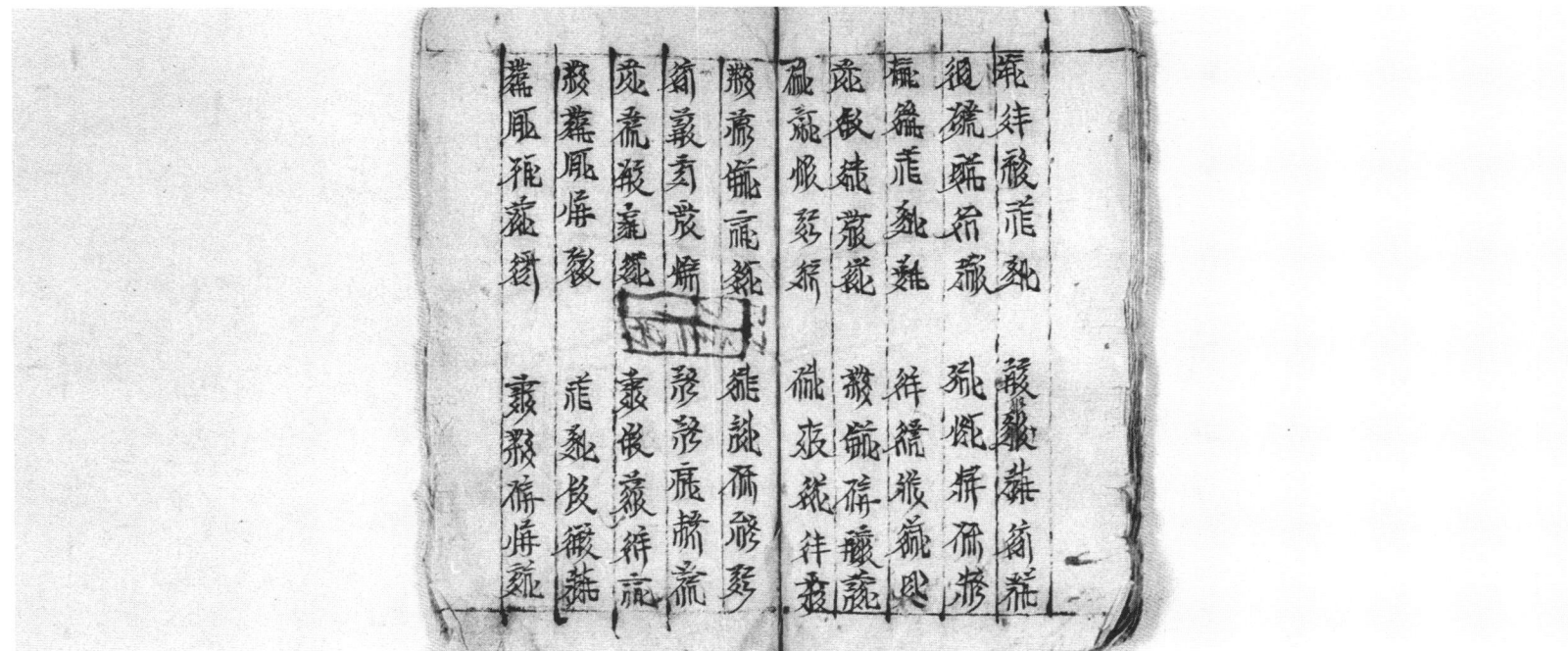

俄 **И**нв.No.2864　　妙法蓮華經觀世音菩薩普門品　　　　（19-14）

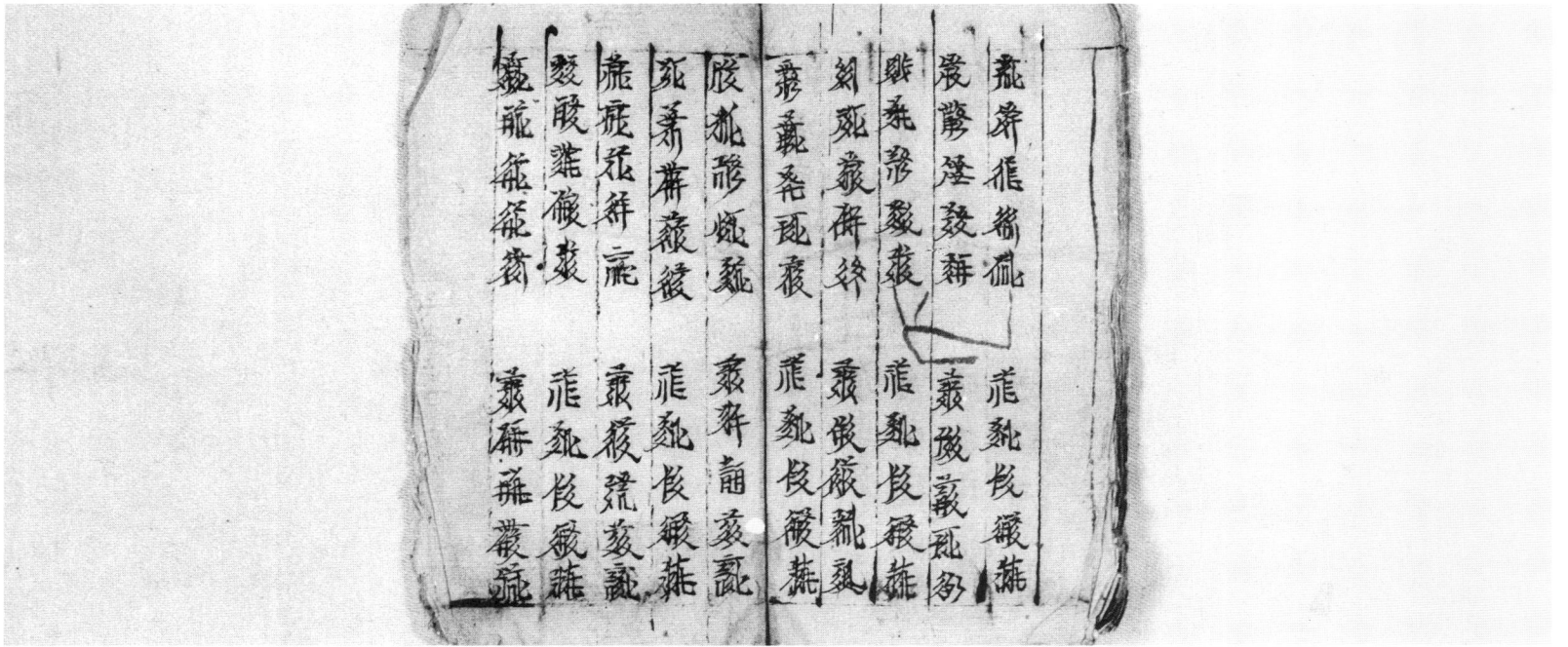

俄 **Инв**.No.2864　妙法蓮華經觀世音菩薩普門品　　　　(19–15)

俄 **Инв**.No.2864　妙法蓮華經觀世音菩薩普門品　　　　(19–16)

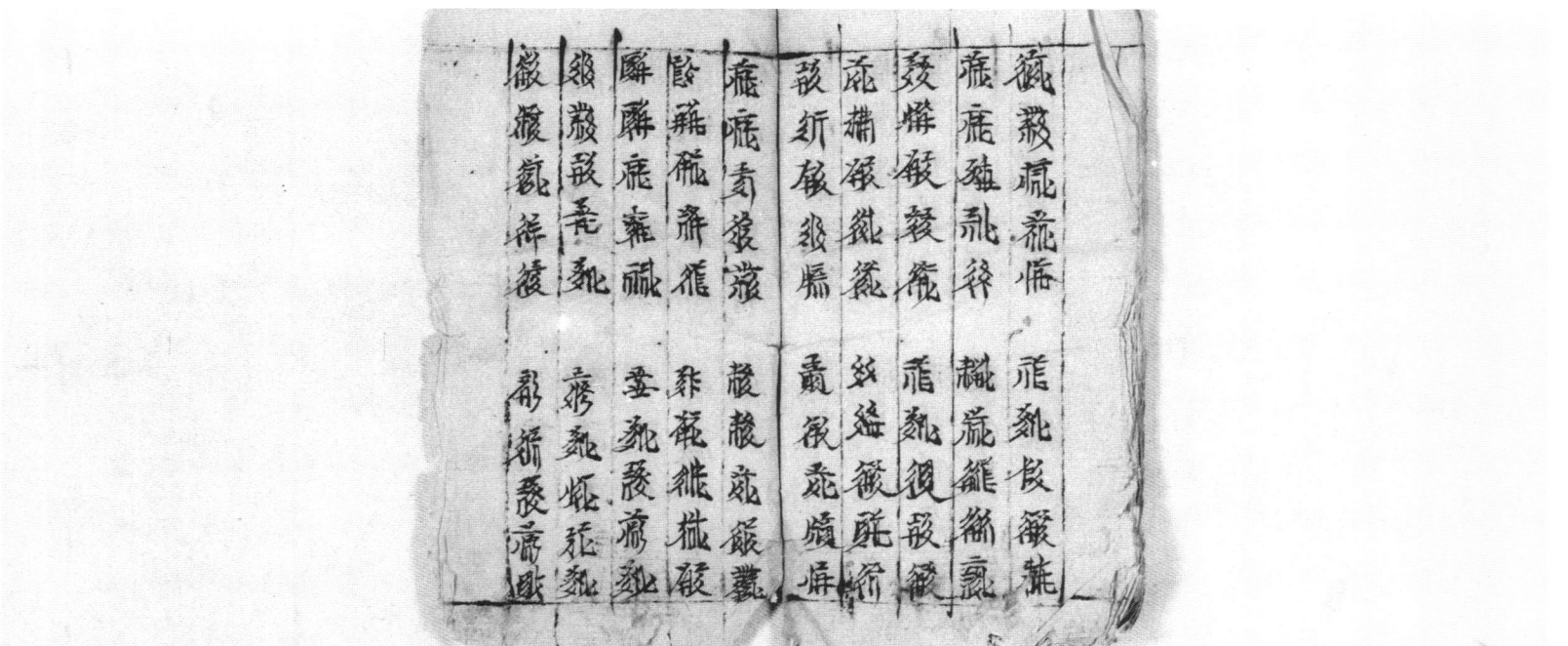

俄 **Инв**.No.2864　妙法蓮華經觀世音菩薩普門品　　　　(19–17)

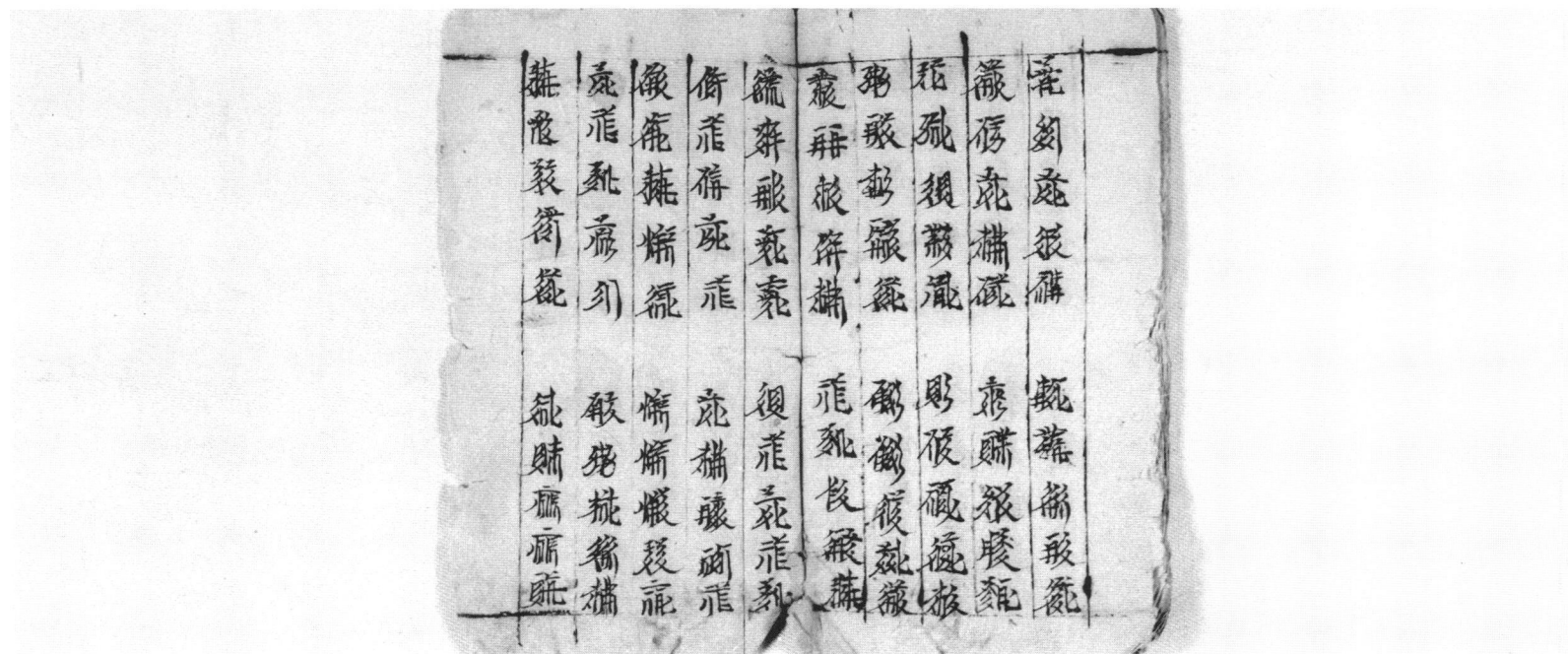

俄 Инв.No.2864　妙法蓮華經觀世音菩薩普門品　　　(19−18)

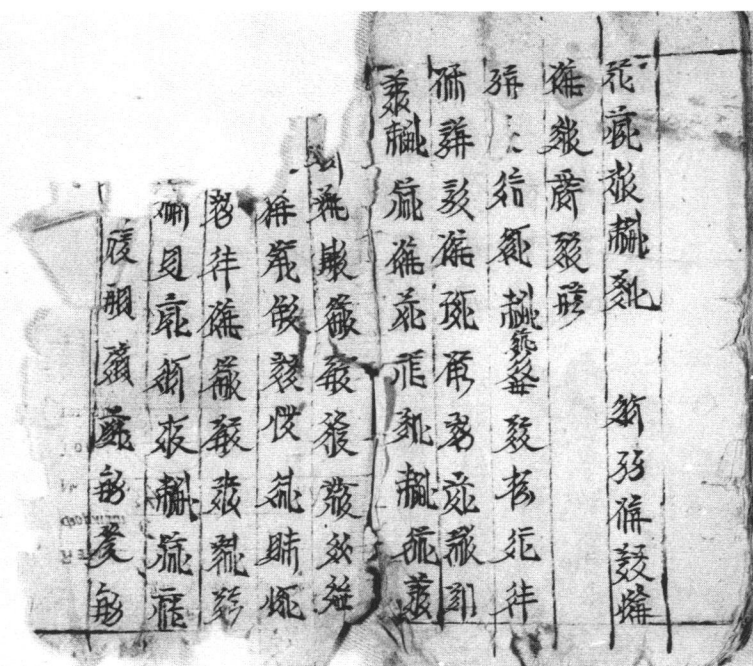

俄 Инв.No.2864　妙法蓮華經觀世音菩薩普門品　　　(19−19)

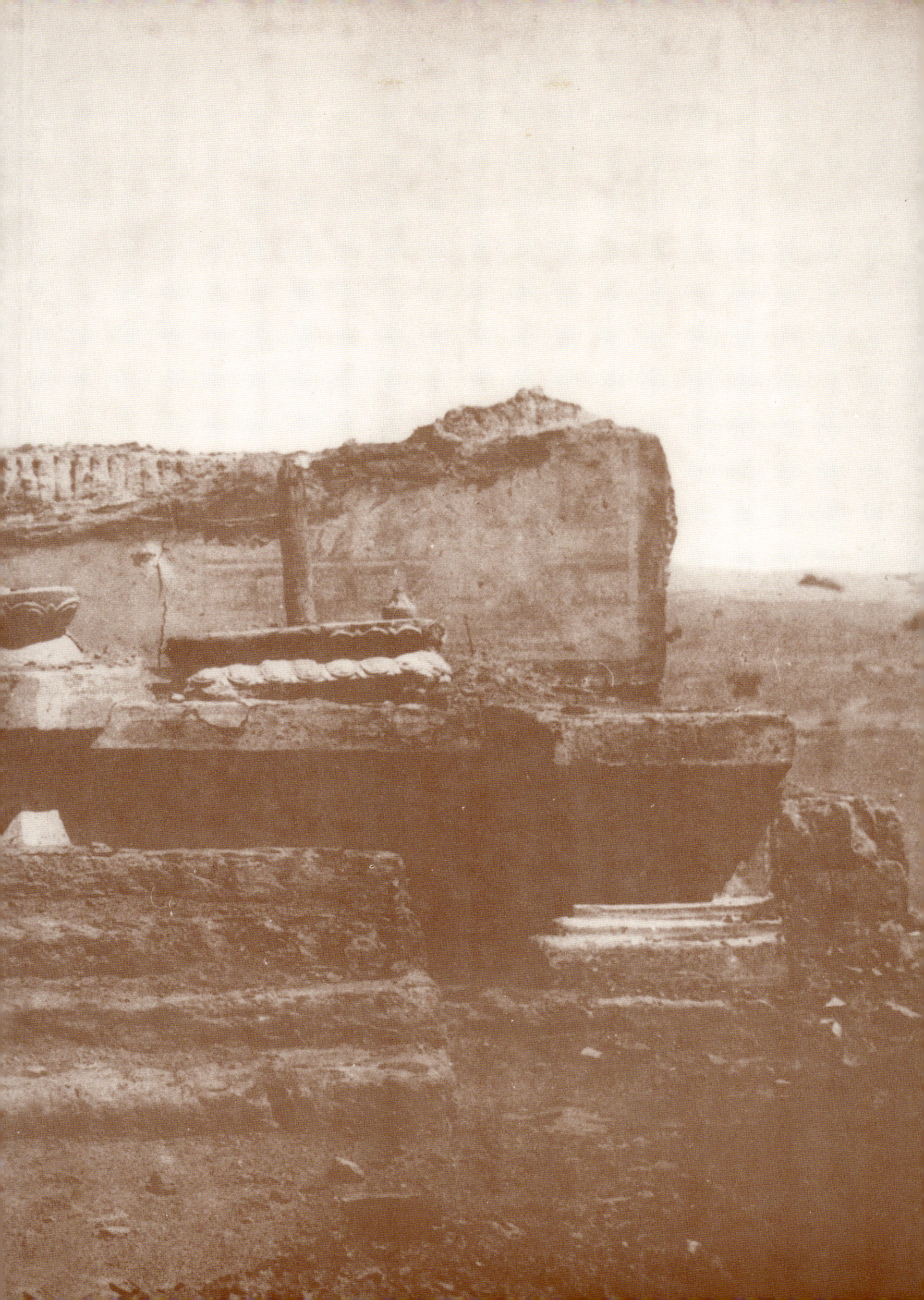

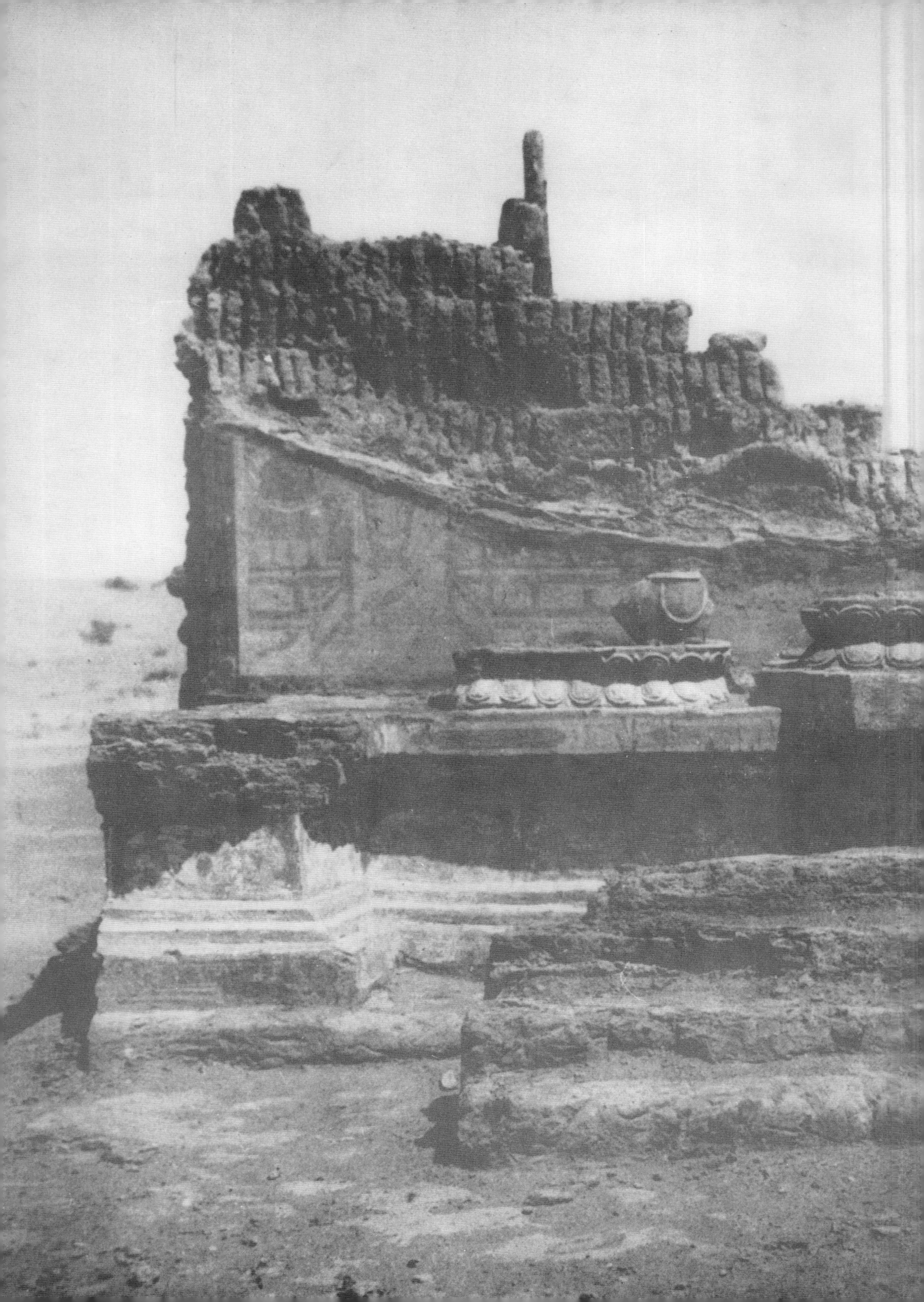

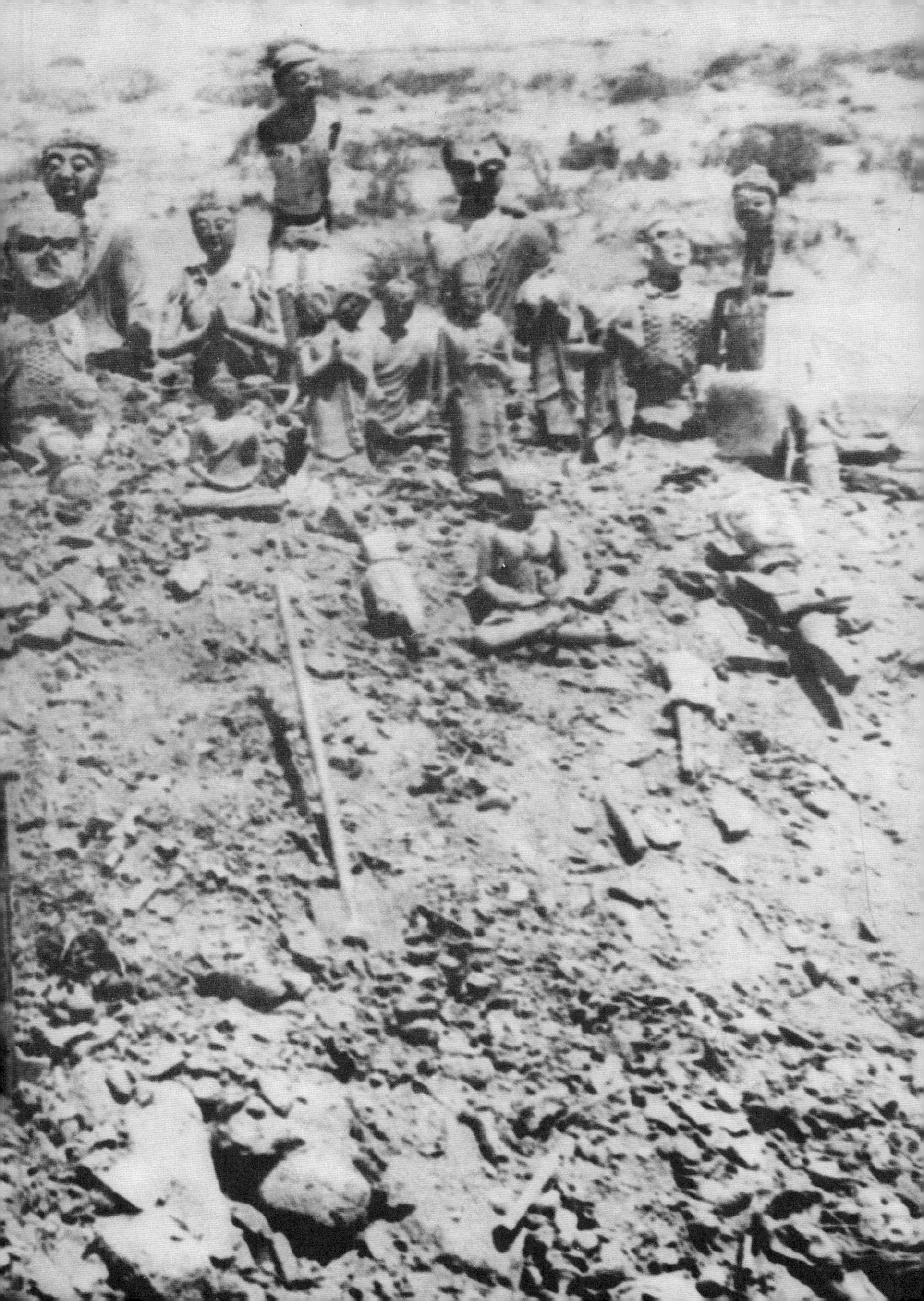

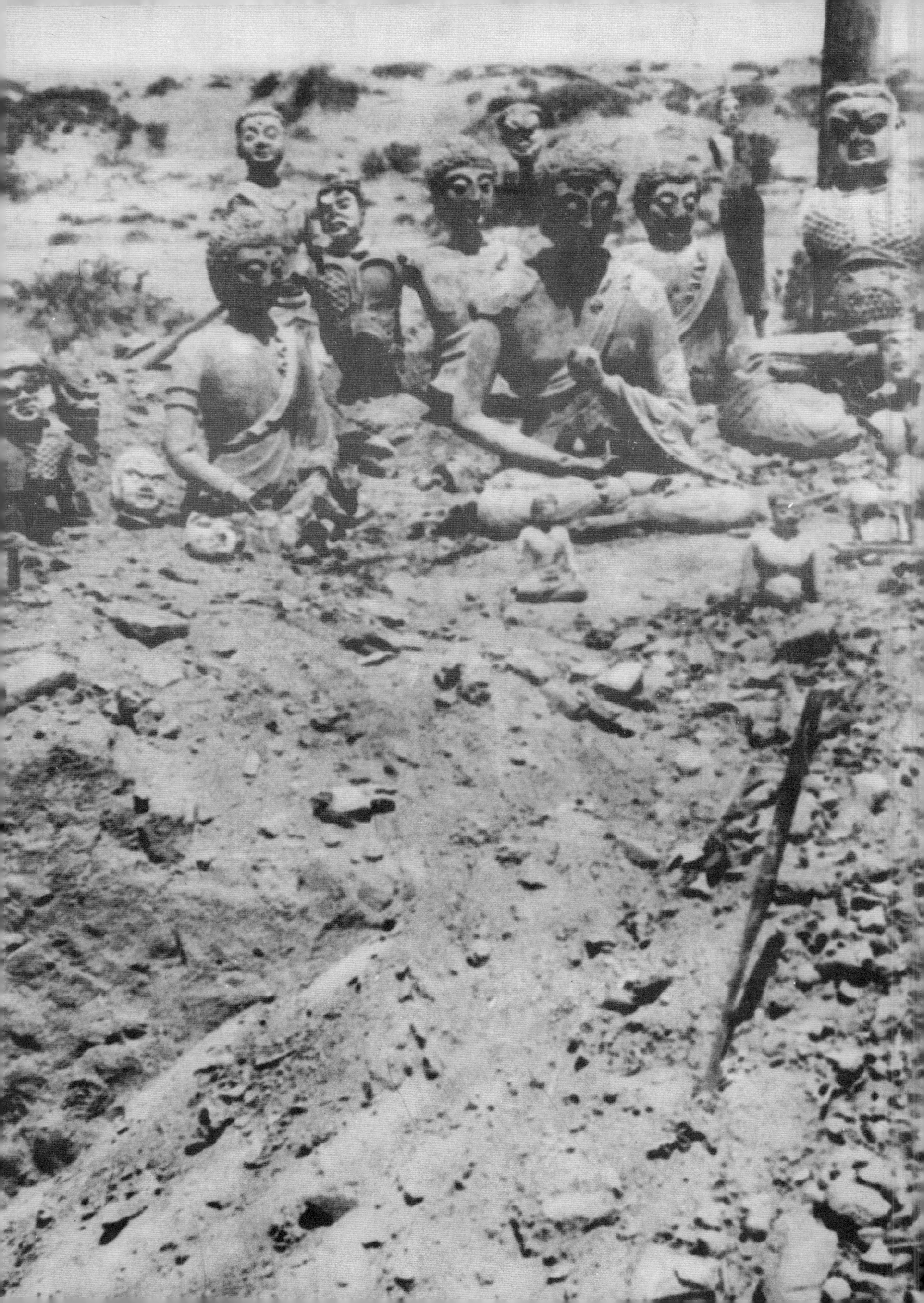

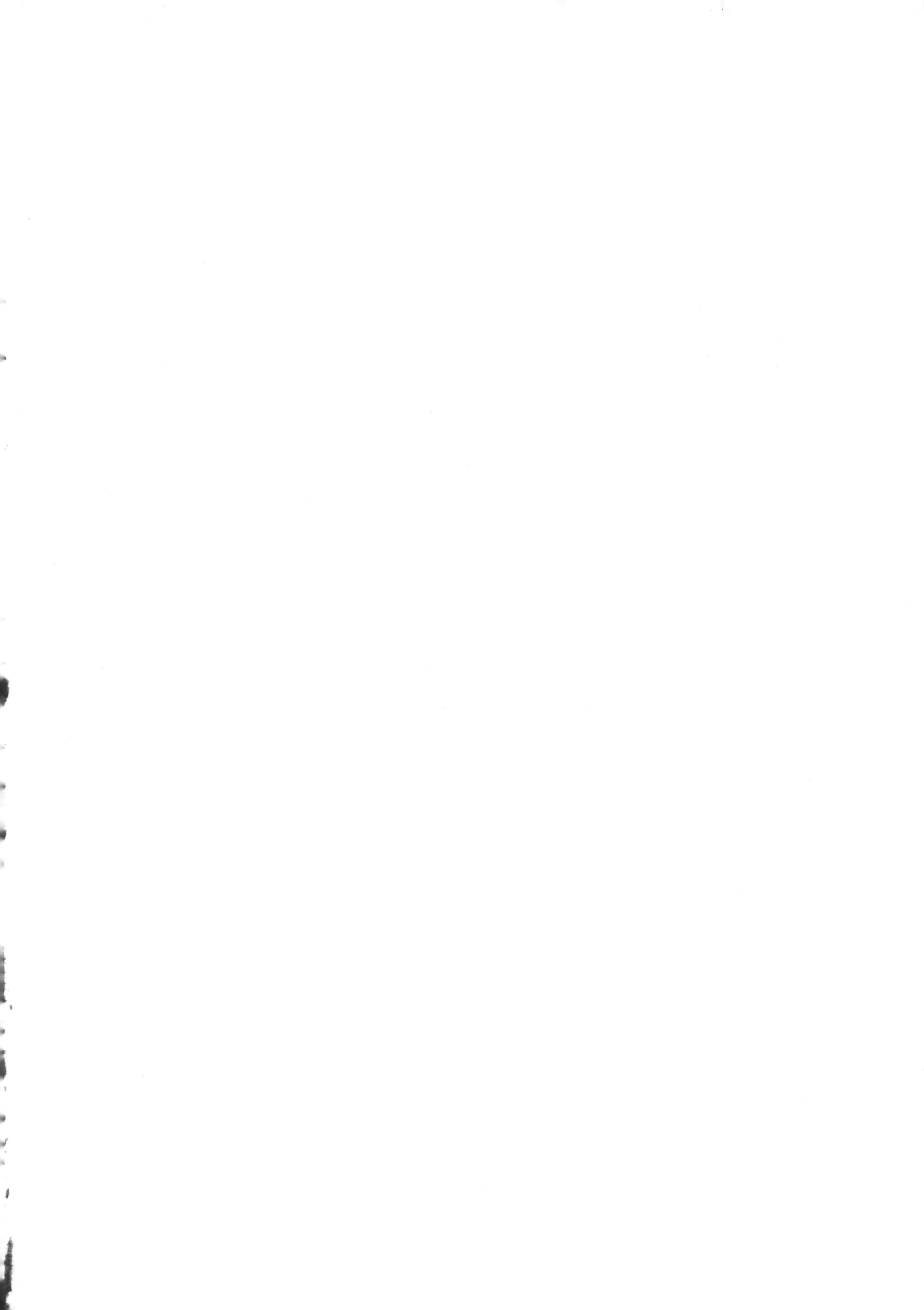